WOMEN, PRODUCTION, AND PATRIARCHY IN LATE MEDIEVAL CITIES

Women in Culture and Society
A Series Edited by Catharine R. Stimpson

WOMEN, PRODUCTION, AND PATRIARCHY IN LATE MEDIEVAL CITIES

Martha C. Howell

The University of Chicago Press
Chicago and London

The University of Chicago Press, Chicago 60637
The University of Chicago Press, Ltd., London
© 1986 by The University of Chicago
All rights reserved. Published 1986
Paperback edition 1988
Printed in the United States of America

97 96 95 94 93 92 91 90   6543

Library of Congress Cataloging in Publication Data

Howell, Martha C.
  Women, production, and patriarchy in late
medieval cities.

  (Women in culture and society)
  Bibliography: p.
  Includes index.
  1. Women—Employment—Europe, Northern—History.
2. Women—History—Middle Ages, 500–1500.
3. Patriarchy—Europe, Northern—History.   I. Title.
II. Series.
HD6134.H69   1986   331.4′094   85-31816
ISBN 0-226-35503-9 (cloth)
ISBN 0-226-35504-7 (paper)

For my mother and father

Contents

Foreword, by Catharine R. Stimpson   ix
Preface   xiii
Introduction   1

Part 1: Women's Work in Medieval Cities of Northern Europe
1. A Framework for Understanding Women's Work   9
   The Northern European Family and the Household
     Economy   9
   Labor Status in Urban Market Economies   21
2. The Sex-Gender System and Economic Systems   27
   The Family Production Unit   27
   Late Medieval Market Production   30
   An Agenda for Research   43

Part 2: Empirical Studies: Leiden and Cologne
3. The Socioeconomic Structure of Leiden   49
   The History of the Drapery   50
   Politics and Government   52
   The Size and Structure of the Drapery   59
   Small Commodity Production   64
4. Women's Work in Leiden's Market Production   70
   Locating Women Workers in the Textile Industry   70
   Women's Work in and Around Leiden   75
   Patterns of Women's Work: The Organization of
     Market Production   87

vii

Contents

5. The Socioeconomic Structure of Cologne   95
    The Problem of Sources   98
    Economic and Constitutional Background   99
    The Transformation of Fifteenth-Century Cologne   108
    Capitalism in Cologne: A Debate   110
    Capitalism in Cologne: The Consequences   116
6. Women's Work in Cologne's Market Production   124
    The Women's Guilds   124
    The Traditional Guilds   133
    Women in Export-Import Trade   137
    Patterns and Explanations   152

Part 3: Points of Intersection
7. The Comparative Perspective: Lier, Douai,
    Frankfurt am Main   161
8. Women's Work and Social Change   174
    Women's Work and Socioeconomic Change   174
    Women's Work and the Patriarchal Order   178

    Appendixes
    1. Income from Leiden's Strikerye   185
    2. Archival Sources for Leiden   189
    3. Population of Leiden in 1498   191

    Notes   193
    Works Cited   261
    Index   279

Foreword

On a two-page map of the world, in a standard atlas, northern
Europe is smaller than a thumb print. Yet, after 1300, this
water-washed, wind-chilled region deeply imprinted itself on
global politics, commerce, and culture. Producing both Queen
Elizabeth I and empires, myths, and markets, it was nothing less
than a matrix of the "modern world-system."* Now, *Women,
Production, and Patriarchy* scrupulously amends its history, and ours.

Martha Howell confesses that she began her book with what she
thought was a simple question: "What kind of work did women do
in the urban market economies of late medieval Europe?" Apparently simple questions often demand more toil to answer than
convoluted ones. Howell has worked with the historical literature
in several languages; with European archives, especially but not
exclusively those of the cities of Leiden in the 1400s and 1500s and
Cologne in the 1400s; and with the insights of the new scholarship
about women, which see gender roles and gender hierarchy as
formidable presences.

Howell refuses to impose an abstraction upon events or places.
She respects stubborn particularities. Indeed, in part she selected
Leiden and Cologne as case studies because they were different;
because they presented dissimilar challenges to her theories. She
reasons thoughtfully, inductively. At the end, she offers hypotheses
for our scrutiny that have immense, and difficult, implications.

Howell begins with the northern European family, a small

* I take the phrase from Immanuel Wallerstein, *The Modern World-System:
Capitalist Agriculture and the Origins of the European World-Economy in the Sixteenth
Century* (New York and London: Academic Press, 1974).

ix

household in the Low Countries, Scandanavia, northern Germany, England, and northern France. Built around a husband and wife who married relatively late in life, such a group was a center of production, in brief, a "family production unit." If the husband was the head of the household, if the husband tended to more public tasks and the wife to more domestic ones, the wife nevertheless had her communal strengths and respect. She could, as well, move flexibly between public and private spheres, a maneuverability that could, potentially, threaten male dominance of the household and, as a result, of the sociopolitical order.

When a family became a part of a market economy, its labor status inevitably became "more differentiated and more complex." To gain high status, a household had to produce much more for the market than for its own subsistence. It also had to control "the economic resources of production and distribution." If the household earned high status, so did the women within it. Single women, and the poor, survived as they could.

Inexorably, markets both change and demand change. Individuals, rather than the family, seemed better able to meet competitive pressures, especially for long-distance markets. However, only men, not women, could function as individuals. Because men, not women, had political standing, only men could participate in government and shape its connections with business. Howell finds that where governments increased, the number of women in market production decreased. Because men, not women, could easily travel, men could more effectively organize trade beyond the neighborhood. Because women were responsible for managing the rhythms of family life, only women, not men, had to place domestic over public obligations.

As men gained authority, women forfeited more and more of theirs. In the zero-sum game of hierarchical relations, some win only if others lose. Although Howell concentrates on the interplay of economic processes and gender roles, she suggests that after women's labor status slipped, so did their legal rights. She believes, too, that "high status" women resisted their historical defeat. They did not go blandly, cheerfully, into responsibility for reproduction alone, into even greater subordination. However, they lacked the social, cultural, and political instruments even to maintain what had been theirs in late medieval families.

Coincidentally, I live in a large urban area. Next to my home, where I study and write, is a small shop that seems like a weak, but appealing, afterimage of the family production unit that Howell analyzes. The shop specializes in locks and keys. A husband, a wife, and the husband's cousin work there. They walk to work, from a building less than a block away. Recently, the couple had a baby. He is now at the shop, in his stroller, much of the day. Neighbors and customers cuddle and cosset him. The husband leaves the shop to make service calls; the wife does not. The wife feeds the baby more than the husband does. However, the husband cares for the baby every day; the wife grinds keys nearly every day. They do not want to do this for the rest of their lives, but for now they are one of the happiest families I know.

Howell does not romanticize Leiden or Cologne. Nor, no matter how much we might both value them, would she sentimentalize my neighbors as survivors of a better world that has largely vanished. However, her book, like all solid and searching work, provokes questions as it provides information and ideas. What can we learn from, as well as about, the history she has constructed?

We can realize, again, that markets are sacred monsters, which can feed us, but which we also feed with our own lives. We can recognize, even more deeply, that something happened to Western women, especially in families that took to the market, in late medieval and early modern society. Modern feminism has had to devote some of its energy to repairing that damage. Finally, we can become even more sharply conscious of the conditions in which gender equality might flourish. *Women, Production, and Patriarchy* shows that productive work is necessary, but not sufficient. Unless women have political and cultural power, unless men have domestic responsibilities, gender equality can haunt us, like a shadow or dreams, but it will not be a material part of our everyday lives, as cloth and other goods were for the men and women of Leiden and Cologne.

CATHARINE R. STIMPSON

Preface

When I began this project over ten years ago, I had what I thought was a simple question: what kind of work did women do in the urban market economies of late medieval Europe? This book is in a sense an answer to that question, but neither the question nor the answer seems as simple as it once did. My initial concern was principally with women's "contribution" to the economy, but I soon came to see that the economic importance of women's work in the late medieval city lay not so much in its quantity but in its role in making the prevailing systems of production possible. Later I came to appreciate that my question required a study of gender itself and of the way work roles created and sustained gender hierarchy. The result is a book less about women's work as such and more about the conditions which allowed some women to acquire high labor-status and about the ways that the patriarchal structure of late medieval society was altered in the process.

I received a great deal of support, encouragement, and aid over the years in which this project took shape. The Social Science Research Council and the Fulbright-Hays Program supported the archival research for my doctoral dissertation on women's work in late medieval Leiden. The Ministerie van Onderwijs en Wetenschappen brought me back to the Netherlands for some follow-up work, and the Deutsche Akademischer Austauschdienst made it possible for me to complete work I had only begun in Cologne during my dissertation research. A Mellon Fellowship in the Humanities at the University of Pennsylvania and a grant from the American Council of Learned Societies allowed me a leave

xiii

from Rutgers University to expand the research base and to write the manuscript.

Friends and scholars here and abroad generously provided essential help. The municipal archivists in Cologne, Ghent, and Leiden kindly and skillfully assisted my research while I was in Europe. A. M. van der Woude of the Landbouwhogeschool in Wageningen made computer facilities available to me in the Netherlands and offered good advice concerning my research in Leiden. Walter Prevenier of the Rijksuniversiteit te Gent and his associates, Thérèse de Hemptinne, Maurice vander Maesen (now at the Archives d'État in Bruges), and Marc Boone, made my work in Belgian archives both fruitful and pleasant. Margret Wensky of the Amt für Rheinische Landeskunde in Bonn was extraordinarily generous; she shared her own data on Cologne's working women with me, she smoothed the way for me during my research trips to Cologne, and she kept me up-to-date on the German scholarship in my field.

My thanks also go to a number of people for reading, and in some cases rereading, parts of the manuscript and offering good suggestions for improvement: Rudolph Bell, Paul Clemens, Robert Gottfried, Suzanne Lebsock, Phyllis Mack, Richard L. McCormick, Herbert Rowen (all of Rutgers University), Robert DuPlessis (of Swarthmore College), Maryanne Kowaleski (of Fordham University), and John Mundy (of Columbia University). Susan Cahn carefully read the entire manuscript more than once and helped reorganize early drafts. Ellin Sarot did her best to help me simplify and clarify my prose. Judith Walkowitz of Rutgers University offered telling comments and valuable advice as I worked to transform the draft into the final manuscript. Kathryn Hollen cheerfully and expertly typed and retyped the manuscript under the pressure of completely unreasonable deadlines. Catharine Stimpson expressed early interest in the manuscript and skillfully helped ready it for publication.

I am especially grateful to J. W. Smit of Columbia University. He sponsored the master's essay that began this project and the doctoral dissertation that followed, but he did a great deal more than those duties required. He was always ready to hear about the turns my research had taken as I worked on this book and did his best to steer me away from dangers along the way. I invariably returned from discussions with him with a deeper understanding of my project and the realization that I had to rethink parts of my argument before I could move on. Although he would never have written this book, it would not have been written without him.

I owe another large debt to the women's movement. The women and men of this movement not only made it possible for me to imagine a scholarly inquiry into the history of women's work but created the intellectual climate and institutional conditions necessary for me to carry out my project.

My husband, Edward Whitney, and my sons, John and William, patiently and good-naturedly bore with me as I tried to combine scholarship, writing, and teaching with family responsibilities and domestic pleasures. They are due my last, and best, thanks.

Introduction

In 1882, Karl Bücher, then the foremost economic and demographic historian of medieval Germany, published a small book called *Die Frauenfrage im Mittelalter* (The Women Question in the Middle Ages). In it he explored how the problem of the "oversupply" of women, a problem he thought the late nineteenth century shared, had been dealt with in the three centuries which closed the Middle Ages. According to Bücher, men were then in measurably short supply because they, more than women, were exposed to war, disease and the hazards of medieval travel. Without husbands to found households for them, many women were impelled into the public world once dominated, Bücher explained, by men. The medieval *Frauenfrage* was thus essentially a *Frauenerwerbsfrage*, a problem of women's livelihood.

Women alone in the world had to fend for themselves. The unlucky became camp followers, prostitutes, vagabonds, and street people. Luckier ones found piecework in textiles, entered domestic service, took up street peddling or found sanctuary in the convent. The luckiest worked in crafts and trade, filling the empty spots in the most prestigious sectors of medieval urban market production. This last route was so common, Bücher claimed, that women "were excluded from no trade for which their strength was adequate. They had the right, as a matter of course, to learn all crafts [and] to practice them, as apprentices, even as mistresses."[1]

By the early modern period, in Bücher's view, the situation had been righted. Women no longer outnumbered men and, thanks to the renewed consciousness of the importance of family life during the Reformation era, the household had been restored to its rightful place at the center of women's lives. Then, according to Bücher, "a new ideal of womanhood" had emerged, one "which laid heavy emphasis on the purity of soul and the unique morality of the German housewife and mother."[2]

In the century since Bücher first published *Die Frauenfrage*, scholars have repeatedly returned to the subject of women's work in the Middle Ages. Soon after *Die Frauenfrage* first appeared, several major studies confirmed its finding that women in late medieval cities of northern Europe practiced skilled crafts, belonged to guilds, and dealt in long-distance commerce.[3] None of these early scholars systematically pursued Bücher's ideas about the causes of this pattern, however, and the medievalists who followed them have also not attempted to improve upon Bücher's theories, concentrating instead on gathering more empirical data about women's work.[4] Hence, while bequeathing us extensive documentation about urban women's work, medievalists have left us unable to explain the data. The few scholars attempting to do so have seldom been historians of the period, and the explanations they have provided are not entirely satisfactory. By and large based on selective documentation, these explanations lack the authority systematic research might have given them.[5]

But the principal difficulty is not an imbalance between empirical and theoretical studies; it is that the evidence gathered since Bücher's day does not unequivocally support his interpretation.[6] The century of research since *Die Frauenfrage* first appeared has in fact undermined, not strengthened, Bücher's case and argues that, at the very least, his account must be modified.

The notion that women throughout late medieval cities had easy access to the skilled crafts and to commerce simply will not withstand close scrutiny, for there were many cities and certain economic sectors from which women were deliberately excluded. Women were forbidden to join the dyers' guild in fourteenth-century Ghent, for example, and were denied the right to make most kinds of clothing in Paris until the seventeenth century.[7] Even in fifteenth-century Cologne where, there can be no doubt, women were active in many skilled crafts and in commerce, there was much work they did not do. They neither wove nor produced export-quality wool cloth; they were forbidden to cut and weigh fish; and they had almost no role in buying and selling commodities such as the silk, saffron, cotton, or tin which were important elements of Cologne's long-distance trade.[8]

The periodization Bücher sketched must also be reexamined because recent research has revealed that urban women were more active in market production during the early modern centuries than his thesis allows. In sixteenth- and seventeenth-century Lyons, women wove silk and managed their own print shops; in eighteenth-century York they practiced skilled crafts; in sixteenth- and seventeenth-century Nuremberg they dominated the distributive trades; in early modern Geneva, they did skilled metalwork in their own shops.[9]

The evidence that the women's work Bücher described was not as typical of late medieval cities or as different from early modern and modern cities as he and his successors thought, while well known and of unquestioned reliability, has so far not been reconciled with the equally well-known and well-regarded studies adopting Bücher's conclusions. Instead, most historians have noted the contradictory data only parenthetically. Kathleen Casey, for example, in "The Cheshire Cat: Reconstructing the Experience of Medieval Women," first reported that "in the ever-widening market for more humdrum products during the later Middle Ages, women in a great variety of crafts actively expanded their control and increased their gains. . . . A process could be very thoroughly learned in a lifetime of collaboration with a man whose workshop was adjacent to the home. Most often, those who attained master's rank in the gilds did so in this way but . . . mastery could be acquired independently in a surprising range of trades. . . . The master's widow operated in nearly the entire range of crafts, including sword making and smelting. We do not know in what strength, or how it may have fluctuated. That she may not literally have been hammering at the forge or wielding the bellows is economically, if not existentially, irrelevant. It was she who collected the profits."

A few pages later, however, Casey appeared to contradict herself: "This promising structure had serious flaws. Certain key gilds would not admit women under any circumstances. . . . Gild regulations as well as market forces set lower rates for day labourers in specifically female trades than in male occupations. And in the one branch of manufacture that already deserved to be called an industry, wool-making, women never did progress to the more highly paid operations."[10]

Casey seems to have been unsure about how to treat evidence of women's exclusion from certain positions in market production, and most other historians have shared her confusion.[11] Some, however, have had no doubt. They have concluded that Bücher's theory is invalid. Kurt Wesoly, for example, has directly attacked the body of scholarship which builds upon Bücher. In an analysis of Wachendorf's *Die wirtschaftliche Stellung der Frau in den deutschen Städten des Spätmittelalters*, one of the most important successors to Bücher's study, Wesoly argued that the author had simply misread his sources. The word *wib* appearing in a late fourteenth-century ordinance from Frankfurt am Main's textile crafts which Wachendorf had read to mean "woman" usually, Wesoly pointed out, is read as "wife" or "widow." Other women mentioned in the same ordinance were not skilled workers, as Wachendorf had described them, but were doing ancillary work. These confusions made Wesoly skeptical about the thesis as a whole: "That women took part in the weavers' guild in Frankfurt as 'full members' . . . while not entirely out of the question, seems to me in no way fully assured."[12] He even more directly challenged Bücher's statement that women were regular members of crafts: "Whether it was really the rule for girls in the thirteenth century to learn a craft and whether, [quoting Bücher] 'in the cities of the high Middle Ages women were generally excluded from no industry for which their strength was adequate' is out and out speculation. The evidence does not suffice for a real proof."[13]

Wesoly's attack is well founded, but by itself his criticism neither invalidates the interpretation he questions nor wholly corrects it.[14] Indeed, the problem is precisely that both Wesoly's point of view and the more widely accepted interpretation, which by and large accepts Bücher's view and treats data in conflict with it as exceptional, can be well supported on empirical grounds. What this means is that new evidence alone, while welcome, cannot resolve the quandary we are in. Instead, we must put Bücher's too-simple account aside and examine anew the data we have, hoping to achieve a better understanding of what was evidently a complex and changing pattern of women's work.

My study offers a hypothesis to resolve the quandary and begins to refine the hypothesis by looking closely at women's work in a few specific settings. Although I have built on Bücher's *Frauenfrage* and am much indebted to other previous studies, I have approached the subject of women's work in late medieval cities somewhat differently from my predecessors. Most of them have examined the changing pattern of women's work in market production in this period as if it were independent of the way gender and the economy were then being constructed. Bücher, for example, thought demographic variables were the key determinants of women's initial access to certain positions and a principal factor in their later retreat from them; others have considered technological developments vital; still others have proposed that fluctuations in general business conditions (measured by the demand for labor) were fundamental.[15] I have not discounted the possible relevance of any of these factors but I have begun my inquiry with the assumption that their effects on women's work were felt only in the context of overarching structures of gender and economy that were then evolving.

Hence, I have treated women's work as the product of an intersection between these two interconnected but analytically distinguishable systems. The first, the sex-gender system, is essentially cultural. Within it, all of women's roles—as mothers, sexual partners of men, citizens, religious persons, or economic producers for subsistence and the market—are located and gender relations are organized accordingly. The second is the economic system which organizes the way material goods and services are produced, distributed, and consumed, which both separates subsistence from market or commodity production and creates a hierarchy that distinguishes between more and less productive work. Because the work of urban women changed as these two systems changed in late medieval Europe, we must locate that work in both as they were then constructed.

In this book, I develop and try to refine a hypothesis about how gender and market production were structurally related in late medieval and early modern cities of northern Europe. Part 1 begins with a description of the sexual division of labor embodied in late medieval household production and of labor status in late medieval urban society. I go on to the hypothesis that women gained positions in market production granting high labor-status through a particular form of the family economy which was viable only under certain economic structural conditions. Part 2, the body of the book, consists of empirical studies of Leiden and Cologne, two important cities of late medieval Europe, in which I explore how variations in the structure of market production there gave rise to changing intersections between the family economy and the market economy, and thus to complex and changing patterns of women's work. In Part 3, I use the conceptual framework developed in these empirical studies to investigate women's work in other cities of northern Europe and to explore how the changes in urban women's work in the region may have been affected by factors other than the conditions of economic structure examined in this book. Finally, I return to the subject of gender, asking how relations between men and women in late medieval and early modern urban society were connected to the changes in women's work traced in the preceding chapters.

Part 1

Women's Work in Medieval Cities of Northern Europe

1

A Framework for Understanding Women's Work

In northern Europe during the late Middle Ages, the household was the most important center of economic production. Work both for the market and for subsistence often took place in the household itself, but even when it did not, as for some artisans and many merchants, the members of the household formed an economic unit by working to sustain themselves as a group. Often they performed closely related tasks, as when household members together raised crops or produced textiles for the market; at other times they performed distinct tasks, as when one person in a household made cabinets, another distributed goods imported from abroad, and a third helped to make clothing.

Most household economies during the period were family economies in that they were managed by the senior members of a family who both resided in the household and had legal control of the assets employed to support the household.[1] The household itself was founded by a married pair, and, once established, the household served as a unit both of market production (the preparation of goods and services for sale) and subsistence production (the preparation of goods and services for domestic use). Most family economies in the Middle Ages were, of course, producers of agricultural goods intended principally for subsistence, but in urban households the emphasis was on market production.

The realms of market production and subsistence production in these households were not, however, as distinct as we might imagine. Many goods made for domestic use were sold; ale,

9

textiles, and clothing that were not needed by the household were often marketed locally. Conversely, goods intended for sale were often consumed by household members; Margarete Runtiger, wife of one of Regensberg's richest merchants and herself an active participant in the family business often obtained fabrics needed in the household from commercial shipments acquired for the business.[2] The line between market and subsistence production in these households was further blurred because individual family members easily moved back and forth between the two spheres. In the course of a few days a housewife might brew ale and sell her surplus, make clothing for household members, help her husband in his shop, and teach her daughter how to spin fine woolen yarn for merchants.[3]

Although men and women shared responsibility for maintaining the household economy, they usually did not perform the same tasks in it, and many historians have argued that the pattern of differences reflected a principle which located women's work in the household and men's outside it.[4] A great deal of evidence, from the countryside as well as from cities, can be marshaled in support of this reasoning. Peasant women, by and large, fed and clothed the household members and supervised domestic helpers, while men in the peasant economy concentrated on field work, fuel and housing supply and, in pastoral regions, care of animals. Even among the rural aristocracy a similar division prevailed, and in cities women specialized in work carried on in the household, while men normally monopolized work that took them away from the home.

But the general rule was often broken. In rural settings, women helped out with the harvest, and in certain peasant communities widows assumed all the economic roles of their deceased husbands.[5] On the estates of Europe's aristocracy, women also took on "male" functions, when supervising agricultural work or overseeing village affairs in their husbands' absences. In cities, women also regularly substituted for their husbands.[6] Some women there even plied trades of their own which encroached upon, or entered, the male "outside" world. Hucksters such as Langland's Rose the Regrator went from village to village distributing consumer goods; women silk makers from Cologne traveled to the fairs at Frankfurt am Main to sell their fabrics; women merchants from Lübeck maintained stalls for selling their wares in Sweden; women in thirteenth- and fourteenth-century Douai served as brokers for foreign merchants.[7]

Nevertheless, whether confined to the domestic sphere or located in a man's world supposedly removed from it, the economic functions performed by women who comanaged medieval household economies were valuable and, what is more, valued. Women married to heads of household in all but the richest landed families generally took care that the members of their large households were fed, clothed, looked after when sick, suitably trained for their domestic duties, and properly married; the women even produced some of the household's food and clothing themselves, and they were usually in charge of the kitchen garden and of the animals raised for household use.[8] Like their social superiors, peasant women saw to it that their household members were clothed and fed; unlike their superiors, these peasant women always had direct responsibility for producing many of the raw materials used to provision the household. Urban women were sometimes less directly involved in producing the goods needed by their households, since the goods and services that could be purchased were often better than those made or available at home, but they also held important economic responsibilities in the household. They planned expenditures for food, for clothing, and for the materials to make them and, depending on the economic status of the household, they executed the plans themselves or oversaw work carried out. Most urban households in the late Middle Ages still kept gardens and animals, and women often had charge of these resources.[9]

The women artisans and merchants of interest in this study, women such as Douai's brokers or Cologne's silk makers, lived in cities where household economies like these flourished. Hence, to understand how these women acquired their privileged positions and how they later lost them, we must understand the parts their families played in market production as it was then constituted. This inquiry properly begins in the following chapter with an analysis of one type of family economy (a type that will be called the family production unit), but as a preliminary to this analysis we need a more generalized description of the families which formed the family economies characteristic of the late medieval and early modern European North. In particular, we will want to examine their demographic characteristics (their size and demographic structure), property relations among their members, and the patterns of hierarchy within them, for these factors seem to have been tied to the economic roles of women both within and outside the household.

11

Each of these factors has been independently examined in some areas of Europe for certain periods within the four or five centuries that constitute the late medieval and early modern era, and some of the scholars involved in these investigations have speculated about how these factors might have been related to one another; for example, how variations in marriage age were associated with variations in inheritance systems, or the way that impartible inheritances strengthened patriarchal authority in households. But the scholars making these speculations have been cautious, since only for a small number of areas in Europe before the late eighteenth or nineteenth centuries is there evidence that would justify confident generalizations. And few have been willing to go beyond speculation unless they are dealing with a small social group like the Italian urban elites of the late Middle Ages who left so many records that reveal their family strategies or unless, like the scholars associated with the Cambridge Group for the History of Population and Social Structure, they have so far limited themselves largely to gathering and interpreting one kind of data.

Despite the uncertainty most scholars feel about generalizations at this stage, however, a tentative consensus is emerging about what is being called the "Western family" or, better, the "northern European family" (more precisely, the "northwestern European family").[10] Principally defined by its demographic features—it was small and was headed by a nuclear couple who had first married rather late and at about the same age—this was the dominant family type among most social classes in England, in France north of the Loire, in Scandinavia, in the Low Countries, and in most of Germany until about 1700.

This demographic pattern, scholars are agreed, was related to the larger economic, political, and legal structures of late medieval and early modern society, but no one has yet mapped these connections, or even traced the chronology of change that occurred in the structure and functions of this "northern European family" as medieval society gave way to modern. Yet it is possible to suggest how that map might look, and in the following few pages, by way of introduction to my own study, I have borrowed from existing monograph literature to sketch that profile, concentrating on the demographic features, internal property relations, and hierarchical structure of these families because I believe these characteristics tended toward a particular configuration in areas where family-run household economies like those just described flourished.

Although my sketch draws upon a well-established body of scholarly literature, it is certainly incomplete and necessarily provisional in that it attempts to link demographic, legal, and gender structures with the economic functions of the family in anticipation of, rather than with the support of, corroborating scholarly research. Tentative as it must be, however, the profile should help place my own study in the history of the European family that has already been written and justify my assumption that the women who, according to Bücher, were doing such untraditional work were doing it as members of a most traditional institution, the family.

Family-run household economies were not unique to northern cities; in much of Europe during the late medieval and early modern period, the household, run by a nuclear couple or its survivor, was the center both of subsistence production and of the relatively small amount of market production that took place outside cities. Where this pattern prevailed, certain distinctive customs affecting marriage, family size, and property relations within families also prevailed.

Both men and women in these families married surprisingly late, if at all (a high percentage of the population did not marry), and husbands and wives were close in age. In Colyton, England first-time brides between the years 1560 and 1646 averaged twenty-seven years of age; their husbands were exactly the same age.[11] In Crulai, France, from 1674 to 1742, women were almost twenty-five at their first marriage, and men were just over twenty-seven.[12] In eighteenth-century Norway, only 11 percent of women had been married by the age of twenty-four, and 35 percent of all married women were older than their husbands (in eighteenth-century Belgrade, in contrast, the figures were 92 percent and 0.5 percent, respectively!).[13] While this evidence and most of the rest we have that is like it comes from the early modern period, it is almost certain that marriage age for first-time brides and grooms was typically as late in the fourteenth and fifteenth centuries as it was in the better-documented early modern period.[14]

John Hajnal, who first systematically described and analyzed this pattern of marriage, ascribed it to the economics of family-run household production.[15] Men and women in cities and in the countryside could not marry until they could set up their own household economies, a step they could not take without land, a shop, or a business of their own, as well as the skills to manage them. It was thus only when their parents or the masters with whom they trained were ready to turn over their assets—or when they had died—that young people could take this step. For this reason, most historians have agreed with Hajnal, first-time brides and grooms were typically both in their mid-to-late twenties.

These families shared other distinctive demographic features. Although the households managed by the men and women who headed the family usually included servants and apprentices, the households were not especially large.[16] In established urban artisanal or merchant families in the North, households regularly contained seven or eight individuals, including on average about two children. Families without an established trade or whose members were past the age of active economic production were smaller, so that the average urban household contained about five persons.[17] This is the household size and structure first scrutinized by Laslett in *The World We Have Lost*; while it was not as unchanging or as universal a structure as Laslett then assumed it had been, it was typical in areas (such as northern European cities) where the family-run household economy, constructed by people who married as Hajnal described, was the chief unit of economic production.[18]

Property relations in families like these also reflected economic realities. By custom or formal agreement, even if according to arrangements which differed in detail, husbands and wives belonging to northern European family economies pooled their property, and in northern European cities frequently did so following some version of community property law.[19] Accordingly, assets acquired after the marriage were treated as the joint property of both spouses; the survivor of the marriage inherited at least half of the property, and could use it as he or she wished, and often had lifetime rights to the usufruct of any communal property they did not inherit. Variations in applying this principle were, however, quite common. In many areas, something resembling a dowry existed side-by-side with communal property. In such cases, a woman retained exclusive ownership of whatever property she brought to a marriage which, although under the management of her husband during her life, reverted to her nearest blood relatives after her death if the couple had no living children. The property with which the husband entered the marriage was similarly reserved for his family of origin. In other areas, however, even "marriage goods," as such property was called, were subject to community property laws.

In many parts of the North, to be sure, traditional law favoring the lineage prevailed, and family property was treated as the husband's, with the wife retaining ownership only of some personal goods, her dowry, and, when widowed, the usufruct of a portion of her husband's property. Even then, however, the wife was protected during and after her marriage. A husband could not alienate his wife's dowry, and she was left a fair-sized portion (usually a third but sometimes more). In areas where traditional law prevailed, moreover, husbands often wrote wills giving their widows full managerial rights over all their property, either for life or until their children reached their majorities.[20]

Whether it was considered as owned communally or separately, family property was legally under the management of husbands, but husbands did not own the assets outright. Instead, they managed family property with duties towards all dependent family members, including their wives. A man's responsibilities for the property on which his family members depended was part and parcel of his general responsibility for them, a responsibility which derived from his position as head of the household. According to traditional medieval law, married women, like children, had no civil status, but were included in the households of their husbands who alone had such standing. When a man married, he acquired the *mundium* of his bride from her parents, a transfer recognized in the early practice of *Muntgeld* payments.[21] Single women were similarly subsumed under their father's guardianship, and only widows were expected ever to gain the civil status accorded all adult males. These customs survived into the late Middle Ages, even into the early modern period in many areas, then, as earlier, testifying to the power of the medieval perception that the (male-headed) household, not the individual, was the constituent unit of society.[22]

The system of *Geschlechtsvormundschaft*, the German term for male guardianship of adult women, and of male control of assets of family members, did not, however, survive the Middle Ages in perfect repair. In cities where women operated their own businesses, it was sometimes possible for married women to separate their business assets from those of their husbands by having themselves declared "feme sole", a declaration always approved by and frequently initiated by the husband; in other instances it was often possible less formally but no less clearly to establish distinctions between a woman's business property and her family's assets.[23] Married and single women also gradually broke free of certain features of the guardianships to which they were technically subject and acquired independent legal status in civil matters; we regularly find urban women giving oaths, making contracts, and conducting their own affairs in civil courts.[24]

Not all families and not all households in Europe during this period, even in cities of the late medieval North, conformed precisely to these patterns, but where they did not, neither did the family-run household economy I have described survive. The families of Italy's urban merchant aristocracy, whose history is becoming comparatively well known, differed most strikingly. Women there were not expected to play a direct role in providing for the household and served only to transfer property, by way of their dowry, from the management of their fathers to that of their husbands. These women were not their husbands' heirs but retained only their dowry and, when widowed, the usufruct of an agreed-upon and relatively small portion which they seldom retained if they remarried. Unlike northern urban women or even women in their own cities from the artisan class, rich Italian women almost never managed the family property bequeathed to minor sons.[25]

If the economic roles of rich Italian women were minimized, however, their reproductive roles were enhanced. Having few responsibilities for economic production and being valued principally for their reproductive capacities, these women could marry very young. On average, they were some eight to ten years younger than northern brides and sometimes that much younger than their neighbors from the artisan class. Largely because they were younger when they began sexual relations, they had more children; women who married at sixteen or seventeen in this period could expect to have three more children than women who married at twenty-five or twenty-six.[26]

Predictably, these characteristics of family size and structure were associated with a socioeconomic system different from that of the Northwest. For Italian aristocrats the household economy as described here did not exist. In some cities men and women did not even form a new household by marrying, for the couple simply moved into the household of the groom's father and lived under his authority. Even where the nuclear unit maintained a separate residence, it belonged to a patriarchal clan, and the clan, directly or indirectly, formally or informally, established the political, economic, and social parameters of the nuclear family's activity. "Family business" was inevitably clan business: clan members owned and operated trading ventures with one another—and not with outsiders; families acted together as political units, and in some cities they almost entirely destroyed communal institutions in doing so.[27] Of course, the household remained a center of subsistence production for these people, and women usually bore responsibility for much of the domestic management; no small task, then as now. But the domestic duties of these women bore no relationship to the commerce, finance, and industry which occupied their husbands, fathers, and brothers. In some places, moreover, women were exempt even from responsibilities for domestic management, for servants not only executed the work but also planned and supervised it on behalf of mistresses increasingly devoted to bearing children or enjoying their leisure.

It was not only among Italian urban elites that deviations from the pattern of household organization typical of most northern European cities occurred.[28] In peasant villages around Florence in the fifteenth century women married at about nineteen years of age and were almost four years younger than their husbands.[29] The explanation for this deviation appears to lie in the economics of the household. In this region, unlike in much of the rural North, the formation of a new family did not always imply the formation of a new household economy. Instead, the bride and groom joined the household of either her or his parents; the parents worked the land as sharecroppers and could take on extra land to accommodate extra workers. It was no matter, then, that brides and grooms had no land, for they could help their parents farm theirs, and no matter that brides were inexperienced household managers, for they could apprentice in the homes of their mothers or mothers-in-law.[30] Although in one sense adult, these young men and women did not assume adult economic responsibilities until their parents or in-laws died.

Certain propertied elites of northern cities also did not precisely conform to the "model," and in some respects they resembled Italy's urban aristocracy. Particularly in the early history of northern cities, patriarchal lineages not unlike the Italian clans played a key role in political, social, and economic organization: members of these lineages had an exclusive claim to political authority and, with it, exclusive rights to certain economic activities, effective control of some other trades, and a secure position at the top of the socioeconomic hierarchy. Although the northern lineages sometimes aligned themselves into opposing factions which, just like Italian clans, vied with one another for political dominance, more often they cooperated: the lineages intermarried, interchanged political offices, and did business with one another.

Although these lineages, or patrician families as they have more often been styled, behaved in some ways more like the Italian urban elite and less like their urban neighbors who were newcomers to commerce or who were firmly located in the artisanate, the household and family structure they established do not seem to have been identical to the Italian. The few pieces of published evidence available for making this judgment suggest that their households served as economic units of some importance and that women played active roles in them: neither women nor men married as adolescents; unlike Italian women of this social group, northern patrician women received portions at least as large as their dowries; women sometimes took part in the market production controlled by their families (as wine importers or cloth merchants, for example).[31]

For my purposes it is not important, however, that deviations from the northern European "model" of family and household structure existed. It is important only to show that the deviations occurred where the household economy I have described was losing or changing its functions. The well-known *Le Ménagier de Paris* of the late fourteenth century seems to reflect a situation like this. The child bride addressed by her aged husband in this text was expected to play no part whatever in his commercial operations; his advice was intended only to help her learn the skills of domestic management. Even here, however, traditional mores had not been entirely abolished, for the young bride was not to be a mere decoration in her rich husband's home but was expected to assume full responsibility for much of the subsistence production.[32]

Deviations from the northern European "model" even before 1500 were sporadic or confined to small sections of the elite, and even thereafter they were limited to areas where social, economic, or political change had been pronounced. The introduction of wage employment in some parts of early modern England led to early marriages for both men and women and to increased fertility because the link between property and marriage had been thereby broken.[33] Other forces seem to have been at work in early modern London. There, according to one study of some two hundred merchant and artisan families, brides were only about twenty to twenty-three years old, and, according to another, may have been five to eight years younger than their husbands.[34] One historian has attributed this marriage pattern to the shortage of women that characterized early modern London; there, even young women with few skills and little property could attract husbands.[35] It may well have been, however, that male merchants and artisans in London married young women because they did not require wives who could comanage a household economy or even see to the domestic economy. For them, young, fecund women might have been acceptable, even preferred, brides. The factors that played a role in establishing their preferences, factors which had led to a decline and reshaping of the household economy, there as elsewhere in early modern Europe, are still obscure, but some of them will be examined in the chapters that follow.

The "northern European family" thus did not reign alone throughout the centuries that closed the Middle Ages and began the modern period of European history, but it did, our evidence suggests, constitute the norm, both in cities and, except for some of the rich, in the countryside. The men and women in these families were expected to manage a household economy together and had to acquire skills and resources before they could do so. In all such households, women concentrated on certain tasks closely associated with day-to-day subsistence and compatible with childcare, but frequently did not confine themselves to purely domestic tasks. As partners and heirs of their husbands and as heirs to the landholdings or trades their parents owned, these women also shared in other aspects of economic production that sustained the family, whether done directly for subsistence or for the market. Hence, the women and men of these households first married in their mid-to-late-twenties; they raised an average of two children to maturity; they made one another the heir of the family property or business they had shared; and they then passed property and skills on to sons and daughters alike.

These households were of course headed by men who had legally recognized authority over all household members—wives, children, servants, apprentices, coresident dependent relatives, and even lodgers. Yet, as we have seen, the women married to heads of household had independent sources of authority as a result of their economic duties and often acted as heads of household in their husbands' absences. We have also seen that a woman's responsibilities for economic production could lead her into market production and, as a result, could free her from her husband's tutelage: having entered market production, many women came to require independent legal capacities, for example, to mortgage assets or make contracts.

Both steps, women's entry into market production in late medieval cities and the improvement in their legal status that ensued, were understandable and entirely pragmatic responses to the needs of the household economy. But, paradoxically, both steps would have weakened the household economy they were instituted to protect. Women working for the benefit of the household, no matter whether they did it as partners of men or on their own, were, to be sure, strengthening the household unit in one way. But in another, they were undermining it, because work that required the institution of feme sole or similar legal privileges removed control over economic resources from the household and its head.

At this point, the unity of the household was being threatened and, with it, the patriarchal structure of late medieval urban society. The male-headed household was, after all, not only the constitutional, social, economic, and political unit of the urban community, it was also the foundation of male dominance in this age.[36] It was in good measure their positions as heads of households and families where economic, social and political power was lodged that gave men dominance over women.

The dimensions of this patriarchal system are well known. While women in late medieval Europe possessed certain discretion and acknowledged responsibility in economic matters, enjoyed privileges as mothers, were given special protection under both secular and canon law, and were permitted separate religious institutions which granted them some autonomy, they were always subordinated to the male-headed household or, as brides of Christ, to its surrogate, the male-supervised convent. As subordinates in institutions controlled by men, women did not participate in the public realm except through men. It was men who wrote the law, and they wrote law which favored themselves; it was men who controlled the Church, the institution of religion and learning; it was men who almost always managed, and usually held, real property, the chief productive resource of medieval Europe and the traditional basis of social standing as well as political, military, judicial, and even ecclesiastical authority. The attitudes expressed in popular and learned culture affirmed the patriarchal order. Women were regularly described as biologically inferior, as, in a common formulation, "incomplete men"; as spiritually deficient and especially liable to misapprehend, distort, or pervert religious teaching; as undisciplined and disorderly thinkers unfit for higher learning.[37]

Tied as it was to the patriarchal household unit, this pattern of male dominance could have been undermined in several ways as women took on roles in market production. Women whose business assets were separated from the household or who gained independent status in civil law would have weakened the household economy because these changes would have fractured the unity of the household. Women who participated in the highly skilled crafts, in long-distance trade, or in international finance would have posed an additional threat because their work required training, capital, and a commitment to a regular schedule which would have made their positions as mothers, as managers of household subsistence, and as subordinate partners of the family economy difficult to fill. An even more direct challenge to patriarchy could have arisen as well: women who bought and sold textiles internationally, who owned and ran a prosperous brewery and pub, or who brokered deals between visiting merchants and citizens of their own city were doing work which could have granted them extraordinary prestige and authority.

The resulting tensions must have been perceptible. Economic needs of the household on the one hand demanded, and seemed to be leading towards, the dismantling of the hierarchical structure of the household and, with it, the unity of the household. The prevailing traditions of male dominance and the continued operation of the existing sociopolitical order, on the other hand, required the preservation of the male-headed household. In the end, I will argue, the patriarchal household was preserved, even strengthened, but not without fundamental changes in its economic functions and a corresponding restructuring of the larger urban society. The remaining chapters of this book examine aspects of this process. Before turning to that examination, however, we should look more closely at the kind of work which seems to have precipitated these changes.

Labor Status in Urban Market Economies

As market production became a larger component of economic production during the centuries that closed the Middle Ages, and as it came to dominate urban economies, certain of its participants acquired extraordinarily high economic, political, and cultural status. It is no wonder, then, that historians interested in women's work have focused on the women who performed tasks in market production which seem to have had this potential. They have done so, however, without specifying why or how this work granted special status, and their imprecision on this point is responsible for some of the confusion about whether the women artisans and merchants of the late Middle Ages had "good" jobs in any relative or absolute sense.

None of the historians who have so carefully catalogued women's roles in market production have apparently thought it necessary to distinguish the kinds of market production they investigated from other kinds or the status each might grant. Bücher, for example, simply told us that women wove cloth in several cities of late medieval Germany, that they were furriers in Frankfurt am Main and in some Silesian cities, or that they were tanners in Nuremberg and beltmakers in Cologne and Strasbourg.[38] Presumably, he did not explain why this list was of interest because he considered it obvious: doing men's work, these women were acquiring the status normally associated with men's work. But it is not clear either that this was in fact men's work or, even if it was, that it necessarily bore the status he and most subsequent historians seem to have ascribed to it.

Many of the tasks Bücher apparently considered men's might just as easily be counted women's. While tanning appears to fall within what was traditionally considered the male sphere in medieval Europe, for women to make textiles, furs, and belts would have accorded with the traditional sexual division of labor, especially since these commodities were normally made in the home or in workshops attached to the home. Even selling these products need not have violated this division of labor if the selling could take place in local markets which women frequented anyway in the course of carrying out their tasks as housewives.[39] In short, if status could be obtained only through "male" tasks, it could not have derived from making or selling food, clothing, textiles, and shoes, or even jewelry and drugs, because most of these tasks could be considered part of the traditional female sphere.

What made this work special, in other words, was not that it was men's, unless we are prepared to claim that any "good" work is men's (and any "bad" work, women's). Otherwise, we must recognize that whatever privilege or honor inhered in work was owed to another quality which gave it special status. The quality could, however, no more have attached to the occupation itself than to the sex of the people doing it, because in late medieval urban society, the status associated with a particular trade was by no means constant. Weavers, for example, might have special status in some cities because they belonged to corporative guilds which participated in government, because they were counted among the taxpaying property owners or even the "well-to-do" who were specially assessed for taxes, or because they were accorded certain deference in social intercourse. Weavers in other cities, however, were neither direct nor indirect participants in government; they were poor and they practiced what was considered a dishonorable trade.[40] Even within a single city some weavers could have attributes of high status which others did not. Certain other occupations that were consistently associated with status of particular kinds in late medieval cities were less well regarded in early modern cities; barber-surgeons or midwives, for example, were respectable members of medieval urban communities, but only a few centuries later the people performing these tasks were considered unworthy competitors of the university-trained professionals striving to replace them.

A role in economic production, then, could imply a great deal about a person, but it was not obvious just what it implied. It could indicate the economic status of an individual, that is, his or her wealth; it could predict one's role in politics and, thus, one's political status in general; it could measure the social benefits accruing from the performance of the tasks; or it could define the kind of training the individual performing the task possessed. None of these associations held consistently, however, and the reason they did not is that in late medieval cities the productivity of some work and the economic value attributable to it were changing so rapidly that, from place to place and even from decade to decade in the same place, a particular task could be differently associated with each of these measures of status. In short, the link between occupation, economic status, and other measures of status was not entirely predictable.

Hence, to decide whether the work of a particular person was "good" or not, we need a definition of status that derives from work but that is independent of occupation itself. I have tried to meet this need by creating a measure of labor status; as it will be used here, labor status refers solely to the economic functions performed by a worker carrying out her or his tasks in economic production. Labor status is not only disassociated from occupation itself, it is also deliberately distinguished from cultural status, political status, legal status, or even economic status as measured by wealth; the term refers simply to the degree to which a person's role in economic production grants access to resources of production and distribution. According to this definition, high labor-status accrues to individuals who, as part of their occupations, independently obtain their own raw materials and supplies (their means of production), and control the distribution of the products of their labor.

This definition can help us to measure changes in labor status as the late medieval economy changed and to chart changes in the relationship between labor status and status of other kinds. In near-subsistence family economies of the late Middle Ages and early modern period, whether they were located in the country or in small towns, the essential attribute of high labor-status (control over the resources of production and distribution) was held by heads of household and their wives who independently managed family economies. Women performing the separate economic roles assigned them as household managers in free, property-owning families had rights to use such production resources as gardens, animals, malt, and tools; they decided what to make with them and whether the family or the local market should use them; they decided whether the family should use them as raw materials for future production or for subsistence and, if the latter, whether or not their consumption should be deferred. From their control over the economic resources of production and distribution, women derived high labor-status. Men who were heads of household had a similar degree of control through their work in agriculture or fuel and housing supply and had comparable labor-status. Both men and women as well as boys and girls who labored at the direction of either of these comanagers of the family had lower labor-status.

In such a world of near-subsistence production, labor status was, of course, a fairly uncomplicated matter. Such status did not vary greatly from family to family, and high labor-status itself brought with it very little in the way of economic, social, or political resources. In the market economies of late medieval urban Europe, however, labor status became more differentiated and more complex. Certain labor was rendered more productive as it was specialized and subdivided or as it was aided by technology. Talent, training, and access to capital (for training as well as for raw materials and equipment and for marketing) became more important in determining the degree to which one's occupation gave control over economic resources, and producers without these advantages fell to the bottom of an increasingly hierarchical economic order.

Where guilds and other organizations of market production provided (or withheld) access to training, materials, and markets, some artisans or entrepreneurs had high and others had low labor-status. A weaver outside a guild had lower labor-status than a guild member because the excluded weaver may have been banned from buying wool or dyes on certain markets, prohibited from hiring certain helpers, and denied access to trade fairs where cloth was sold; he or she thus had less control over resources of production and distribution. At the same time, this weaver obviously also suffered a loss of competitive position since production was not so cheaply or so well done, nor was distribution so effective, as for the weaver favored with guild status. Eventually a weaver denied guild privileges might have lost economic independence and become a wage worker, with little control over the resources of production and distribution and consequently with very low labor-status.

In market economies, it is evident, labor status became a comparative measure of competitive advantage in the marketplace, and high labor-status was allotted only to full-time market producers. Those who produced principally for subsistence gradually lost labor status when many of the raw materials they needed were controlled by market producers and when the demand for the surplus they would have sold into local markets was diverted to better-quality goods produced directly for sale. The highest labor-status became the exclusive possession of those market producers who enjoyed privileges which enhanced their competitive position and consequently who alone retained the essential attribute of very high labor-status, full control over the resources of production and distribution.

Labor status also acquired new importance in market economies because work came to be related to status of other kinds in a way not true of nonmarket economies.[41] Labor status sometimes came to determine political status, for example, because guild membership granted rights to participation in government or because people who played key economic roles were recruited for government posts. Labor status may also have indicated legal status in that laws may have been written and rewritten to facilitate the industrial and commercial activities of those who had high labor-status. Labor status may also have determined economic status, because wealth in market economies was increasingly derived from the application of labor to productive tasks and because only people with high labor-status, by definition, were able to perform the most productive, and hence the most remunerative, work. For these reasons, in fully developed market economies labor status frequently became the single most important indicator of status of any sort.[42]

Using this definition of labor status, we can decide what made some women's work in late medieval cities different from women's work elsewhere; what, for example, made a woman who wove wool cloth in Douai different from a woman who wove wool cloth in Frankfurt am Main, or what made a silk weaver in fifteenth-century Cologne different from a woman making the same kind of fabric with the same kind of tools in the same kind of household workshop in early modern Lyons. This definition of labor status becomes a tool to help resolve the confusion about whether or not the women Bücher and his successors found in medieval sources had "good" jobs and whether these positions were "better" or "worse" than the positions women did not hold. Knowing what made a position "good" and knowing where and when women held these positions, we can go on to the questions that motivated my inquiry into women's work in these cities: did women have, but then lose, positions in market production which granted high labor-status? If so, did these women acquire these positions through the family? Did women lose them at the end of the Middle Ages? If so, why? Was it because the positions they held lost status or because the positions disappeared entirely? Alternatively, was it because women were excluded from the positions which granted high labor-status? The next chapter offers a hypothesis which addresses these questions and introduces a research program designed to test and expand the hypothesis.

2

The Sex-Gender System and Economic Systems

The women who earned high labor-status in urban market production were, my working hypothesis proposes, members of families who managed independent household economies much like those described in the previous chapter. These units were of course "family economies" as the term is generally used, but they were a special kind of family economy. Like all family economies, theirs were institutions in which, as Tilly and Scott have put it, "the labor needs of the household defined the work roles of men, women, and children. Their work, in turn, fed the family. The interdependence of work and residence, of household labor needs, subsistence requirements and family relationships constituted the 'family economy'."[1] In fundamental and important ways, however, the family economy through which women gained high labor-status differed from others existing at the same time and, in some cases, surviving beyond it.

Such an economy can be clearly distinguished, on the one hand, from the family economy producing for subsistence. While these two family economies resembled one another in their demographic characters and in the way they managed family property (and belonged to the same northern European family type), the family economy of interest here differed from the family subsistence unit in that it did not produce principally for household use but for sale in the marketplace. It can also be distinguished, on the other hand, from the family economy whose members worked for wages to meet the household's subsistence needs, a kind of family economy

27

characteristic of capitalist Europe, because it did not simply sell the labor of its members but instead produced goods and services for sale. The defining characteristic of this family economy—what will be called here the "family production unit"—is that it alone could earn its members high labor-status in a market economy because it alone of the three kinds of family economies could have full control over the economic resources of production and distribution in a market society.

All family production units, while sharing this essential feature, were not identically positioned in the market economy. In some, family members were independent entrepreneurs; in others, they were skilled artisans who owned their own tools and had independent access to materials but who produced for sale to merchants rather than in the open market.[2] Still others were not direct producers in the usual sense but were the professionals of their day—government officials, medical people, or teachers. Similar in some respects to those providing more traditional services, these people had high labor-status because their skills allowed them control over economic resources and, concomitantly, status in noneconomic spheres.

More than its focus on market production separated the family production unit from the family subsistence unit, its undoubted progenitor. The men and women of family production units more easily worked independently of one another than men and women of family economies concentrating on subsistence. In the latter, a strict division of labor by sex was the rule presumably because it insured the most efficient allocation of productive time and thus best served the consumption needs of the family. Accordingly, women's labor consisted of childbearing and nursing, preparation of food and clothing, while men's consisted of agriculture and of supplying fuel and housing. This division was violated only in times of real need or only for short periods of time, such as during the harvest when women did field work. But so strict a division of labor was economically unnecessary in market economies because, with its earnings from commodity production, the family could buy what it did not produce. Productive energy in these families could therefore be best allocated according to the income-generating capacity of each task and the availability of subsistence goods in the marketplace.

The traditional sexual division of labor was not done away with, however, even in well developed urban market economies. Cultural norms, it seems, continued to distinguish between masculine

28

work and feminine work, perhaps partly because of inertia, partly out of a need to maintain clear gender distinctions and partly because women's physical capacities and their roles as mothers made them less suited for certain work. In consequence, while a more flexible division of labor by sex often prevailed in families producing commodities for urban markets, sexual division of labor itself did not disappear. In some families all members joined in the common task but each assumed a different aspect of the task; a family might together run a bakery but the husband might specialize in baking and wife in sales. In other families, tasks were shared or at least interchanged as needed. In still others, each member might have a separate business; the wife might make cloth or beer or might work as a municipal employee, while her husband might work as a butcher, as a grocer, or as a cabinetmaker.

Even families like these, whose members pursued separate trades, can be counted family economies. As Tilly and Scott have pointed out, family economies were defined not by the common participation of their members in one productive effort but by the way their members shared economic, social, and political resources.[3] The unit *could*, however, break down if wives and husbands who had separate businesses came to regard these as individual enterprises. The well-known legal convention of feme sole, which allowed wives to register their business assets and liabilities as their own, may have marked the beginning of this process. Yet, that such a declaration had to be made and that it was in some areas difficult to make are measures of the strength of the family economy.[4]

Although distinct from the rural family enterprise which produced largely for subsistence, the urban family production unit was its recognizable heir. The nuclear family was the core of both units, and both shared demographic and legal structures. In both, coresident nonkin and kin members helped in the family trades. In bakers' households, natural children as well as servants—many of them still children—picked up and delivered goods; in fullers' households, subordinate coresidents helped with the tedious handwork involved in this craft; in smiths' households, they tended fires. In almost all households, they attended to small children, thus freeing the skilled adult women, who in any case had the rights of family position, for more valued tasks.

Both, moreover, were property owners, and consequently had economic incentives to save, to invest, and to adjust family size to the earning potential of their property. The late age of marriage among people in both family economies suggests, of course, that they did respond to economic forces in this way, but we can not therefore assume that such forces affected them as they would have in a fully developed capitalist society. Scholars studying the rural family subsistence unit and the family wage economy into which, in some areas of early modern Europe, it was transformed have observed that these families usually responded to consumption needs rather than to opportunities for accumulation and thus tended to increase production—at whatever cost, so long as it was not ruinously above income—to assure subsistence; but they tended to decrease production, even in the face of apparent chances to increase wealth, when subsistence needs had been met. While it is doubtful that urban family production units serving market economies were entirely unresponsive to the economic opportunities available in a market economy, it may be that the profit motive may not have played a key role in the economic decisions they took.[5]

Although the only kind of family economy which directly produced for the market, and therefore the only possible *familial* routes to high labor-status, family production units were not guaranteed routes to high labor-status in late medieval cities, because they were not always at the center of market production. To explain how women acquired and lost high labor-status in late medieval cities, we must therefore identify the conditions which permitted the family production unit to control market production.

LATE MEDIEVAL MARKET PRODUCTION

Structural economic conditions principally determined the family's role in urban market production and, hence, women's access to high labor-status. At first glance, my hypothesis bears a strong resemblance to that of Alice Clark, who argued that the advent of capitalism in early modern England destroyed the family economy and, with it, women's status in market production. But Clark's thesis is not satisfactory because neither she nor the scholars following her gave sufficient thought to the family economy or to the economic systems with which it intersected.

In *The Working Life of Women in the 17th Century,* first published in England in 1919, Clark argued that during the sixteenth and seventeenth centuries capitalism in England destroyed what she termed the family economy. It did so both by removing the workplace from the home and by subjecting work to schedules that did not harmonize with the rhythms of the household; hence, capitalism effectively eliminated the base from which women had entered production.[6] Subsequent studies have adopted important elements of Clark's thesis. In *The Liberation of Women* Roberta Hamilton explicitly stated that women in early modern England lost access to jobs in capitalist production because industry then moved "out of the home." Susan Cahn, in *Descent from Paradise*, echoed and extended Clark's argument. According to Cahn, the market economy (which she generally equated with the capitalist economy) destroyed the production function of the home because goods and services once made or provided by men and women at home were now purchased outside the home; capitalism intro-duced wages as the basis of productive relations and compelled laborers faced with relatively fewer jobs to compete for what little work there was; and patriarchy assured men access to the scarce wage and to the skills needed to secure it. Inevitably, women were left out of many sectors of the new market production.[7]

A generalized version of Clark's notion has been developed in recent Marxist literature. Eli Zaretsky, in *Capitalism, the Family and Personal Life*, used a similar framework to describe how capitalism (a form of production he seems oddly to regard as a nineteenth-century phenomenon) affected women:

> As in precapitalist society, throughout most of capitalist history the family has been the basic unit of "economic" production—not the "wage-earning" father but the house-hold as a whole. While there was an intense division of labor *within* the family, based upon age, sex, and family position, there was scarcely a division *between* the family and the world of commodity production, at least not until the nineteenth century. ... With the rise of industry, capitalism "split" material production between its socialized forms (the sphere of commodity production) and the private labor performed predominantly by women within the home. In this form, male supremacy, which long antedated capitalism, became an institutional part of the capitalist system of production.[8]

More recently, M. Coulson located women's separation from valued economic production in preindustrial, rather than indus-trial, society:

> As long as production was for use values only, or pro-duction for the market was only a subsidiary element of

general economic activity, production and consumption were fused within one labour process. Although women tended to be employed in some labour processes rather than others, the sexual division was more in terms of different concrete labours or stages of labour process than in terms of men producing for the surplus while women produced for consumption. . . . The growth of the market, based on increasing differentiation of labour, took out of the family most production capable of generating a surplus.[9]

It has become almost a commonplace among many Marxist and feminist historians that capitalism diminished women's roles in economic production by diminishing the family's role in market production. But as it stands, this theory can explain very little about women's work in the period. In part, the problem is that the theory does not distinguish one kind of family economy of this period from another. Clark defined the "family economy" far too generally, as one in which "father and mother and children worked together, and the money earned was regarded as belonging to the family, not to individual members of it," while others have used the same term to mean anything from a household-based workshop, to a subsistent unit, to a wage economy.[10] These are, however, not identical units. Each provided women different kinds of work and in each the meaning of work was different. Undoubtedly, each was affected differently by capitalist development, and if we are to understand the effects of capitalism or of any economic change on women's work, we must take account of these differences.

A second objection to Clark's theory and to those derived from hers is that they do not define capitalism in a way which explains how it changed either the family economy or women's work. Most theorists seem simply to have equated capitalism with market production or with industrialism, and all of them seem to have concluded that capitalism removed work from the household, thus destroying the family economy and eliminating women's access to market production. But market production does not necessarily equal capitalism, and even in obviously capitalist settings the family economy can and did survive. Well into the nineteenth, even the twentieth, century, a kind of family economy was in fact the locus of the putting-out system, the form of capitalist production typical of early modern Europe. It has long been known that women played key roles in these family economies.[11]

The definitions of labor status and of the family production unit offered in the preceding pages can help clear up the confusion resulting from this imprecise terminology. While it is apparent that women did not lose access to market production because the "family economy" was destroyed by "capitalism," it is possible that women lost access to *high-status positions* in market production because the *family production unit* was destroyed by capitalism. It is also apparent, however, that if we want to pursue this hypothesis by looking at urban women working in late medieval economies, we must answer some questions about late medieval market production: in what settings was this production capitalist? Was it in capitalist economies that the family production unit disappeared and that women lost access to high labor-status? If so, how did these changes occur?

To answer these questions, we must turn to the development of urban market production in the late medieval period of northern European history. The general line of development is well known. By definition, the emergence of market production involved a shift from production for use to production for sale. With this shift came an increase in the degree of division and specialization of labor, the application of better technologies to production, and more sophisticated organizations for allocation, distribution, and consumption of goods and services. These changes occurred most rapidly in economic sectors involved in long-distance trade, partly because producers for international markets had to meet particular and specialized demands but even more because the competitive conditions of trade in international markets promoted, indeed compelled, these changes. In these markets, there was no single authority to apply regulations and curtail competition; as a result, producers could survive only if they could supply better goods and services more quickly and more cheaply than others. To do so, they needed sufficient flexibility to divide and specialize labor, to train artisans and to add technology.

These pressures did not eliminate local supervision and control over international trade and industry but they did ensure that the guilds, hansas, staples, municipalities, ecclesiastical authorities, and princes who exercised this control did so within limits. It was in the context of this competitive market situation that early forms of capitalism arose, usually when long-distance merchants, using the leverage over artisans and local tradesmen which access to imported raw materials or markets gave them, took over production processes themselves. In these early days of the development of

Europe's market economy, however, there were several routes to and no single form of early capitalism.

From about 1300 to 1800, the long period when the transition to capitalism occurred, economic change came in various ways and rates. In trying to understand this complexity, scholars have produced a rich literature on the rural agricultural and industrial economies as on well as the urban economy but they have arrived at no consensus on the nature of the transition in any of its temporal or geographic settings. Questions remain about the most basic issues: the ultimate causes of the development of capitalist production relations, the role early capitalists played in production, the character of the social and economic systems capitalism replaced, the locus and forms of capitalist development, and the role of the state in this process.[12]

Used with caution, this literature can nevertheless help us to identify the structural economic changes which may have affected the family economy and women's labor status. With it, we can construct three "ideal types" which categorize the various forms of production, along with their associated social structures, typical of late medieval cities of northern Europe. The first two types, medieval craft production and capitalism, are familiar, if not always well understood. The third, small commodity production, is less familiar. It describes economies which had developed stable, noncapitalist production structures well adapted, as medieval craft production was not, to competition in international markets.

At one end of the spectrum lay medieval craft production, which most historians regard as the immediate predecessor of urban capitalism. In this form of production, small producers serving local and regional markets controlled industry and commerce. A hallmark of the system was the household-based shop staffed by a master artisan and helpers; the subordinate status of the helpers was transient and reflected their youth, their comparatively meager experience, and their slight expertise, rather than permanent relegation to a social sector employed by, rather than employing, productive resources. Another hallmark was the guild or artisanal corporation which preserved the economic egalitarianism of the system and the personal basis on which production relations were managed. The system of medieval craft production thus promoted producer autonomy, rough equality among members of a craft, and, above all, shared control of the resources of production and sale. In this form of production, master artisans and independent shop-owners had high labor-status while their helpers and trainees had lower labor-status.

While medieval craft production may have been typical of most late medieval urban communities, it seldom survived in cities devoted to production for long-distance markets. There, most historians agree, some form of capitalism was emerging, but just what this capitalism was and how it emerged are subjects of debate. The description used in this study owes something to many of the definitions which have been proposed, but it owes its largest debt to a Marxist definition which focuses on the social relations of production and the associated sociopolitical order.

The term "capitalism," as used in this study, refers to a form of production which grew up in cities involved in production for long-distance markets where merchants transformed themselves into merchant-producers by taking over the production functions once carried on by independent producers. The merchants accomplished this in a number of ways. Some transferred trading profits (obtained through long-distance merchandising of commodities or luxury goods) to industry, initially at least to industry serving long-distance markets. In this way, merchants came to monopolize raw materials needed by producers and to control access to their sales outlets; in the process, they assumed the entrepreneurial role of the artisan, turned craftsmen into wage laborers, and eventually by similar avenues moved into nearly all trades, even those serving local markets. Other merchant-capitalists arose differently, by using rural, female, or immigrant labor to undermine urban artisans. Sometimes artisans themselves entered long-distance trade, only to abandon their craft allegiances and, like merchants elsewhere, become owners of putting-out systems. Whatever the means by which artisans lost control of production and sales, the consequence was lost labor-status. It did not matter that throughout the late Middle Ages and into the early modern period in some industries—in metal working and textiles, for example—wage-earning workers remained highly skilled, nor did it matter that their wages exceeded those of unskilled workers. The artisans lost labor-status both absolutely, as they lost control over production and distribution of economic resources, and relatively, as the entrepreneurial position they had lost—which was now the exclusive province of the bourgeoisie—was elevated by the money, prestige, and political power capitalist entrepreneurships could bequeath.

Wherever capitalism was the dominant mode of production, we

find certain features of social, economic, and political structure. Fundamental to capitalism's definition is the nature of the class relations that prevailed and the social hierarchy it bred. In capitalist economies, the property-owning class was, of course, rich and their employees were poor, but differences in wealth alone did not distinguish one from the other. Instead, each was defined by the production relations which reciprocally bound it to the other: the employers owned the means of production and, without access to them, their employees could not have survived; the employers, for their part, could not have survived as capitalists without their laborers.

In economic sectors characterized by such production relations, the object of production was to increase profit. This object could be achieved by revenue growth and production efficiencies, but the methods available to late medieval urban capitalists were limited by the economic conditions of the age: markets were hard to reach, specialized, and small; technological limitations meant that equipment was not readily available for reducing labor costs. Compared to nineteenth-century industrialists, capitalists of late medieval cities had few tools with which to achieve profit growth, but, as participants in the same kind of production relations, they behaved in quite similar ways. The capitalists of late medieval cities sought to cheapen labor by subdividing the production process, a goal often achieved by circumventing the established labor force and, as we have seen, by employing women or workers from the countryside. Capitalists also struggled against each other for markets and materials, seeking constantly to insure and expand sales revenues.

These features of capitalism led to economic, social, and political unrest that was manifested in several ways. The competitive atmosphere in which capitalism flourished, and which it bred, freed entrepreneurs (and forced them) to seek ever higher profits. Consequently, capitalists followed perceived profit opportunities, frequently abandoning individual businesses and starting new ones. No economic sector, no enterprise was secure, and the instability was heightened because many, perhaps most, new ventures did not turn out to be so profitable as hoped and so were quickly abandoned. It is easy to understand why in this atmosphere capitalists themselves were insecure. Often they vied for political power with the city's traditional elite who still held pivotal positions in government, despite their loss of economic hegemony. Capitalists also competed against each other not only for resources, labor, and markets, but also for political power to promote their economic interests.

Another source of instability in capitalist societies derived from the capitalists' efforts to destroy small producers. Unable to resist the economic pressures capitalists could bring to bear but unwilling to submit to their fate, artisans sometimes revolted. In some places, this unrest was so widespread and so permanent a feature of urban life that it is fair to speak, even in such early days, of class consciousness—to assert, in other words, that a working class had emerged, conscious of its own interests and perceiving its employers as its social and political enemy.[13]

The descriptions of urban capitalism and medieval craft production offered here are ideal types and do not describe the actual socioeconomic structure in any city of late medieval Europe. Nevertheless, the terms are widely used, and the definitions I have provided will be familiar. For many historians, these terms not only refer to ideal types but are also used, explicitly or implicitly, to describe urban economic development in this period. In this argument, cities of late medieval Europe are thought to have progressed from medieval craft production towards capitalism as a result of their involvement in the international market economy.[14] Accordingly, cities of the era can be classified as belonging to one type or another, or as being in transition from the first to the second, and the differences in classification will reflect the degree to which the international market has penetrated the local economy.

My study will differ from existing scholarship on the nature of the transition to capitalism in late medieval cities on exactly this point, for I will argue that many cities involved in international trade did not fit either type and were not in transition from one to another. In fact, even in cities devoted to production for long-distance markets a transition to capitalism was not inevitable. Because they had strong and individual traditions and institutions, because they participated in different markets and industries, and because they had entered the international market economy at different times, some cities had developed another production structure, a structure neither of the two ideal types can easily accommodate. To understand the urban history of Europe during the four or five centuries that make up the transition to capitalism, we cannot ignore these situations. Less predecessors of, than stable alternatives to, capitalism, they constitute another type, and to analyze them we need a third definition, "small commodity production."[15]

Small commodity production shared certain elements with medieval craft production. Commodities were manufactured by independent master artisans who owned their means of production and worked in individual small shops assisted either by members of their households or, at best, by a handful of skilled and semiskilled employees, some of whom they were training to take over the business or to establish one on their own. Social and personal ties as well as wages formed the basis of economic relations. Corporate associations, which were variously known as guilds or "crafts" and which had varying degrees of independence and corporative power, supervised the acquisition of output, terms of employment, and training practices. In addition to these traditional features, however, small commodity production incorporated important new elements which also characterized capitalism. Expansion of output, achieved by the application of additional labor or by the introduction of new technology and new products, was one of its objectives. Like the late medieval urban merchant-producers of capitalist societies, small commodity producers directed their output towards export markets and required significant amounts of capital for raw materials, equipment, operations, and sales.

Small commodity production was not a stagnant holdover from earlier days found in economic sectors which were in decline. It was, rather, a system compatible both with growing, market-oriented industries and with traditional urban societies. Competition and investment, although intrinsic to this form of production, were nevertheless circumscribed in accordance with certain firmly defended values. Full employment, a "reasonable" standard of living, producer autonomy, and rough equality among artisans rather than unbridled growth and profit maximization were the goals of those responsible for the system. Production for the market which was accomplished with infusions of capital naturally meant a constant impetus, even pressure, for innovation and change, but the mechanisms established by those in control of the system succeeded in preventing its subversion.

No precapitalist city, of course, whether characterized as dominated by medieval craft or small commodity production, was egalitarian. In these cities, populations were rigidly stratified on the basis of age, economic function, and birth. The young were poorer than the old and lacked their elders' social and political status; sons and daughters of master artisans, for example, worked as servant-apprentices in their own or in their neighbors' homes. A distinct hierarchy existed among crafts as well; butchers and artisan-producers of wool cloth, for example, were often richer, better represented in whatever form of corporative government existed, and awarded greater social deference than were barbers and linen weavers. Finally, in most of these cities, a group of wealthy property owners formed both a distinct economic elite, which was sometimes active in commerce, and a distinct political elite, which controlled office by virtue of birth or juridical status. Usually, the elite claimed descent from the founders of the urban constitution.

It is probably because precapitalist urban societies were often highly stratified and because the degree of this stratification often reflected the economy's involvement in long-distance trade that many historians have believed that these societies were capitalist or quickly becoming so. Horst Jecht has provided one of the fullest explications of this argument. Proposing that the progression towards capitalism could be measured by the extent to which wealth was inequitably distributed among taxpayers, Jecht constructed, as his own measures of this progression, three ideal types of situations: the agricultural market town ("die Ackerbürgerstadt"), the diversified medium-sized industrial city serving local and regional markets ("die allseitig entwickelten Gewerbestadt lokalen Gepräges"), and the export-oriented industrial city dominated by merchants ("die Exportgewerbe- und Handelsstadt"). Sixteenth-century Augsburg, where more than 50 percent of the population was judged too poor to pay taxes and more than 1 percent of the population could afford over 100 Gulden in taxes, exemplified for Jecht an export-oriented city in which capitalism had been established.[16]

While Jecht's analysis helps to show how the economic orientation of a city could determine its economic hierarchy, it must be used with caution. A highly skewed wealth-distribution curve is not, contrary to Jecht's assumptions, necessarily evidence of capitalist production relations. In many cities, to be sure, where merchants grew very rich, local townspeople did not; but this pattern was not the consequence of capitalism. Rather, the wealth of the elite reflected ties to long-distance trade and finance, not to the local establishment of capitalist production relations; only when the merchants used their wealth to take over production did they become capitalist. Instead of involving themselves in local industry, however, merchant elites often ignored it or sometimes even protected it, and local industry then went on as it had. In some cities, moreover, capitalists with roots in the artisanal community were far from being as rich as established long-distance merchants.

Capitalism in late medieval cities was not, therefore, the inevitable result of an orientation toward long-distance trade nor was it indicated by the presence of great wealth.

Rather than measures of economic stratification, measures of social and political stratification may better indicate a city's socioeconomic structure in this age. Late medieval cities of the North developed comparable political institutions and comparable social structures which tended to change in predictable ways in response to socioeconomic change. Erich Maschke, in a series of studies, has constructed a typology of late medieval urban social structure, which can be adapted to examine these links.

Beginning with the premise that the social system of late medieval cities was sui generis, Maschke argued that the urban citizenry, the *Bürgerschaft,* was not a unit in the society of orders that Mousnier, following Weber, had described.[17] As Maschke pointed out, these were not homogeneous but highly, indeed uniquely, stratified societies. At origin in the eleventh through the thirteenth centuries, many of these cities were governed by an entrenched, often legally defined elite who alone had citizenship, a group which many historians have considered a social order new to medieval society, unique to cities and characteristic of noncapitalist urban societies. They have called this social order a "patriciate," replacing a variety of terms used at the time (such as *meliores, potentes,* or *Geschlechter*) to describe families who governed, controlled wealth, and claimed social status, all by right of birth.[18]

This patriciate, Maschke tried to show, lost its essential privileges and homogeneity, however, when the city fully entered international markets. Thanks to the expansion of commerce, often accompanied by the growth of a population of artisans oriented towards long-distance trade, both social and political change occurred. The societies became more "open" than cities dominated by a true patriciate, and vertical social mobility occurred more commonly; legal or juridical differences between the old patriciate and the rest of the urban residents were disappearing, if not already gone, and social as well as economic distinctions among the patrician residents, as measured by consumption patterns, were both more varied and more marked.

Maschke insisted that these changes did not, however, signify the emergence of classes. The term "class," he claimed, was created to describe the social stratification system peculiar to industrial capitalism and cannot be usefully applied to late medieval urban society. For Maschke, a class was "a collection of individuals whose life chances are determined by disposition, under a market economy, over economic goods (property, income) or the lack thereof, as well as by similar interests and who are conscious of their position."[19] Late medieval urban society only occasionally and in part met these criteria. He also insisted that since, according to Marx, classes are distinguished by their relationship to the means of production and, since the most important distinguishing economic factor in late medieval cities was not ownership of the means of production but participation in trade, the term "class" cannot be applied to social groups in late medieval cities.

Rather than adapt either of these two inappropriate concepts to the late medieval city, Maschke borrowed a concept from modern sociology, that of a stratum (*Schicht*), which he defined as "a number of persons horizontally grouped according to a social system who, on the basis of certain indicators, are judged as approximately equal and, in comparison to other groups, [are judged] as higher or lower, as [being] under or above [them]."[20] In the late medieval cities he studied, two objective, identifying marks (*Lagemerkmale*) located an individual in the urban hierarchy: wealth and honor (*Ehre*, perhaps better described as professional or occupational status). Wealth played so key a role that laws in some places set a minimum to the fortune required of a holder of city office. Occupational status similarly had social and political consequences; artisans' wives could not dress as sumptuously as merchants' wives; barbers and linen weavers in fifteenth-century Cologne could not stand for office in the guild government.

Using this analysis, Maschke divided the population of a typical late medieval city into three *Schichten*. The first was originally confined to the patriciate—usually rich merchants and *rentiers*—but Maschke acknowledged that these men frequently shared political status (citizenship and right to office) with nonpatrician merchants and sometimes with artisans and guildsmen who belonged to the *Mittelschicht*. In such cases, the middle group was itself becoming stratified, being headed by nonpatrician merchants and artisan-merchants who were distinguished by wealth, life-style, and political influence from lowly artisans in less honorable trades such as woodworking and construction. At the bottom of the hierarchy was a poor and propertyless group of workers without skills. Despite the sharp differentiation among these *Schichten*, individuals could move from one to another. Many young immigrant journeymen who belonged first to the lowest stratum, for example, often moved up to the second after completing their training. Often, too, aged widows of artisans fell to the bottom. Mobility at the top was possible as well, since, as we have seen, the barriers erected by the patriciate were being scaled by new men who married into or pushed their own way to the top.

Maschke used this typology to describe what he regarded as the social, economic, and political order typical of late medieval cities in the North and seems to have regarded this order as self-perpetuating. In fact, however, he described a stratification system which could and did change, in a pattern which accords with the typology I have offered to describe the socioeconomic systems possible in late medieval cities.

Certain features of the system Maschke described incorporated, on the one hand, features reminiscent of both medieval craft production and small commodity production. Where a patriciate still controlled trade and government, a rigid social hierarchy prevailed. Each stratum (*Schicht*) in the hierarchy was nevertheless free of binding economic ties to the others; patrician merchants, for example, ran long-distance trading operations with little economic connection to the industrial and service economy managed by small, independent producers. In such cases, however, the *Schichten* had strong political and social ties to one another because the merchant patriciate provided the city with government and military leadership in exchange for political obedience, social deference, and some financial support for the city's governors.

Maschke's analysis also illuminates, on the other hand, how this socioeconomic system would have been transformed in a transition to capitalism. In such a scenario, the patriciate, having been undermined by the development of industry and the further expansion of trade, would have lost its claim to political and social status to the new competitors emerging from the artisanal sector and the citizenry of new merchants who once made up the now disintegrating *Mittelschicht*. As merchants of industrial goods who increasingly ran putting-out systems, the new elite would have had little in common with the artisans from their own guilds whom they now employed as wage workers. These artisans would have slipped into the new proletariat while their employers were taking on the role of a preindustrial bourgeoisie.

Maschke's typology, while it does not describe a stable social order, does illuminate the possible links between the sociopolitical system of a city and its economic structure. Patrician rule, his work suggests, is compatible both with what I have called medieval craft production and small commodity production, while the disintegration of a patriciate, and its replacement by a mercantile and industrial elite without juridical or familial claims to rule, indicates, if it is not an infallible guide to, the emergence of capitalist socioeconomic order. The chapters that follow will employ Maschke's typology to help identify these links.

AN AGENDA FOR RESEARCH

Women's labor status in late medieval cities of the North, we can now hypothesize, depended upon the functions of the family production unit during the development of the market economy. The hypothesis has three parts, which together will be the focus of examination in the following chapters. (1) Women gained access to high-status positions in urban market production in late medieval Europe because the family production unit survived the transition from subsistence to market production and because women retained their position in the family economy during this shift. (2) Since family position gave women access to high-status work, principally married and widowed women earned such status, and women who belonged to families with high labor-status themselves had high-status positions. (3) As a result of still undetermined changes in the way production for the market was organized, the work which granted high labor-status was soon removed from the family production unit, leaving it a center of low-status work.

I designed the empirical studies that immediately follow, on fifteenth- and early sixteenth-century Leiden and on fifteenth-century Cologne, to help determine how variations in the structure of market production affected the family production unit and, hence, women's place in market production. My analysis consequently emphasizes economic factors, and I have not directly investigated the families which gave birth to the work. The questions I have set out to answer do not, however, require direct study of family structure, because we can be reasonably sure that in both cities families by and large conformed to the "northern European" pattern typical of the region.

We know, for example, that the demographic profile of Leiden's families matched that described in the previous chapter. Small nuclear families formed the core of the household, but most households lodged apprentices, servants, or dependent relatives as well, bringing their average size during the period of my study up to about five.[21] It is also evident from some scattered data that even among Leiden's traditional elite, women married in their late twenties or occasionally in their early thirties, and men were on average only a few years older when they married. Furthermore, to judge by the few statistics available, it was not uncommon for women to marry men a few years their junior.[22] If the rich in Leiden married according to a pattern not too far removed from the "northern European" one described by Hajnal, we can assume that ordinary people in the city very likely followed customs even closer to this cultural tradition. The legal historians who have looked at private law and women in the Low Countries have concluded that legal conventions there also fit the pattern typical of family-run household economies in the urban North. Women and men shared family property, and women were technically subject to the guardianship of their husband in civil law; both practices testify to the strength of the household economy in the city.[23]

Demographic evidence permitting even similarly tentative inferences are much more scarce for Cologne, but we do know that Hermann van Weinsberg, a member of Cologne's sixteenth-century merchant class, was first married in his late twenties to a widow six years his senior; his second marriage was also to an older woman. Both of his wives were businesswomen. The legal evidence from Cologne is much more extensive than the demographic, and it leaves little doubt that the family-run household economy was well entrenched there. Customary law treated the property of the nuclear family and all its members as community property; sons and daughters typically inherited almost equally. While men and women in Cologne made marriage contracts and wills which distinguished one partner's property from the other's, they seldom deviated very far from the principle that husbands and wives, sons and daughters, shared the economic resources of the household. So closely knit was the household economy in this city, in fact, that husbands and wives were for certain purposes forbidden to separate the property they brought into the marriage from the marital property.[24]

My empirical studies in the chapters to follow presume, therefore, that in size, structure, and function the families of Leiden, Cologne, and the other cities at which I look more briefly in a later chapter fit the pattern I have described as typical of northern European cities in the period. The studies do, however, test this presumption and examine the ways in which this pattern altered as women left market production. In fact, the marital status of the women whose work I am cataloguing is one of my principal concerns, and in the empirical chapters I will be both recording and commenting on how the position of working women in their families and the position of their families in market production were correlated with variations in the structure of market production.

Leiden and Cologne were both important cities in the region comprising northern France, the Low Countries, and the Rhineland. This was the most urbanized area of northern Europe from about 1300 to 1600 and, not coincidentally, the source of much of our evidence about women's high-status work. These two cities were chosen as the centerpieces of my study principally because, as a pair, they provided the best opportunity available to me for exploring my hypothesis. Unpublished and published sources from medieval archives in both cities are abundant, and aspects of the history of both cities have been the subject of careful research by past scholars. Thanks to these sources, I could locate women's work in its economic, social, and political context and test my idea that the family production unit and women's labor status changed as this context changed. Even so, I had to go beyond the existing scholarship which described this context, for my predecessors were often concerned with different questions or had arrived at conclusions about the context that I thought necessary to modify. Consequently, a good part of the empirical studies that follow is devoted not to cataloguing women's work but to describing the world in which they worked.

Although other cities might seem more obvious choices for an investigation of women's work in the period, none proved to be as appropriate as these two. The great Flemish textile centers—Ypres, Ghent, or Bruges—had to be excluded because the archives of each were incomplete or inaccessible. Amsterdam's and Antwerp's histories belonged more to the modern age when a world economy and centralized states were developing and forever changing the urban history of Europe. Paris, as the seat of the French crown, could not be considered typical. Of course, many other cities might well have proven good subjects for study, had I the time to investigate every possibility. In some others that seemed promising, I began research, and the results of that research are contained in chapter 7, where I show how the hypothesis developed in the studies of Leiden and Cologne might be applied to explain women's work elsewhere. While each of the three cities described in that chapter, Lier, Douai, and Frankfurt am Main, provide interesting comparisons with Leiden and Cologne, none could have served as a centerpiece of this study because archival material would not have sufficed or because none would have provided so useful a test of my hypothesis.

It is principally for the last reason that Leiden and Cologne were chosen for this study; they differed from each other in ways that are crucial for testing my hypothesis. Leiden was a medium-sized city firmly linked to the international market economy through its devotion to the manufacture of drapery, the heavy cloth made of English wool which was the foundation of northern Europe's long-distance trade in industrial products. But, as I shall argue in some detail in chapter 3, Leiden's economic and social structure was not capitalist. Instead, the dominant mode of production in the city during the period covered by this study was small commodity production. The pattern of women's participation in Leiden's industry and commerce provided significant opportunities to study the ways that this production structure could accommodate—or close out—the family production unit.

Cologne was very different. One of northern Europe's largest cities in the fifteenth century, it was just ending a long period as Germany's most important trade and industrial center. At the same time its traditional two-part economic structure, made up on the one hand of long-distance merchants and financiers and on the other of independent artisans, was collapsing into one economic enterprise centered on production of industrial goods for sale in distant markets. The resulting merger produced a new class of artisan-merchants and merchants who functioned as capitalists. Cologne was different from Leiden not only in its economic orientation and socioeconomic structure but also, and surprisingly, in that it provided women more opportunities for high-status work. It is these two differences which made Cologne so appropriate to pair with Leiden.

PART 2

Empirical Studies
Leiden and Cologne

3

The Socioeconomic Structure of Leiden

For almost a century and a half, from the second quarter of the fifteenth until the third quarter of the sixteenth century, Leiden was one of the most important producers of the heavy cloth made of English wool, known as drapery, which then dominated northern Europe's international textile trade. So important was this industry that a study of any facet of Leiden's history at the time must take it into account, and a study of economic matters must be centered on it. The drapery employed well over half of the adult male work-force; it was responsible for the almost threefold increase in the population which occurred during the fifteenth century; it contributed significantly to the prosperity of individual members of the city's elite; it underwrote a good part of municipal expenses; and, as a consequence of its importance, it generated, directly or indirectly, most of the records we have about the economy of Leiden during the time.

The drapery was also a premier employer of women. N. W. Posthumus, the eminent historian of Leiden's textile industry, thought that the city's drapery offered women almost unparalleled opportunities for paid work: "Leiden's industry," he claimed, "offered [women] a wide field . . . [and] in this respect had thus discarded its medieval character in contrast to those trades in which medieval craft production remained the prevailing mode . . . almost exclusively female labor was used in the lighter processes [of textile production]."[1] Jenneke Quast's study of Leiden's municipal records also revealed that women were active in the drapery, indeed in the entire textile industry.[2]

49

Neither Posthumus nor Quast thoroughly examined women's place in Leiden's market production, but their leads provided the impetus for the research summarized in chapter 4. There, women's roles both in the drapery and in other sectors of market production are investigated and the pattern of women's gain and loss of these positions is sketched. The preceding chapter examines the socio-economic structure of Leiden in order to identify the features which rendered market production more or less hospitable to the family production unit, the agent, according to my hypothesis, of women's entry into market production.

This study is confined to a period which began about 1430, when the drapery first expanded, and ended around 1570, when the drapery collapsed. The period belongs to the Middle Ages, not to the early modern era which in Leiden began only after the 1570s, when the "new drapery" was founded, an industry which was destined to grow even larger and achieve even greater significance in the European economy than its predecessor. The 1570s also marked the early stages of the Dutch Revolt and inaugurated Leiden's emergence as an international political, religious, and intellectual center. As home to thousands of refugees who fled north from the southern Netherlands after the Spanish triumph there and as survivor of the siege mounted by the Spanish in 1573, Leiden became a center of political resistance. Thanks to its success against the siege, Leiden was made the home of a new university. During these same decades Calvinist practices took hold, upsetting the religious status quo as neither Lutheranism nor Anabaptism had done. The 1570s decisively ended one era in the city's history and began another.

THE HISTORY OF THE DRAPERY

The economic, social, and political structure of late medieval Leiden reflected its ties to the drapery; so to understand Leiden's economy, we must understand its drapery. Until Holland's amalgamation into the Burgundian lands of Philip the Good in 1434, Leiden, then a small city of perhaps 5,000 inhabitants, had only regional importance as a market and political center of the Rijnland. Residents of Leiden had been producing textiles for regional markets since the fourteenth century, and, probably in connection with its involvement in the wool trade, the city had acquired a place in northern European commerce. But it was only when Leideners achieved regular access to English wool, at some point in the early fifteenth century, that the city's producers shifted to manufacture for distant markets and the population began its expansion, reaching about 14,000 by the end of the century.[3] Although the drapery made in Leiden never equaled the best cloth from the southern Low Countries, it came to rank as the finest from the northern Netherlands. By the third quarter of the fifteenth century, the city annually exported some 20,000 cloths bearing the city's seal and bought on average at least 15 percent of the English wool exported through Calais.[4]

The industry owed its dramatic growth to several factors. Flanders, having suffered almost continuous social and political upheaval since the early fourteenth century, was losing its dominant position in the traditional international cloth market.[5] Leiden easily found buyers for its cloth, particularly since the producers from other Continental centers and from England who were eventually to dominate textile markets had not then reached their full capacities. Tensions between the Hansa merchants and the Flemish gave the Dutch an opportunity to improve their own position with the Hansa, then a key supplier to prosperous Baltic and eastern European markets. Amalgamation into the Burgundian empire was a further benefit, because it gave Leiden better access to materials and markets. Hansa merchants bought most of Leiden's sealed cloth, and because they demanded a single kind of heavy, good-quality cloth made entirely of English wool, Leiden imposed rigid production standards and had a very narrow product line.[6] After about 1450, Leiden stopped producing textiles of Continental wools for export, and most cloths of Continental wools made after that date were intended for local and regional markets.[7]

After the rise which began in the 1430s drapery production remained high for decades, but the industry was always threatened by competitors, by changing markets, and by its vulnerability to disruptions of English wool supplies. Competition from rural manufacturers had become a major problem by 1500 when Leiden began to ban textile production as well as other industries in the area around the city. Periodic recessions, many of them tied to shortages of wool supplies, plagued the drapery. The industry entered its final decline in the 1530s when the costs of wool rose sharply and its quality fell because the best English wool was reserved for the growing English industry.[8] Marketing arrangements with the Hansa merchants broke down because their eastern markets demanded less of the heavy cloth which Leiden made but more of the lighter, cheaper cloth from places like Hondschoote. Leiden did not respond quickly to this shift in the market, and in trying to retain traditional markets while simultaneously trying to move to southern markets where new Continental competitors making light fabrics were already established, the city's rigidity hurt it. The English entrance into the Baltic markets with their own products (and, to the detriment of Hansa merchants, with their own ships) compounded the effects of declining northern and eastern markets. Leiden's shortsighted policy of taxing wool imports, which did not end until 1545, when it was too late, made matters worse.[9] When the English lost Calais in 1558 and closed the wool Staple, Leiden finally turned to Spanish wool, but not in time to save the old drapery. Its final collapse occurred between 1562 and 1573; the *strikerye* figures in Appendix 1 testify to its extent and speed.

Although the medieval drapery was totally destroyed during the Dutch Revolt, a new textile industry was founded soon afterwards by refugees from the textile cities of the southern Low Countries.[10] For over a century after they began to arrive in 1582, they made Leiden the single most important wool-cloth producer on the Continent, with annual exports of well over 100,000 cloths. The city grew in population as well; by 1600 Leiden had about 24,000 residents and by 1623 approximately 45,000.[11] The new textile industry was hardly just a bigger version of the old. Its practitioners were different—initially Flemish, then Walloon, and only much later Dutch. Its raw material was different. Instead of English wool, it used Spanish and other Continental wools. Its product, too, was different. The new industry began with "light" textiles, like sayes or fustians, and it was only after the 1630s that drapery reminiscent of, but not the same as, old medieval cloth was to have importance. Its markets also were different; instead of northern and eastern Europe, the new textiles were directed towards southern European markets or markets outside of Europe.

POLITICS AND GOVERNMENT

The municipal government of late medieval Leiden closely supervised the drapery. From the late fourteenth century on, the government issued extensive regulations covering every aspect of production and trade in sealed cloth and made certain they were enforced. Many of its members produced and sold cloth, and themselves provided the day-to-day supervision of drapery production and sales. From time to time, it even supplied the drapery with capital equipment and made direct loans to drapers.[12] Because the sources we have about the drapery were produced by this municipal government, we must look at it more closely.

From 1434, when Philip of Burgundy granted Leiden control of its own administration and courts, until well into the sixteenth century, when the Hapsburg government began to encroach on its autonomy, all city affairs were legislated, executed, and adjudicated by the government of Leiden. During this period of effective autonomy, Leiden's communal government was headed by eight aldermen (*Schepenen*) who shared judicial functions with the *Schout*, the count's representative in Leiden. The aldermen were joined by four mayors whose offices had first been established in the fourteenth century, and together these thirteen officials formed the *Gerecht*. By the mid-fifteenth century, the *Vroedschap*, whose members had usually served on the Gerecht, had come to play a powerful role in government and, in fact, constituted its legislative arm. Other government officials in Leiden, including the wardens of the drapery, who oversaw all aspects of cloth production and sale, were appointees of the Gerecht and were responsible to that body.[13]

The important offices in Leiden's government were held by members of the city's traditional elite, a group of long-resident families, a few of whom bore titles, most of whom had rights to income-producing properties outside Leiden, and many of whom had direct connections to the drapery. This elite controlled government not by means of laws explicitly excluding others but through the procedures by which offices were filled. Beginning in 1434, when Philip the Good issued the Privilege which served Leiden as a constitution until well into the sixteenth century, the aldermen were chosen by the count from a slate of candidates proposed by the Vroedschap, itself composed of former aldermen and mayors, while the mayors were in turn chosen by the aldermen and the Schout. The Schout, although the count's direct appointee, had to be a citizen of Leiden. By the mid-sixteenth century, the Vroedschap had become the most important governmental body, and its heir was Leiden's early modern patriciate, a body known as the Regents.[14]

While a great deal of work has been done on the social, economic, and political character of the urban patriciates in early modern Holland, very little research has focused on these elites during the Middle Ages.[15] The data available leave little doubt, however, that Leiden's late medieval elite can be considered a patriciate even in the most narrow sense of the term and was the direct predecessor of Leiden's seventeenth-century patriciate. In both periods, the key offices of government were rotated among a small group of the richest families who not only monopolized political power but also controlled urban property and managed its industry, all by right of birth. Many of the families who ruled in fifteenth-century Leiden had descendants in the seventeenth-century patriciate.

The hold medieval Leiden's patriciate had on political power can be illustrated with data drawn from a variety of contemporary records.[16] In fiscal year 1495 (beginning November 1494 for the mayors and July 1495 for the aldermen) twelve men were appointed to the office of mayor or alderman. All held at least one of these two offices at another time during the thirteen-year period from 1490 to 1503, and, on average, each held one of the two positions for four and one-half of these thirteen years. In total, these twelve men held 56 of 156 terms of office in the Gerecht (excluding the post as Schout). In addition, one of the men served as Schout for at least four years of this period. All but one of the six in this group whose kin can be identified appear to have been related to men who held one of these two posts twenty times during the same thirteen years, so that at a minimum these men and their close relations held over half the major posts in Leiden during this period.[17] Many also held lesser posts. Jan Conninxz, for example, mayor in 1490 and 1496 and alderman in 1494 and 1495, was also drapery warden in 1490 and 1492. Jacop van Boschhuysen, mayor in 1490 and 1494 and Schout at least from 1498 to 1501, was also a treasurer in 1493 and 1494.

Measures computed somewhat differently illustrate that two generations later a similar pattern prevailed.[18] For the twelve years from 1540 through 1551, twenty-four men held fifty-two available terms as mayor (in some years there were more than four appointments). The same men also held over three-quarters of the aldermen's appointments so that, on average, they held about 90 percent of the Gerecht offices. Further, all but eight served in the Vroedschap during the period.

Most members of the patriciate were involved in the drapery, either directly as producers or indirectly through their families. So common was it for Gerecht members to have such ties that, to prevent conflicts of interest, until 1578 ordinances were regularly issued which forbade members of the Gerecht to produce cloth during their terms of office.[19] To comply with the law, Leiden's elite had to alternate government service and cloth production, and many men did so, even within periods so short that switching from one to another must have been both inconvenient and expensive. Between 25 and 30 percent of the appointments to alderman or mayor made during the twelve years from 1490 through 1501 were held by men who produced cloth in the same period, although never during those years of active government service. For the twelve years from 1540 through 1551, the figures range from 25 percent to 39 percent.

Gerecht members had few industrial or commercial interests other than the drapery and did not take on new ones, even during the mid-sixteenth century when cloth production was declining. Of the fifty-six men who sat on Leiden's Vroedschap from 1540 to 1565 whose principal occupations are known (out of a total membership of ninety-nine), eighteen were drapers, twelve were otherwise involved in the drapery (as large retail cloth merchants [*wantsnijders*], as wholesalers and financiers [*uutreeders*], or as wardens of the drapery), and four were both drapers and brewers. In total, these men made up about 60 percent of the group identified by occupation. The only other industry that attracted more than occasional Gerecht members was brewing; seven men (plus the four who also produced cloth) were brewers.[20] Many Gerecht members who did not themselves produce cloth had family connections to those who did.[21]

Like the patriciates elsewhere in late medieval cities, the patriciate of Leiden was both an economic and a political elite. The men of this elite had long-standing financial interests in the rural economy of the region and must have derived a good part of their income from these holdings, but they did not actively undertake commercial farming there.[22] Instead, they devoted their energy to importing wool, to cloth merchandising, and to government. Just as the economic activities of its members help to identify Leiden's elite as an urban patriciate, so does the security they enjoyed as municipal governors. Although they quarreled among themselves, even joining in the *Hoekse* and *Kabeljauwsche* battles which divided Holland's aristocracy for two centuries, their rule in Leiden was unaffected by the disorders. The city supported Philip of Burgundy's opponents in these battles before his succession, but under him it acquired greater autonomy than it had before, and members of the two opposing parties shared power in Leiden after 1434.[23]

Fiscal problems prompted the single internal challenge to the rule of the patriciate. One group of men, who were apparently excluded from government and dissatisfied with the way the Gerecht handled the city's financial affairs, forced the Gerecht to create special fiscal officers to be elected in the districts, presumably by members of the adult male citizenry. The first *homans* were chosen in 1398 but the citizenry lost control over them when the Privilege of 1434 gave mayors the right to name them (with the consent of the citizenry). The homans, now called treasurers, thereafter steadily lost influence until the city's financial plight of the late fifteenth century and early sixteenth century engendered new reforms.

As a patrician government, the municipal authorities shared rule with no other communal or religious institution. The many artisans of Leiden had not established themselves as a political force, and the trade-associated brotherhoods, which were supervised by, even founded at the orders of, the Gerecht, had only religious and social functions.[24] The municipal authority forbade independent guilds, but instead organized some of Leiden's artisans into "crafts" (*ambachten*).[25] An ambacht was typically a formal body, sometimes with a charter and always with clearly defined functions, work rules, and membership requirements. The ambachten regulated production and set requirements for training and membership by orders of and often under the eyes of municipal officers. The senior official of the drapery who oversaw drapery ambachten, the warden, was a Vroedschap member who had himself temporarily relinquished production in order to hold office. Ambachten were an unusual form of public body, almost government agencies. Unlike artisanal associations of many other late medieval cities, these had no strong roots in family or in communal institutions and, unlike the corporative guilds which shared political power in some cities, no independent role in government.

The weavers and fullers of the drapery each formed an ambacht, and the finishers were similarly organized after 1508. The linen weavers were elevated to ambacht status in 1563 and the makers of coarse woolen and wool-blend textiles were given regulations in 1562 which began their transformation into an ambacht. Other drapery trades seem not to have been accorded such institutional status. The dyers, for example, were subject to controls over production methods and over some aspects of business organization, but for most of the period these artisans were not formally organized. The drapers were entirely unorganized. They were free to make any kind of cloth and as little of it as they wished, and could do so while practicing almost any other trade so long as they did not exceed production limits and met quality standards. The nontextile trades, including the less important crafts and most retailers serving local or regional markets, were usually less closely controlled than the ambachten and always less well organized.

The municipal government that dominated economic affairs in Leiden created most records treating these matters. The Privilege of 1434 awarded Leiden extensive judicial and legislative authority, and almost all the documents available for this study consequently date from the inception of the Burgundian period and were produced by the small bureaucracy which operated then. Not until the late sixteenth century, the end of the period on which this study focuses, was a wider range of documents produced, which was generated by a more complex governmental structure and by private institutions or individuals.

Among the surviving document series, judicial sources proved to be particularly important for this study. During the years on which the study focuses, civil cases in Leiden were settled in three ways, but records were normally kept only in appeals to a Kenning (where the aldermen heard and recorded both sides of the case and then issued their findings).[26] Punishments assigned in criminal cases were recorded in the Corrextieboeken; the offenses included infractions of health and police ordinances, murder and rape, as well as violations of industrial and commercial regulations.[27] The government also served as record keeper in settlements of personal injuries between citizens and increasingly as arbiter in these cases; the Zoenboeken contain these records. This study also relied heavily on city accounts which survive incompletely in various forms for the entire period covered in this study, on the city ordinances which were issued from the late fourteenth century up to the years of the siege, and on legislative and executive records such as decisions taken by the Vroedschap or executive orders promulgated to the citizenry (*Vroedscap Resoluties* and *Aflezingen*).

While it was not possible to read these documents for each of the 150 years they covered, it was possible to approximate such a survey by sampling each series. The samples were taken at thirty- to forty-year intervals, and nonserial records produced during these intervals were used to fill out the picture only sketched by the serial documents. (Appendix 2 describes these sources in more detail.)[28]

Because my survey had almost exclusively to rely on records produced by the government, it reflects the biases of this bureaucracy. Not unexpectedly, the records contain a disproportionate amount of information about the drapery and other regulated industries such as fish and meat sales; they emphasize information about wool imports and beer sales, for both were taxed. The records also provide the names of many of the drapers responsible for the largest production quantities and of many of the fullers, too, who, alone among the skilled artisans, regularly staged protests for better working conditions. But they reveal much less about construction, wood and metal working, or clothes making, since these industries were neither directly regulated nor directly taxed, and they almost never name the combers, spinners, weavers, dyers, finishers, and retailers in the drapery, or the shoemakers, seamstresses, cutlers, and tavern keepers in other economic sectors who went about their work without drawing the attention of the government.

A second, less obvious bias of the records also threatened to distort my results. The government was controlled by prominent families with direct or indirect ties to the drapery, the only industry in Leiden at the time in which members of the elite were significantly involved, and it showed an extraordinary interest in the health of the drapery. The private interests of government members did not make them insensitive to public interests—in fact, the government displayed surprising sympathy with ordinary people in Leiden—but that government was dominated by the large producers of drapery means that we can know about the drapery only what seemed important to them.

The records used in this study contain still a third, even less apparent, bias. They tend to misrepresent women's work in market production either by ignoring it or by describing it inaccurately. Several reasons account for this tendency. As will become evident, women's exit from a sector of the market frequently coincided with an increase in the ties between that sector and the government. Since documentation about an economic sector increased with the increase of ties between it and government, those economic sectors for which we have the best records often had the fewest women participants.

Other features of record-keeping could further distort the picture of women's work. Sometimes, as the bureaucracy began to keep records on a particular trade, it wrote regulations or charters which described the trade as if it were practiced entirely by men, yet other documents show that women were in fact active in it. In other instances, the bureaucracy used language from old charters or legislation for new regulations, thereby describing women's role as it had formerly been, not as it was when the document was actually issued.

The biases could not be eliminated but I believe they were minimized because they were taken into account as the records were read, and the survey which resulted should fairly represent Leiden's economy and women's place in it.

THE SIZE AND STRUCTURE OF THE DRAPERY

The health of Leiden's economy and its structure were determined by the health and the structure of the drapery. All of Leiden's commentators seem agreed on this point. Contemporaries regularly remarked on the drapery's importance and occasionally provided statistics to demonstrate it, as in 1542 when it was recorded in the Vroedscap Resoluties that Leiden had "but one industry" on which more than two-thirds of the population depended.[29] Historians of Leiden, confronted with the reams of documents produced when the drapery prospered and with the dearth of information about any additional industries in the city (other than the usual urban crafts devoted to providing food, shelter, and clothing), have accepted contemporary reports.

Despite its general acceptance, this conclusion finds little support in published literature. The major study of the industry, N. W. Posthumus's *Geschiedenis van de Leidsche Lakenindustrie*, contained an analysis of a head-of-household tax roll taken in 1498 which indicated that just 35 percent of the population worked in the drapery, including only 60 weavers and 127 drapers—this at a time when cloth production was near its peak. In other principal textile cities in the Low Countries, however, the populations were considerably more concentrated in this industry. From the 1560s to the 1580s in Hondschoote, a city of about 15,000 to 20,000, some 4,000 weavers and finishers were newly enrolled in the textile business. In fourteenth-century Ghent, at least 60 percent of the population (of about 60,000) was dependent on the drapery, and at least 5,000 weavers worked in the city. In fifteenth-century Ypres, long after the city had passed its peak as a textile producer, about 50 percent of the working population identified in one of four districts (probably *not* the principal residential area for textile workers) was in textiles.[30]

Evidently, either Posthumus's figure is too low or the claim that the drapery dominated medieval Leiden is overstated. Since the drapery must serve almost as a proxy for the economy itself, few records concerning other economic sectors being available, it is important to know just how dominant the drapery was, or the entire textile industry was, in late medieval Leiden. Fortunately, it can be easily shown that errors of statistical reasoning render Posthumus's computations doubtful. It can be shown, too, that the tax roll alone is an inaccurate guide to the population in Leiden, because it comprises only the heads of household and excludes all journeymen, all apprentices and helpers of either sex, and all women who did not head households.[31]

Other records provide a better way of estimating the size of the industry, and they confirm the impression that textiles dominated Leiden's economy. With the strikerye figures, an almost direct measure of sealed cloth production (reproduced in Appendix 1) and the six editions of the drapery regulations issued between 1363 and 1568 (the *Draperiekeurboeken*), we can relate production volumes to a production cycle recreated from the regulations and thus estimate the size of the labor force.[32] City accounts and judicial records can be used to test and refine these calculations. This analysis, which measures the drapery's dominance of Leiden's economy and provides information for understanding the structure of the industry, is so important to this chapter's inquiry that it must be presented in some detail.

The relation of production volumes to a production cycle allows us to estimate the size of the five principal groups of producers and artisans: the large drapers, the small drapers, the weavers, the fullers, and the dyers.[33] The most important group was the drapers, who organized cloth production. They owned the wool brought from Calais, saw to the manufacture of the finished product and then sold the cloth, sometimes to agents who visited Leiden, sometimes to consumers (or distributors) in nearby and distant cities, and most often to wholesalers who frequented regional trade fairs. A good many drapers produced large quantities and concentrated their energies simply on buying wool, supervising cloth production, and managing sales; they had little to do with the manufacturing process itself and even occasionally hired weavers to supervise manufacturing. Another group of drapers, many of them artisans—and most of them weavers—also produced cloth. These drapers did not travel to Calais but bought their wool from the men who did—a privilege city statutes guaranteed—and, relying instead on the well-developed markets in Leiden and the region, they did not journey to distant markets to sell their few cloths.

Posthumus tended to ignore or minimize the importance of the small drapers, believing instead that most drapers were large producers, with sales of some 200 cloths per year, and that most of them were continuously organizing production and sales. Consequently, he estimated that perhaps 100 drapers with volumes close to 200 cloths a year produced some 80 percent of the total cloths sealed in any year and that they employed some 400–500 weavers.[34] Evidence more extensive than Posthumus's or drawn from different sources shows, however, that his estimate is not correct. For one thing, not all "large" drapers were regularly active.[35] Indeed, no more than sixty to ninety large drapers could have produced cloth in any year. Among these were the twenty to thirty large drapers who went to Calais for their own account and another forty to sixty large drapers who produced from wool inventories or from wool acquired through syndicates. For another, not all these sixty to ninety drapers made 200 cloths a year. Instead, they averaged closer to 150.[36] Together the large drapers produced, not 20,000 cloths per year, but about 10,000 to 13,000. Small producers, some of them responsible for just ten to twenty cloths per year, thus made close to half of the cloth taxed for export.[37]

While it seems Posthumus ascribed too much importance to large producers, he was correct to point out that large producers were a distinct group. They were part of Leiden's patriciate and thus played a key part in determining how the drapery was structured and regulated. The small drapers, in contrast, lacked political power and had no ties to the patriciate. These drapers were members of Leiden's artisanal families, and many of the small producers were themselves weavers or artisans of other trades.[38]

There were, then, about 150 to 200 large producers and about 200 to 300 small producers in late fifteenth-century Leiden, but not all of them produced every year. With this estimate we can derive an estimate of the weaving population. Perhaps half of the small producers were also weavers who presumably worked, on average, half-time as producers and half-time as weavers. To produce the 24,000 cloths Leiden sealed in peak years, these part-time weavers would have been supplemented by perhaps 450 full-time weavers who worked both for large producers and for those small producers (many of them women) who did not weave. There would thus have been 550–600 weavers in Leiden.[39]

Fullers seem to have been at least as numerous as weavers. Official records, such as documents listing signators to loyalty oaths, imply that there were more than 700 fullers and fullers' journeymen in the late fifteenth century.[40] It is much harder to estimate the number of dyers in Leiden, but the count surely exceeded 200, a third of them masters.[41]

In total, at least 2,000 skilled adults, half of them journeymen and only about 100 of them women, worked in the drapery. This count includes some 150 large drapers who were not continuously active (that is, who produced only seventy-five cloths on average per year); 125 small drapers and 125 draper-weavers (who each made about thirty cloths every year); 550–600 weavers (300–350 journeymen); 750 fullers (500 journeymen); and 225 dyers (150 journeymen). It excludes small groups of such skilled workers as finishers or pelt sorters, and all unskilled workers. The total population of Leiden in 1498 was about 14,000 and the adult male labor force (not employed in domestic service) totalled about 4,300; the 2,000 adult males working as drapers or in these skilled drapery crafts constituted, then, about half the adult male labor force (which was not in domestic service).[42] If we were to add the remaining skilled workers and the unskilled workers, the count would be much higher.

Such figures indicate that Leiden's drapery was indeed as large as contemporaries believed and as historians have reported, and it must have dominated the economy as they have supposed. The remaining problem is to describe the structure of the industry. Posthumus thought that it was capitalist, which is understandable given his emphasis on the very large drapers in Leiden. These large drapers, we have seen, were neither so numerous nor so large as he supposed, but this evidence does not allow us to dismiss Posthumus's argument, because he did not base it entirely on this misconception. He also tried to show that other principal elements of capitalism were in place. Closely following Pirenne's analysis of how early capitalism developed, Posthumus described the large drapers as merchants who had entered production, usurped the entrepreneurial functions of artisans, and created an industrial proletariat of textile workers.[43] Some, he showed, even organized certain work in their own shops, such as preparing wool for spinning, weaving, dyeing, or finishing.[44] The resultant polarization between worker and capitalist merchant led in Leiden, as in cities of the southern Low Countries, to the kind of political instability characteristic of capitalist cities. The fullers, he pointed out, had begun to strike as early as the fourteenth century and continued into the sixteenth century. Leiden's drapers also used unskilled rural labor, another indication for Posthumus of the capitalist character of the industry.[45] That drapers were rich and artisans poor seemed to Posthumus additional proof that capitalism had arrived. He cited, for example, data from the 1498 tax roll which indicated that the average tax paid by drapers was 19.0 times that of fullers, 18.2 times that of weavers, and 1.4 times that of dyers.[46]

As we have seen, however, the typical cloth producer in Leiden was an artisan, usually a weaver, who worked for himself, and even Leiden's typical large producer was hardly a magnate. Other artisans also survived. The dyers retained entrepreneurial independence until well into the sixteenth century, and, even then, when some dyers fell to proletarian status, others emerged as owners of substantial enterprises, sometimes themselves undertaking cloth production. The one group of skilled artisans to fit the capitalist model Posthumus described was the fullers. Mobile, unstable, obstreperous, most fullers were journeymen employed in shops of five or six men headed by a master fuller in the direct employ of a draper. It is easy to see why Posthumus viewed the wage exploitation with which they were threatened—and from which, to some extent, they suffered—and their walkouts as evidence of class formation. The condition of the fullers, however, was not typical of other artisans in the industry, and, in any case, the government tried to halt their proletarianization.[47] The government often banned the use of rural labor in all crafts except for spinning, and it frequently forbade even that, rather than encourage the creation of new proletarians in the countryside.[48] Leiden's drapery, with its large group of drapers and draper-weavers, its numerous family-run dyeing establishments, and even its master fullers and weavers, who subcontracted themselves to drapers, obviously does not yet fit the capitalist "ideal type." The drapers who controlled imports did not attempt to take over the production process but left production management to the artisans themselves, especially to the weavers and dyers.

This production system was a conscious product of Leiden's Gerecht, and all the steps the Gerecht took to create and preserve the system are recorded in the legislative, executive, and judicial documents it generated. Beginning with the first separate set of drapery regulations of 1363, wool merchants were normally forbidden to resell wool and were required to use their purchases in their own production. Other laws prevented large drapers from expanding: restrictions were placed on the number of looms and workers each might employ and on the number of cloths each might make. There is proof these laws were enforced: the Corrextieboeken are full of cases in which large drapers were fined for exceeding production or employee limits.[49] The government also sought to support the small draper: laws required journeyers to Calais to execute purchase orders for small drapers and to register all their buying syndicates so that the government knew who had bought wool and how much had been bought; money was spent to provide dyeing facilities for small drapers; efforts were made to keep master artisans in Leiden and to give them work when times were hard.[50]

SMALL COMMODITY PRODUCTION

If capitalism did not emerge in the drapery, it is not likely to have emerged elsewhere in Leiden, for conditions elsewhere were even less conducive to capitalist innovation. No other industries could have bred merchants or industrialists of sufficient stature. Municipal records confirm the conclusion. The records of appeals in civil cases (the Kenningboeken) from a single year, for example, depict Leiden as a city, just like countless others of the period, made up of small-business people, not of industrial or merchant magnates. Typical disputants included a bricklayer and a smith who quarreled over the quality of construction of a house; a basket maker who brought suit (for his wife) against a man who allegedly had taken possession of property from the estate of the basket maker's mother-in-law (she was a midwife); a miller who was accused of building his mill too near city gates; a butcher who denied owing a cattle merchant for animals; a printer who claimed a book he had produced was not done on commission but on his own account.[51]

The socioeconomic structure of the city as a whole also firmly located Leiden in precapitalist Europe. The city's elite, as we have seen, was a traditional urban patriciate whose power derived from inherited political authority. The members of the elite were not so rich as merchant patricians in contemporary cities because they did not directly participate in long-distance trade. In fact, while Leiden's large drapers were much richer than typical draper-weavers, other artisans, or unskilled laborers in the city, they earned less than we would expect because they produced so little. Annual profits brought in by the typical large draper may have been 200 to 400 £ Holl., about three to six times the total earnings of a skilled master artisan in Leiden. Leiden's patriciate had additional sources of income, but it was not until the late sixteenth century and more often until the seventeenth century that other commercial or industrial investments, for example, in brewing or brickmaking, yielded Leiden's patricians substantially higher earnings. Real estate, although a substantial portion of the assets of prominent families, typically consisted of scattered pieces of farmland let to tenants; no family appears to have been a landowner of size in a single area. Within the city real estate holdings were usually minimal, and it was not until the post-siege expansion of the city that urban property development became one route to a fortune.

Leiden's 1498 tax roll helps to confirm this conclusion. At the very top of this tax-paying hierarchy were 207 male and female heads of household whose taxable property was valued at more than 4,000 £ Holl. The city's single wealthiest taxpayer paid taxes on property valued at about 14,000 £ Holl. Of the 207 taxpayers at least 38 were drapers, and the average value of the property on which the drapers paid taxes was about 7,400 £ Holl. By local standards, to be sure, these men and women were rich: 7,400 £ Holl. represents about 100 times the annual earnings of a fully employed master fuller then working in Leiden.

Members of the economic elite in other cities, however, were far richer. In 1450, a merchant from Cologne left an estate valued at about the equivalent of 80,000 £ Holl., that is, more than ten times the value of the taxable property of Leiden's richest draper.[52] A fourteenth-century Flemish financier in a single deal bought a collection of rents for the equivalent of about 125 times a fuller's yearly wage at the time.[53] In Augsburg in 1498, a full generation before the emergence of merchant capitalists like the Fuggers, there were relatively twelve times as many taxpayers with taxable property valued at the equivalent of 10,000 £ Holl. than in Leiden, and the wealthiest taxpayer had about four times as much taxable property as Leiden's richest.[54] When in 1490 Bruges imposed a forced loan on its wealthiest citizens, it collected the equivalent of 1,636 £ Holl. from each of its biggest lenders, about twelve times the single highest assessment in 1498 Leiden.[55]

Fortunes made elsewhere during the sixteenth century, even when adjusted to reflect the precipitous decline in the value of money during the period, were much larger than fortunes in late fifteenth-century Leiden, where 10,000 £ Holl. made one rich. In 1556 an Antwerp capitalist left an estate of 112,000 Gulden (equivalent to about 40,000–50,000 £ Holl. of 1498), but even this estate did not make him Antwerp's richest resident; of 552 individuals contributing to a loan in 1552, 77 gave more than he did. Other estates from the sixteenth century were even larger: 151,000 Gulden in 1568 (perhaps 50,000 £ Holl. in 1498); 408,258 Gulden in 1582 (perhaps 100,000 £ Holl. in 1498).[56] In Augsburg in 1540 a widow was taxed on property valued at 167,000 Gulden (perhaps 80,000 £ Holl. in 1498), and five others were taxed at over 80,000 Gulden (perhaps 40,000 £ Holl. of 1498).[57]

Because wealth is often considered an indicator of capitalism, Posthumus and others after him, like Jecht, tried to link distribution of wealth with socioeconomic structure.[58] But great wealth alone, even wealth derived from trade and finance, need not be associated with a capitalist socioeconomic structure, as that term is understood in this book.

In any event, even if these relationships held in general, they did not apply in the case of Leiden. Leiden's wealth-distribution curve was not so highly skewed as Posthumus thought, and was in fact much closer to the pattern Jecht considered typical of noncapitalist cities. In Frankfurt am Main in 1495, when the city was neither so large nor so important in international market production as it would become in the sixteenth century, wealth and property were distributed very much as they were in Leiden. In both cities, about 55 percent of the population had less than the equivalent of 50 £ Holl.; in both, about 40 percent of the population had more than 50 but less than 1,000 £ Holl. The only real difference is at the top of the economic pyramid: 1.8 percent of Frankfurt's taxpayers had more than 10,000 £ Holl. while only 0.4 percent of Leiden's had reached this level.[59]

Early sixteenth-century Erfurt, then a university town of 18,000 involved in regional trade and woad production, provides another telling comparison. According to a 1511 tax roll, the top 7.4 percent of the taxpayers owned 66.4 percent of the taxable wealth, the next 16.9 percent owned 24.1 percent, and the bottom 75.6 percent owned 9.5 percent.[60] For approximately comparable strata of Leiden, the wealth concentration figures are, respectively, 60.0 percent, 25.3 percent, and 14.7 percent. If anything, wealth in Leiden was *less* inequitably distributed than in Erfurt.

It is also useful to compare wealth distribution in 1498 Leiden to that in Kaufbeuren, Memmingen, and Ravensburg at about that time. All were industrial centers of linen and barchent (a fabric made of cotton and wool) manufacture which served an export market dominated by merchants, some local and some from larger cities like Cologne and Nuremburg. The smallest of the three centers, Kaufbeuren, had 3,000 to 4,000 residents while the largest, Memmingen, had only 5,000. We have one tax roll from Kaufbeuren (1479), two from Memmingen (1450 and 1521), and two from Ravensburg (1497 and 1521).[61] All but one roll suggest there were more poor in these cities than in Leiden, for all four exempted a larger proportion of potential taxpayers judged too poor than in Leiden; only Kaufbeurgen's 26 percent was lower than Leiden's 29 percent. Even greater differences seem to have existed at the top of the pyramid. In Memmingen in 1450, eight individuals had wealth greater than 10,000 Rheingulden; in 1521, fifteen individuals did. In Ravensburg in 1497, there were ten such persons and in 1521, twelve. In 1498, in Leiden, which was three times as large as Memmingen or Ravensburg, there was only one such person. Similarly, wealth was more concentrated at the top of the pyramid in Kaufbeuren, Memmingen, and Ravensburg—consistently the top 2 to 3 percent of the taxpayers there owned 70 to 80 percent of taxable wealth—while in Leiden the top 2.1 percent owned only 38 percent.

Finally, we can show that wealth in Leiden was distributed much as it was in fifteenth-century Mulhausen i. Th., Frankfurt am Main, and Basel, the cities Jecht typified as noncapitalist, and not as it was distributed in sixteenth-century Augsburg and Gorlitz, where Jecht believed capitalism had been established. For example, 29 percent of Leiden's population, at most, was unable to pay the 1 percent tax imposed on property while in Augsburg in 1526 over 54 percent were so classified. In late fifteenth-century Basel, on the other hand, a city which in Jecht's view exemplified the "allseitig entwickelten Gewerbestadt lokalen Gepräges," about 28 percent of the population was credited with property worth between 100 and 1,000 Gulden; in Leiden almost the same figures obtained. In both Basel and Leiden, the remainder of the population was divided between those with less than 100 Gulden and those with more than 1,000 Gulden in roughly comparable ways.[62]

In Leiden the transition to capitalism occurred not in the late Middle Ages but after the siege, when the new drapery was established and the patriciate had almost completely abandoned textile production. Most of the large producers and cloth merchants of seventeenth-century Leiden were newcomers, both to wealth and to the city. The early saye (light wool cloths) drapers, weavers, and other workers were mostly Flemish and the later immigrants—even the rich *lakenbereiders*, *lakenkooplieden*, and *lakenreeders*—often were Walloon. The economic elite of the new textile industry differed in another way from their counterparts of the late Middle Ages: they did not as a group belong to Leiden's richest families. In 1599, for example, textile producers were never listed among Leiden's wealthiest; the richest Leideners were still members of the old patriciate, who had aggressively moved into brewing, finance, and long-distance trade and earned fortunes far greater than any imagined in the fifteenth century.[63]

The organizers of Leiden's new textile industry, while not part of the city's political elite and not yet dominant as an economic elite, were nevertheless capitalists. They often had large shops of their own (atéliers) and regularly ran extensive putting-out operations. As early as 1595 one producer employed thirteen looms;[64] in 1610 another had a shop with thirty-seven mechanical *passamentier* looms, each of which did the work of twelve handloom weavers;[65] in 1643 one lakenreeder directly employed thirty looms;[66] by the 1630s, lakenreeder firms with capital (most of it simply cloth inventory) of over 100,000 guldens were common;[67] in 1640, eleven lakenreeders tied up 30 percent of all skilled workers in the drapery.[68] In keeping with the stereotype of an early modern capitalist, these men were constantly on the lookout for ways both to cut labor costs and to undermine the traditional artisan: as early as 1588, they were closing small drapers out of the market for spun yarn by making exclusive contracts with spinners;[69] they sought and won permission (for twelve years) to introduce the power passamentier loom;[70] and, perhaps most dramatic, they annually imported hundreds of workers from orphanages and employment agencies in Liège, Brielle, and Maastricht, making Leiden infamous as an employer and exploiter of children.[71]

To say that the social and economic structure of late medieval Leiden was not capitalist is not, however, to argue that it was a backwater where medieval craft production and a medieval social structure were artificially preserved. The city's links to international markets, its devotion to a single industry, and the weakness of its artisanal organizations firmly located it elsewhere. The production system of late medieval Leiden approximated small commodity production as described in chapter 2. Although in many other cities the institutions responsible for this system—for the small shop and the socioeconomic structure associated with it—were controlled by artisans, in Leiden the control was held by the patriciate who, closely tied to the drapery, might be expected to have welcomed, even nurtured, capitalist practices.

It is easy to show that Leiden's production system was established and preserved by the patriciate, for the municipal government's efforts—and its success—are easily documented. But it is not easy to explain why the patrician governors chose to preserve the small shop and restrict long-distance trade in Leiden or why they were able to do so without any significant dissent from those among them who were large drapers. We might begin to explain the consensus by arguing that the measures were perceived as necessary. The large drapers, as captives of the Hansa and Calais, perhaps saw little real chance for expansion in international marketing and so were willing to forgo the limited profits available from amalgamation of production at home. They may also have thought that the inconveniences of managing production themselves and the economic risks of production expansion could not be offset by the limited profits which could be made in industry. They may even have feared that their efforts to deprive master artisans of independence would have engendered uprisings like those experienced in the southern Low Countries, in Bruges, Ghent, and Ypres, for example. Finally, it may be that they placed other values above economic growth—that they saw themselves as members, indeed as fathers, of a civic community for which they were responsible and on which their life-style depended.[72]

The pressures of production for international markets had thus moved Leiden's drapery from medieval craft production, but not towards capitalism. Instead, the direction of development was towards small commodity production where industrial expansion, investment, and innovation were tolerated but where both the individuals who ran certain key trades and those who worked in them were subjected to extensive municipal controls which sought to preserve the traditional social and political order. Many of the changes associated with this development could have affected the family and women. In the next chapter, we will try to assess these effects, first by describing the work women did in the drapery and, where possible, in other industries where the traditional medieval mode of production might have survived longer, and then by relating the pattern of women's work to the pattern of economic, social, and political change that occurred in Leiden as small commodity production replaced medieval craft production.

4

Women's Work in Leiden's Market Production

Women in Leiden had access to high-status positions in textiles, even in the prestigious drapery, but it is necessary to search widely and carefully to find them. Most sources treating the drapery mention women only as practitioners of low-status trades. Observing that the regulations in the Keurboeken concerning spinning, combing, wool sorting, and other exclusively low-skilled tasks usually employed the feminine form of the noun to describe workers, Posthumus concluded that women even dominated in these trades.[1] The 1498 tax roll reinforces his impression: the nine female textile workers identified by occupation were all employed in low-skilled jobs. Few documents concerning more prestigious positions refer to women at all. Among some 200 large drapers who appear in governmental documents from fiscal 1491 to fiscal 1500, only two are women, and one of them, the only woman to import a significant amount of wool and to work during more than one of these years, was the widow of a draper. Similarly, although excise tax records of imports between 1449 and 1543 name 3,490 men, they name only eleven women.[2] None of the dyers, finishers, weavers, or fullers identified by trade on the 1498 tax roll was female. The sampled Corrextieboeken confirm that women did not weave and full drapery; thirty-five male weavers and twenty-seven male fullers were named in them—but no women.[3] None of the other miscellaneous lists of weavers and fullers in the cloth-industry records contain an even remotely significant number of female names. Of the 343 fullers who signed a loyalty oath in 1447, only two were women and both of these apparently were widows of fullers. No women were listed among the 488 additional fullers registering their oath between 1447 and 1452.[4] Only one of the 127 master fullers who signed a similar oath in 1478 was a woman, and she, too, was a widow.[5] Of 57 weavers and 117 fullers identified by name as having paid fines to the Schout for the seven years between fiscal 1487 and 1503 for which records have survived, not one was a woman.[6] Finally, the drapery regulations never refer to women as independent masters, journeymen, or apprentices in weaving or fulling.

Compelling as they may seem, these data are misleading. A more careful look at these and other records—the drapery regulations (from the Keurboeken) and miscellaneous judicial and financial records—indicate that women did practice skilled trades and held entrepreneurial positions both in and out of the drapery. Two sectors of the drapery, both of them providing almost exclusively high-status work, seem to have been especially hospitable to women, the organization of production itself (draping) and the large-scale retail distribution of cloth (wantsnijden); the women who held these positions were at the top of the drapery.

The evidence regarding women drapers is especially rich. Records of the fullers' walkout of 1478, for example, contained the demand that

> no masters' wives enter the frames [the area where cloths were framed] except Saturdays after the weavers' clock has struck; the fine is 3 lbs. . . . *except in cases where the cloth belongs to the woman and she has produced it herself.* (Emphasis added)[7]

Other documents from the early fifteenth century through the mid-sixteenth century refer to women drapers by name.[8] The estate of a weaver, sold in 1412 to settle his debts, included a basket of wool sold for 50 bot to "Lijsbet Johannes die coster's dochter, Adriaen's wijf."[9] The estate of an *uutreeder* auctioned in 1417 named eleven drapers for whom he was working; one was a woman, Alijt Aelbrant Willemsz's widow, who owned one "good quality black half-cloth" (*voirwollen zwart half laken*).[10] Five of forty-two syndicate members who sued for losses suffered in 1424 while bringing wool from Calais were women.[11] A 1437 Kenning recorded a claim against the estate of a woman for debts incurred in purchasing wool yarn, sackwool, and pelts.[12] The city accounts of fiscal 1475 listed sums spent by city officials to investigate charges that cloth below city standards was being sold as genuine, sealed *Leidse laken*; the suspected drapers were a group of four headed by a woman, Griete Goeswijns.[13] A 1476 Kenning settled a quarrel between a woman who claimed to have inherited a loom from her husband and a man who claimed her husband had sold it to him; the woman was awarded the loom, with which she planned to continue to make cloth.[14] One of fourteen members of a 1492 syndicate was female.[15] An ordinance of 1519 required two drapers accused of exporting inferior cloth to bring their cloth in for inspection; the drapers were Kerstijn Dirck Meesz's widow and Willem IJsbrantsz.[16] Perhaps most telling, a group of ninety-two drapers selected six of their number as *Kantoormeesters* in 1552 to handle sales of their black cloths in various markets. Among the ninety-two names, thirty-three were female.[17]

The Corrextieboeken and Scoutsrekeningen supplement such anecdotal material. Close to 20 percent of all the names appearing in Correxties assigned to drapers for violations of cloth manufacturing regulations in the seven sampled periods between 1436 and 1541 were female. A larger percentage—close to 30 percent—appeared in all the Correxties Posthumus included in his published source collection. Even in the Scoutsrekeningen which have survived from between 1487 and 1503, a source which is probably incomplete, over 10 percent of drapers' names were female.[18]

The records show not only that women were numerically well represented as drapers but also that they practiced the trade much like most of their male colleagues. The cloth women produced was apparently indistinguishable from that produced by men; among the cloths both identifiable by color or quality and assignable to a particular draper which were mentioned in the Corrextieboeken in all sampled years, those owned by female drapers were about the same quality as those owned by men.[19] The offenses women committed in producing cloth, too, were very much like those of their male colleagues, and, again, the punishments they were awarded were like those meted out to men.[20]

As wantsnijders, women also sold good-quality cloth in Leiden, at least during the late fourteenth and early fifteenth centuries, the only period for which adequate records survive. During sampled years between 1371 and 1419, forty men and ten women were named as retailers. On average, each female retailer sold the same amount of cloth and at the same price as her male colleagues.[21] Some of these retailers may have been drapers themselves, for the drapery regulations from the period anticipated that drapers would retail their own cloth, but all sold cloth made both in and outside of Leiden.[22]

Although the principal records misled us about the extent of women's involvement in the production and sales of high-quality cloth, the records seem to have reported accurately women's absence from weaving and fulling. Further research into these and even less accessible records does not suggest that women belonged to these ambachten, but they do suggest that fullers' wives had once helped their husbands. A document of 1478 contained a request that fullers' wives not be permitted to enter the drying frames (presumably the wives were prohibited from delivering or collecting cloths), either to do textile work for their husbands' clients or to do hand finishing, and the same document asked specifically that household members be prohibited from removing cloths from the frames.[23] Scoutsrekeningen listed fines for infractions of rules intended to keep wives out of their husbands' fulling business: in 1493/94 Clais Thijsz was fined for allowing his wife in the framing area; Cornelis Dammesz was fined for allowing his wife to collect money for him from his drapers; and Joncker Rauwert was fined because his wife "trimmed her clients' cloth."[24]

While excluded from weaving and fulling, women had an accepted role in two other trades in the drapery, finishing and dyeing. Both of these trades required skill, and dyeing also required significant amounts of capital for equipment and materials. The earliest evidence we have about the finishing trade dates from its establishment as an ambacht in 1508, when the prologue of the founding ordinances referred to an existing brotherhood of St. Ursula as "the brotherhood and sisterhood" (*tbroederscap ende zusterscap*). Not in itself evidence that women practiced the trade, brotherhood membership at least suggests that women shared ownership with their husbands. Another section of the document made clear, however, that women had actually practiced the craft: the sixth article required that girls and women "henceforth" no longer shear *scepwerck* of any kind or train to shear or help with dry finishing. But the document did permit women and girls already in the trade to continue if they joined the brotherhood. Presumably, this right to membership was extended to women without husbands or fathers in the trade.[25]

In the dyeing trade, women seem to have had, and long retained, a place, if only as partners of their husbands. Requirements, regularly reiterated in all editions of the regulations, that dyers, their wives, and their master journeymen swear to adhere to rules regarding quality standards, demonstrate that a man and his wife often worked together as partners in the household shops where dyeing was typically done. The 1541 edition of the drapery regulations showed that they not only worked together but jointly ran the business: "It is always to be understood that a man and his wife who have given the aforesaid oath shall be considered a single person."[26]

It is difficult to know whether women always owed senior positions in the dyeing industry to their husbands or whether some women worked on their own as dyers. Most legislation treating master artisans or apprentices of the trade referred only to men, although the occasional ordinance suggests that women on their own had dyeing shops.[27] References to dyers in judicial records hint further that a few women practiced the trade alone. The collection of cases from the Corrextieboeken published by Posthumus, for example, contained twelve cases treating dyers: three cases involved women dyers, and only one of them was identified as the wife of a dyer.[28] A 1525 Kenning recorded the complaint of a woad merchant against twenty dyers working in a city dyeworks who, he claimed, owed him for delivered woad; one of the twenty was a woman, and she was not identified as married.[29]

Outside the drapery, in other sectors of the textile industry not tied to international markets until much later, women were also active. The first set of regulations issued in 1563 for the newly formed ambacht of linen weavers, for example, described women as full-fledged members of the trade.[30] The prologue of the ordinances, like the one establishing drapery finishing as a "craft" in 1508, referred to the "brotherhood and sisterhood," and the initial article began,

> First, that no man or woman may set up a mastership of linen weaving unless he [sic] is a citizen, and a member of the brotherhood of the *Heylige Drievoudicheyt*.[31]

Later articles referred to mistresses and to female apprentices (*jonckwiven*); one article provided for masters' widows:

> Likewise, should a master of the aforesaid trade die, his widow may maintain the mastership as long as she likes without paying new fees; however, should she remarry with a man who is not a master (in this trade), she is obligated to satisfy the requirements of the brotherhood and all else required of those setting up masterships anew; the fine for non-compliance is as stated above.[32]

Women also regularly owned and manufactured coarse wool and wool-blend cloth, a product which found first a regional and then an international market in the second half of the sixteenth century when improvements in Continental wools, in manufacturing techniques, and in the market for lighter and cheaper textiles, along with the increasing unavailability of sufficient good-quality English wool and reduced prospects for marketing Leiden's traditional drapery, began to reverse the relationship of the two industries. Cloths of this type (*voerlakens, schortecleetlakens, tierenteinen, baaien,* and *warpen*; later additions were *saaien* and *saajetten*) had been manufactured in and around Leiden, as in most areas around northern European textile cities, since Leiden's own drapery had begun, and had probably given birth to the high-quality cloth industry. During the drapery's prosperity, the coarse cloth industry had been kept entirely distinct from the drapery and was unquestionably subordinate to it. In 1562, in recognition of the coarse cloth industry's growing importance in regional and international trade, the government of Leiden issued the first set of ordinances for voerlaken production and sale.[33] A document from about 1572 identified three of seventeen voerlaken producers as women and another from 1563 named two of five as female.[34] A survey taken in 1540 by the government at Brussels of businesses within 500 *roeden* (ca. one mile) of Leiden named eighty-five households and 118 individuals; sixteen of the 112 working individuals made textiles (schortecleetlakens, groff lakens, voerlakens or tierteinen), and nine of the sixteen were women.[35] Women may also have traditionally fulled these fabrics, for the complaint of 1572 which named the seventeen voerlaken producers charged them with doing their own fulling, in apparent contravention of the regulations requiring that all fulling be done by ambacht members.

WOMEN'S WORK IN AND AROUND LEIDEN

Although we now know that some women in Leiden held high-status positions in the drapery as well as in other sectors of textile production, we do not yet know how women obtained high-status work nor what the links were between women's access to high-status work, the family economy, and the structure of market production. Without this analysis, we cannot answer the first question posed by this study's working hypothesis—whether women had high-status work where the family was the unit of production— or explain why some high-status positions in market production were available to women and others were not.

To answer these questions, we need a more systematic survey of women's roles in all sectors of market production as well as of the marital or family status of all working women, both those with high and those with low labor-status. The needed information is not directly available, but we can piece together a statistical profile of Leiden's working women, using three difference sources that have survived from the period, each of which focuses on a different kind of laborer and treats a different aspect of market production. When supplemented by the more detailed material about women's work in textiles just summarized, the profile provides an overview of women's work in and around late medieval Leiden.

The three sources, which have been introduced already, are the 1498 tax roll, the 1540 survey of Leiden's suburban industry, and the data collected in the sample of Leiden's Corrextieboeken. Each source is biased in favor of a certain kind of work: the first inclines towards the low-skilled, low-paid work of the city's single women who appeared on the tax roll because they were heads of household; the second, towards the comparatively high-status work, often semiskilled and not highly differentiated, done by the men and women of Leiden's immediate suburbs; and the third, towards the high-status work of Leiden's married and widowed women. Tables 1, 2, and 3 summarize the information from each source. The tables are similarly arranged. Each identifies, where possible, the marital status of the identified worker, the relationship of the woman's work to her husband's, and the economic status of the woman. This last category is measured quite simply by the woman's property, her job, or her husband's job.

Methods of categorizing each working woman according to her marital and economic status differ from table to table.

Marital status. The 1498 tax roll provided only one method of identifying married women, that is, if the woman was named as someone's wife ("Alijt, Jan's wijf"). Since the tax roll selects only heads of household, it is reasonable that few married women appear on the roll; these were probably women whose husbands lived away from Leiden. The roll provided two ways of identifying widows: one was by name ("Alijt, Jan's wede") and another by the fact that the woman was accompanied by her own children ("Alijt met hoir 3 kinderen"). All women identified as someone's daughter ("Alijt, Jan's dochter") were assumed to be single. Further, all *joncwiven* and *maechten* were assumed to be single. Women listed without any sort of marital identification were categorized as "widowed or single" ("Alijt die naeyster" or "Alijt van Goude") except for midwives, who were assumed to be widowed even if not specifically identified as widows. I suspect that a large portion of the "widowed or single" category were widowed but that, because the tax assessors identified single women by job more often than they did widowed women, the overwhelming majority of the women in the "widowed or single" group and identified by occupation were single.

The 1540 survey clearly identified all married women and usually indicated whether other women were widowed or single. The categorization of marital status in table 2 is the most certain of the three.

The method used to categorize women in the Corrextieboeken was similar to that used in the 1498 tax roll.

Economic status. Determination of economic status for individuals in the 1498 tax roll was straightforward. Women who paid none of their assessed tax, unless a reason was given that indicated otherwise, were judged "poor." Women who paid up to 2 £ Holl. were categorized as "middle class," and those who paid more than 2 £ Holl. were judged "rich." The text of the 1540 survey generally included a brief description of the family and its workers so that it was often possible to make a judgment about the relative wealth of the family.

Categorization of economic status in table 3 (women identified in the Corrextieboeken) was usually based on the job the women had, the size of the fine (as an indication of ability to pay), and sometimes on some external information I had about the economic status of the women drapers named. Possession of a skilled trade or of position in the drapery was assumed to indicate at least "middle-class" status.

Before sketching the profile these tables combine to make, I should clarify the biases in each table. The 1498 tax roll (table 1) selected almost exclusively widowed women or single women who were the most likely to have been identified by trade, since they had no husband or known family to provide the tax collector another means of social identification. For reasons that will later become clear, the women on the tax roll were also much poorer than the average. Table 2, covering the 1540 survey of suburban industry, treats a group of people who produced for local or perhaps regional markets. While their labor status was high when measured in comparison to that of their neighbors in this suburban commu-

Table 1. Occupational, Marital, and Economic Status of Women on 1498 Tax Roll

Occupation	Married					Widowed									Widowed or Single					Single				
	Total No.	Economic Status				Total No.	Husband's Business				Economic Status				Total No.	Economic Status				Total No.	Economic Status			
		(5)	(6)	(7)	(8)		(1)	(2)	(3)	(4)	(5)	(6)	(7)	(8)		(5)	(6)	(7)	(8)		(5)	(6)	(7)	(8)
Clothing and Cleaning																								
seamstress															10	3	7			1	1			
hat knitter																				1		1		
Metalworking																								
knife maker	1								1			1												
fastener maker	1									1		1												
Textiles																								
comber															7	5	2							
spinner															2	2								
Food Production																								
baker															1				1					
Trade																								
apple seller															1		1							
peat seller															2		2							
old clothes seller															1	1								
pubkeeper & wine merchant															3	1	1		1					
retail merchant								1				1												

	(1) Related	(2) Same	(3) Other	(4) Unknown	Subtotal	(5) Poor	(6) Middle class	(7) Rich	(8) Unknown	Subtotal	Total
Wage Labor/Domestic Work											
maecht							4	3	1	4	4
werckwijf						1	1				
jonckwijf								4		4	
huysvrouwe						2	1	1		4	
Other Occupations											
bewaerster						1	1				
midwife								4		4	
tackwijf						1	1				
Subtotal	15	15	2	0	32	4	6	0	0	10	7
Women Not Identified by Occupation	85	92	19	0	196	118	71	15	0	204	317
Totals	100	107	21	0	228	122	77	15	0	214	324

KEY: (1) Related (2) Same (3) Other (4) Unknown (5) Poor (6) Middle class (7) Rich (8) Unknown

Table 2. Occupational, Marital, and Economic Status of Women on 1540 Survey

	Married									Widowed									Widowed or Single					Single				
	Total No.	Husband's Business				Economic Status				Total No.	Husband's Business				Economic Status				Total No.	Economic Status				Total No.	Economic Status			
Occupation		(1)	(2)	(3)	(4)	(5)	(6)	(7)	(8)		(1)	(2)	(3)	(4)	(5)	(6)	(7)	(8)		(5)	(6)	(7)	(8)		(5)	(6)	(7)	(8)
Basic Production																												
farmer	1	1					1																					
Earthernware Mfg																												
potter	1	1						1																				
Clothing and Cleaning																												
seamstress	1			1			1																1					1
Textiles																												
spinner	15	2	12	1	1			1	14	4	4	1				3			1		1			1		1		
producer	7	2	4	1			6	1																				
weaver	2	2					1	1																				
pelt washer	1		1				1																					
fuller	1	1					1																					
Food Production																												
baker	1	1					1																					

	Total	(1)	(2)	(3)	(4)	(5)	(6)	(7)	(8)
Trade									
pub keeper	4		3	1		3			1
toll collector	1		1			1			
Other Occupations									
midwife	1			1					1
Subtotal	35	2	12	19	2	19	0	0	16
Women Not Identified by Occupation	5	0	0	0	5	0	0	0	5
Totals	40	2	12	19	7	19	0	0	21

KEY: (1) Related (2) Same (3) Other (4) Unknown (5) Poor (6) Middle class (7) Rich (8) Unknown

Table 3. Occupational, Marital, and Economic Status of Women in *Correctieboeken*, selected years, 1435-1541

Occupation	Married									Widowed									Single					Unknown				
	Total No.	Husband's Business				Economic Status				Total No.	Husband's Business				Economic Status				Total No.	Economic Status				Total No.	Economic Status			
		(1)	(2)	(3)	(4)	(5)	(6)	(7)	(8)		(1)	(2)	(3)	(4)	(5)	(6)	(7)	(8)		(5)	(6)	(7)	(8)		(5)	(6)	(7)	(8)
Textiles																												
draper	12	1		3	8	1	11			14		1		13		13	1		1	1				9		9		
spinner																												
comber	1				1		1																					
Lighting Material																												
oil presser										1			1			1												
Food Production																												
baker	2		1	1			2																					
Trade																												
peat seller	1		1				1																					
fish seller																			3		3			1		1		
Wage Labor/Domestic Work																												
jonckwijf																			12	2			10					
werckwijf																								2				2
Subtotal	16	1	2	4	9	1	15	0	0	15	0	1	1	13	0	14	1	0	16	3	3	0	10	12	0	10	0	2
Women Not Identified by Occupation	0	0	0	0	0	0	0	0	0	0	0	0	0	0	0	0	0	0	0	0	0	0	0	18	0	0	0	18
Totals	16	1	2	4	9	1	15	0	0	15	0	1	1	13	0	14	1	0	16	3	3	0	10	30	0	10	0	20

KEY: (1) Related (2) Same (3) Other (4) Unknown (5) Poor (6) Middle class (7) Rich (8) Unknown

nity, in comparison to that of more productive urban workers they had low or at least declining labor status. Table 3 summarizes women's work as described in sampled Corrextieboeken and, consequently, its bias is towards work in organized, regulated industries, thus towards high-status work.

Read together, the tables point to two generalizations about Leiden's working women. First, women's work was concentrated in a narrower range of economic sectors than was men's. Ninety-six percent of the women on the 1498 tax roll, 96 percent of those in the 1540 survey, and 95 percent of those in the Corrextieboeken worked in clothing and cleaning, textiles, commerce, wage labor, domestic service, and miscellaneous odd jobs. For men the figures are, respectively, 59 percent, 52 percent, and 87 percent.[36] In construction, woodworking, leatherworking, metalworking, printing, as in most professions, women, both in the suburbs and in the city itself, appear not to have worked at all or only by rare exception. Women were most strongly concentrated in textiles, where they produced and sold cloth, prepared wool for weaving, and helped to dye and finish woven cloth. Sixty-three percent of working urban women (who appeared in the sampled Corrextieboeken) worked in textiles and 68 percent of suburban women (those in the 1540 survey) did so. They were also heavily represented in retail merchandising of foodstuffs, agricultural products, and household goods, in innkeeping, and in general clothesmaking and repairing.

Working women both inside and outside Leiden thus shared a key attribute: they were concentrated in industries that had obvious roots in the tasks in which women in subsistence households specialized. Nevertheless, there were important differences between the two groups of women. City women were often absent from trades that the division of labor by sex ought to have assigned them, for example, from skilled textile crafts, like fulling and weaving, and from butchering, milling, brewing, and specialized clothing manufacture. Women in the suburbs, in addition to performing the kind of textile work which accounted for most high-status work available alike to suburban and city women, also made pots, wove and fulled cloth, and more frequently than women in the city ran bakeries and pubs. This first generalization must, therefore, be modified, because the urban women had an even narrower range of occupations than the suburban women, and they had a smaller share of the high-status positions available.

We can see these differences more clearly by comparing the

urban and suburban female labor forces in their entirety. In the suburbs, women made up 42 percent of the identified workers. Almost 90 percent of them (the women whose economic status is indicated in table 2) were "middle class" or rich (20 out of 23). About 55 percent of the women had jobs which implied independent status or skill, thus implying high labor-status (25 out of 47) and, of those women, 44 percent were in textiles (11 out of 25).[37]

We have no comparable profile of the female labor force in the city, but we can piece one together. According to the occupational identifications in the 1498 tax roll, only 8 percent of the urban work-force was female. Since 26 percent of the taxpayers were women, however, and since very few of them were rich, we can assume that most women did work but were simply not identified by trade on the tax roll. Conservatively, then, we could raise the 8 percent to 20 percent, a figure intended to represent both widowed and single female heads of household. This gives us about 600 head-of-household working women, perhaps half widowed and the other half never married.[38]

Domestic servants must be added to this figure if we are to obtain a realistic overview of the female labor force in Leiden because, as tables 1 and 3 separately hint, domestic service was a major employer of women in Leiden.[39] This was true of other late medieval cities as well, and, comparing Leiden with mid-fifteenth-century Nuremberg, Posthumus estimated Leiden's servant population at 1,960. Other comparisons of the sort that Posthumus made plus data on the servant population in Leiden in 1581 not only confirm the reasonableness of his estimate but also permit a guess that about 80 percent of the servant population was female.[40] On the basis of these figures we can put the female servant population at 1,500.

Finally, we must add married, non-head-of-household working women. While we have little direct information about such women, it is certain that a good many of the women drapers, cloth merchants, pubkeepers, and other high-status workers were married, and we have occasional hints in sources like the Corrextie-boeken and Kenningboeken that many of Leiden's spinners, combers, peddlers, and odd-job women were married. Many married women who unofficially helped out in their husbands' shops are invisible in the records, and it is extremely difficult to know whether or not those who occasionally appear should be counted as "full-time" participants in market production. If so, we might estimate the married female labor force at perhaps 1,200, about 70 percent of the female population estimated in Appendix 3. At the other extreme, we might exclude all the wives who "helped out" and put this labor force at just 300. Using this conservative figure, we arrive at a female labor force in Leiden of 2,400, only 900 of whom worked outside domestic service, as compared to about 4,300 men who did not work as servants.

Thus, only about 17 percent of the urban, nondomestic labor force was female, as compared to almost half of the suburban labor force. Although textiles employed 63 percent of the urban working women who appeared in the Corrextieboeken (37 out of 59) and accounted for 80 percent of the high-status positions held by women in the Corrextieboeken (35 out of 43), this industry was not a major provider of high-status positions to women. In Leiden as a whole, we can estimate that at most only about 25 percent of the medium-to-small drapers were female, or, in total, certainly no more than 100. A few women wove and produced linen and coarse cloth, sold cloth at retail in Leiden, dyed both good and cheap cloth, and did some occasional (illegal) fulling. But these women may not have numbered many more than another 100, so that the total number of women working in textiles who had even moderately high labor-status could have been little more than 200. In sum, only 200 of the female labor force of 2,400, or less than 10 percent, had high-status positions in textiles, as compared to about 25 percent of suburban women.

The second generalization we may make about Leiden's working women requires no modification when the urban and suburban labor forces are compared. In both places, there was a significant correlation between marriage, high labor-status, and high economic status on the one hand, and spinsterhood, low labor-status, and low economic status on the other.

In the city, most women with high-status jobs were married or widowed, and many owed their jobs to their husbands. Twenty-six of thirty-six drapers in the sampled Corrextieboeken were identified as married or widowed, and most of the nine drapers whose marital status was not identified were probably married or widowed. A significant portion of these married or widowed women were in the same jobs as their husbands. One of the twelve married drapers shared her trade with her husband but three worked in entirely separate businesses; one of the fourteen widowed drapers practiced her deceased husband's trade. One of the two married bakers was her husband's partner, but neither the married peat seller nor the widowed oil presser practiced her husband's trade.

The 1498 tax roll analyzed in table 1, which depicts life for the women at the other end of the city's economic and social spectrum, shows that single female heads of household in Leiden were concentrated in low-status jobs. Although few single women were identified by trade, all could be placed in one of the three crudely defined economic categories used in the tables, and their poverty leaves little doubt that single women held Leiden's worst jobs. Over half were "poor" and less than 10 percent were "rich." In contrast, Leiden's taxpaying widows, a group usually considered the poorest element in urban society during the period, were much better off: less than 30 percent were "poor" and almost as many—25 percent—were "rich."

In the suburbs, the same relationships held. Seventy-five percent of the working women were married and they dominated the high-status positions held by women. Married and widowed women together held 90 percent of the high-status positions. No married woman who worked was categorized as "poor" while one of eight widows was so judged, as was one of two single women and one of two women whose marital status we do not know (who were either widowed or single). Married women in high-status jobs often shared the work of their husbands. The three women who wove or fulled cloth did so as their husbands' partners, as did the sole baker, the sole potter, and the sole market farmer. This was not, however, an invariable pattern: although two of the seven cloth producers did the same work their husbands did, four were in entirely different trades. (We do not know the occupation of the seventh's husband nor those of the husbands of any of the eight widows.)

The records do not tell us why there was such a strong correlation between labor status and marital status. Common sense suggests that some married women probably helped their husbands in their work, and then took over for them when their husbands died. Others may have benefited from marriage in that it gave them access to capital for setting up their own businesses (for example, for entering the drapery). Possibly, a third factor was even more significant. Labor status and marital status were statistically associated with each other, not because there was a direct causal relationship between them, but because women with a trade or with the money, talent, ambition, health, or intelligence needed to acquire a trade would also have made the most attractive marriage partners. According to this reasoning, single women would have done low-skilled work, not because they were unmarried but simply because they were unhealthy, poor, unintelligent, untrained, very old or very young.

PATTERNS OF WOMEN'S WORK
THE ORGANIZATION OF MARKET PRODUCTION

Women's labor status in Leiden was clearly associated with family position. In both the city and its suburbs, married and widowed women disproportionately dominated the positions granting high labor-status. Because a smaller proportion of these women in Leiden worked, fewer high-status jobs were awarded city women than suburban women. This evidence is therefore extremely good support for the hypothesis that women gained access to high-status work through the family.

For most of these women, the family provided the training they needed, and for many of them the route to high labor-status was as their husband's partner or heir. Women with their own enterprises were concentrated in trades that could be learned in the family; either they practiced skilled crafts like weaving and fulling cheap cloths or they took on managerial functions which required skills any good housewife would have already honed. The evidence also explains why single women had such low labor-status: young, unmarried, possibly immigrants, they were subordinate to the married pair or to the widowed head-of-household with whom they lodged, and consequently they had labor status below that of the senior household members.

With good indirect evidence that the family was the vehicle of women's access to market production, we can now predict that the family's absence from production for the market can account for women's absence from high-status work. How and why the family production unit lost these roles remains to be explained. A pattern revealed in the past few pages offers a crucial hint, that is, the clear inverse association between women's participation in a trade and its status in Leiden's ambacht system. An analysis of this relationship suggests that two particular features of ambacht organization in Leiden weakened the family production unit and, with that, the labor status of women who had achieved high labor-status through this unit.

One feature was the close association between ambacht membership and political status. The trades in Leiden to which women did not belong were those which had links to political bodies, took organized political action, or granted access to government. The

87

artisanal trades in Leiden with these characteristics were its ambachten; although without formal, independent political power, they were organized to carry out municipal policy as agents of the government. Some of the ambachten even overstepped the limits of their authority and sought to change official policy. The fullers, in particular, frequently staged organized protests for better pay and working conditions and negotiated as a single body with their employers, the drapers, or the municipal government itself, which represented the drapers' interests.[41] At these moments, the fullers' ambacht even assumed the role of a corporative guild which shared in government.

Women did not belong to these ambachten because in late medieval cities political roles were the exclusive preserve of men.[42] Accordingly, women did not weave or full drapery because to do so would have required ambacht status; but they continued to dye cloth and finish it and to weave, full, and finish linens and voerlakens until these trades acquired ambacht status.

The inverse association between the political status of a trade and women's place in it held even outside the ambachten. Women drapers, for example, never took on the political roles sometimes associated with the trade. A mid-sixteenth-century document that records the plans of ninety-two drapers to set up a sales office in Amsterdam dramatically illustrates this correlation: although thirty-three of the drapers were women, not one of the association's officers was female.[43] This may be one reason why women did not join the ranks of large drapers. Leiden's large drapers were responsible for negotiating with the Calais wool merchants; they represented the city in discussions with other cities concerned with Leiden's cloth trade; and through the offices they held in the ambacht they supervised manufacturing. Many, as I said earlier, were members of the government.

Important as this political dimension undoubtedly was in making it difficult for women to practice a trade, the process of excluding women from a trade once it had taken on such associations was seldom a straightforward one. In the case of the finishers, the process began with the ambacht's founding ordinance of 1508 which forbade women to train for masterships, but it was some decades before women were written out of the regulations entirely. While the 1508 ordinance referred to a "brotherhood and sisterhood of St. Ursula," the version of 1552 mentioned only the "brotherhood of the dry finishers and trimmers." By then, the reference to women workers in the first article, which had allowed currently practicing female mistresses to continue in the trade, had been eliminated. A new article established burial rights for a "dead brother or sister." Another new article provided that a widow accompanied by a master journeyman who had produced a masterpiece might continue her husband's business, but also stipulated that, should she remarry outside the trade, she would lose her trade rights. By 1563, when the ordinances were again revised, all references to women were gone. Even widows' rights were not mentioned; in addition, the 1552 article that required attendance at funerals had disappeared, and in a new one, requiring aid to sick brothers, women were not mentioned at all, not even indirectly.[44]

With the linen weavers it was the same. As we have seen, the ordinances establishing this ambacht in 1563 explicitly referred to women mistresses. Five years later an announcement by the government implied that women were no longer normally considered when membership and work rules were established. While repeating the requirement that all who produce linen cloth in Leiden must be members of the brotherhood, it, unlike the first article of the founding ordinance, did not refer to female members.[45] The change in language is not easily explained. We have almost no external information about the trade which might tell us more about who actually made linen textiles. It is possible that the first ordinances were simply transcriptions of old, less formalized brotherhood rules which were, in fact, out of date by the time the ambacht ordinances were written. It is also possible that the later omission of women from the ordinance reflected only the attitudes and presumptions of the bureaucracy that formulated trade ordinances; although a few women may still have actually worked in the trade, they were not considered "official" and were not of real concern to the authorities who prescribed entrance standards.

The latter argument may apply also in the case of the voerlaken makers. The legislation first issued in 1562 for this textile sector did not even mention women; nor did any of the subsequent editions, except when describing the low-skilled labor of piece-workers.[46] Yet, as we have seen, other evidence leaves little doubt that women were active—and legitimate—voerlaken producers in the last decades of the sixteenth century. The officials who made and wrote government policy for this trade probably could not imagine women as full ambacht members and so ignored the few women who did make this cloth. The bureaucracy, it would seem, wrote a self-fulfilling prophecy, for by the seventeenth century women do not appear as independent producers and artisans in the records of this industry.

These examples illustrate some of the ways that establishment of an ambacht could lead to women's loss of membership in a trade. When we recognize that Leiden's ambachten were political bodies of a kind and if we acknowledge that women could not be granted full political status in this culture, it becomes clear that women would have had to surrender trade rights when these rights implied political status. This connection becomes easier to understand when we realize that women could not have political status because they were subordinate to the male head of the family (who alone had political status) and were publicly defined through the family. A woman's family status—single, married, widowed, head of household or not—defined her public status and she was not regarded as an independent member of any public body except the family. As urban politics developed in this period in the North, however, the individual—the male individual—not the family or the household, participated or was judged as a participant. Only males nominated or elected members or officials of governmental bodies and it was increasingly their position as merchant, craftsman, property owner—effectively, their position as citizen—which gave them this right rather than position in a household or a particular family. For similar reasons, only the individual males in a trade signed oaths to uphold work rules; and only individual males whose civic status obligated them to do so actually bore arms for the community. In these cities, it seems, the growing political organization of work weakened the bond between work and family which had prevailed for centuries because in these communities the male individual, not the female, was made the unit of participation.

Even when these political associations had drawn work from the family, it did not necessarily follow, of course, that what was now "men's" work had no residual ties to the family and the household. A man's family might well help him in his trade, the family might even succeed to the assets of the trade, and a man's work might very well be located in the household. Nevertheless, because the political system which regulated his work gave him status in his trade that it did not extend to his household or family associates, they were not regarded as having fully shared his work.

Organization as an ambacht seems to have weakened the family production unit in an equally important and more familiar way as well. Ambacht organization almost always involved the establishment of work rules and schedules which were incompatible with family life. For example, weavers and fullers in Leiden's drapery were required to have served one to three years as apprentices and another three as "free journeymen" before they could acquire masterships; weavers also were subject to a daily schedule of work regulated by a clock; fullers labored in teams of one master and two journeymen who were expected to deliver a finished product in a fixed time period and who were paid as a team by the job. None of these arrangements allowed the flexibility needed by someone bound to the rhythms of a household.[47] Because ambacht rules were directed at individuals considered free of household tasks, ambacht membership separated a worker from his household, even if he continued to locate his work in the household.

Records from the 1470s about the fullers help to illustrate how these two aspects of ambacht formation could undermine the family production unit. One document forbade the wives of master fullers to handle their husbands' accounts along with their own.[48] From this evidence we can deduce that women entrepreneurs had once performed certain tasks simultaneously in their own trade and their husbands', for both were considered the family's. When ambacht rules required wives to separate their work from their husbands', the ambacht weakened the unit. Another document contained a complaint by journeymen fullers that the wives of master fullers were infringing on their territory; one of their demands was that fullers' wives no longer remove cloth from the drying frames on which it was stretched and finished, a task the journeymen were presumably claiming for themselves.[49] This demand can be read as a spearhead of the ambacht's attack upon the family enterprise, one prompted no doubt by the journeymen's wish to reduce competition, but one they advanced on the basis that rights to skilled crafts did not belong to families but to individuals.

The large drapers, too, instituted business practices that could have weakened the traditional family production unit and made it impossible for women, even as wives and widows, to work as large drapers. Large drapers in Leiden traveled much of the time; they made at least one annual trip to Calais, and they regularly visited regional markets in cities such as Bergen op Zoom, Amsterdam, and Bruges. Keeping such a schedule would have been difficult for women, who had pressing household tasks and who, in any case, would seldom have found business travel feasible, given the cultural norms they faced and considerations of safety. Women with important household duties—and perhaps even some men unwilling to give up household duties—would have found the demands of producing cloth in quantity too burdensome.

Even the men able to keep these schedules had to rely on someone to manage the local aspects of the business while they were away—to oversee production, to receive shipments, and to deal with any local purchasers. While, in some cases, wives could have taken on these tasks, this was not the practice in Leiden, where, from at least the mid-fifteenth century on, women very seldom helped or succeeded their husbands in their businesses of importing wool and selling wool cloth. The reasons they did not undoubtedly had something to do with the way the drapery business was managed. Much of the business of being a large draper was done away from Leiden, at Calais, where negotiations were difficult and prolonged, and at regional fairs where contracts for sales, delivery, and payment were arranged. Wives who remained at home could have learned nothing of this part of the business and would have known only about the local affairs, over which they had only indirect control when their husbands were away. Women with only a partial knowledge of the business might well have been regarded as inadequate agents for their husbands, and it may have seemed preferable for men to arrange things among themselves. Men who already cooperated in certain phases of the business during their journeys to Calais and regional markets could easily cooperate in other phases as well, so that one traveled and another handled local affairs. The practice of forming buying syndicates which sent representatives to Calais for large groups of drapers was undoubtedly such an arrangement.

The contrast between the city and the suburbs already explored illustrates particularly well the force with which these two factors— which I am labeling the political and the business organization of work—affected the family and women. Work in the suburbs was unorganized in both senses, and married women there were active and obviously valued members of the family production unit that reigned in this relatively unsophisticated and undifferentiated economy. Young and single women there, on the other hand, had very low status. Few were even mentioned in the survey, probably because they had left home.[50] Many had surely entered domestic service in the city, where they did housework, ran errands, watched children, and perhaps helped out in the trade(s) being carried on in the household. In the process they learned a bit about weaving, fulling, potting, or beer brewing and, when they later married, they brought these skills to their new households, thus moving into what Maschke labeled the *Mittelschicht* and acquiring higher labor-status.

In contrast to work in the suburbs, work in the city had become more organized in both the political and the business sense, and married women were found in few sectors of market production. Still defined by their family status and restricted to economic roles compatible with their family roles, married women could fully participate only in those trades not yet subject to such organizational features. In contrast, single women were not closed out of market production, because most of the low-status work they had traditionally done for the market, as woolcombers or knitters for example, was not organized in either of these senses.

While very few high-status trades in Leiden itself were not organized in these ways, those which were not still employed women. One of the trades was drapery production itself. Since it was possible in Leiden to be a small, part-time draper whose product—not training, institutional membership, or production schedule—provided the sole standard of suitability to practice the trade and to participate in wool-buying syndicates and sell cloth through agents, women were active at this level of the drapery. They also practiced other skilled textile trades which were not yet highly organized but provided moderately high labor-status and they continued to run pubs and to make and sell cheese, butter, beer, and clothing. All the while, nevertheless, they suffered a decline in labor status as these functions were taken over by better-organized tradesmen.

The pattern of women's work in Leiden also owed something to cultural traditions that defined men's work and women's work as separate. Few of the women in Leiden worked in industrial sectors like construction, metals, or wood, and instead usually performed functions which had grown from the household chores that had been the province of women in the traditional family economy. Widows who carried on their husbands' trades were the sole apparent exceptions to this rule, but in carrying on these trades they were, in fact, upholding the traditional system because they obtained their positions in market production through their position in their family. The traditional sexual division of labor, however, was not responsible for all features of the pattern. Women did not hold *all* the jobs in the market economy that precedent should have awarded them. Leiden's brewers, embroiderers, hatmakers, weavers and fullers of drapery, butchers, and medical doctors—all of them subject to varying degress of business and political organization—were male.

The data permit one final observation about women's work and the socioeconomic structure. Until the political and business organization of work occurred, women of Leiden's *Mittelschicht*—the group made up of small merchants and producers—were active in market production and did work commensurate with the socioeconomic status of their families. Like the men of the *Mittelschicht,* these women, when young, served as helpers and trainees and as adults took over masterships and proprietorships. During the fifteenth and sixteenth centuries, this pattern gradually changed, however, and such women either retreated from market production to devote themselves entirely to managing their households or, driven by economic necessity, took on low-status work which was incompatible with the social status they once would have had as the wives of artisans.

In summary, then, we can tentatively confirm and refine the working hypothesis of this study. The family production unit was, indeed, the vehicle for women's access to high-status jobs in market production and, so long as it retained its role, women of Leiden's *Mittelschicht* held jobs commensurate with their status in the social hierarchy. But developments directly associated with small commodity production, developments that both secured political control of industry and preserved social order and that enhanced the efficiency of the individual producer, weakened the family production unit. These developments were not capitalist innovations but were products of a system—small commodity production—which even retarded the emergence of capitalism. The effect of these developments was to lower women's labor-status by closing many of the positions that granted high labor-status to women, forcing women of Leiden's *Mittelschicht* to retreat from market production or, more rarely, to take on work incompatible with their social position.

5

The Socioeconomic
Structure of Cologne

The women of late medieval Cologne played prominent roles in commerce and industry. Karl Bücher drew attention to their importance in market production in his *Frauenfrage*, but it was Wilhelm Behagel's study published about the same time that provided the confirming data; in Cologne, he showed, most guilds provided for women members, and three guilds as well as a branch of a fourth were almost exclusively for women.[1] Understandably, later scholars returned frequently to Cologne's women. Bruno Kuske's articles and document collections on trade in late medieval Cologne offered many examples of women active in commerce, and Helmut Wachendorf's examination of Bücher's idea that women once had but later lost labor status in late medieval German cities relied in part on evidence from Cologne for proof that women in the late Middle Ages had been valuable, and valued, participants in industry and trade.[2]

Contemporary reports from the men of Cologne's merchant elite confirm the findings of historians. In 1580 one of the city's prominent citizens, for example, left a testament advising his nephew to marry a woman with a shop "for through wives [sic] a man gains entry into commerce [*kaufhandel*] and a livelihood which [he] did not learn from the ground up"; in 1542, another member of Cologne's elite explained in his will that he had remarried after the death of his first wife both "because of the children and because of his trade."[3]

Margret Wensky has recently expanded on the work of previous scholars. Using a somewhat wider range of published documents than was available to her predecessors and some important unpublished documents from the fifteenth century, she corrected a few details of their reports but reached the same conclusion: in the fifteenth century Cologne's women had easy access to a wide range of prestigious and skilled positions which clearly can be characterized as high-status. As Wensky summarized it,

> In late medieval Cologne there were but a few economic sectors in which women could not be found. Only a few guilds (the tailors, the harnessmakers and the cloth cutters) restricted women's right to work, and even then, the restrictions were in effect for only limited periods or had only partial application. . . . The great independence, which Cologne's women enjoyed in commerce and industry, was matched in no other late medieval German city. . . . The administration and structure of the women's guilds differed from the rest of the guilds only in that they counted virtually only women as members.[4]

While Wensky and the scholars who preceded her have provided a rich collection of evidence for the study of women's work in late medieval Cologne, none of them has addressed the hypothesis raised here. To be sure, Wensky used biographical data about some of the most visible women artisans and merchants in Cologne to conclude that they had gained access to their jobs through their families, but her evidence was not conclusive.[5] In order to prove that women's positions in their families were directly associated with their positions in market production, we must show not only that the economic sectors in which women worked made use of a family production unit but also that those sectors from which women were excluded could not accommodate this unit. Then, to test the hypothesis as it was elaborated in the study of Leiden, we will need to show that the family production unit lost its place in market production—and that women lost theirs with it—as the political and business organization of production increased.

We will also want to go beyond the conclusions that could be drawn from the study of Leiden. The information about working women in Leiden came almost entirely from one industry, and most of the women, indeed a majority of all the city's workers with high-status jobs, belonged to the traditional urban artisanate. Cologne's economy and society were much more complex, and the pattern of women's participation in market production there appears to have been equally complex. Women held or had access to a much wider range of high-status jobs than in Leiden and they came from more diverse backgrounds. They were perhaps even better represented in the traditional crafts in Cologne than in Leiden, and while many of them belonged to artisanal families, just like the craftswomen in Leiden, some did not. Three of the women's guilds—the silk makers, yarn makers, and gold spinners—were dominated by women from a sector of Cologne's economic and political elite, a group almost unrepresented in market production in Leiden. Women in Cologne also held a number of official and semiofficial city posts rarely assigned to women in Leiden—commodity broker or host to foreign buyers, toll collector, appraiser and lender (the somewhat elevated ancestor of our pawnbroker), and gatekeeper. The role women played in long-distance trade in Cologne provides perhaps the clearest contrast with Leiden. Not only did women in Cologne invest in cooperative long-distance trading ventures, they also financed and managed their own deals. They exchanged wine, wool cloth, fish, chemicals, and metal wares in markets north, south, east, and west of Cologne; within Cologne, they bought and sold imported raw materials as well as industrial and luxury products in local markets and over the Staple.

It is not simply because more of Cologne's women had high-status work, as a result of their social backgrounds being more diverse than in Leiden and the range of high-status positions available to them being wider, that Cologne makes an interesting partner to Leiden in this study. Even more significant, Cologne's socioeconomic structure was quite different from Leiden's. By examining the links between women's labor status in Cologne and the place of the family production unit in market production there, we have an opportunity to test whether the features which seem to have determined the role of the family production unit in Leiden had the same effects under different socioeconomic circumstances. If so, we have a persuasive case for a hypothesis that can be generally applied to women's work in urban market economies throughout northern Europe.

This study of Cologne's working women depends, as did the study of Leiden's working women, on close examination of the city's socioeconomic structure. Only with such a detailed analysis can we identify the differences between Cologne and Leiden which helped account for the differences in the work roles and labor status of women in each city.

THE PROBLEM OF SOURCES

To understand the social, economic, and political structure of fifteenth-century Cologne we must turn to the city's earlier history, one we can reconstruct in some detail, thanks to the work of past historians.[6] Late medieval Cologne has attracted such interest, in part because of its importance. It was the home of about 30,000 to 40,000 people, among them an archbishop as well as the members of his court and the officials who surrounded him, the faculty and students of a major university, a small nobility, merchants and financiers counted among Europe's wealthiest, and artisans of some of Europe's finest specialty textiles, weaponry, and clothing. Cologne has also proved to be an accessible subject. Its archives are rich, well organized, and in part published. Most of the documents on which historians of medieval Cologne's secular history have depended were produced by urban institutions, many of them by the municipal bureaucracy. Such institutions as guilds, which in their early history were not part of the city government, generated their own records, and less formally organized bodies such as business associations or families have provided Cologne's historians with other kinds of documentation for the late Middle Ages.

This study of Cologne relies heavily on the work of past scholars and the sources they used.[7] Without them, the analysis of the economic, social, and political structure of late medieval Cologne and the detailed documentation of women's work necessary for this study would not have been possible. Adapting the sources and the findings of others, however, occasionally required a return to the original sources, and the results of reexamination appear here as critical appraisals of the ways in which the borrowed data have been collected or interpreted.

My comments on Wensky's work are especially extensive since her study, *Die Stellung der Frau in der stadtkölnischen Wirtschaft im Spätmittelalter* is the principal source for my analysis of women's work in Cologne in the following chapter. Her search of the sources was so thorough that only someone able to undertake systematic analysis of the huge document series not yet published could hope to improve on it. While my sources are Wensky's and the material on which she drew and while I have reproduced her research in a distilled form, my study is different from hers because it concentrates not on gathering empirical data but on interpreting the data.

Wensky primarily relied on three major source collections. One was the set of documents relating to the guilds long ago published by von Loesch and supplemented by other documents not known to him but for the most part catalogued in published material.[8] Many of Cologne's guilds, or the brotherhoods from which they sometimes had grown, originated as early as the twelfth century but it was only in 1396 that they received corporative status; most of the information about the guilds comes from the founding statutes of 1397 and the documents subsequently generated. The records used are principally legislative, the available judicial and financial documents being so scarce that no systematic study of Cologne's artisanal sector can be based on them. Second, Wensky relied heavily on the collection of records concerned primarily with long-distance trade that were published by Kuske. Court cases, wills, government correspondence, records of Hansa meetings, excerpts from the books of businessmen, and portions of the city's accounts make up the bulk of the collection.[9] The third set of sources Wensky used developed from Cologne's right to tax commerce, and includes records of fees paid to sell luxury cloth or wine and of excise taxes paid on goods brought through individual Staple markets. Good series of both kinds of records have survived for much of the fifteenth century. Those covering trade in stapled goods exist in a series from 1452 to 1495, broken only by the decade of the 1480s, and in incomplete form for short periods of the early sixteenth century.[10]

ECONOMIC AND CONSTITUTIONAL BACKGROUND

Cologne's economy, as well as its political and social systems, underwent fundamental reorganization during the fifteenth century. This transformation and its importance can be best understood by looking, first, at the history of the three preceding centuries during which Cologne grew from a small ecclesiastical center into a city of as many as 40,000 individuals, the largest and most important city in medieval Germany.

By 1100, Cologne had begun its growth.[11] Merchants settling on the Rhine in what had once been a Roman administrative center and was then the seat of an archbishop, had by that time begun long-distance trade which linked southern and eastern Germany to the North and West as well as to lands beyond. Taking advantage of their pivotal role as middlemen and of Cologne's location as a natural off-loading place on the Rhine, western Europe's greatest inland waterway, the merchants were able to establish Cologne as a

Staple in 1259. Through Cologne and then northwards, especially to England and the Low Countries, Cologners shipped German wine and metals, as well as luxury goods bought from the Italians; southwards through Cologne they sent wool and cloth from both England and the Low Countries as well as fish, grains, and raw metals. As this trade involved Cologne's merchants in international finance, they became some of northern Europe's most prominent lenders and dealers in metals and coins.

Trade with England was especially important. In the thirteenth century, Cologners typically took metal goods (especially weapons) and German wine to England and brought back wool, raw metals, and agricultural products. By the fifteenth century, the terms of trade had changed. By then, England was buying much less wine from Cologners than formerly (having switched to French wines), but had increased its demand for yarn, silk cloth, and barchent (a linen and wool mixture). England was then also exporting wool cloth more often than wool, but Cologne was as active in the new trade as it had been in the old. In the second half of the fifteenth century, Cologners handled about 30 percent of English cloth distributed by the Hansa or about 5 to 6 percent of total English cloth exports. Cologne's merchants were active in the Low Countries too, especially in Bruges from the thirteenth century and in Antwerp from the fourteenth century. Between 1488 and 1513, 532 of 1,227 German merchants in Antwerp were Cologners— more than from any other German city. Other northern markets of significance to Cologne were Dordrecht, where heavy goods such as steel and wood were traded, and Kampen and Hamburg, which were used when the markets of Brabant and Flanders were closed. Southern Europe was equally important, especially Venice, as the source of spices and raw silk from the East and the Levant.[12] Finally, Cologne was active, in particular as a cloth supplier, in the eastern European markets centered in Vienna, Prague, and Pressburg.[13]

Cologne's prominence in trade was due, of course, to the city's geographic position and its Staple rights, but what distinguished Cologne, and perhaps accounted for the city's economic strength well into the sixteenth century, was its industry. From the thirteenth century on, at least, Cologne's artisans produced for export. They made fine metal products of gold and silver as well as heavier metal goods, like weapons, armor, wheels, tools, and locks; textiles of wool, linen, and silk, especially linen yarns and decorated fine fabrics; leather goods and certain articles of clothing. At this point in Cologne's economic development, regional trade fairs became very important, for these were often the entrepots where Cologne's artisans obtained raw materials and distributed their products.

By the fifteenth century, marked changes had occurred in both the commercial and industrial sectors of the economy, many of them reflecting shifts in the European economy during the late Middle Ages when demographic crisis, climatic change, political instability, and monetary mismanagement combined to produce what has been called the depression of the Renaissance.[14] Some historians have held that Cologne, too, suffered a depression during this period, but others have argued persuasively that, while the fifteenth century was clearly not a period of continuous or evenly distributed economic growth, it was not for Cologne a time of depression.[15] Instead, it was a time of reorganization. Decreases in production or sales occurred in certain sectors, but increases in other sectors largely offset them. Both the decreases and the increases mirrored, to some extent, changes in long-distance trade throughout Europe. Certain products of traditional importance in Cologne, such as English wool, were withdrawn from trade. Others were driven from traditional markets; German wine lost the English market to French wine, and wool cloth made in Cologne lost the eastern European market as a result of upheavals caused by the Hussite wars and the collapse of the Bohemian silver mines. Replacing them, products such as hopped beer grew because they were new and better, while still others, such as silk, grew because there was a new demand for them.

Franz Irsigler has traced these developments, most fully in *Die wirtschaftliche Stellung der Stadt Köln*. In the late fourteenth century, Cologne was regularly producing about 10,000 wool cloths, which, although far less than the 15,000 to 20,000 made fifty to seventy-five years earlier, were enough to maintain Cologne's strength in the markets of central and eastern Europe. After 1415, the volume sank to about 5,000 per year, a level sustained until the late fifteenth century when the manufacture of wool cloth virtually disappeared from Cologne itself. Around 1372-74, about 8,000 *Tirtei* (cheap blended fabrics) were produced in Cologne, but by the mid-fifteenth century Tirtei production had fallen to negligible quantities. Counteracting these losses, barchent production and sales of English cloths rose. Barchent output reached a peak in about 1450, at 9,000 pieces, and sales of imported wool cloths in Cologne by *Gewandschneider* hit almost 3,000 per year in the early 1440s. During the second half of the century, the production of silk also reached impressive heights, and silk became Cologne's single most important export industry.[16] In the late fifteenth century, Cologne annually imported enough raw silk for its own industry to produce silk fabrics worth 150,000 to 200,000 Gulden, about equal to the wholesale value of wool cloth produced during any year in the previous century when wool-cloth production in the city had been at its height.[17]

Dramatic shifts in the volume of production and patterns of trade occurred in other sectors of the economy. The spice trade fell off, a result of declines of price and of volume; commerce in raw metals contracted while that in finished or semifinished metal goods expanded; and during the fifteenth century the leather goods business seems to have boomed. Most significant were the marked changes in the wine and beer businesses. Traditionally, wine had been Cologne's single largest business, with an annual wholesale value of over one million Mark in the first half of the fifteenth century, when total volume in *all* imported dry goods (spices, leathers, cotton, metals, and chemicals) was between 400,000 and 500,000 Mark a year. By the mid-fifteenth century, however, wine imports had fallen and by the 1460s were but one-third of the late-fourteenth-century level. The decline in wine sales was largely offset by an increase in beer sales that reflected the improved brewing methods of the late Middle Ages. First in northern Germany, which sold beer to Cologne, and later in Cologne itself, a beer was made with hops and herbs which was longer-lasting and tastier than the old *Grutbier* that was once the common people's unloved alternative to cheap wine. Hopped beer was such an improvement on its predecessors that even the upper classes enjoyed it. The sales of hopped and herbed beer in the late fifteenth century sometimes reached 100,000 hectoliters (10 million liters) a year and never fell under 40,000 hectoliters.

As striking as the mix of products made or traded in Cologne, and of more importance to this study, was a shift in the structure of trade and industry. The kinds of goods handled and the kinds of people who handled them both changed. Long-distance commerce in Cologne, begun as a carrying trade centered on luxury goods—spices, wine, metals, jewelry, fine wool—had been conducted by merchants who handled large volumes, dealt in a variety of goods, and were represented in markets throughout Europe. By the fifteenth century, Cologne's merchants dealt much more often in manufactured goods made in and around Cologne, sometimes at their order. Not all were luxury goods but those which were—silk and embroidered fabrics, jewelry, ecclesiastical vestments, furs, finely worked metal and leather boxes as well as decorative objects—often were manufactured in Cologne. Other goods commonly traded were medium-quality fabrics (made of local wools, linen, cotton, or blends of these materials), weapons, tools, and beer—again, for the most part, goods manufactured by or under the direction of Cologners. Cologners, as mentioned before, turned from trade in English wool to the distribution of English cloth and from the wholesale trade in wine in England to the distribution of it in northern Europe and in Cologne.

As fifteenth-century trade differed from earlier trade so, too, the fifteenth-century merchant was different. As a dealer in locally and regionally produced goods, he or she was often closely involved in the production process itself; in fact, many merchants began their careers as artisans or came from artisanal families. These fifteenth-century merchants were more specialized than their predecessors. Often they traded only a few related products or they traded in one set of markets, for example, along the north-south Rhine axis or between England and Cologne.

The long-distance trade of fifteenth-century Cologne was, as never before, linked to industry, especially local industry, and local industry was thereby transformed. Craftsmen of textiles, metals, and leathers increasingly produced for long-distance markets, and to reach them they had to deal with long-distance merchants or become merchants themselves. They did both. Some artisans of Cologne grew into merchants and employers of other artisans; others were reduced to employees of merchants; still others remained independent producers who sold their goods to long-distance traders.

The wool cloth industry was the most important to undergo this transformation.[18] After the availability of English wool declined, beginning in the fourteenth century and continuing, with ever more drastic effects, in the fifteenth century, and English wool cloth exports through Cologne increased, Cologne's weavers turned to Continental wools and to new regional markets where their coarser, cheaper product was welcome. Many weavers also set up putting-out operations to increase production; they supplied weavers in the area with wool and distributed their products, usually at regional fairs or in distant markets.[19] After the Gewandschneider's monopoly of cloth sales was ended, weavers also sold imported cloth in Cologne, but they were never dominant in the *Gewandschnitt*.[20] Instead, many members of the *Wollamt* became significant exporters of the cloth made in and around Cologne. A list of eighty-three wool cloth exporters that covered eight months of 1428-29 contained forty-eight members of the Wollamt, who accounted for 55 percent of sales. The eight largest merchants among the forty-eight Wollamt members, who alone accounted for 25 percent of the sales, were among the ten leading sellers.[21] Wollamt members were also active in the wine trade and in the trade of some luxury dry goods during the fifteenth century. By the fifteenth century a large group of wool, cloth, wine, and dry goods merchants had emerged from the old Wollamt, many of whom were also managers of putting-out systems through which they procured the cloth they sold.

Equally dramatic changes occurred in what had been the most important commercial sector of Cologne, the wine trade. In the late fourteenth century, members of Cologne's traditional commercial elite dominated the trade; 68 percent of this elite (who comprised just 12 percent of all importers) were in the category of "large importers" (those 27 percent of the importers who handled 81 percent of the wine).[22] Few of them, however, exported wine to distant markets; instead, they resold it in Cologne, in a business they dominated as members of the exclusive *Weinbrüderschaft*.[23] In 1396 the right to sell wine in Cologne was made available to anyone who could pay the stiff fee. Thereafter, according to figures for 1414/15 and 1420/21, the old elite virtually abandoned large-scale wine trade, and both men and women from this group now imported solely for their own use; for these years only 4.7 percent of the importers were from the traditional elite. A new group of merchants had replaced them in positions of dominance; in 1420/21, 25 percent of these new merchants accounted for 74.4 percent of sales.[24]

In the course of the fifteenth century, total wine import volumes declined, and as they did, so did the amounts handled by individual merchants. From 1466/67 to 1478/79, only 2.6 percent of the importers brought in more than 100 Fudern per year, while 24.7 percent of importers had done so in 1420/21. The volume declines obviously reflected the falloff in demand from England, but that the sales declines were not accompanied by comparable decreases in the number of merchants is testimony to the trade's continued profitability.[25]

Along with changes in Cologne's economy came dramatic alterations in the city's social and political structure. To understand their importance, it is necessary to begin with a sketch of Cologne's constitutional history during the late Middle Ages. This history comprises three distinct periods: the first, from the eleventh century to about the mid-thirteenth century marks the establishment of municipal government; the second, which lasted, with one short interruption in 1370-71, until 1396, covers the period when Cologne was governed by an entrenched elite; and the third, which continued until 1513, distinguishes the period of so-called guild rule.[26]

By the thirteenth century Cologne was independent and self-governing. A well-entrenched political elite, *Schöffen* and members of the *Richerzeche*, provided courts and administration, and were completing their takeover of Colgone's parish organizations, where self-government had begun. By 1305 a new organization had developed, the *Rat* or Council, and it replaced both the Schöffen College and the Richerzeche in the course of the century. The council was composed of fifteen individuals, all well-established Cologners who elected their successors annually. The council's many officers and two major courts administered finance, defense, the docks, many aspects of trade, and maintained the peace. After 1321, this council was supplemented by a Large Council (*weiter Rat*) whose eighty-two members were selected, in a more democratic fashion, from the administrative parishes that concentrated on financial matters while the old council came to be called the Small Council (*enger Rat*).

This system was fundamentally revised in the late fourteenth century. Changes began in 1370 when, through their guild, the Wollamt, the wool weavers forced the government to include them in the political process. They abolished the Richerzeche, but left the Schöffen College and the Small Council in place. In matters of finance and foreign policy the Large Council was made more powerful; its membership was reduced to fifty, with the majority being weavers and the rest, by and large, members of select industrial guilds. The "weavers' rule" did not, however, last long; the weavers did not have the support of certain key guilds or the merchants that had newly entered trade in Cologne, and without these groups the weavers could not retain control. Their trade and tax policies alienated many Cologners, including several of their former allies. In November 1371, just about a year and a half after the weavers took power, the old elite staged a successful coup.

The victors reinstated traditional government and, despite tension among some of their numbers, and even open conflict between one faction of conservative, more established families and another of families less securely placed, their government survived until 1396. Then, an alliance between new merchants who had been excluded from the government and some leading craft guilds, like the Wollamt and the *Goldschmiede*, overthrew them and established their own rule. Their new constitution, the *Verbundbrief*, established a guild government, and the new council provided to replace the old Small and Large Councils was elected by twenty-two *Gaffeln*, sort of political-military guilds to which henceforth all citizens would belong.

Until these uprisings of the fourteenth century, the guilds in Cologne had been without political power. At first they had existed at the sufferance of the Richerzeche and the council; the political elite of Cologne had not directly interfered in their economic or internal affairs but had left them surprisingly independent— perhaps because, as long-distance merchants, the elite had little interest in craft production.[27] For their part, the craftsmen had abstained from the communal affairs of concern to the political elite. Few were even citizens, because citizenship was expensive (6–12 Gulden when 10 Gulden a year rented a worthy, if not elegant, house and when wage-earning artisans made but 40–50 Gulden a year), and necessary only to practice a few crafts and join a few guilds.[28]

As institutions of the artisanal community, the guilds emphasized religious and social services as much as economic matters. They had no power of incorporation and no right to impose their will outside their own membership without the consent of the authorities; until the early twelfth century, authority was the archbishop, until the guild uprising of 1370 the Richerzeche, and thereafter the council. Only after the twelfth century were the guilds, one by one, able to obtain the right of *Zunftzwang*, the requirement that all who practiced a craft belong to the associated guild.[29] But even then entrance to the guilds was generally open to all, fees were low, and membership was neither restricted nor heritable.[30]

Throughout the entire late Middle Ages, however, as the "weavers' revolt" of 1370 indicates, the craft guilds were far from quiescent; from the mid-fourteenth century on, they repeatedly sought a larger share in government and freer reign in the economy. The wool weavers, in particular, as masters in the city's single most important craft, fought to keep cloistered men and women out of their trade and to open the Gewandschnitt, the right to trade in wool cloth in bulk in Cologne, traditionally a trade reserved by the elite for themselves.[31]

The craft guilds were not the only challenge to traditional order. Even before the fifteenth century, as the composition and nature of long-distance and regional trade in Cologne were transformed, merchants who specialized in the new commerce, who were not themselves part of the Schöffen College, the Richerzeche, or the Small Council, and who were only inadequately represented in the Large Council, had formed guild-like organizations of their own called Gaffeln. The merchant Gaffeln and the leading artisanal guilds led the takeover of government in 1396, and the constitution they wrote, largely revised in 1513, served Cologne until the end of the Old Regime.

The structure and composition of the twenty-two Gaffeln are not entirely clear. Originally, it seems, they comprised the four existing merchant Gaffeln (*Eisenmarkt, Windeck, Schwarzhaus,* and *Himmelreich*), the Wollamt (to which all the woolworking guilds were subordinated), and the remaining forty-odd guilds, grouped roughly according to the industries served. All other citizens were assigned to a Gaffel arbitrarily so that, even at the beginning, the members of a Gaffel were not necessarily associated with a particular trade. During the next three centuries, as old industries died out and new ones developed, the disassociation between Gaffel membership and occupation became even more common, so that by the early modern period, membership in a Gaffel was no longer a guide to one's economic role and status. Until at least the sixteenth century, however, the Gaffeln largely kept their original economic identity even if they were not entirely composed of the industrial or trade interests with which they had originally been identified, and they were always dominated by these interests.

Although these new Gaffeln were not direct heirs of the already existing merchant Gaffeln which had been without formal political power, the new government was dominated by the old Gaffeln and by the new Wollamt (now a Gaffel). The Wollamt sent four members to the council, and the eleven Gaffeln representing major crafts or the old merchant Gaffeln sent two each. The remaining ten industrial Gaffeln each sent one.[32] In turn, these thirty-six representatives selected a complement of thirteen members of certain Gaffeln (called the *Gebrech*). The council chose the senior municipal officials, the most important among them the mayor (*Bürgermeister*). From 1396 until 1513, the council and the mayor ran Cologne with only a little help (or interference) from the

Schöffen College or from any other governmental bodies or officers.

The constitutional changes of the late fourteenth century were part of a political, social, and economic transformation which was marked by the withdrawal of Cologne's old economic elite from commerce and its loss of political hegemony. In terms of its social and political position, if not its economic position, this patriciate very much resembled the patriciate which continued to rule in Leiden. Its members controlled wealth, and claimed social status, all by right of family connections.

As with the patriciates of most northern cities, the origins of Cologne's patriciate are obscure, but most historians agree that for much of its early history its members were involved in trade and finance. An early and still well-regarded study of this elite claimed that trade and finance were in fact the basis of patrician wealth.[33] A later study compared some of Cologne's patricians to Jean Boinebroke, the rapacious merchant-industrialist of thirteenth-century Douai made famous by Espinas.[34] In the latest full examination of Cologne's early constitutional history, the importance of trade in establishing these families has been reaffirmed.[35]

Historians have also agreed, however, that not all the leading families of eleventh- and twelfth-century Cologne began as merchants. Some were descended from Pirenne's wandering merchants, many of them Jews, but others were the heirs of imperial administrative officers, the *ministeriales*, who acquired wealth and land through office.[36] It was not until well into the twelfth century that these two groups had shed their separate social and economic identities and joined in a struggle against the archbishop. By then, it seems, all of them were involved in trade, all owned land, and all helped to govern the city.[37]

Despite its early, firm commitment to trade, the patriciate shifted from commerce to real estate and finance from about 1200 on. While a few important families were still merchants in the late thirteenth century—the Overstolzs, for example, were important cloth traders—many others had severely limited their commercial interests, confining themselves to wine sales and cloth wholesaling (Gewandschnitt) or had turned wholly to passive investments. (A few of these financiers were rich enough to take a 9,756 Goldgulden mortgage on the crown jewels of Edward III of

England.) Most owned real estate in and near Cologne, and some of them married into the landed nobility.[38] A century later, most patricians had given up long-distance wine commerce and the prestigious Gewandschnitt as well. Instead, they owned land out-side Cologne, controlled wine distribution in the city (*Weinzapf*), and, probably as a consequence of their financial activities, were heavily involved in coin making. Even when active in trade, patricians showed no interest in industry. As one scholar summa-rized it, "we never . . . encounter industrial enterprises under the direction of Cologne's patriciate."[39]

Birth or family connections and political office were the key determinants of patrician status, but family and politics alone were never enough: wealth remained essential. So rich was the typical patrician that one could spare 16,000 Rheingulden for a loan to the city in 1390.[40] Another was a real estate tycoon whose family, in 1379, owned a variety of substantial properties: a lease on property which earned 300 Mark annually in addition to a complex of houses used as a residence; an interest in a group of houses and a bakery in Cologne; outside Cologne, five Morgen (perhaps 3.5 to 4 acres) of vineyards; a *Hof* with 40 Morgen of land and two-thirds of another; three smaller *Hoffstätten*; a portion of another *Hofstatt*; 340 Morgen of grain-producing land (*Ackerland*); 16 Morgen of scrubwood (*Busch*); 10 Morgen of pasture land (*Wiese*); and a 6 Malter income of rye from another property (perhaps 900 liters). They also owned bullion, plate, and valuable household objects.[41] About the same time another member of the patriciate had a yearly income of 940 Rheingulden from property he owned in Cologne alone. Like most members of the patriciate, this man probably owned extensive property outside the city as well.[42] None of the nonpatrician Cologne residents had local real estate income this high, and few then owned land outside the city. The richest nonpatrician earned only about 600 Rheingulden annually from his properties and the second richest just 300 Rheingulden. As one recent scholar put it, "name and tradition alone did not suffice to guarantee participation in the ruling circle, . . . the financial basis was crucial."[43]

Once won, a family's place in the patriciate was not assured indefinitely. Families who lost their money, no matter how well-born or well-connected they were, lost political and social position. Even family size played a role in maintaining status: families with few children might have none with the necessary talent for rule, while a family with a great number of children might be unable to leave each of its many heirs fortunes adequate for rule. Other families might lose place by choosing the losing side of whatever internal battle was going on or by making bad marriages.

Uncertain as membership in the patriciate occasionally could be, the composition of the order was amazingly stable; thanks to the privileges of birth, generation after generation of the same families retained the wealth and nurtured the talent necessary for rule. The order itself also retained its almost exclusive hold on government and on social prestige long after it had left commerce. Yet, as the patriciate abandoned trade and ignored industry, others eagerly undertook them and, by the fourteenth century, these newcomers were pressing for social and political changes which an increasingly exclusive patriciate denied. The patriciate's refusal to open its ranks to the new members or to share political power, combined with the growing economic powers of new merchants and some artisans, together explain the revolts of the late fourteenth century and their success.

Capitalism in Cologne: A Debate

The new elite which took over Cologne's government in 1396 was not a replica of its predecessor. Unlike the patricians whom they replaced, whose political and economic status derived from birth, these men were capitalists, and their political and economic status derived from their role in production. The support for this argument comes in the work of many historians and from several kinds of sources, but it has been most thoroughly worked out by Franz Irsigler, especially in his *Die wirtschaftliche Stellung der Stadt Köln im Spätmittelalter*.

Two principal points underlie Irsigler's argument. First, he disassociated capitalism from long-distance trade and finance as such, where, after all, Cologne's patriciate had for centuries been involved, and linked it to industries directed towards export. The most active new merchants often came from industry or had direct ties to it and, moreover, had no links to the old merchant-patricians of Cologne or to the carrying trade they had managed. Instead, they had direct ties to industrial production, and these ties permitted the establishment of capitalist practices. Capitalist wage relations first appeared in wool cloth production, barchent manufacture, silk making, metal-goods making and leatherworking. In each of these industrial sectors, guild brethren who had entered trade made wage workers of other artisans, and merchants from artisanal backgrounds as well as those without direct links to the crafts used laborers outside Cologne to produce these goods for long-distance trade.

Second, Irsigler argued that the new merchants and merchant-producers belonged to a newly fluid social and economic environment, one in which rank was determined only by success in business. Unlike in centuries or even decades past, when the Weinbrüderzapf and Gewandschnitt, for example, had been patrician privileges and certain economic activities had for generations been associated with certain families, in fifteenth-century Cologne trade and industry were opened to everyone and a family's hold on a trade route or on the distribution of a product was sustained only by ability to compete economically.

Extensive lists of importers and exporters that survive from fifteenth-century Cologne illustrate how readily newcomers were welcomed; the names on these lists (in effect, the register of most importers and exporters who were citizens of Cologne) are of craftsmen-turned-merchants and of merchants newly resident in Cologne. Some of them were evidently just beginning in long-distance trade. Conrad Schutz, for example, a *Harnismaker*, who appeared on the 1497–1500 and 1507/78 excise tax list for iron gloves, in second place with 19 percent of the market, traded goods worth just 412 Gulden. Schutz was obviously an artisan-entrepreneur whose business was beginning to expand. Others, already more established, had similar backgrounds. In 1495–1511, for example, the largest importer of metal disks (*Pfannenscheiben*) came from a toolmaker's family.[44] The lists for 1497–1501 and 1506–9 of thirty-five traders in iron cauldrons (*Kessel*), most of whom lived in Cologne as citizens or legal residents, included at least twenty who had come to Cologne from towns where foundries had been set up. These men had, presumably, started out by building and running foundries to supply the Cologne market.[45] The largest trader of barchent in 1452–59 in Cologne represented a Ravensburg firm; others had links to Nuremberg firms.[46]

Another feature typical of fifteenth-century trade was the rapidity with which new names entered the lists of merchants and old ones disappeared.[47] An immigrant to Cologne, Johan Kemper, in 1497–1501 and 1506–11 the largest importer of iron and steel products and a member of the *Harnismaker* guild, had not even shown up in the records for importers of 1495 and early 1496.[48]

Even in economic sectors where this mix of industry and commerce could not occur, the competition and instability of capitalist enterprise became characteristic. The spice trade, once the secure preserve of a few old patrician families, came to be controlled by a constantly changing group of families new to trade in Cologne.

Irsigler's general point, that the economic elite of fifteenth-century Cologne was often directly involved in industry and, in many instances, established capitalist wage relations, has been widely accepted. Nevertheless, key elements of his argument have encountered criticism, especially in a series of studies by Klaus Militzer. In one article, Militzer questioned whether capitalist wage relations had been established in wool cloth production in Cologne as early as the late fourteenth century, as Irisigler claimed.[49] In a fuller critique, Militzer undertook his own analysis of the socioeconomic system of late medieval Cologne from 1360 to 1410, the period of fundamental political reorganization in Cologne. Using data indicating that wealth in Cologne was more equally distributed than in Augsburg (where, he assumed, merchant capitalism had been established and had destroyed the artisanal "middle class" by the late fifteenth and early sixteenth centuries), Militzer concluded that Cologne was not capitalist.[50] Neither was it a society of *Schichten*, however, as Militzer and his followers would have it.

Rather than invalidating either Irsigler's or Maschke's frameworks, however, Militzer's data can be read as indirect corroborations of both. In his analysis, Militzer used statistical data drawn from the records of property transfers contained in Cologne's *Schreinsbücher* to place Cologne's population into one of Maschke's three *Schichten*, categories Militzer initially defined according to wealth alone.[51] None of the categories so constructed, Militzer found, fit Maschke's requirement that they be composed of individuals who shared life-style, politics, and self-consciousness. The *Oberschicht*, Maschke charged, comprised three distinct groups, one of which, the patriciate, had its own criteria for membership (birth, length of residence, source and amount of wealth) and its own life-style.[52] This group also considered itself a separate order from, and better than, the remainder of the economic *Oberschicht*. Many intermarried with local nobles, and even those who did not aped the life-style of landed nobility. The *Oberschicht* also contained a second group of families who, long resident in Cologne and long involved in trade, were still distinct from the patriciate; not members of the pre-1396 Small Council or the other bodies defining patrician status, they had few informal ties to that elite. A third group in the economic *Oberschicht* was the merchant-producers. Although often involved in post-1396 government, they were otherwise unlike other members of the economic elite: their money was "new" and came from different sources; they centered their lives on trade and industry; they had few kin in Cologne and few ties to other members of the *Oberschicht*.

The craftsmen of Cologne who ought to have made up the bulk of the city's *Mittelschicht* similarly could not be accommodated by Maschke's model. The Wollamt offered a particularly complex case. While most of its members belonged to the economic *Mittelschicht*, a good number were part of the *Unterschicht* and the rest were merchants of the economic *Oberschicht*. The guild itself was controlled by and represented the interests of its elite members. The guild houses, built before 1396, located on the Heumarkt next to the meeting house of the society of Gewandschneider— hardly a section of Cologne associated with the poor—and described by a contemporary as "eine grosse pallis,"[53] suggested the Wollamt's wealth and prestige. The "weavers' revolt" of 1370 also shows that the Wollamt had forgone its artisanal origins: hardly the expression of working-class unrest earlier historians had assumed it to be, the revolt marked a bid for political power by a newly rich element who, as leading members of the Amt, were neither concerned for nor in solidarity with artisans in Cologne, many of whom had now descended to employees.[54]

Militzer's data seem unassailable, but his argument, even if adopted without qualification, does not seriously undermine either Maschke's or Irsigler's case. His study might even be read as evidence that many of the elements of capitalism were already in place in 1400 and, as indirectly anticipated by Maschke's model, were effecting a transition from the traditional medieval urban social structure to a capitalist social order. After all, Militzer's claims that the *Mittelschicht* excluded the members of many of Cologne's guilds, that the economic *Oberschicht* was made up of men who did not share backgrounds and interests, and that the *Unterschicht* counted even some skilled artisans in its membership, implicitly describe capitalist development in Cologne. At best, Militzer only demonstrated the unsurprising point that around 1400 Cologne was not yet a fully developed capitalist society.

Information from other sources, much of it reviewed above, reinforces the impression that capitalist development was proceeding apace, practically as it has been anticipated by even the most simplistic evolutionary models: social and economic divisions between employers and employees were increasing; competitive advantage, rather than birth, determined an individual's place in the economic hierarchy; and economic status directly determined political status, rather than the reverse.

One of the easiest ways to appreciate these changes is to look at the financial power of Cologne's newest elites. Around 1400 the patriciate was, to be sure, probably still the richest element in Cologne—it members could apparently easily afford the 20,000 Mark fine imposed upon each of the leaders of the defeated opposition in 1396—but the new merchant-capitalist class was quickly closing in on them. During the period of 1493–95, Heinrich Struyss, for example, annually passed about 180,000 Mark of goods through the collectors of Cologne's excise tax.[55] In 1509, Bartholomeus Byse, nephew and heir of a merchant, contributed, from his legacy alone, 8,000 Gulden towards the 11,000 Gulden price of a sugar plantation and refinery in the Canary Islands.[56] In 1498, the widow of a coppersmith (turned investor and merchant) left 2,000 Gulden as a dowry to each of three daughters and bequeathed thirteen houses to her sons and two grandchildren.[57] In 1422, Johann van Sectam's heirs received part of his portion of an investment in a salt-mining venture which was worth more than 14,500 Gulden.[58] One woman, Neegin Schrijn-mechers, can be credited with the purchase of 7,800 Gulden of debt instruments over a six-year period; the widow of a merchant, she had herself been active in trade.[59] The dowry of Grietgen van der Burg, wife of one of Cologne's most active merchants in the late fifteenth century, was 5,000 Gulden. In 1487, in one administrative parish alone, she owned thirteen houses which rented for 210 Gulden annually, as well as several heritable annuities.[60]

Cologne's underclass bore equally compelling witness to capitalist development. The large underclass in Cologne, made up of immigrants, unskilled workers, the old, the sick, the mentally deficient, and actors, peddlers, barbers, and perhaps linen weavers, was expanding and its character was changing.[61] In earlier days, most urban residents had belonged to the *Unterschicht* only during a stage of life, but many now endured a lifetime there. Apprentices and domestics, probably around 20 percent of Cologne's population, constituted the largest group suffering this change.[62] Almost all of them young, they lived with their employers and were paid a small cash wage plus room, board, and training. As actual apprentices, which some of the girls and most of the boys had traditionally been, they could look forward to masterships, to running their own households, and to higher incomes and places among the artisanal population of the city. Servants not in training for a craft, most of them immigrant girls, could only hope that marriage would lift them out of the *Unterschicht*. Many seem to have achieved their dream. Having worked five to ten years, having learned on the way a bit of the trades carried on in the household, and having saved a bit of cash, servant girls did in fact marry young men who, completing their apprenticeships, set up shops of their own.

But these avenues of upward mobility in Cologne, as elsewhere during the late Middle Ages, were gradually closing. One aspect of the closure affected female household servants. In 1494, the harness makers prohibited further use of maidservants in production, and the ordinances which founded the conreiders made the same exclusion. According to an ordinance of 1397, pocket makers allowed women or girls in the trade but forbade entrance to "unsuitable" female helpers. In 1378 the felt-hat makers forbade all female help—wives, daughters and maids.[63] Another series of regulations made it difficult for apprentices to assume masterships. The development, common to all of Europe in the late Middle Ages, usually took the form of longer periods of apprenticeship, increased costs of masterships, and restrictions on the number of masters. As a result, a new socioeconomic group emerged, the journeymen or *Gesellen*, self-conscious of their status and organized to improve it. Having completed their training but, unable to set up shop, they worked for wages. They had generally moved out of the masters' houses where they had served, rented space in another's house as lodgers, or sometimes married and set up households of their own. In some areas and in some industries, being a journeyman came to be a lifetime occupation, and these men sometimes formed cooperatives to protect their own interests. In German, the term *Gesel* suggests the fraternal spirit that characterized this group of men, and where we hear of *Gesellen* instead of *Meisterknechten*, we can be fairly sure that the traditional system of occupational advancement had broken down.

In many areas, this breakdown seems to have occurred during slow economic periods or in troubled industries. In Cologne, it occurred first in industries from which the small, independent shop was disappearing under the pressure of capitalist competition. For instance, the *Lohgerber* (tanners) Gesellen formed a brotherhood in the fifteenth century in response to a move by merchants (especially leather-artisans with big businesses who used tanned leather) to import either tanned hides or raw hides which they then tanned themselves or hired nonguild workers to tan.[64] It was circumstances such as these which led to social unrest, compelled geographic mobility, and prompted searches for new routes to masterships. One of the favorite new routes was marriage with the widows and daughters of masters.[65]

The effects of the marriages of young male apprentices to widows and the exclusion of young female servants from informal craft work combined to yield a surplus of unmarriageable, untrained women who had no conventional access to the *Mittelschicht*, this in an age when women, for reasons still not understood, probably outnumbered men. In every case where it can be measured, women—usually single but very often widowed—made up a disproportionate share of the economic underclass of late medieval cities.[66] The same was undoubtedly true of Cologne, where many of the same factors present in other cities were at work: guild entrance requirements were tightening, female servants were gradually banned from craft work done on the premises of the household, and some guilds made it impossible for widows who did not remarry to carry on their late husbands' trades.

In the abstract, and certainly in fact in some cities, the creation of a permanent, female-dominated underclass in the late Middle Ages can be attributed to hard times, to economic malaise produced by European-wide *conjoncture*. So general an explanation will not, however, suffice for Cologne, where hard times were not general and where it was often in the most prosperous industries that artisans and workers lost status. While we cannot ignore conditions of supply and demand in analyzing these changes, we cannot hope to understand them fully unless we take account of structural shifts associated with capitalist development.

CAPITALISM IN COLOGNE: THE CONSEQUENCES

Understanding how capitalism emerged in Cologne, we can begin to understand the political and constitutional changes of the period. Militzer's analysis of the crucial decades from 1360 to 1410 exposes the connections. The *Oberschicht* grew mightily during the decades, in large part thanks to the entry of new immigrants into Cologne's commerce and industry.[67] Indeed, the richest man among the nonpatrician property owners in 1410 had acquired citizenship just twenty-three years earlier.[68] Yet, as new men entered and as the patriciate left commerce, government remained unchanged until 1396. As Militzer suggested, the latter two phenomena may have been related: patricians left trade to concentrate on politics and retained their political ascendancy only because their replacements in trade themselves had no time for government.[69] Even nonpatrician merchant families of sufficient longevity shared this characteristic. Many of them had long ago won places in patrician-dominated economic activities now closed to newcomers, such as distribution of wine locally, and many of them now were simultaneously leaving long-distance trade.[70] Some among them were well entrenched in the new Large Council, if not in the patrician-dominated bodies. But the new citizens who had only recently entered commerce had none of these chances; they were not well represented even in the Large Council, and members of craft guilds were totally excluded from rule prior to 1396 (with the exception of 1370-71).

It was this new elite, with the help of some of their more established nonpatrician brethren, who made the revolution of 1396. Thereafter, the social composition of government changed dramatically. The patriciate had only a few minor representatives on the new council, while the craft guilds took 25 percent of the seats; new citizens also increased their representation to about 21 percent of the council.[71] Although Militzer identified this shift, he was unwilling to attribute the transformation to capitalism. Yet it seems attributable to nothing else.

The contrast between government in Cologne before and after 1396, as most thoroughly explored by Wolfgang Herborn, provides clear evidence of the connection between capitalist development and sociopolitical change. Before 1396, particularly between about 1325 and 1396, when rule in Cologne was reserved for certain patrician families, it was virtually impossible for newcomers to enter government. In the more than seventy years studied, only ten families entered the group and of these only three achieved positions of real power. During the same period, only five families in the group disappeared.[72] Government after 1396 was fundamentally different. Few leaders came from old patrician families: of 110 mayors elected between 1396 and 1450/51, only thirteen came from that background.[73] Of the forty-two leading families in government between 1396 and 1420, only three were old patrician families while twenty-two came from the old Large Council and seventeen belonged to neither group.[74] Another difference, after 1396, was the constant turnover among the leading families. In the years between 1420 and 1450, twenty-seven families held the mayorality; twenty-one families lost places in the council during this period, and fourteen new families entered the council. Herborn showed that only six of the forty-one families holding the mayoralty from 1396 to 1450/51 held office both before and after 1420/21.

Above all, the new political elite derived directly from trade:

> The new ruling elite after 1396 was much more active in trade than the old patriciate. . . . riches opened the way to the political elite, to the leading municipal offices and to a top position in the council . . . the new ruling elite was a monied aristocracy. [Familial links to the old order] remained secondary. Feuds waged in battles among members of the group did not exist. Expressions of economic power had first rank and were decisive in [determining] political careers. In the first half of the fifteenth century there were marked fluctuations among the families holding power.[75]

Well into the sixteenth century government in Cologne remained relatively open to newcomers despite its domination by rich merchants.[76] Early in the fifteenth century, to be sure, a few Gaffeln obtained a disproportionate number of Gebrech seats, but this concentration of power did not imply a return to patrician rule. The new government had little choice, Herborn argued, but to privilege a few councilors because most members of the new council had no experience in government; after all, few had held office before, and the old patriciate which had monopolized office was now out of service (and sometimes prudently out of town). Until about the mid-fifteenth century, the Gaffel Eisenmarkt (consisting primarily of wine merchants and Gewandschneider), whose members had, in 1396, both some political experience (as former members of the nonpatrician Large Council) and the wealth that encouraged concentration on government service, dominated the council by their representation in the Gebrech and their hold on the mayoralty. Moreover, this Gaffel, unlike the wealthier Windeck, had not supported the patrician losers during the 1396 takeover.[77] Later in the fifteenth century, other merchant Gaffeln took the lead, obtaining a disproportionate place in the Gebrech, and, still later, industrial Gaffeln possessed the majority of places in the Gebrech. Herborn reasoned that by the time this occurred, however, control of the office of Bürgermeister, not numerical dominance in the Gebrech, signified real political power in Cologne, for the office had come to be a property of certain Gaffeln rather than one which the electors truly controlled.[78] Even after 1513, when changes made to the constitution (through the *Transfixbrief*) opened the council, the office of Bürgermeister remained in the hands of a few.

Although the oligarchic government described by Herborn appears not to have fulfilled the democratic promise of the *Verbundbrief*, government after 1396 was unlike government in the previous centuries of patrician rule. Even when, at any one time, only a few families in Cologne dominated the office of mayor and, with it, all important executive posts, these families still had short tenures and no heirs. Sons, sons-in-law, uncles, male cousins, and nephews did not follow one another as during the period of patrician rule. The old days when government was a right of birth and a way of life were gone. While Herborn did not characterize the political revolution as a takeover by the bourgeoisie—surely such a description would be anachronistic—his argument and his evidence about the nature of political officeholding in fifteenth-century Cologne strongly support the claim that Cologne was in transition to capitalism. The reigning political elite owed its status to its economic might, which was rooted in industry. The merchant-capitalists who dominated fifteenth-century Cologne had quite often begun either as distributors for or suppliers to local or regional industry or as artisans specializing in the goods they now traded. Even those members of the post-1396 council who lacked industrial roots—by and large, members of the old merchant Gaffeln—increasingly involved themselves in organizing production. Many guilds which had lost their roots in artisanal society without gaining much in exchange, although ostensibly corporative bodies, were dominated by the leaders of the Gaffeln to which they belonged; in every known case (all those of importance) their leaders were merchant-capitalists who had emerged from the craft.

The shift from a traditional to a capitalist social order in Cologne is surely best analyzed in terms of generalized changes in economic activity, distribution of wealth, social mobility, political crisis, and constitutional reorganization. But it is perhaps best appreciated in terms of individual lives. Both Irsigler and Herborn have published biographical sketches of a few of late medieval Cologne's most prominent men which help us gain this appreciation.

Herborn's study of two families, one patrician and one "new," is based on journals kept by the head of each household.[79] The first, Werner Overstolz, was descended from merchants who had established themselves in Cologne at the turn of the twelfth century. As leader of the successful uprising of 1268 which, Herborn argued, established patrician rule in Cologne, the Overstolz family was thereafter always in the council, the Richerzeche, and the Schöffen College. Sons and daughters married with other patrician families, and in the late fourteenth century one Overstolz was titled a knight (although no records indicate that family members ever married landed nobles). The two brothers who headed the family in 1396 were fined 2,050 Mark by the city and expelled from the government for their opposition to the revolt. One, who was later involved in the patrician counterrevolution, was banned from the city for a time.

His son, the Werner Overstolz of Herborn's study, served in Cologne as soldier, diplomat, and judge (a member of the Schöffen College). True to his origins, however, he represented conservative patrician interests and was involved in the attempt to establish independence of the Schöffen from the new council, a transgression for which he was sentenced to prison. After his return to community service as a judge, in the 1440s he joined the Teutonic Knights, to whom he had already dedicated his two eldest sons, and at the same time made his youngest son, who died without issue in 1453, his heir.

Werner Overstolz's journal expresses an ideology fully in keeping with his life. Part of the journal lists, somewhat unsystematically, the family properties. The rest tells a highly imaginative family history; it traces the Overstolzs to one of the fifteen Roman families reputed to have founded Cologne during the reign of Emperor Trajan. This story apparently was current among Cologne's patriciate by the early fourteenth century, but Overstolz amplifies it, naming the families and specifically tracing his own connections to them, including, as he goes, a few marriages with landed nobility. Herborn argued that this was not conscious fabrication; Overstoltz believed in these origins and considered them so central to his life that they constituted the largest—and most lovingly prepared—portion of his journal.

The "new" man with whom Herborn contrasted Overstolz, Johan (or Jan) Sloegins, had quite a different life and kept quite a different journal. Born in Nijmegen in 1389, he joined the Cologne citizenry and, in 1417, the merchant Gaffel Windeck, members of which specialized in trade with England. In the next years, he progressively enlarged his fortune, married, built an impressive home, and fathered twelve children. His family firm specialized in the cloth trade that dealt in England, the Low Countries, upper Germany, and at the fairs of Frankfurt am Main. His children went on to establish trade relations in Venice and to fortify those he himself had begun in England. To celebrate the engagements of his six daughters he gave each 700 Rheingulden and, for dowries, 8 Mark 12 lot of silver bullion. His journal is filled with business affairs, financial records, and accounts of the education and careers of his children. He never discussed his family's history, its service to Cologne, or its supposed distinction.

In another biographical sketch Irsigler provided an equally revealing account of the mentality of the fifteenth-century merchant in Cologne.[80] His sources were records of a protracted court battle between a merchant and his wife's nephew. The merchant and the younger man were newcomers to trade and wealth and each was an aggressive and tough businessman. Although the younger man lived more grandly and moved gradually into social and political circles beyond the narrow world of Cologne's new entrepreneurs, he devoted his energies and subordinated his politics to trade. The case recorded in the dossier started when the older merchant tried to deny his nephew a portion of the family property and, having failed in that attempt, tried to ruin the nephew's business. Just why the uncle had come to despise his nephew, with whom he had for many years done business, is not clear. Whatever the reasons, both the uncle's actions and his nephew's dogged efforts to gain redress clearly reveal disdain for traditional values of family and community. The nephew not only used his power, gained in diplomatic service to the Burgundian court, to exclude Cologne's merchants from certain markets, a tactic to force the courts of Cologne to hear his case, but also gave up his citizenship rather than impede the conduct of his suit against Cologne and his uncle. Irsigler commented that the men portrayed in these legal documents fit the description Maschke provided elsewhere of the typical late medieval businessman: "his characteristic traits were rationality and lust, restraint and unrestrained profit seeking, both aversion to and propensity for risk."[81]

To the extent that any real fifteenth-century city of northern Europe conforms to an abstract "model" of late medieval urban capitalism, Cologne does so. Yet the city itself does not constitute an ideal type. In fact, the institutions of market production themselves and the way these combined to constitute a "society in transition" were unique to Cologne. The most unusual aspect of Cologne's transition was that it occurred through guilds, or, more precisely, the guild-like organizations called Gaffeln with their roots in and their residual ties to artisanal society. The brief history of late medieval Cologne in this chapter delineates the pattern. Because the artisanal sector of Cologne had developed independently of long-distance trade, the artisanal organizations had for many generations been free of direct interference by the patrician government. Consequently, guilds established a legitimate economic and social, if not a political, role, and some long-distance merchants similarly organized themselves to further their own interests. Capitalism, as we have seen, developed *within* these organizations, which, in the process, were transformed into hierarchical organizations stratified along economic, social, and political lines. When the men who ran these now hierarchical organizations took control of government in Cologne, they used the corporative guild to build the new government.

Consequently, the guild system after 1396 (and the system of Gaffeln to which it was now subordinated) had oddly hybrid functions. Guilds provided access to participation in government and were the means by which the government regulated the crafts; through them a trade gained legitimacy and only they preserved artisanal independence as well as the egalitarian principles on which artisanal organizations were originally founded; and the guilds were the means by which capitalist wage relations were intensified and the political hierarchy was legitimated. Obviously, these functions were in many ways incompatible. All of them could be performed but only so long as each guild did not do them all. Some guilds, without exception those made up of small craftsmen not directly tied to long-distance markets, functioned as they traditionally had, as egalitarian social and economic organizations. Despite *de jure* participation in government through their membership in a Gaffel, these guilds in fact had no political authority and were controlled by dominant Gaffel members. Other guilds were entirely new organizations, formed because the practice of a trade in Cologne was now eased by guild status. The new guilds in fifteenth-century Cologne—the silk makers, the silk spinners, the gold beaters, for example—were the creations of capitalist entrepreneurs and were controlled, directly or indirectly, by these merchant-producers. While these were not all alike, none had a membership that resembled the independent master artisans once usually associated with guild membership. Other established guilds—those organized crafts serving long-distance markets such as the wool weavers, goldsmiths, harness makers, tinsmiths, and leather workers—had, of course, been transformed into hierarchical organizations composed of capitalist entrepreneurs on the one hand and skilled wage workers on the other. The old merchant Gaffeln seem to have retained a uniformly elite membership, but these merchants increasingly took on roles in organizing production. The guild structure in Cologne, therefore, institutionalized old, new, and transitional modes of production. Consequently, to assess the economic, social, or political meaning of work in fifteenth-century Cologne, it is never enough to know simply that a worker was a guild member.

The women producers and merchants to be studied in the next section took part in what has been revealed as a complex and changing economic and social structure organized by complex and changing institutions. It is already clear that women held high-status jobs in all economic sectors of Cologne—in industries that capitalism dominated, in others that served markets controlled by capitalists but which maintained traditional production relations, and in those still free of capitalist pressures. It is clear, too, that under all of these systems women could not gain access to all high-status work. The first problem of the next chapter, therefore, is to discover as many places as possible in which women found high-status work—and also those in which they did not—and, then, to identify principles according to which a pattern was established. The second problem is to determine whether or not that pattern can be explained by the hypothesis outlined in the previous chapters.

6

Women's Work in Cologne's Market Production

The Women's Guilds

The existence of guilds restricted to women evidences, as little else could, the special place women enjoyed in Cologne's economy. Three of the guilds—the yarn makers (*Garnmacherinnen*), the gold spinners (*Goldspinnerinnen*), and the silk makers (*Seideweberinnen*)—produced high-quality export goods of great value to the city's economy and, with only a few exceptions, the women of these guilds did so as independent, highly skilled artisans with their own shops, their own apprentices, and their own materials. Although normally dependent on merchants for distribution of their products outside Cologne, the guild mistresses were not the commissioned employees of merchants. These women, with the control over allocation and distribution of productive resources their guild status gave them, unquestionably had high labor-status. By contrast, the silk spinners, who were accorded guild status somewhat later, possessed none of the attributes associated with high-status work because they were piece workers in the employ of silk mistresses.

Three special attributes seem to explain the unusual membership of the three leading women's guilds: all of them organized import-export businesses run by families, not individuals; all drew their principal membership from Cologne's new merchant-capitalist class; none had power in Cologne's government.

The first point is easily shown in the case of the silk makers, the most important of the women's guilds and the one about which most is known. According to biographical data assembled by

124

Wensky, the silk mistresses typically had obtained their positions through their families. Most were married, usually to men in related businesses or from families connected to related businesses. Of the 113 silk mistresses active in the trade between 1437 and 1504 (years for which membership lists are available), at least 78 were married or widowed; many more may well have been, for of the 68 most active, the group about whom we have the best information, all but one were either married or widowed.[1] As some of these biographical sketches demonstrate, many silk mistresses were married to (or widows of) silk merchants. Druytgin van Boele, for example, came from a family who traded in dry goods and metals and she married a Gewandschneider and importer of raw silk.[2] Another Druytgin, of a very powerful merchant family, the Rinck family, married a man from an important trading firm with its headquarters in Frankfurt am Main.[3] Niesgin van Cleve, who had been registered as a silk maker for twenty-nine years before she enrolled her first apprentice (her daughter), had had two husbands, each active in trade in copper, wine, and silk.[4] Grietgen Becker, another relatively inactive mistress, also came of a merchant family; her husband, another merchant and a member of the Buntwörtergaffel, was a council member and an officer of the Seideamt.[5] Tryngen Loubach, who came of a silk working family and had apprenticed under her own mother, married a successful merchant who traded in silk; it seems they made silk together.[6] Perhaps one of the most active silk makers was Fygen Lutzenkirchen, whose husband was one of Cologne's leading merchants and an active member of the guild's administration.[7] Another among the largest producers was Grietgen van Berchem; her husband Jacob was a member of one of Cologne's most active merchant families and traded wine, silk, and wool cloth. Jacob and Grietgen (she was his first wife; his second was also a silk maker) participated in the Amt's administration.[8] Druytgen van Attendarne was married to Heinrich Vurberg and was part of a family business run by her husband; together they were involved in Italian trade, including the importation of raw silk, although Heinrich alone sent silk fabrics and other goods to Antwerp.[9] When Druytgen died, Heinrich married another silk maker.[10] Druytgen Furstenberg, long active in silk making but apparently not one of the largest producers, married a member of one of Cologne's important merchant families, whose business included silk trading.[11] Even the only unmarried woman among the sixty-eight women in the silk-making guilds apparently was in business with her widowed sister; both of them were, almost certainly, daughters of a married couple who together had made and sold silk.[12]

While these thumbnail biographies indicate that many women in the Seideamt belonged to families in the silk business, they do not tell how many of the 113 mistresses had such connections, and it is impossible to obtain that information. For twenty-five among the most active sixty-eight silk makers, however, such detail is available. The husbands, fathers, or other close relatives of twenty of these women were either in the silk trade or active in importing wool cloth from England. Since the exchange of wool cloth for silk was the backbone of trade between England and Cologne in the fifteenth century, it is almost certain that a Gewandschneider married to or closely related to a silk maker was paying for his wool cloth imports with silk exports.[13] If these twenty-five women are representative of the whole, we can conclude that about 80 percent of women silk makers had direct family connections to long-distance silk trade.

If almost all silk makers were married and if most were wives or daughters of men with interests in the silk business, it seems perfectly reasonable to suppose that the women who controlled silk making in Cologne did so as members of families in which the men traded raw and finished silk themselves. This conclusion is supported by evidence that women rarely dealt in raw or finished silk. Between 1452 and 1459, for example, only three women appeared in records of import taxes owed on imported raw silk and these three together accounted for less than 1.5 percent of the volume booked for the period.[14] Women seem to have marketed their silk fabrics almost as infrequently, for of the many records from the period covering sales of finished silk very few contain women's names.[15]

Less extensive evidence about the two other women's guilds, the gold spinners and yarn makers, points to exactly the same conclusion: the women in these guilds managed the production ends for family import-export businesses. The founding ordinances (1397) of the Goldspinnerinnen, the female branch of the Goldschläger (gold beaters), clearly expressed the view that the *family* was the production unit and the wife was the producer in it; the legislation made specific provision for husband/wife teams: a gold beater whose wife was a gold spinner was permitted three apprentices but an unmarried gold spinner was permitted four. This statute does reveal that not all spinners were married to beaters, a point made plain again by a document of 1514 in which some spinners claimed that gold beaters were entering the trade illegally by registering their wives—who, the spinners claimed, did no spinning—as mistresses, but both suggest that single or unaffiliated spinners were at a disadvantage, compared to those married to gold beaters.[16] Spinners who were married to goldsmiths, a guild closely associated with the gold beaters, must be counted as members of similarly functioning family production units.[17]

The yarn business appears to have had an analogous structure. Yarn makers normally employed yarn twisters to prepare their thread, and a complaint from 1373 about the prices charged for these semifinished fibers indicates that the yarn business was run jointly by husbands who were merchants and their wives who were artisans: the merchants who submitted the complaint described themselves as men "who customarily sell the yarn abroad" and their wives as women "who customarily make the yarn inside the city."[18]

The mistresses in all of these three guilds, then, were part of family businesses, but these were, indeed, special businesses. Although artisans themselves, these women did not belong to the artisanal sector disappearing from Cologne but to the capitalist class then emerging in the city. Wensky's biographies of many of the silk makers illustrate this point. All twenty-five women among Cologne's most active sixty-eight silk mistresses whose socioeconomic backgrounds could be identified showed these links. As earlier reported, twenty of them belonged to families known to deal in wool cloth or silk; the remaining five belonged to families who traded in wine or metals. The pattern appears throughout the guild: of 157 women registered as mistresses between 1437 and 1504 (not all of them active), at least forty-one were married to merchants, and another fifteen were themselves active in trade while four others had fathers in long-distance trade. As additional evidence of their social status, we have information showing that these silk mistresses were related to men of the new political elite which had risen to prominence after 1396. At least thirty-nine of the 157 are known to have been daughters or wives of members of the council, and probably many more had such connections.[19]

It should be emphasized that the merchants linked to silk making were not from Cologne's traditional patriciate or even from long-established merchant families but from the ascendant merchant-industrialist class. Of the thirty-two men who were married to or were the fathers of silk mistresses whose Gaffel Wensky was able to identify, only seven belonged to one of the four prestigious merchant Gaffeln—Windeck (4), Himmelreich (2), or Eisenmark (1); there were none in Schwarzhaus.[20] The men who belonged to the craft Gaffeln, however, were by no means craftsmen; all but eight of the twenty-two in these Gaffeln were explicitly identified as merchants, most of them wholesalers of wool cloth (Gewand-schneider).[21]

The trading interests and the political positions of the men who were, through their wives, daughters, and nieces, involved in silk making provide one kind of evidence that the Seideamt repre-sented the family production unit of the new capitalists in Cologne. The actions of these women, as producers and employers, provide another. Many mistresses in the guild hired other guild members or trained apprentices (the latter were called Gesellen), about whose marital status and social background we know little. In these actions, we witness the process Irsigler described in other sectors of Cologne's industry—the proletarianization of some artisans and the embourgeoisement of others.

Council records from the period offer further documentation of this development. A report of 1490 written for the council about conditions in the industry claimed that four to six women, each of whom imported 2,000 to 3,000 Mark a year of raw silk (enough for five to seven *Zenter*—about 500–700 pounds—of finished silk), dominated the industry.[22] While most historians consider this an overstatement, the claim evidently had a basis in fact. By 1469, for example, the council already required wage-earning silk makers to be paid in cash and specifically prohibited the truck system (whereby workers were paid in kind), a usual step in the beginnings of proletarianization. In 1479, the prohibition had to be repeated and even extended to include the silk spinners.[23] A *Transfixbrief* for the guild issued in 1506 contained another provision clearly intended to combat such tendencies: it required each silk maker to work only her own silk.[24] The Seideamt's relationship with the silk spinners underlines the point that proletarianization in the indus-try was proceeding apace. The spinners had long been the wage employees of silk makers and even after 1456, when their guild was founded, nearly twenty years after the silk makers had first founded theirs, they did not establish entrepreneurial status.[25]

While the Seideamt was dominated by merchant-capitalist fam-ilies, not all silk makers belonged to this new elite. Some, as we have seen, were employees of others. Many apprentices, and presum-ably some mistresses, came from families of artisans or even of unskilled workers, and some came from villages in the region.[26]

Wensky identified the occupations of the fathers of fifty-six (8 percent) of the apprentices registered between 1437 and 1513; the list included a barber, a baker, a pastry baker, and a Gaffelknecht as well as a council secretary, along with brewers, goldsmiths, and Schöffen. But few of the apprentices became mistresses, and the small number of those whose careers we can trace from apprenticeship to full mistresship normally had ties to Cologne's elite, a pattern which suggests, again, that most important mistresses of the guild had either been born to or had married into the guild's elite. Hence, while it may have served as a vehicle of social mobility for some women, the craft evidently filled its senior positions from a small elite.[27]

Evidence about the gold spinners and yarn makers, although less extensive, indicates that their industries, too, were run by merchant capitalists. Many gold beaters, it appears, taking advantage of their control over the needed raw materials, hired women as wage workers, women sometimes who were not even guild members. Women married to gold beaters who were themselves registered guild members often did the same.[28] The statutes of the yarn makers imply similar practices in that industry, for they allowed a yarn mistress who could not complete her work in her own shop to put the work out to others for a limited period of time.[29]

The third feature of significance for this study has two aspects: the guilds themselves had no political power in Cologne and the women who belonged to the guilds did not run them. The Seideamt illustrates this pattern especially well. When the Seideamt was founded in 1437, it seems not to have been assigned to any Gaffel, presumably because its members, who already held citizenship, were thereby attached to one or another of Cologne's twenty-two Gaffeln. Consequently, the Seideamt had no direct political role in Cologne. The guild was administered by a board made up of two female and two male members who owed their jobs to their wives and whose only functions were the managerial and juridical tasks their wives were presumably thought unable to perform. The women officials were, in contrast, charged with technical supervision of the craft, and the guild as a whole was supervised by a (male) member of the council. The other two women's guilds were similar in structure in that the men on their boards had broad supervisory and judicial roles, while women, as the technical experts, were the technical supervisors. Both the gold spinners' and yarn makers' guilds were founded in 1397, at the inception of corporative government in Cologne but, apparently alone among the craft guilds, neither was then assigned to a Gaffel—a striking illustration of their political impotence.[30]

These women's guilds were not, however, bogus organizations. While they did not have the political structure or stature of men's guilds, their powers over their craft were real and their very existence testifies to women's importance in some of Cologne's key industries. After all, through these guilds women exercised the same control over production and over their apprentices as did other masters in Cologne. Their power to give membership rights to their spouses was greater than in most guilds, since their ordinances not only provided widowers' rights but also granted husbands access to leadership posts.

The guilds thus accommodated themselves to the family production unit chiefly by reserving the political aspects of guild membership to men. There seem to have been some logical reasons for doing so—that is, for neither forcing women from the guilds as they were being forced from Leiden's ambachten or, alternatively, for barring the trades practiced by women from the guild system.

The second decision is easier to explain than the first. If the government set up in 1396 was to survive, then all trades had to be incorporated, because the government was defined as a body representative of all persons, male and female, active in market production whose interests were expressed and addressed through the corporation—the guild. To exclude one trade, particularly an important one such as silk making, in which, it must be recalled, men had direct interests, was to invite political instability. Then, too, the members of the trades themselves desired guild status, because only trades organized as guilds were recognized as having control over markets, production, and membership.

An explanation for the first decision, to keep women in these guilds, emerges from the history of the trades themselves. The skills involved in making decorative yarn or gold thread and in working with silk had long been the preserve of women from "good" (*vornehm*) families, those families that were able to obtain expensive raw materials and that alone had access to long-distance markets. By the time the crafts were formally organized, they were firmly in the hands of women from families of the new elite, and could not be turned over to men from ordinary artisanal backgrounds.

The case of the Goldschläger and Goldspinnerinnen is perhaps most to the point. The expensive raw materials these craftsmen needed—gold, precious jewels, and other metals—had to be imported and required a substantial outlay of capital. Craftsmen capable of dealing in these materials were necessarily men of substance who were in a position to enter import-export markets themselves and to bypass the long-distance traders who traditionally provided such access. The craft itself, among the most highly skilled and thus most lucrative, was one these early artisanmerchants were reluctant to relinquish. Hence, trade and production in the gold-working industry were not separated as they were in many other export-oriented industries. Nevertheless, it was convenient to be able to separate these tasks within the family of the goldsmith or gold beater by allocating production to women. The technique of gold spinning, related to that used in spinning textile fibers, was one of the highly skilled crafts involved in making the luxury textiles which had long been the specialty of Cologne's well-to-do women. So it was natural for wives of these men to spin gold and easy to reserve this task for them because no pre-existing artisanal guild was present to claim manufacturing rights.[31] As members of one of the newly powerful Gaffeln, the smiths/beaters thus had the motivation and the opportunity to protect their trade rights by institutionalizing the family business.

The evolution of the silk makers may have followed a similar, if more complicated, pattern. This trade had two quite distinct roots. One was silk making as it had been practiced in the thirteenth and fourteenth centuries. Then as later, the trade depended on imported raw material and on a market for luxury goods both inside Cologne, which the archbishop helped provide, and outside the city. What information there is about the silk makers of this period, most of whom enjoyed fairly high economic status, suggests that very few of them were women.[32]

But silk making probably owed its further development to the craft of silk embroidery, in which women traditionally had taken an active part. Very early both the church and the regional nobility used decorated fabrics, especially the *Borten*, half-silk cloths embroidered with silk and linen threads and sometimes with gold filament in pictorial designs. Scholars have guessed that the demand for such products spurred the growth of silk making. Most silk embroiderers of the thirteenth and early fourteenth centuries were female, and many belonged to "good" families, and some married men involved in commerce, such as the wife of one Gerhard the Good, a rich merchant of early thirteenth-century Cologne.[33] But by the middle of the fourteenth century, when the guild of Wappensticker was formed, women had lost their monopoly, and by 1397 the ordinances issued to the guild granted full membership and training rights to men as well as women.[34]

This history suggests how women from Cologne's rising artisan-merchant class might have obtained an exclusive hold on the manufacture of silk fabrics. While women had monopolized neither of the two trades from which the fifteenth-century silk-making industry grew, they had taken part in both, once even dominating what became the Wappensticker, and thus established a claim for their sex in the craft. In the burgeoning industry of the fifteenth century, control of the craft may have gone to those claimants with the easiest access to raw silk, markets, equipment, and training. While members of the Wappensticker and the small silk makers from the traditional artisanal sector of Cologne would have enjoyed access to some of these essentials, women from families with links to long-distance markets would have had *all* of them.

The advantages to keeping these three luxury crafts within the family seem obvious, and for this reason it is easy to understand why the silk, gold, and yarn merchants would have chosen to do so. Just why, for about two-thirds of a century, these families institutionalized a rigid division of labor by sex in these crafts is somewhat less obvious. It may have been that the men who controlled the export industries regarded this system as a way to insure their own control of production: had the crafts been open to men, male artisans could have claimed rights to production. By reserving the crafts for women the guild structure further served the interests of these merchants and merchant-producers, by assuring that they themselves were the only men with influence in the crafts (since only husbands of mistresses could join the Amt). Women, too, benefited from the system: this was a profitable and important business, one of the few open to them.

In the end, the institutionalized division of labor by sex within the household disappeared. Even early in the sixteenth century, it seems, men frequently belonged to the Amt, and all three guilds seem to have become less important in the early modern period. Their later history has not yet been traced, but it seems that the nature of these crafts changed when competition from other cities made such industries less profitable. Women of the new elite in Cologne may then have left these trades.[35] Their departure might have reflected changes in the life-style and mentality of this elite, for at some point the notion that rich women should work at the same tasks as rich men may have come to seem absurd. Without a study of these later developments, we can only speculate about their causes, but we will return to them briefly in the concluding section of this book.

THE TRADITIONAL GUILDS

The history of the traditional crafts, and of women's place in them, is very different from the history of the women's guilds. Like crafts in many other cities, they seem to have begun as artisans' associations rooted in the family and devoted to meeting the religious and social as well as the economic needs of their members. In the late fourteenth century, when most had moved a considerable distance from these origins and become hierarchical organizations chiefly concerned with political and economic matters, they still bore vestiges of their origins. Typically, their regulations described a small shop which was run by a master and his wife assisted by helpers; a branch of the leather workers (*Riemenschneider*) in 1398, for example, issued legislation describing a family business to which widows could succeed as full mistresses in charge of apprentices, so long as they kept a journeyman.[36]

The familial roots of Cologne's guilds are further demonstrated by the history of Cologne's brotherhoods. In many medieval cities, brotherhoods founded to serve religious and social ends had preceded more politically oriented guilds. While some brotherhoods in Cologne did in fact precede the guilds, others were founded after them, presumably when the social and religious functions of craft association could no longer be contained in guilds which had become newly political.[37]

By the fifteenth century, where my study (and most documentation about the guilds) begins, many of Cologne's guilds had already moved far from their artisanal origins. In almost every measurable instance, a particular guild's disposition towards women appears a direct reflection of the degree to which the original functions of the guild had been superseded. While we can seldom observe the entire process by which a guild was transformed from an association of family shops into a political organization made up of individual male artisans (by the late fourteenth century this process was far advanced), we can often witness its end. By the fifteenth century, for example, the records of nine of the forty-one existing guilds contained no references to women.[38] While the omission does not necessarily mean that women did not practice these nine trades, it probably means they did so rarely.[39]

During the period under study, three of the thirty-three remaining guilds expressly forbade some kinds of female work, and these instances suggest how the process of exclusion occurred. The hat makers (*Hutmacher*) in 1378 forbade wives, daughters, and female servants to help in the trade; in 1397 the cloth cutters (*Tuchscherer*) forbade wives to help their husbands cut cloth; in 1484 the council forbade a widow of a sword maker (*Schwertfeger*) to assume her husband's craft.[40] Six other guilds—Lohgerber, Maler, Riemenschneider, Sattelmacher, Harnischmacher and Lederzurichter—granted only severely limited widows' rights and made no provisions for other women mistresses.[41]

Eighteen of the remaining twenty-four guilds restricted women's access less severely, yet these nevertheless appear to have been almost exclusively male trades. The wool weavers and goldsmiths both provided widows' rights, but the abundant documentation we have about the activities of members of these trades reveals few instances when women practiced the craft, and most evidence suggests that widows did not very often actively continue their husbands' trades. In fact, not a single woman is included in the membership lists of the goldsmiths surviving from 1395 to 1500.[42] Six of the eighteen guilds—Kannengiesser, Kupferschläger, Decklackenweber/Scharzenweber, Schuhmaker, Böttcher, and Drechsler—provided membership rights to widows and sometimes to the husbands of masters' daughters, but the surviving records of these trades do not suggest that widows actually practiced the craft.[43] Three other guilds—the Färber, the Schmiede, and the Barbiere—apparently permitted widows to carry on after their husbands' deaths; although their statutes did not specifically grant such rights, their records contain occasional references to female mistresses who are often identified as widows.[44]

The ordinances of the last seven of these eighteen guilds specifically provided for women members or otherwise anticipated that women would practice the trade, and there is no direct evidence to show that these rights were available only to widows. Two of them, however, placed severe restrictions on women members. The tailors (*Schneider*) admitted women but instituted rules which, from the mid-fifteenth century on, restricted women to remaking old clothes or a limited assortment of new clothes, especially women's underwear made of light fabrics. As Wensky has pointed out, these restraints excluded women from the profitable and prestigious side of the business.[45] The ordinances of the fish dealers (*Fischhändler*) indicate that women had limited access to this trade as well; women were forbidden to cut or weigh fish for sale and, thus, were relegated to dealing in fish that could be sold whole—again, the less prestigious side of the business.[46] The remaining five—the Sartuchweber, Beutelmacher, Taschenmacher, Buntwörter and Fleischhauer—admitted female members apparently without restriction, but neither the statutes nor the scarce reports we have about these businesses suggest that women joined these trades in significant numbers.[47]

In sum, by the fifteenth century all but six of the forty-two guilds seem to have become virtually male preserves, either openly restricting women's participation (typically by limiting widows' rights) or counting so few mistresses in their membership that they cannot really be considered mixed guilds. That four of these six— baking, linen weaving, beer brewing, and silk embroidery (*Bäcker, Linenweber, Brauer,* and *Wappensticker*)—should have retained female mistresses is not surprising: all required traditional skills of women household managers. These four guilds probably originated as trades *exclusively* involving women, so their lag in closing women out, in spite of their metamorphosis into guilds with public status, is easily understood.

Naturally, specific reasons for the favor shown women differed in each case because the history of each trade was different. The first, baking, was a business that women could easily share, a feature which undoubtedly explains why most of the female bakers in the records were described as co-owners and co-managers of bakeries.[48]

The second, brewing, was another household-based task which, originally, had been almost exclusively the province of women.[49] Many of the small producers of "bitter beer" (*Grutbier*) and of herbed beer (*Keutebier*) and the beer retailers mentioned in fifteenth-century records (*Hockers* and *Höckerinnen*) were women, although such women were not members of the Brauerzunft that organized the producers of hopped beer. The women of that guild probably had achieved their status by one of two routes.[50] Some may have started as producers of Grutbier or Keutebier and had then managed to upgrade their product because imported hops and the new production technique were available, even to small producers. When beer production became organized, these women would of necessity have been absorbed by the new guild. Other producers may have been wives of merchants who entered the business with the introduction of hops, which made a long-lasting and much better-tasting product that could be produced in volume. Consequently, many members of the fifteenth century guild were not small producers but important entrepreneurs who imported and traded hops (often even investing in hops production in the Rhineland) and put their capital into equipment for producing, storing, and transporting beer in quantity.[51] These merchant-producers, who could offer an uninterrupted supply of high-quality beer and could often undersell small producers and sometimes corner the market for hops, herbs, and malt, threatened the traditional structure of the industry.

The third, linen weaving, was another "woman's" craft, and there is even evidence that women from merchant families made and traded linen cloth throughout the late Middle Ages.[52] In Cologne the status of the guild was specially limited because, like members of the barbers' guild, linen weavers were barred from participation in Gaffel elections. Maschke thought this provision reflected the low cultural or social esteem that he claimed linen weavers were accorded (he classed it as a "dishonorable" trade), but contradictory evidence shows that many women from prosperous and respected families practiced the trade.[53] The bar against participation in voting may be directly related to women's domination of the industry, a feature which did not make the trade "dishonorable" but which would have rendered it politically impotent.

The fourth, the silk embroiderers, had developed from a craft originally practiced by women, for women had been the first specialists in the production of Borten and other decorative fabrics used by the church. The guild's name, however, refers to coats of arms which later became a regular product of this craft, and it is possible that this aspect of the business had developed as a male specialty. Guild statutes that so clearly anticipated male *and* female members may have originated from this merger of male and female specialties.[54]

The two last cases—needle making and belt making (*Nadelmacher* and *Gurtelmacher*)—are more difficult to explain. One contributing factor undoubtedly was that both trades required traditional female skills, since both demanded a certain amount of fine handwork, an explanation supported by evidence that the pieceworkers increasingly employed in needle making as the fifteenth century progressed were female. But the women who appeared in Wensky's records were not pieceworkers. Some, according to Wensky, were small, independent producers. Many of the bronze importers recorded in Staple trade were women, and, since bronze was the raw material for needle making, it may have been that small needle makers brought in their own materials.[55] Others from both crafts may have been members of capitalist family production units like those in silk making. To judge by records of the belt makers, however, even wives of Gaffel members lost access to the craft in the course of the century. In 1500 the separate brotherhood of the belt makers listed, along with fifty-four male members, thirty-six female members, twenty-nine of them wives of and seven widows of masters. In the guild itself, however, few women were ever named, and most of them were presumably masters' widows.[56]

The pattern of women's participation in traditional guilds in Cologne was very similar to the pattern in Leiden. Women owed their trade rights to family status and retained them only so long as the familial nature of the guild was preserved. The greater political importance a guild assumed, the less likely it was that women held a place in it. Thus, the wool weavers, the goldsmiths, the important leatherworking trades, and most metal workers included, as a rule, no female participants. Conversely, the guilds in which women both enjoyed full rights and actively exercised them usually had little political status (as shown, the linen weavers were expressly denied political participation) and usually represented trades still closely associated with the family-run shop of earlier days. While it would be unreasonable to disregard evidence that most guilds allowed women some form of participation—there were, after all, many cities in which women had no such rights—it would be equally unreasonable to overlook evidence that their rights depended on an institution, the family production unit, which was vulnerable to the new political institutionalization of market production. To be sure, the process of exclusion seldom occurred abruptly, and we consequently find many instances in Cologne as elsewhere of women holding masterships in guilds with corporative power. But just as surely, we find fewer and fewer women in these guilds within decades of their change in corporative status.

WOMEN IN EXPORT-IMPORT TRADE

A feature of women's work in Cologne that has justifiably impressed historians is the role women played in import-export trade. Until Wensky's study, however, the evidence about the nature and extent of women's work in this kind of commerce was merely anecdotal. To provide a more precise account, Wensky systematically mined the published collections that contain this anecdotal information and analyzed records of taxes or fees charged by the city of Cologne for rights to trade certain products in the city. One set of these records covered the excise taxes collected at one of two principal markets through which most goods entered the city or passed through it. The privilege of collecting the taxes was normally leased, but in a few exceptional years the city kept the accounts itself, and for those years we can identify many of the merchants and the goods they traded. The principal records cover goods imported over one of the city's scales, the *Kraut-* and *Eisenwaage* on the *Malzbüchel*, for 1452–55–59, 1460–69, 1470–78, and 1491–95; partial records of goods imported from 1497 to 1509/11 have also survived.[57] Many of the most important dry goods imported into Cologne, including spices, chemicals, raw materials for textile production (except wool), textiles (except wool cloth), cheese, wax, and many metals and metal goods came through this market.[58]

While these records reveal much about Cologne's export-import business, they are significantly limited because they treat only a certain group of importers and do not include all their imports. Except for incomplete lists from the late fifteenth century and early sixteenth century, the records pertain only to individuals whose payment was deferred, a privilege known as *Akzisestundung* and afforded only to citizens. As a result, these tax records exclude all foreigners who did business in Cologne, unless a Cologner represented them in the city. At best, then, the Akzisestundung records tell us only about the minimum imports of certain goods by certain Cologners.[59]

Another set of the fiscal records Wensky used covered the fees paid upon entrance to the Gewandschnitt and sales of cloth by Gewandschneider; partial records of both kinds have survived from several periods in the fifteenth century.[60] Her final source consisted of records of taxes on wine imports and on sales of wine for local consumption as well as of membership lists for the Weinbruderzapf (which granted retail licenses). Of the three kinds of records Wensky examined, only these provide information about women's place in the export-import business both before and after the change of government in 1396.[61]

All three sets of records treat only sectors of trade linked to the import and export market in Cologne and therefore tell little about retail trade or about wholesale trade of products neither imported nor made from imported materials. Furthermore, these records can tell nothing about products imported tax-free or, in the case of the Akzisestundung lists, the totality of importers. Yet these sources cover a great deal of what we already know to have been the most important areas of commerce in Cologne—wine, wool cloth, other textile products, metals, and leathers. Since they cover a good half-century, they also constitute a statistically meaningful series that can measure change over time. These records document Wensky's essential thesis that women were well represented in the export-import trade of Cologne and that most women were involved in family businesses.

The trade in raw metals provides a good example of the significance of women's participation. Between 1460 and 1469 women accounted for about 10 percent of lead imports; between 1452 and 1459, they brought in 5 percent of the copper, 30 percent of the bronze, and some 40 percent of the sheet metal.[62] Many of these women were either agents for their husbands or their heirs. Gutgyn van Gerestorp, for example, acted for her husband, a lead importer, in 1450 and after his death continued to run the business for a few years.[63] Another lead merchant active in the 1460s, Druitgin zo dem Atfange, was evidently her husband's partner and later his heir.[64] Hilgin Schecters, who appears in another record as a copper dealer, was surely an occasional agent for her traveling husband, one of Cologne's largest copper traders.[65] Niesgin Yss, an inactive mistress in the silk-making guild, assisted both of her husbands in their trade in the Baltic, and, during each widowhood, carried on trade for the late husband; she is mentioned in several sources as a merchant of wine and copper goods frequently exchanged between Cologne and the East.[66]

Records of steel imports and of semifinished metals document another of Wensky's claims: many of the women who imported raw materials, especially metals, were not members of merchant families but acted as commercial agents for their husbands, small craftsmen still rooted in Cologne's artisanal community, or were themselves, occasionally, craftswomen. Eight of the ninety-four merchants named, for example, in the records of steel imports available in the years 1497–1501 and 1506–9 were women. Of the twenty-six largest importers, four were women, two of whom acted for their husbands. One of the four was indeed from a merchant family (the daughter of a council member and wife of a mayor) but the rest seem to have represented their husbands who worked the raw material. Others responsible for smaller volumes, according to Wensky, sometimes acted for themselves and bought for work in their own shops.[67]

The women who imported iron gloves may also have been artisans. It was women who trimmed these imported gloves with leather and then exported them again, so it seems reasonable to suppose, along with Wensky, that the many women who appeared on the import lists cataloguing these imports often bought for their own shops.[68] Because women played almost no role in importing other semifinished metals, their importance in importing iron gloves had, it would seem, such particular causes.[69]

The Akzisestundung lists underline women's importance in trading products used in the "female" crafts such as linen making and retail sales of food.[70] In the years 1497–98 and 1507–8, the two periods for which we have records, women accounted for nearly half the linen and flax importers. They, like their male colleagues (there were twenty-six women and twenty-seven men), had small businesses. In 1497, thirty-eight merchants, for example, imported linen with a total taxation value of 1,094 Gulden; the twenty-two women merchants together accounted for just 626 Gulden. In both periods, a man and wife who together brought in 538 Gulden of linen cloth accounted for the largest imports attributable to a single shop.[71] At least nine of the twenty-six women named on all the lists were lingerie seamstresses who apparently bought for their own shops.

The records of spice imports reveal a similar pattern. The women who imported large volumes seem to have specialized in the kinds of goods stocked by grocers—nutmeg, sugar, almonds, paper, and wax, for example. This is just the mix of goods that importers supplying local retailers would have handled; if so, we can explain why women's importance in the spice trade declined as the century wore on. In the later fifteenth century, foreign firms gave up their market share in the entire spice-trading business to members of Cologne's rising merchant-capitalist class; and unlike their predecessors who had specialized in the carrying trade destined for commodity markets such as Antwerp, Cologne's merchant producers moved into the Cologne market by selling to redistributors there, thus undercutting smaller wholesalers who had filled a niche in the market which the larger foreign firms had ignored.[72] A list of buyers of imported spices from the years 1491–95 helps confirm that most of the women importing spices were distributing their goods to retailers in Cologne. These buyers, obviously retail distributors, bought just the kind and mix of goods these women, but not their male colleagues, could supply. Like their suppliers, many of these distributors were women: seventeen women bought 5 percent of the cinnamon, 10 percent of the pepper, and 15 percent of the nutmeg.[73]

It is equally revealing of women's place in Cologne's export-import trade to consider the kinds of commerce they did not do. Women were concentrated in small, specialized sectors of the import trade, and, although they sometimes directly handled large volumes of a single product or material, they were not, either as individuals or as a group, important in any single *group* of products. In fact, many products or materials were rarely, if ever, handled by women. They were seldom involved in business with large firms, whether foreign or domestic, and their importance in import-export trade seems to have declined over the half-century studied. Finally, women very often dealt in odd lots rather than in standard units.

Table 4, which lists the approximate wholesale value of major spices imported into Cologne, helps illustrate these points. While the approximations are very rough, they provide the means for assessing women's importance in the business. The table shows, for example, that pepper, ginger, and saffron accounted for the bulk—almost 90 percent—of the spice trade. Yet, in the decade (the 1450s) when their participation in the spice trade was at its height, women accounted for only about 10 percent of the pepper and ginger imports and about 5 percent of the saffron. In later decades their share was even lower.[74] Without the benefit of this table, the figures showing that women accounted for 27 percent of the Muscatbluten imported in 1452–59 or 24 percent of certain sugars (*Melzzucker* and *Brotzucker*) imported in 1460–68 seem more significant than, in fact, they are. These products accounted for just 3 percent of spice imports. For instance, Karyssen under Helmslegern, one of the period's most important woman merchants, can be credited with some 20 to 25 percent of caraway (*Kummel*) imports, but this spice made up only 1 percent of imports.[75]

The Akzisestundung records further show that women bought and sold goods in nonstandard measures and that, while they often almost monopolized trade in these odd units, the total volumes they handled were small compared to volumes handled by men. Wensky's tables, which provide in detail women's share in the imports of single groups of products or the imports of a single woman merchant, obscure this point by ascribing to women an importance in the Staple trade they did not have. Because the units women dealt in were not standard, equivalent values are rarely

Table 4. Approximate Wholesale Values of Leading Spices Imported into Cologne, from *Akzisestundung* Records, 1452-59

Spice	Weight in lbs.	Wholesale price in Mark/Zenter	Total wholesale value in Mark (00)	% of total
Ingwer (ginger)	45,354	195	8,844,030	21
Pfeffer (pepper)	91,342	227.5	20,780,305	50
Melzzucker (sugar)	17,444	32.5	566,930	1
Brotzucker (sugar)	12,667	52	658,685	2
Kassuyn (sugar)	14,196.5	39	553,663	1
Lorbeer (bay)	2,761	13	35,893	—
Kummel (caraway)	20,119	29.5	593,511	1
Zimt (cinnamon)	1,114	487.5	543,075	1
Muskat (nutmeg)	3,407	195	664,365	2
Muskatblüten (mace)	261.5	650	169,975	—
Reis (rice)	18,053	19.5	352,034	1
Safran (saffron)	3,169	2112.5	6,694,513	16
Datteln (dates)	532	45.5	24,206	—
Nelken (cloves)	3,011	325	978,575	3
Mandeln (almonds)	13,173	39	513,747	1
			41,973,334 Mark	100

Spices for which prices are not available

Mächlin (?)	4,208
Muskatnuss (nutmeg cloves)	847
Grüner Ingwer (green pepper)	800.5
Lang Pfeffer (specially pepper)	111.5
Zucker (sugar)	50,829
Kandiszucker (sugar)	173
Zwiebelsamen (onion seed)	7,975
Weihrauch (incense)	1,920
Lakritze (liquorice)	1,263
Venys (?)	51
Rosinen (raisins)	772
Silber Montanum (?)	535
Galgant (galanga)	232
Wurmkraut (parsley fern [anthelmintic herb])	1,591

Quantities are from Irsigler, *Die wirtschaftliche Stellung der Stadt Köln*, table 86, p. 290, and prices are wholesale prices from the year 1495, table 89, p. 298. Table 86 lists *Zucker* (sugar) volume at 329 lbs. but in "Kölner Wirtschaft im Spätmittelalter," p. 293, Irsigler reported that 50,829 lbs. of *Zucker* were imported in the decade, a figure in keeping with his table 88, p. 295 ff. in *Die wirtschaftliche Stellung der Stadt Köln* which lists annual *Zucker* imports for the decade at some 6,000 lbs. These available, yet even very rough conversions illustrate the point. Karyssen under Helmslegern, for example, did not have some 28 percent of the pepper market but, rather, 28 percent of the pepper imported in *Sack*. If a Sack was equal to 200 pounds, she had only 6 percent of the market recorded for that period.[76] Similarly, her ginger imports counted not for 17 but 5 percent. Other reductions would surely be made by converting other units. For example, Wensky showed Helmslegern with 4 percent of the rice imported in pounds, 61 percent in Ballen, and 15 percent in Sack. During the period, 18,053 pounds of rice were imported, 87 Sack, 4 Fass, 28 Ballen, 5 Korb, and 2 Pack. Helmslegern's 716 pounds, 17 Ballen, and 13 Sack were clearly not insignificant, but they gave her a share of the market closer to the 4 percent represented by her imports in pounds than to the 61 percent represented by her imports in Ballen.[77]

Perhaps even more indicative of the specialized role women played in the import trade is their concentration on odd lots and their underrepresentation as dealers in pound lots, the usual unit of trade. About 20 percent of importers of ginger between 1452

---

figures provide at best only a very rough approximation of the relative economic importance of the spices imported into Cologne by a specialized and possibly small group of merchants afforded the city's credit.

The prices relate to a period about a half-century later than the period from which the import volumes were taken. As Irsigler's table 89 shows, many wholesale prices may have fallen during the half century and were in any case changed. Despite the inevitable inaccuracies that result from using prices and volumes from time periods so widely separated, I chose the 1452-59 volumes because this was the period of greatest activity by women.

There were many items for which no price data was available. Few of these appear to be individually significant, but taken together they might have increased the total value of imports another 20 to 40 percent. *Zucker* may have been the same thing as *Brotzucker* (refined blocks of sugar). If so, the totals on the portion of table 4 with prices would climb to 44,616,442 Mark and *Zucker*, at the same 52 Mark/Zenter price as *Brotzucker*, would have amounted to 6 percent of the total. All sugars together—*Zucker, Brotzucker, Melzzucker* (molasses), *Kassuyn* (raw sugar)—except *Kandiszucker* would have amounted to 10 percent.

Many goods were measured in units other than pounds; entries in these units have been ignored (see Irsigler, table 86, p. 290, for the complete listing). While such omissions probably do not substantially distort the principal point of the table, they certainly detract from its accuracy.

The price quotations are in Mark/Zenter and the import volumes are in pounds. The Zenter was equal to approximately 100 pounds, but varied depending on the product weighed (see Irsigler, p. 340). The table assumes all Zenter equal to 100 pounds.

and 1459 were women (10 out of 48); they traded only about 6 percent of the ginger sold in pounds, none sold in Fass, Kemlade, Sackchen, or Stück, but 100 percent sold in Fässchen. Comprising almost 25 percent of the licorice importers (3 out of 11), women handled less than 10 percent of the trade in pounds but over 50 percent in Sack. Some 13 percent of the pepper importers (6 out of 45), women accounted for only about 3 percent of the poundage but over 33 percent of the volume traded in Sack. The incense trade provides one last example: although a good third of the incense importers were women (4 out of 11), they had no dealings in pounds, and brought in the only Sack, 3 of 16 Fass, and all the 3 Fässchen; men, for their part, brought in 1,920 pounds and 1 Säckchen, but had no further dealings in odd units.[78]

Another distinguishing characteristic of women merchants was that they were active only in selected areas of trade and almost entirely absent from others. Women rarely imported saffron, one of the most important areas of the spice trade, and, especially after the 1450s, had only small roles in pepper importing, the other dominant sector of the spice trade. Women played an insignificant part in the importation of most dyes and chemicals.[79] They were well represented only in one area of the semifinished- or finished-metal business (iron gloves, as already discussed) and were almost never present, especially after 1460, in the tin trade. Very few women imported barchent and they handled very small volumes. As we have seen, women brought in little raw silk.

Moreover, women steadily lost market share during the half century studied. In the spice trade, for example, women were 11 of 120 persons named on the lists of 1452–59, but only 5 of 98 in 1460–69; only 6 women's names appeared in the 1470s.[80] This decline seems to have occurred in dyes and chemicals as well and is easily documented in the case of metals. Between 1460 and 1469 women accounted for about 10 percent of lead imports; between 1452 and 1459 they brought in 30 percent of bronze and some 40 percent of the sheet metal. By the end of the century, in contrast, few women were importing these three raw metals.[81]

Women importers shared several additional characteristics not typical of men. They were not members of the large firms which usually dealt in markets both inside and outside Cologne. This can be deduced from evidence that women usually did not trade in the goods concentrated in the hands of large firms (barchent, pepper, saffron, and perhaps tin) and that they lost market share as big firms entered the market sector—importing for local redistribution—where women seem to have specialized. Women's tendency to deal in a diversified list of goods, a visible characteristic of their trade, is evidence of their role as redistributors, and this tendency may explain why they were likely to trade in odd lots or in nonstandard units of measure.

The finding that women were small, specialized merchants is unsurprising and entirely in accord with a hypothesis linking women's work to the family. Women were small merchants because they belonged to family businesses which, almost by definition, did not have the permanent staffs, fixed procedures, and complex structures for finance and management that increasingly characterized larger firms.

It is more surprising to find that the most active women in Staple trade were not partners in family businesses. The merchant Karyssen under Helmslegern, a leading woman trader who ranked in the second quartile of all Staple merchants, was evidently single.[82] Durgin van Zutphen, another well-positioned merchant, *may* have been related to one of two men of the same last name who were active in the dry goods trade at the time, but she seems not to have been involved in any deals with them.[83] Greta zom Barde, the largest spice importer among the women, managed not only her own spice business but had other substantial interests, in cotton, chemicals, wax, and paper, and managed these businesses without any apparent help from her husband (whose occupation is a mystery).[84] Tryngin van Lynge, the largest importer of bronze and the fourth largest importer of tin plate (*Blech*) listed between 1452 and 1459, seems to have been single.[85] Cathringin Broelmann, the second-largest importer of steel in the years 1497–1501 and 1506–9/11, with, according to Wensky, almost 20 percent of the market, was in business for herself.[86]

Yet these women also owed their occupations to their families. Broelmann, for example, married a member of the Wollamt who served as mayor. She herself was the daughter of a council member from a merchant Gaffel, and her family (Broelmann) was closely related to leading merchant families in Cologne.[87] Greta zom Barde was married and, although we know nothing about her husband, we know that her son was in business with her.[88]

We should take into account, in evaluating the importance of the family unit in providing women access to trade in Cologne, that *most*—if not always the most active—women merchants were married. A good many of them were simply agents for their husbands, such as Lempgin, the wife of Johann van Gelre, a merchant of spices, textiles, and other luxury goods, who—certainly as a receiver for her husband—was taxed only in 1452.[89] Hilgin Schecters, mentioned earlier, was occasionally an agent for her husband, a copper trader.[90] Others were widows who carried on their husbands' trades. Yrmgin Wachendorp, the daughter of a merchant of barchent, as a widow in the 1460s carried on her husband's business—he had been one of Cologne's important long-distance merchants—although she had not appeared in any sources as his partner or agent until his death.[91] Grietgen van der Burg provides another example of the working widow. As the wife of Alf van der Burg, one of the most important merchants of Cologne, she had trading interests of her own and after his death she continued many of his lines, including spices.[92] Gutgyn van Gerestorp acted for her husband, a lead importer, in 1450, and after his death continued to run the business for a few years.[93] Another lead merchant active in the 1460s, Druitgin zo dem Atfange, evidently was in partnership with her husband and later his heir.[94]

While it is obvious that not *all* women owed their position in commerce directly to family businesses, it remains incontestable that *most* women merchants were married and owed their place in trade to their husbands. Some of the most important were indeed single or independent of their husbands, but these were most likely the women with time and energy for business. The few married women who worked independently may have been childless or may have been married to men whose political interests left them without time for the family business. The single or independent women of the merchant class in Cologne, women like Karyssen under Helmslegern, were able to establish themselves in trade, it is very likely, only because wives or widows who worked as part of family businesses had already made a place there for women.

The pattern of women's participation in wholesaling imported wool cloth in Cologne (the Gewandschnitt) was very similar to the pattern in Staple trade. Until late in the fourteenth century, commerce in good wool cloth was restricted to the patriciate, but by 1388 the privilege was open to all citizens who could pay the stiff entrance fee of 10 Gulden.[95] The earliest surviving membership list from the period of patrician dominance dates from 1378: it named the members but did not list their sales and indicates that six women and seventy-five men were Gewandschneider.[96] Records covering the years 1414–42, when the Gewandschnitt was opened, are summarized in table 5. It both identifies all the active members and measures their activity.[97] Women, excluding Stina Waveren, accounted for a small but not insignificant number of cloth wholesalers and for a smaller portion of sales; through the years, about 10 to 15 percent of the membership was female, and about half that percentage was theirs in sales. At least 50 percent of the women were joined in the trade by other family members. Of the seven most important, including Waveren (who accounted for 98 percent of the sales by women) five were their husbands' heirs.[98] The two women who did not succeed their husbands were both active in the wine trade (as were a great many of all male and female Gewandschneider), and one of these women married an important wine merchant. Stina Waveren, by far the most important woman cloth merchant, was her husband's heir, but she carried on the business with undiminished vigor for a full twenty years after his death (in 1419) and passed it on to their son in 1440. Irsigler has shown that Stina Waveren's husband had produced trousers—as many as 10,000 pairs a year—under a *Verlag* system; whether his widow continued this aspect of his business is not certain, but it may well be that she did.[99]

Small numbers of women were involved in the Gewandschnitt during the last periods for which we have records of membership in the trade. Of 221 new members admitted between 1465 and 1500, 7.2 percent were female; of the ninety-seven members who joined between 1501 and 1527, only two were women.[100] We have no information about the volume of sales attributable to any Gewandschneider for these years. Seven of the eighteen women admitted in 1465-1527 belonged to the Seideamt, a connection attributable to the mutual compatibility of exporting silk to England and importing wool cloth into Cologne.[101]

This information shows that women by and large owed their place in the Gewandschnitt to their family status and that most women played a secondary role in trade. But it also reveals, as do the records of trade in other kinds of goods, that the system allowed the exceptional woman—such as Stina Waveren—to establish herself as an important merchant.[102]

Almost the same pattern of women's work obtained in the wine importing business. Surprisingly, despite the transformation of the wine trade and the turnover of its membership, the pattern was maintained throughout the fifteenth century. Although about 16 and 22 percent of the importers in 1390–92 and 1392–94, respec-

Table 5. Women's Participation in Sales of Wool Cloth in Cologne (*Gewandschnitt*), 1414-42

	All Merchants				Women Merchants				Women Merchants ex Waveren			
	Cloth Sales		No. of Merchants	Sales per Merchant	Total Cloth Sales	% of Total	No. of Women	Sales per Woman	Total Cloth Sales	% of Total	No. of Women	Sales per Woman
Year	Total	Domestic										
1414	1,595	n.a.	29	55	211	13.2	7	30	211	13.2	7	30
1415	1,672	n.a.	27	62	124	7.4	5	25	124	7.4	5	25
1416	1,438	n.a.	27	53	106	7.4	4	27	106	7.4	4	27
1417	1,711	n.a.	29	59	139	8.1	7	20	139	8.1	7	20
1418	1,420	n.a.	24	59	65	4.6	3	22	65	4.6	3	22
1419	1,360	n.a.	19	72	465	34.2	2	233	52	3.8	1	52
1420	1,396	n.a.	26	54	408	29.2	5	82	38	7.2	4	9
1421	1,368	n.a.	25	55	454	33.2	7	65	83	6.1	6	14
1422	2,052	n.a.	24	85	472	23.0	4	118	94	4.6	3	31
1423	1,881	n.a.	24	78	376	20.0	3	125	41	2.2	2	21
1424	1,823	n.a.	26	70	401	27.0	5	80	60	3.3	4	15
1425	1,460	n.a.	21	70	380	26.0	5	76	88	6.0	4	22
1426	2,149*	35*	27	80	559*	26.0	4	140*	39*	1.8	3	13*
1427	2,182	42	22	99	471	21.6	3	157	144	6.6	2	72

1428	1,874	45	23	81	582	31.1	4	146	142	7.6	3	47
1429	1,868	41	25	75	607	32.5	4	152	95	5.1	3	32
1430	1,967	23	23	86	429	21.8	3	143	77	3.9	2	38
1431	1,802	49	21	86	532	29.5	5	106	106	5.9	4	27
1432	2,249*	69*	26	87	580*	25.8	5	116*	173*	7.7	4	43*
1433	2,067	50	29	71	566	27.4	5	113	184	8.9	4	46
1434	2,067	66	27	77	434	21.0	5	87	91	4.4	4	23
1435	2,025	64	31	65	417	20.6	6	70	134	6.6	5	27
1436	1,706	90	33	52	336	19.7	5	67	82	4.8	4	20
1437	1,858	47	31	60	437	23.5	5	87	232	12.5	4	58
1438	1,763	42	31	57	418	23.7	5	84	159	9.0	4	40
1439	2,735	18	30	91	465	17.0	4	116	202	7.4	3	67
1440	2,832	188	34	83	252	8.9	4	63	252	8.9	4	63
1441	3,029	188	35	87	260	8.6	3	87	260	8.6	3	87
1442	2,633	131	39	68	147	5.6	3	49	147	5.6	3	49

Sources: Irsigler, *Die wirtschaftliche Stellung der Stadt Köln*, table 11, p. 65, and Wensky, *Die Stellung der Frau*, table 45, p. 244. These figures exclude six women who sold 58.5 cloths as agents for their (absent) husbands.

* Based on records of delayed tax payments (*Akziestundung*).

tively, were women, they brought in just 5.8 percent and 12.3 percent of the wine. While women from patrician families or from families represented in the Large Council (the latter being an indication that the family was well established in long-distance trade) were more numerous than men, they were not well represented in long-distance trade, and among the largest importers there were no women.[103] Most of the patrician women were carrying on their late husbands' trade and were, like them, local distributors. Among the nonpatrician women, more may have been single or at least in business without their husbands, but most of them were still importing for the local market.[104]

In 1414/15, women made up about 8.8 percent of importers but brought in just 4.1 percent of the wine. In 1420/21, there were more women importers but they did not rival men: 14 percent of the importers were women and they handled 7.1 percent of imports. Of the ninety-six women in both periods, some 40 percent were wives or daughters of council members. Again, while women wine merchants came disproportionately from Cologne's elite, they by and large did not engage in large-scale trade but apparently bought for family use and for local redistribution.[105] For the twelve and one-half years between 1466/67 and 1478/79, women made up some 12.3 percent of importers and brought in 8.3 percent of the wine. A greater number of women in these years than previously were among the top importers; 1.1 percent of the women imported more than 300 Fudern per year and 3.5 percent imported between 100 and 300 Fudern (as compared to 0.3 percent and 2.0 percent, respectively, for men).[106] Reflecting their greater concentration among the large importers, women occupied two of the ten top places for the period and eight of the top thirty-seven.

Thanks to Irsigler and Wensky, we know a lot about some of the women. Of the eight largest women importers, six, at least, belonged to families active in the wine trade and six had male relatives on the council. Only one of the eight was involved in trade of other products, while twelve of the twenty-nine men in this group had other commercial interests. The sole woman was Grietgen van Merll (mentioned earlier as a dry-goods importer). Heir to her husband's business, she was also independently active in trade. Her daughter and two of her sons were included among the largest thirty-seven wine importers, and the daughter served as a representative of her own husband with whom Frau van Merll often did business. Frau van Merll was even sometimes a partner in trading ventures with another son-in-law, Gerard von Wesel.[107]

Third among women importers after Frau van Merll and her daughter was Styngen van Nyle, her husband's heir and a member of a wine-trading family, and fourth was Styngen zo der Kuylen, who also came from a wine-trading family.

Wensky collected information about other women who did not handle such large volumes but who were nevertheless buying in volumes too large for household use; these women belonged to the category of importers who brought in between 5 and 20 Fudern per year.[108] In the period from fiscal year 1466/67 to 1478/79, fifty-one women were included in this group. Like the large importers, they belonged to families engaged in the wine trade (at least twenty-one of them and perhaps as many as thirty-one) and to families who governed Cologne (at least 25 percent had family members in the council). A good number of these women (at least fifteen, perhaps as many as nineteen) sold wine at retail in Cologne, a business, in contrast, in which only one of the eight largest importers was engaged.

As late as 1513–19, this pattern was repeated.[109] Annual wine imports had then fallen about 20 percent from the levels reached in 1466/67 and 1477/78, and the average volume per importer had fallen about one-third, to 10 Fudern per year. As was true in the late fifteenth century, women were well represented among the top echelon of importers in 1513-19; but on average, although 9 percent of the importers, they imported less than the men, taking in only 5.1 percent of the wine. The three largest importers, all widows of important wine merchants, were also merchants in their own right.[110] Women who imported smaller amounts during this period resembled those of the preceding generation in their family connections: of the thirty-two women who imported between 5 and 20 Fudern per year, at least sixteen, and possibly twenty-three, belonged to families in the wine trade and between ten and sixteen, at least, had relatives in the council.[111]

The women who were the largest wine merchants in the late fifteenth and early sixteenth centuries never handled anything near the volume handled by the typical large merchant, male or female, of the late fourteenth or early fifteenth century. In 1390–92, for example, 8 percent of the total number of importers brought in over 150 Fudern each and almost 20 percent annually imported over 75 Fudern. In the period from 1466/67 to 1478/79, fewer than 3 percent brought in over 100 Fudern. The average import quantity per merchant in 1414/5 was about 68 Fudern, but in 1466/67–78/79 it was just 15.5 Fudern. In the period from

1513/14 to 1519, only 1 percent handled more than 100 Fudern and the average import quantity per merchant had fallen to 10 Fudern.[112]

Although women were sometimes involved in the direct sale of wine they do not appear to have been important factors in this trade. Between 1357 and 1371, about 10 percent of the admissions to the Weinbruderschaft, then a patrician organization, were women, but we do not know what amount of wine these women sold.[113] Their membership may well have been used to import for family use. From 1467/68 to 1477/78, ninety-nine women members accounted for just over 2 percent of direct sales; all but two of the largest fifteen women retailers also imported wine in those years.

Women's roles in wine export cannot be as closely followed, for we have only anecdotal information about this business. Most women, like Guetgen van Moubach, represented their husbands and they appear in records simply as their husbands' agents.[114] Some women worked alone, but the sources suggest that very few of these were active regularly.[115]

Like women who dealt in Staple goods or in imported wool cloth, the women who imported wine into Cologne shared several characteristics. Most were acting for their families: they imported wine either for household use or for family businesses. Women who redistributed wine in Cologne and the few women large importers who did not serve local markets typically belonged to families involved in the wine-carrying trade. While women were sometimes involved in the direct sale of wine in Cologne as well, their role in this trade was less than might be expected, a reflection, no doubt, of the rather formal organization and high entrance fee of the Weinbruderzapf which made wine retailing in this city a less casual business than it perhaps was in other places.

Patterns and Explanation

These three studies—of the women's guilds, the traditional guilds, and the import-export trade—help to answer the questions with which this chapter began. Did women's access to high labor-status depend on the survival of the family production unit? Did the political and business organization of market production separate it from the family production unit? How did capitalism affect women's roles in market production?

The family production unit obviously served as access to high-status jobs for women in Cologne. This was as true for women from prominent merchant families, who represented, aided, and later served as their husbands' heirs, as it was for women from artisanal families, who bought raw or semifinished materials for their husbands' shops. The few women merchants who actively imported a wide range of goods on their own and the women artisans who brought in materials for their own shops—linen, iron gloves, and bronze, for example—were indirectly beneficiaries of the family production unit's resilience. Many, indeed most, of these women were married or widowed, but even when they were in business on their own they regarded themselves—and were regarded by others—as members of the family to which their assets and earnings belonged.

The unity of family businesses found legal expression in Cologne where a man and wife regularly obligated themselves jointly in leases, mortgages, purchase contracts, and the like.[116] To insure that debts could be collected, Cologne's council required all property brought into the marriage (*hijlichsguet* or, in modern German, *Heiratsgut*) to be considered community property and, thus, part of the estate inherited by the surviving spouse and liable to seizure by creditors. The first record of such a ruling is from 1406, when the council responded to complaints that surviving spouses were claiming that the *Heiratsgut* was not part of the estate. The council ordered that husbands and wives in business together were severally and jointly responsible for each other's debts and that, while a married woman could undertake no debts without her husband's approval, a husband and wife might each run separate businesses with separate obligations, provided the surviving spouse would assume all liabilities as well as assets of the estate.

Women's ties to family in Cologne seem to have been even stronger than in Leiden where, it should be recalled, women regularly ran businesses separate from their husbands'; Cologne, where so many of its high-status workers were partners in a single family enterprise, was atypical. Women's dependence upon the family production unit for access to high-status work is even more evident in Cologne's guilds. The women's guilds were straightforward embodiments of family production units, and the traditional guilds employed women as full mistresses only so long as the family production unit survived.

The processes that destroyed the family production unit are most easily observed in the traditional guilds where we can often trace the development of political organization which led to women's expulsion, or else, in many cases, infer that these occurred. In the women's guilds, which organized production in capitalist families, we can see how important political organization was in determining women's access to a trade, for these trades had to make allowances for the political impotence of their female members. Women merchants were subject to the same business and political constraints as women in the guilds. They did not belong to large firms with permanent, bureaucratic structures, nor did they, except rarely, deal directly with foreigners. As large firms became more important in Staple trade or when it involved overseeing production or distribution abroad, women necessarily retreated from Staple trade. The women distributors who represented their husbands and bought raw materials in small quantities for their husbands' shops were compelled to work around the constraints imposed by their political incapacities and their ties to the household; since the artisanal guild limited their rights as wives to help in the shops or even to carry on the business as widows, they specialized in commercial aspects of the enterprise which the guild did not control.

An interesting, somewhat surprising feature of the pattern of women's work in Cologne is that the business organization of work was less significant in restricting women's access to market production there than it was in Leiden: the women's guilds instituted apprenticeship and training rules every bit as strict as in the typical male guild; some of the women merchants in Cologne traveled to regional fairs; some of the most active silk mistresses and Staple merchants were mothers.[117] Clearly, for certain women in Cologne the limitations imposed by the duties of housewifery and mothering were not especially severe. But they were present. After all, a disproportionate number of the most active women merchants were single, and the female Staple merchants, the Gewandschneider, the wine merchants, and the silk mistresses—those women whose level of activity we can measure—were, on average, far less active than men in comparable businesses. What this suggests is that women had less uninterrupted time for market production than their male counterparts had. Further, the women who were apparently able to combine market production with running a household and raising a family were rich. In the few cases about which we have detail, the women merchants had abundant household help—younger relatives, apprentices, servants—as well as the money to purchase the beer, wine, bread, cured meats, cheeses, furnishings, and clothing they themselves had no time to make for their families.[118]

In the most significant sense, the pattern of women's work in Cologne was very much like that in Leiden: women depended on the family production unit to provide the access to high-status work that they lost when shifts in the business and political organization weakened the family production unit. In other respects, however, Cologne was different. The proportion of women who had high-status jobs was much higher in Cologne than in Leiden; women of Cologne's elite participated in market production while in Leiden they did not; women took part in Cologne's long-distance trade but not in Leiden's. Each of these differences, which amounted to higher labor-status for Cologne's women than for Leiden's, can be attributed to capitalism or to the economic and social climate which fostered it.

More women in Cologne than in Leiden had high-status jobs, partly because there were several routes to high-labor status in the city's dynamic economy. In Leiden, only the skilled crafts, the management of drapery production, or limited local and regional commerce offered women (or men) opportunities for high-status work. While these were available to women in Cologne, there was also long-distance trade and the management of many kinds of industrial production.

But the breadth of Cologne's economy alone cannot explain the wider availability there of high-status work for women.[119] Its socioeconomic system offers part of the explanation: many women with high labor-status in Cologne came from a new elite which created new kinds of work—and opened it to women. Women with high-status positions in Leiden came overwhelmingly from only one socioeconomic background, but the women of Cologne came from two. Many were members of the artisanal community which made up Cologne's disintegrating *Mittelschicht*, the locus of the independent craft shops and the small retailer. These women, by and large, were the linen weavers, iron-glove importers, grocers, bakers, and belt makers, as well as widows who ran their late husbands' tailoring establishment, shoemaking shop, or smithy. Many other women producers and merchants were members of Cologne's emerging capitalist class. A good number came from artisan families in Cologne while others were from merchant families, some of whom had long been resident in Cologne although many had only recently arrived from villages, towns, and cities of the region. The women who represented this new elite were the silk makers, yarn makers, gold spinners, lead merchants, pepper traders, Gewandschneider, and wine importers about whose lives Wensky gives so much detail.

During the fifteenth century, both the artisans and the new elite were changing. Many artisans and small shop-owners descended to the status of wage workers; others clung to their shops but lost their ability to compete with larger producers or more efficient distributors; a small number, of course, rose to join the capitalist class. Some members of the new elite, then in the process of formation, could in some respects still be regarded as artisans while others who had retained their original identity as merchants had not yet fully entered production. Consequently, the boundaries between these two groups—either between the surviving artisans and the emerging proletariat, or between the new merchant-capitalist class and the purely commercial element in Cologne—were not always clear. Women from both groups—as well as from the indistinct borders of the groups—participated in market production, and can all be credited with high labor-status although the status of some women was more secure than that of others.

The women of Cologne's elite who were involved in market production belonged to a class which did not exist in Leiden. The only elite in Leiden was a patriciate which, in economic, social, and political character, was much closer to the patriciate that in 1396 lost control of government in Cologne. What scarce evidence we have suggests that the women of Cologne's old patriciate, like those of Leiden's still viable patriciate, rarely participated in market production. Only a small number were involved in the wine trade, the last commercial stronghold of the patriciate during the late fourteenth century, and nearly all of them bought for household use. The few who seem actually to have managed an import-export trade were widows, successors to their husbands, a pattern that accords with the limited role women of Leiden's elite played in the Calais trade.[120]

The last major distinction between Leiden and Cologne—that Cologne's women were active in long-distance trade but Leiden's were not—reflects major differences in the economy, society, and politics of the two cities. First, and most obviously, Leiden was not a commercial city, so any opportunities for long-distance trade were limited there. Second, the one important area of external commerce—the Calais trade and the regional distribution of cloth—was both limited and highly organized. The largest drapers in Leiden, men who bought wool and sold cloth outside Leiden, were only middlemen between, on the one hand, the Calais merchants and Leiden's producers and, on the other, the producers and the Hansa. These men normally worked in teams which traveled together, first to Calais and back, and then to such places as Bruges, Antwerp, Bergen op Zoom, Dordrecht, and Frankfurt am Main where they met wholesale purchasers. Involving them in constant travel and in constant negotiation with foreigners, their trade led them into credit purchases at Calais which were afterwards liquidated at the regional markets where cloth was sold. With these activities it is no wonder that the wool and cloth trade in Leiden accommodated few women.

These limitations were not part of the Staple trade at Cologne, and we must concentrate on the Staple to elucidate the third reason for women's easy access to long-distance trade in Cologne. As the center of Cologne's commercial life and the guarantor of municipal fiscal health, the Staple trade was, in many respects, highly organized. Goods coming into and leaving the city were measured, weighed, and taxed; lists of taxpayers were kept, foreign agents were registered; brokers were employed for trade between foreigners and locals. But Cologne prospered and managed to enforce its Staple rights primarily because it provided easy access, for citizens and foreigners, to a wide range of raw and finished materials and provided ready availability of the services merchants needed. As a result, commercial life in Cologne was open to all, even to women, and the organization or practices which might have confined women were to grow more slowly there.

In a more fundamental sense the Staple was the agent of women's participation in long-distance trade because it made Cologne itself a center of trade and provided the connections and facilities for trading in long-distance markets without the necessity of leaving the city. This feature made trade more accessible to women, and may even explain why a few women who managed their businesses did sometimes travel: since women had already established their legitimacy in the thriving international trade which took place on the local Staple, it would have seemed almost natural for a woman from Cologne to travel for business.

Capitalism, too, originated in the long-distance trade handled in Cologne and by Cologners, so, in an indirect way, both the prominence of women in commerce and the precocious development of a capitalist economic order in the city were owed to long-distance trade. Early capitalism and the environment it created in turn were responsible for many of women's roles in market production in Cologne, because they helped to keep the family production unit alive and opened up new economic opportunities for fortunate families. Scattered references in the sixteenth century, such as the testimonies of merchants which opened this chapter, suggest that the family production unit survived in commerce for some time, and there is evidence that it also continued in industry. The wife of the son of Christian von Weinsburg, a university-educated member of the Gaffel Schwarzhaus and a wine merchant, was a Scharzenweberin, and as late as 1553 a daughter of a council member apprenticed for silk weaving.[121] But at some point in the early modern age women lost high status in market production in Cologne just as they had lost it earlier in other cities. We have traced a good part of the process in traditional guilds and can assume that women of capitalist families, who depended on a family production unit which itself was as vulnerable to the same forces that impinged on the family production unit of artisanal society, lost their elevated places in market production when work entered politics or took on rhythms incompatible with the rhythms of family life. Part 3 of this study lends support to this reasoning.

PART 3

Points of Intersection

7

The Comparative Perspective: Lier, Douai, Frankfurt am Main

Women acquired high-status positions in market production in Leiden and Cologne because the family economy was directly involved in production for the market, and they later lost them because the kind of work that could confer high labor-status shifted from the family production unit to the individual. This shift occurred as further development of market production intensified changes in the political and economic organization of work.

Women who pursued high-status work under the new conditions of production would have been forced to surrender many of their functions as household managers, the very functions that first gave them access to market production. Had the household economy lost its manager, it would have been destroyed, and, without the subsistence goods provided by their households, men could not have taken on the newly organized high-status work in market production. The political domain also would have been transformed by women's assumption of newly organized high-status work, for these women would have been obliged to assume active political roles. Such changes threatened the patriarchal order of the society.

The changes in the political and business organization of work which occurred in Leiden and Cologne were themselves products of the competitive pressures of production for long-distance markets. To prosper in the international economy, the producers of Leiden and Cologne had to match costs of other suppliers and standards of quality. Specialization, uniform training of labor, and effective quality control, all achieved in the course of the business and political organization of work, were the means to these ends.

Industries which could regulate the size and composition of the labor force gained additional competitive advantage. Guilds, ambachten, and other associations of workers, sometimes controlled by municipal authorities, provided this regulation, and industrial and commercial sectors often came under the control of such bodies as they achieved economic prominence.

Although these processes drove women from high-status positions in market production in both Leiden and Cologne, the organizational developments responsible for the shift of market production away from the family production unit did not occur in the same way in both cities. Hence, the immediate consequences for family production units and women were different in each. In Leiden, increases in the political organization and in the business organization of work began early and often happened at the same time; as a result, it was only in a few places—the small drapery shop, the work places of finishers and dyers, and the rooms or even outbuildings where linen and coarse cloth were made—that the family production unit and women held their own. In Cologne, the two processes did not always occur together and did not immediately reinforce each other. Perhaps this difference helps to account for women having freer access to high-status positions in market production in Cologne than in Leiden. Women might have retained their hold on silk making because the trade was almost completely free of political association, even though it was subject to strict rules of business organization. The women merchants in Cologne, for their part, might have owed their continued high labor-status to roles in market production which did not require schedules incompatible with other gender roles.

Despite marked differences in the range of high-status work available to women and in the rates at which they lost it, women's access to high labor-status depended in both Leiden and Cologne upon the same intersection between the sex-gender system and the economic system, an intersection which located market production in the family and conferred high labor-status on its principal workers. In both cities, it was the combined force of the political and business organization of work that took high-status positions away from the family. The distinct histories of women's work in Leiden and Cologne together, then, tentatively confirm my working hypothesis linking structural economic change, the decline of the family production unit, and women's loss of labor status.

It does not of course follow that the same constellation of forces similarly affected women's labor status in other late medieval cities.

After all, the political and business organization of work that occurred in Leiden and Cologne did not have precisely identical consequences for women's labor status, and in other settings results may have been different enough to lessen, even negate, the usefulness of the conceptual framework so helpful for understanding women's work in Leiden and Cologne. Demographic changes, wage levels, or other changes in the socio-economic domain might elsewhere have been related to the shift of market production away from the family economy. Surely economic crises would have altered the political and business organization of work. Surely, too, the changes that occurred as market production developed and as the sexual division of labor was altered precipitated further changes throughout urban society which, in turn, affected women's labor status.

These last two chapters look at such possibilities. First, women's work in other late medieval cities of northern Europe is examined within this framework. Second, alternative or supplementary explanations for changes in women's labor status are explored.

Whether urban women throughout northern Europe gained and lost labor status as they did in Leiden and Cologne is a question we cannot answer without countless studies as detailed as those in the last four chapters. But the framework which emerged from those studies can be tested by applying it in other settings where market production was differently organized. The three cities I chose for this test, Lier, Douai, and Frankfurt am Main, serve this purpose well, for each had an economic structure different from one another's and different from either Leiden's or Cologne's.

In some ways, the economy of fifteenth-century Lier, a medium-sized city near Antwerp, resembled Leiden's. The city, long active in the textile business, gained new prominence after Flanders lost its hegemony in this industry, and the heavy, medium-quality cloth it produced was destined for Continental markets. In one respect, however, the economy was different from that in either Leiden or Cologne: the drapers of Lier belonged to a politically autonomous guild of weavers which had an important role in municipal government. The studies of Leiden and Cologne lead us to predict that women would not have been full members in such a guild nor, for that reason, would they have produced cloth in this institutional structure.

The most important study of this period in Lier's economic history, van der Wee's "Die Wirtschaft der Stadt Lier zu Beginn des 15. Jahrhunderts," seems to confirm this prediction.[1] Cloth in Lier, as in Leiden, was made by a few large merchant producers and a great number of small artisan producers. The merchants, however, did not dominate small producers. Instead, according to van der Wee, the large merchants acted as wool-buying agents for artisan-producers, who also occasionally imported wool on their own.[2] Most of the small drapers were weavers who hired fullers, spinners, and combers, and some of them were financially well-off. Surprisingly, these men were consistently listed as officials of the cloth guild (the only textile guild) and sometimes even as aldermen (*Schepenen*), while the large wool merchants performed neither function. Thus, although the mode of production in Lier resembled the small commodity production of Leiden, the political organization in Lier was different.

The records van der Wee used indicate that women were not included among Lier's drapers and draper-weavers, hence confirming that women were excluded from high-status work associated with formal politics. The importance of the link between politics and work in eliminating women's access to high-status work is further emphasized by the evidence from Lier; here women did not participate in work associated with the formal exercise of public authority even when the production system otherwise favored their participation.

In thirteenth- and fourteenth-century Douai, one of the most important of the early Flemish producers of fine-quality woolen cloth, the pattern of women's work appears to have been entirely different. There, women bought and sold cloth and wool; they produced cloth and hired skilled artisans to make it for them; they wove cloth, occasionally on their own and frequently in the employ of others. To understand whether or not this pattern, so different from Lier's, can be explained in terms of the framework used to analyze Lier's drapery, we must look more closely at Douai's economy.

Douai was a leading producer of luxury wool cloth and, along with other Flemish and northern French cities, quite early had established trade links both with its Italian buyers, through the fairs of Champagne, as well as with its English suppliers. During the 150 years when the Flemish industry dominated northern Europe's drapery, the city was run by a group of merchants closely involved both in the cloth and the wool trades. According to Georges Espinas, medieval Douai's eminent historian, this was a merchant patriciate which established capitalist production relations and reduced artisans to wage workers.[3] His path-breaking study of Jean Boinbroke, a merchant-producer apparently ahead of his time, provided much of the evidence for his conclusion. Boinbroke not only exploited his own skilled and unskilled employees and constantly sought to undermine independent artisans whose markets and sources of raw materials he could often control, but he even set up workshops for some production processes.[4] The brief period in the late thirteenth century when a popular element in Douai joined similar movements elsewhere in Flanders against the French-supported patricians of these cities convinced Espinas that capitalist relations were in place, for he regarded these uprisings as an attempt by artisans to resist the economic and political oppression which marked their proletarianization.[5]

Even a cursory look at the sources that Espinas used in drawing his conclusions—chiefly legislative records, business accounts, and municipal financial and judicial records—suggests that we must modify those conclusions. Some particularly skilled craftsmen, like the dyers whose special skill with red dyes made Douai's wool cloth the most expensive from northern Europe, retained entrepreneurial freedom. Many fullers, weavers, and finishers had their own shops, and some worked as cloth producers alongside the bigger drapers who often employed their counterparts in the crafts.[6] Furthermore, even after the industry's decline in the mid-fourteenth century, independent artisans and draper-artisans emerged to claim a place in municipal government, a development which suggests that the earlier conditions of artisanal independence had not been totally destroyed.

But during the twelfth, thirteenth, and fourteenth centuries, as Espinas was entirely correct to emphasize, Douai's merchant patricians monopolized governmental authority. The *échevins* (aldermen), who came from their ranks, alone wrote and enforced all cloth industry ordinances, employed wardens to supervise production, and punished all infractions of their rules. There is no evidence to show that, before the fifteenth century, artisans, even the dyers, were consulted in the formation or execution of these laws. The échevins regulated the fullers, finishers, and weavers particularly closely, and even formed organizations which resembled Leiden's ambachten, except that they did not protect artisanal status and apparently allowed merchant-producers such as Boinbroke to hire pieceworkers. Like Leiden's Gerecht, the échevins of Douai left drapers free from direct supervision, requiring only that their cloth meet quality specifications.

While Espinas may have overemphasized the evidence of capitalist development in Douai, it is nonetheless apparent that during
the period from which most of our evidence comes—1200–1400—
Douai was moving towards a capitalist production structure. The
city's merchant patriciate, like Cologne's new ruling elite and
unlike Leiden's traditional elite, did not restrict commerce in wool
or cloth, or limit the quantities of cloth any draper could produce,
or control the use of casual wage labor in the skilled trades. As a
result, the internal market in wool and cloth was active and open,
and there were a great many drapers, some of them small, and
many skilled wage workers. At the same time, however, it seems
that capitalism was not dominant. The small drapers may have
been vulnerable to takeover by large merchant-producers like
Boinbroke, but they were nevertheless protected by the easy
availability of wool and of customers in Douai. For similar reasons
the artisanal shop survived in many other trades.

Women workers in Douai seem to have fared reasonably well
under this system. In the drapery, women had access to skilled
work, much of it high-status. According to legislative documents,
they dyed and finished cloth; they set warps on weavers' looms;
some even worked as independent weavers and fullers, but most in
these trades were in the employ of others.[7] As if to underline the
importance of women in the drapery crafts, these legislative
documents consistently used feminine as well as masculine forms in
describing those who "faire mestier qui afiere a draperie," a phrase
which appears to refer to all kinds of artisanal labor, both skilled
and semiskilled.[8]

Women are even more visible in the sources as cloth producers
(drapers) and as merchants of wool and cloth. Legislation specified
female merchants, the *marchandes* or *bourgoisses,* and female drapers, the *drapieres, bourgoisses,* or, simply, *femmes.*[9] An ordinance of
1250, for example, required that "no *ourdre* or *ourderesse* may warp
cloth or *couverture* for a *home* or *feme* unless he [sic] is a citizen of the
city."[10] Another ordinance from a series of 1250–98 forbade a
drapier or *drapiere* from taking cloth to a master [fuller] without
providing the butter as well.[11] The nonlegislative documents
confirm these ordinances: many contract disputes and summaries
of judicial proceedings, for example, involved women who were
merchants of wool and cloth or organizers of production.[12]

While the sources used provide little direct information about
the family status of these women, indirect evidence argues that
they owed their positions to the survival of the family production

unit.[13] Commerce in Douai—even commerce in valuable imported wool and in luxury cloths—appears to have been open to the general population and to have attracted a great variety of merchants; in this atmosphere the family production unit could easily have survived. The organization of cloth production—draping—was also unrestricted, and it is reasonable to suppose that women in Douai, like women in Leiden, would have found such work compatible with their roles as household managers. While independent artisans in the skilled trades were organized more formally (almost, it seems, into something resembling Leiden's ambachten), neither these artisans nor the government which regulated them sought to restrict the use of wage labor in the skilled trades. This would explain why Espinas found women weavers in Boinbroke's employ but why at the same time so few women were mentioned in the ordinances that regulated weaving: the women working for Boinbroke were members of families who had lost their independence and now worked for wages, while the others were members of the few surviving family shops.

The direct evidence that does exist regarding the family's role in market production confirms that many women merchants, drapers, or independent artisans were senior members of family production units. For example, an ordinance of about 1250 referred to a dyer's wife as a partner of her husband: "and if the wool were not dyed the color the *drapier* or *drapiere* had commanded of the dyer, the wife or his journeyman. . . ."[14] A later ordinance treated a fuller's wife similarly.[15] An ordinance from about the earlier date prohibited both wives of finishers and unmarried women from entering the *halle a draps pour tondre;* the regulation expressly required unmarried women to send a male worker in their place, implying that married women sent their husbands.[16] Perhaps many of the merchants, drapers, or craftswomen cited in the regulation were widows who carried on the business they had shared with their husbands.

Tentative as any conclusion drawn from such evidence must be, it seems reasonable to claim that Douai's women, like those in Leiden, Cologne and Lier, had high-status positions only in the sectors of market production free from the organizational features that weakened the family production unit. To find that these relationships held in cities as different as these in economic orientation, socioeconomic structure, and political organization lends support to my argument that the patterns and causal relationships observed in Leiden and Cologne held throughout the region. To find that the same relationships held consistently in Frankfurt am Main under entirely different circumstances further strengthens the argument.

From the late fourteenth until the late sixteenth century in Frankfurt, women steadily lost ground in the many guild-controlled crafts of the industrial sector in this economy. Once regularly described as partners, independent mistresses, and even as formal apprentices in trades, women in Frankfurt appeared in later urban records as heirs to but rarely as managers of their husbands' shops, or as unskilled laborers in the employ of others. This deterioration appears to have been associated with a reorganization of market production, itself the result of changes in Frankfurt's economy.

In the early fifteenth century, Frankfurt was a medium-sized city of some 10,000 artisans, market farmers, small merchants, and organizers of the large fairs held there twice annually.[17] A few of the city's industries were directed towards regional markets, presumably through the fairs, but resident patricians only gained a role in long-distance trade in the early fifteenth century, when wine began to be regularly exported in volume through Frankfurt. As early as the mid-fourteenth century, most of the city's crafts had been organized and, in most cases, guild membership was required of those practicing an organized trade, but the guilds had a limited role in municipal government and, in 1366, had even failed in their single recorded effort to gain real political power. Instead, patrician families ran Frankfurt. Although they controlled the external trade which took place in Frankfurt, principally the wine trade, these families concentrated their assets in land.[18]

Like many other cities of northern Europe, Frankfurt suffered a depression in the middle of the fifteenth century, but its economy revived in the sixteenth, and its population grew dramatically, largely as a result of immigration.[19] The immigrants to Frankfurt, mostly Protestant refugees from England and the southern Low Countries, brought new methods of textile manufacture with them, and three new guilds begun in the middle of the sixteenth century organized the specialty textiles trades they introduced.[20] Later immigrants, Jewish as well as Flemish, Walloon, and Dutch, introduced luxury trades such as goldsmithery, jewelry making, and silk weaving, all of which were organized for export.[21] By the end of the sixteenth century many of these people had displaced Frankfurt's patricians as the richest residents in the city.[22] The trade fairs in Frankfurt had by then grown to European importance; the book trade, which had developed around the fairs, gave the city a distinct importance in international culture and commerce. As a center of currency exchange and banking, activities in which Jews were often involved, Frankfurt claimed a special role in European financial affairs.[23]

By the early seventeenth century, Frankfurt had become a city of merchants, merchant-producers, artisan-merchants, and wage workers and was on its way towards a capitalist mode of production, a change reflected in the preceding two and one-half centuries of guild history in Frankfurt.[24] At the middle of the fourteenth century, Frankfurt counted twenty guilds, all of them representative of trades characteristic of a small craft-producing center and regional market. Some 200 years later, thirty-one guilds existed; the guilds added to the original list were concentrated in luxury goods production and merchandising—for example, in book printing, bookbinding, the furrier trade, beltmaking, silk and lace making, goldsmithery, and felt-hat making. By then, several older guilds had merged or been abandoned; the cartwrights and plowwrights, the coopers and the small shippers were among the casualties. Over the period, the guild ordinances had also become more elaborate and specific; instead of general statements about the rights and obligations of trade practitioners, they now contained explicit and often restrictive listings of membership requirements and of training or work rules.[25]

Many of the new guilds composed of immigrants were staffed by merchant-producers and their employees, not by independent artisans. The traditional guilds without institutional power strong enough to preserve the small shop took on a structure similar to that of the new guilds under the pressures of competition for international trade. Those able to adapt the small shop to production for long-distance markets introduced elaborate work rules and training procedures.

The records that survive from late medieval Frankfurt, all of them published before the near-total destruction of the medieval archive there during World War II, include the regulations of these guilds. While hardly sufficient for a full history of Frankfurt's artisanal sector, the collection, which contains the complete legislative history of the city's guilds through two and one-half centuries, accurately measures what the legislators considered possible and likely in the city's regulated industries. The collection becomes a guide to the structure of Frankfurt's industrial sector and an indicator of women's place in the organized crafts as the city grew from a regional market and craft-producing center to a cosmopolitan participant in international trade, finance, and industry.

The ordinances amply document the full rights to practice many trades that women possessed during the fourteenth and fifteenth centuries but show that during the late fifteenth and sixteenth centuries they steadily lost their positions. Of the twenty guilds or brotherhoods that existed in the fourteenth century, nine appear to have had women practitioners.[26] Only three of the nine retained provisions for women after 1500, and only two of these three did so after 1550.[27] Of seven guilds established in the fifteenth century, five originally mentioned women practitioners, but only one did so after 1500.[28] Of nine guilds first established after 1500, only one (the knitters of clothing) seems to have had women practitioners.[29]

Admittedly, "practitioners" is an ambiguous term, but it reflects accurately the imprecision of the language in these ordinances. Especially in ordinances written before 1500, masters and mistresses were seldom described as such; instead, the regulations simply referred to people "in the trade," "active in the trade," or who "practiced the trade."[30] The ordinances are far from clear about how the women who "practiced the trade" had acquired their skills and their rights, but the language suggests that many women owed both to their membership in a family economy, which they comanaged. For example, an ordinance of 1355 of the slaters and tilers (*Steindecker*) described journeymen who worked either for *eyme* [sic] *manne adir eyner frauen,* and an ordinance of 1469 of the wool weavers referred to individuals who "produced cloth in Frankfurt, practiced the craft of wool weaving, cut cloth or prepared it and had not inherited the trade from . . . parents or ancestors. . . ."[31] A later ordinance of 1499 required that "any person, whether *manne oder frauwe*," who did not 'possess [rights to] the trade' [and who] became engaged [in marriage] to another person in the trade, pay 12 schillings. . . ."[32] The tailors (*Schneider*) required, according to ordinances from about 1479, that a man who wanted to join the guild pay extra entrance fees for his wife so that "he and his wife and his children will have rights to the craft and everything belonging to the right of membership. . ."; when masters' widows remarried, their husbands also paid additional fees.[33]

The records further suggest that many women obtained their trade rights, whether in a craft or business they shared with their husbands or managed on their own, through inheritance from their parents. In 1377, the linen makers required, for example, that "if a master's son or daughter wishes to practice the trade, they [sic] must give the craft 10 s for its general use."[34] Similarly, many women inherited shops from their husbands. A council ordinance from the middle of the fifteenth century which required citizens to maintain equipment necessary for city defense made widows "in the craft" responsible for their deceased husbands' military obligations.[35] The husbands of masters' widows and of masters' daughters were regularly allowed special favor in entering the guild.[36]

A few women seem even to have obtained their skills independently of their husbands. An ordinance of 1377 of the tailors (*Schneider*), for example, made provision for any "woman [who] wishes to practice the trade but has no husband."[37] In 1479 a renewed set of ordinances explicitly welcomed women who had no indirect trade rights, that is, women who were neither widows nor daughters of masters.[38] Another ordinance of 1499, from the tanners and workers of fine-quality leather (*Weissgerber, Pergamenter, Beutler, Nestler und Taschner*), similarly distinguished between widows and other women but treated both equally: "any woman or widow who henceforth wishes to practice the trade ... must annually pay her house tax as though she were married."[39]

The great majority of trades women regularly practiced as full members, no matter how the membership had been acquired, utilized skills which had long been in women's traditional preserve and which therefore could have been learned in the course of ordinary domestic work in making textiles, clothing, and food. But other trades fell into the "masculine" realm. According to language from a council ordinance of 1388, for example, women worked not only as sellers of fish but also as independent fishers with their own equipment: "No fisher, whether woman or man, may have more than two nets, and they must be placed alongside one another. . . ."[40] While it may be that these women were wives or widows of fishermen, it is significant nevertheless that they practiced on their own a trade they could not have learned in training for housewifery.

Hence, the early guild legislation and regulatory provisions appear to describe women who belonged to family production units, women usually involved in trades they inherited or learned from parents or husbands. Later legislation from the fifteenth and sixteenth centuries reveals, however, that these production units were transformed, apparently as a result of the increased political and business organization of work. Because the processes occurred more slowly and with less force in Frankfurt than in either Leiden or Cologne, women retained trade rights in Frankfurt's guilds longer than in the formal associations of traditional crafts in either of the other two cities. The reasons for the delay in Frankfurt am Main may be that no industry in Frankfurt had the economic importance achieved by the drapery in Leiden (and hence all were less closely controlled by political actors) and because the artisans as a group had not assumed the political roles in fifteenth-century Frankfurt that they had in Cologne.[41]

It seems certain that women were able to acquire high-status positions in Frankfurt's guilds because the guilds were originally made up of family-centered production units which had few associations with government and did not impose elaborate work rules on their members. From guild ordinances which suggest that as industry grew away from regional towards international luxury trade many guilds converted to more formal structures, we can deduce that women left these positions because the family production unit lost its place at the center of Frankfurt's market production.[42] Most of the evidence available to show that women lost privileged spots as this development occurred is, however, indirect, since, in all but two cases, the only proof we have that women were excluded from guilds is their omission from regulatory provisions which had once included them.

One case of apparently direct exclusion concerned the tailors. A regulation of 1565 revised earlier ordinances which, it will be recalled, provided even for women with no family connections to the trade. The new regulation apparently limited membership to wives and daughters, requiring that "no master may teach a woman the trade unless she is his lawful wife or daughter."[43] In addition, we have an ordinance of 1593 from the *Weissgerber, Pergamenter, Beutler, Nestler und Taschner* which appears to overrule the earlier ordinance of 1499 which had granted unattached women, as well as widows, trade rights. The new ordinance restricted trade rights to widows: "Whichever widow will practice the trade without a husband must annually pay her shop tax as though she were married."[44] Significantly, in both cases only women who were neither married to nor fathered by the male master in the trade were written out of the ordinances. In its strictest sense, then, the family production unit still survived in these two guilds, because the processes of political and business organization of work were only beginning.

A few of the guilds record aspects of the introduction of capitalism into Frankfurt's guilds, and show, as we surmised, that some of the guilds established in the sixteenth century were composed of merchant-producers and of wage-earning employees (skilled and unskilled, female and male). With capitalism came a female proletariat, whose members are evident in the legislative records of the *Posamentier* (the members of which produced expensive fabric trimmings for export). The guild's first ordinances foresaw that women and girls would train for the craft, along with men and boys, but in 1596, just thirteen years after the founding of the guild, new regulations enjoined masters from using apprentices for casual help. They were required, instead, to register any "[boy] apprentices" (*lehrjungen*), "servants" (*gesindt*), or "girls" (*magdlin*) they were employing.[45] These rights apparently were abused when some masters imported girls (probably from nearby villages) as unskilled workers, and a new ordinance issued in 1597 required masters to employ only their own kin or the daughters of citizens as helpers.[46] In 1607, because this privilege had been "misused," the rule was tightened so that only the daughters and children of masters—and not all relatives—could be employed. But later that year this article, too, was overturned to allow "merchants" and "masters" to employ no more than two girls, "whether citizens' daughters or not."[47] Evidently, a struggle had taken place between those who wished to preserve traditional production relations in the craft and others eager to introduce capitalist wage relations; evidently, capitalist interests won.

The analytical framework drawn from the empirical studies of Leiden and Cologne, in combination with comparisons from Lier, Douai, and Frankfurt, lends convincing, if not conclusive, support for the thesis that women's work throughout late medieval European cities, even throughout preindustrial Europe, was determined by ways in which the sex-gender system intersected with the economic system.[48] This intersection, we can now be reasonably sure, produced changes in market production which eventually led, in turn, to women's departure from high-status positions in the businesses they often had helped to found. So fundamental were these shifts in the sexual division of labor and in the organization of market production that their effects could not have been confined to economics alone. In the concluding chapter we will look at ways in which the changes might have been felt elsewhere.

8

Women's Work and Social Change

In the previous chapters I have emphasized, in order to identify and understand them, the relationships between women's labor status and structural economic change in late medieval cities. As a result, the importance of these factors has probably been over-stated and the importance of others surely minimized. Here I will try to rectify this imbalance by considering several other plausible causes for the diverse patterns of women's work we have encoun-tered. The first is the effect of cyclical economic and demographic factors; the second, the role of the traditional sexual division of labor; and the third, the connection between law and changes in women's labor status.

Change in the supply and demand for labor obviously affected women's work in this period, just as it has in other times and places. But is it possible that women's acquisition of high-status positions in market production simply reflected changes in the availability of or the need for female labor? Bücher thought so. He suggested that late medieval women entered the labor force only because there were too few men and too many women and he concluded that women later left it in part because this demographic imbalance called the "women question" was righted.[1] Other scholars have suggested that women's access to positions in market production depended more directly on the demand for labor: when times were good, women were hired; but when times were bad, they were fired.

Let us consider the evidence that supports these hypotheses.

174

Most historians agree that in many late medieval cities there were more women than men.[2] Several have pointed out that the period during the fifteenth century of women's exodus from high-status positions in market production coincided with the economic and demographic malaise which afflicted many urban communities. In some ways, this demographic and economic argument is complemented by my own findings. Economic downturns, it cannot be disputed, often were the occasions for formation of corporative guilds or promulgation of strict work rules which in many cases called for women's exclusion from the work being regulated.[3] It is easy to understand why insecure artisans, particularly journeymen, would have wanted to shrink the labor force; no wonder, then, that they pushed for restrictive legislation when they were in a position to do so. It is also evident that expansions of industries in which women had traditionally been involved—the booms in textiles, for example, which many cities enjoyed—would have created new demand for female labor.

But it does not follow that women's access to high-status work was only a function of swings in economic activity and shifts in sex ratios. While women's employment in market production may have increased in response to a shortage of labor, it increased only in economic sectors and positions which granted high or even low labor-status where structural conditions favored women's employment. Otherwise, women would not have steadily lost high-status positions in textiles almost everywhere in northern Europe during the sixteenth century, when women in most cities still outnumbered men and when on the whole textile production increased.[4] Conversely, women would not have lost access to commerce and the crafts whenever they were organized or took on political status, no matter the state of the economy. Women in sixteenth-century Leiden, for example, would not have lost their places as master finishers when their trade *expanded* in the early sixteenth century and would not have *retained* their positions as drapers when production fell so dramatically after 1530. Women would not have enjoyed higher labor status in fifteenth-century Frankfurt than in fifteenth-century Leiden, where the economy was stronger and women just as overabundant. Finally, women in early seventeenth-century Frankfurt would not have had *lower* labor status than their fifteenth-century counterparts.[5]

The role of the traditional sexual division of labor needs more attention as well. Natalie Davis has commented that in sixteenth-century Lyons, "the crafts of the weaponmaker, of the smith and of the caster, which had a marked masculine quality about them, probably drew little on wifely aid." Paraphrasing a contemporary observer, she reasoned that "here the craftsmen had to be very strong; here they looked brutish, with their faces full of powder and half burned," and implied that such working conditions were unsuitable for women.[6] Davis suggested a cultural interpretation for the sexual division of labor, but other historians have argued explicitly that the factor dividing male work from female was physical strength. Posthumus, for example, explained the prominence of late medieval women in urban textile crafts and their absence from others on the grounds that textile work was "light."[7] In her study of late medieval Cologne, Wensky used the same reasoning to explain why women wove silk but not wool cloth. Making wool cloth, she pointed out, required the use of heavy frames and shuttles which she thought beyond the strength of the average woman.[8]

A sexual division of labor something like what these scholars described surely did characterize market production in late medieval Leiden, Cologne, Douai, and Frankfurt. Women were concentrated in food and clothing preparation and sale and they seldom undertook tasks which led them away from the home or required great strength. Leiden's small textile producers, Cologne's linen makers and small retailers of beer, and Frankfurt's glovers often were women, while Leiden's butchers, Cologne's carpenters, and Frankfurt's coopers were almost always men.

But the actual division of tasks in these cities could and did change in response to the structural conditions identified in this study. In families which devoted themselves to market production, the fundamental precept that women's work must be centered on the household was often enlarged. In Douai, women entered the male world of public business negotiations when they acted as brokers for visiting merchants, and they acquired independent status in commercial law when they bought and sold wool on credit; in Cologne, they traveled to regional fairs, took oaths guaranteeing the quality of their products, and dealt, both in cash and on credit, in international markets. The precept could even be overturned: wives who performed important functions in family production units or daughters raised to join this economy assumed "men's" roles as smiths or knife makers in order to aid the male head of household in his work or to substitute for him in his absence.

When men took over the high-status jobs in market production that could no longer be contained within the family production unit, the traditional division of labor by sex was, in one sense, altered again. Many of the positions men acquired, in brewing, weaving, and innkeeping, for example, once had been women's. But, looked at another way, this change did not involve a reorganization of the traditional sexual division of labor so much as a reassertion of it, if we regard the "tradition" not as if determined by the average physical capacities of the sexes but by cultural norms dividing communal from domestic concerns and locating women in the latter; the positions the men acquired had entered a business and political sphere separate from the family, a sphere, according to the principle underlying this even more fundamental and perhaps the truly "traditional" division of labor by sex, reserved for men.

A sexual division of labor based on average physical strength alone may have set certain parameters for women's work but it did not determine women's gain and loss of high labor-status. The role played by the legal system seems to have been similar. Historians have not yet systematically studied changes in women's legal status in relation to changes in women's work in late medieval Europe, but there can be little question that the connection between legal and economic change for women in this period was close. Community property laws were adopted in many northern cities during the period, daughters there often inherited equally with sons, and wives were increasingly exempted from the guardianships to which traditional law had relegated them, all just as women's roles in market production came to require such adjustments.[9] In the centuries that followed, moreover, just as women lost labor status, women also lost legal status. These developments have been even less thoroughly studied, but the trend is clear. Petot and Vandenbossche, for example, noted that women in France lost the legal capacity to act for absent husbands and to conclude certain "actes et contrats," a loss that "reinforced more or less according to a strictly juridical system, the inequality established in the interests of the man."[10] Legal scholars specializing in other regions have made the same argument. Gilissen saw a "slow retreat" in women's legal status in the southern Low Countries during the seventeenth and eighteenth centuries.[11] In England, we are told, "Tudor-Stuart legal practice hardened against women," a consequence, undoubtedly, of the triumph of common law.[12]

Exactly how the rise and subsequent decline of women's legal status was connected to changes in women's labor status is hard to determine. Surely the changes reinforced each other, but without careful research we cannot know if law responded to economic change or vice versa. I am inclined to suspect, as I explained in chapter 1, that the apparent rise in women's legal status from about 1200 to 1500 was a response to the need for new legal capacities required by the work women were doing. I am inclined also to suspect, however, that the changes which restricted women's legal capacities in early modern Europe were part of a prevailing effort to restrict women's economic and social autonomy so that, in this period, the direction of causality was reversed. Some published evidence supports this supposition. For example, in sixteenth-century France, community property laws were changed to insure explicitly that widows could not control their husbands' estates.[13]

Not enough is known about changes in demographic patterns and in family structures in northern cities during the early modern centuries to judge whether changes of this kind paralleled the changes in work and law which seem to have been so closely related. The evidence we have, however, suggests that urban merchant families by the eighteenth century at least, sometimes long before, were beginning to look and behave like merchant families of the South. Marriages between middle-aged men and young women became more common, and families consequently became larger. By the same time, aristocratic urban women had by and large not only left active participation in family businesses but had also begun to withdraw even from management of the domestic economy.[14] Confirmation of these suppositions about the links between work, law, and family structure towards the end of the ancien régime will require more research, and until it is available, the principal defense for this reasoning is that it fits so nicely with what we already know about gender relations in early modern Europe. The roles of women and the definitions of womanhood were changing at this time, and women's lives were increasingly centered in a newly constructed patriarchal household. It seems reasonable that law changed to accommodate this change.

WOMEN'S WORK AND THE PATRIARCHAL ORDER

Women's work in late medieval cities changed, we can conclude, essentially because the patriarchal order required it. Men gained a monopoly over the high-status work outside the family production unit because men alone could assume the political status associated with such work and because they alone could rearrange their own work schedules to meet the demands of production in competitive markets. When this shift occurred, women who could dispense with earnings from their work left market production. For some three or four centuries afterwards, privileged women of Europe entered market production only for short periods of time during predictable moments in their life cycles—when they were young and single or, if the privileges of their class did not protect them from want, when they were old and widowed. Married women in this period, the very women most likely to be the most productive workers were they trained for work in market production commensurate with their economic and social status, almost never worked in market production. Poor women of all ages and of every marital status constantly worked in market production of course, taking on varying tasks in the informal labor market—domestic service, cottage industry, casual retailing—as age, marital status, and family responsibilities permitted and as poverty dictated.

Scholars who concentrate on women in modern European capitalist society have explored the implications of this pattern, to show how it perpetuates patriarchal gender relations. Bourgeois women do not enter market production except as low-status workers, and do not acquire the social, economic, political, or cultural status which in capitalist societies attaches to middle-class work; instead, they owe their status to the men in their families.[15] Women's work is so unimportant to their social status that even when bourgeois women undertake low-status jobs, neither their status nor that of their families is affected. According to this analysis, patriarchy in capitalist societies is achieved partly by excluding women from high-status positions in market production.

My study of women's work in late medieval cities suggests that this pattern of women's work did not start in modern capitalist society but, rather, in the early development of a European market society and was neither exclusive to late medieval capitalism nor necessarily associated with it. In both Leiden and Lier, women were excluded from sectors of market production which were decidedly noncapitalist; in both Cologne and Douai, women very often owned and managed capitalist enterprises. Revising interpretations of the relationships between changes in the mode of production and women's work in late medieval and early modern Europe, we can say that capitalism did not compel women's departure from market production, as Clark and many of her successors believed. Capitalism could take root, as it did in Cologne and Douai, in the family production unit and could spur the growth of the family wage economy, where women took an active part, as it did elsewhere in early modern Europe.

Admittedly, it was not everywhere that women had high labor-status in late medieval and early modern urban capitalist economies, and even in places like Cologne where women had secure positions near the top of capitalist enterprises, there were very few such women. By definition, capitalism allows few people places at the top, and most women in these cities, like most men, as employees of capitalists, had low labor-status. Furthermore, many capitalist economies of the period had been preceded by small commodity production which had already destroyed the family production unit, and the capitalist enterprises there consequently did not begin in family-run shops, as they did in Douai and Cologne. By the modern period of European history, it is also true, women capitalists like those of Cologne and Douai were rare, surely, in part, because the family production unit could not survive the emergence of the formalized and impersonal systems of management and investment embodied in modern versions of corporate and finance capitalism.[16] For late medieval society, however, many of these changes were only in the future, and as a result it was then small commodity production, not capitalism, that proved the less hospitable to women. Paradoxically, the organizational developments which made small commodity production an effective alternative to capitalism also made it the enemy of the family production unit.

The family production unit survived best, of course, neither under capitalism nor small commodity production, but in medieval craft production where it must have begun. There, few of the organizational changes necessary for survival in competitive markets had developed. Even the guilds and craft associations typical of this mode of production proved no threat to the family unit because these associations derived from the family economy and the artisanal community. But this mode of production could not secure women's high labor-status in the long run because it was insecure itself. In time, the better organized, more productive workers of small commodity production and capitalism could and did undermine the small, independent artisans characteristic of medieval craft production.

Even when the family production unit survived the emergence of small commodity production or capitalism, as it did in parts of Leiden's drapery and in Cologne's new export-oriented industries, its tenure was short because under these systems work was eventually organized in ways which removed it from household control. In accordance with the prevailing patriarchal order, women could not retain these work roles because they could not abandon the household and could not independently participate in politics. To preserve this patriarchal order was, in this circumstance, to strengthen it. When high-status work was removed from the family production unit and became inaccessible to married women, women surrendered an important source of authority to men. Men gained even more than women lost, because the identical work now acquired greater economic, political, and cultural importance than when it had been contained within the family production unit. In this way men's authority inside and outside the household was increased at the expense of women's.

Although women held high labor-status in the European market economy for only a short time and lost it just when high labor-status came to confer unprecedented cultural, political, and economic status, they must have threatened the patriarchal character of Europe's sex-gender system during the period they held it. Such a threat, and its resolution (accomplished by women's withdrawal from high-status positions in market production), must have been perceptible outside the realm of economics, in a realm where attitudes towards gender roles were formed. To explore the connections between changes in women's labor status or, more generally, the sexual division of labor, and the ideology of gender in this age, we need a great deal more research, but we can be certain that the inquiry will be fruitful. The late medieval and early modern period, as we already know, was an age of great uncertainty, even disagreement, about appropriate gender roles. By its end, the divisions between public and private had been newly and clearly drawn, and women, by and large, were firmly located in the private realm centered on the patriarchal nuclear family.[17] Women's gain and loss of high labor-status in market production has to have been involved in this shift, and the tensions bred by the shift must have been reflected in contemporary sources. To close this book, we can look briefly at some of the evidence which reveals associations between women's roles in market production and contemporary struggles over gender relations—and their resolution.

In judicial records that survive from cities very much like Leiden and Cologne, we have straightforward evidence that women sometimes resisted new laws which denied them entry to certain trades. For example, a dyer's daughter in fourteenth-century Ghent sued to inherit her father's place in the guild (and lost); a widow in fourteenth-century Paris sued to keep up her husband's trade as candlemaker.[18] The literature of urban popular culture less directly, but even more eloquently, records such conflicts. Comedies and satires of the period, for example, often portrayed market women and tradeswomen as shrews, with characterizations that not only ridiculed or scolded them for taking on roles in market production but frequently even charged them with sexual aggression.[19] Chaucer's Wife of Bath was an expert at sex—who delighted in playing the aggressor—and at weaving. In Chaucer's words, she "bettered those of Ypres and Ghent," and, as Chaucer undoubtedly knew, the weavers in Ypres and Ghent were men.[20]

A great many of the women portrayed in literature who were accused of sexual aggressiveness were, of course, not involved in market production, but they had trespassed upon other male spheres. Marijke, titular protagonist of *Marijke van Nijmegen,* a fifteenth-century Rederijker play from Antwerp, becomes the Devil's lover in order to enter the male preserve of learning: "Before I'll let you sleep with me/You will teach me the seven liberal arts/For I take great pleasure in learning about all things."[21] Marijke regains her soul only after she abandons the Devil, illicit sex, and male learning. She had transgressed against both God and men: the forbidden learning she sought was male, and she violated God's order to obtain it. Her pact with the Devil, it is clear, involved something of divine concern—her soul—and something of male concern—her sexuality.

While no actual women of the ordinary classes in late medieval and early modern European cities, as far as we know, boldly challenged the male preserve of higher learning to the degree this created character does, the women who held high-status positions in market production did challenge male preserves, and the male fears and hostilities expressed by this play may very well reflect the turmoil over gender relations brought to life partly when working women acquired new status. The *fabliaux*, most of which are set in northwest Europe, often in the cities—the merchant and his wife of "Le souhait reprimé" are even from Douai—recapitulate these themes, tension about gender roles combined with tension about heterosexual relations; one scholar recently claimed that the tales "gave European literature a new theme: sexuality that betokens not a personal fulfillment, but rivalrous interpersonal struggle."[22]

The popular literature of late medieval and early modern urban culture seems, then, to express unusual hostility towards aggressive women, women whose aggressiveness in some measure attends their positions in market production, and it seems to equate such aggressiveness with sexual aggressiveness, even sexual misconduct.[23] But are we justified in seeing these implications? Are examples such as these representative of late medieval and early modern urban culture? Do they truly reflect tensions in urban society or do they simply repeat literary conventions held over from other cultures? Are the themes really so transparent? These are difficult questions to answer. If any of them can be answered affirmatively, we can ask yet another: how did the lessons expressed in this literature help to ease women's departure from market production, help to restrict their sexuality and shore up the patriarchy?

It is tempting to suppose that the relationships between work, economics, politics, and law explored in this study were tied to changes in religion, literature, and sexuality, that women's temporary admission to high-status positions in market production seriously threatened the patriarchal order, and that the literary artifacts mentioned above were produced in a struggle to reinforce that order. With the authority granted by their roles in market production, these women may have begun to assert themselves in other spheres, frightening men, other women, and perhaps even themselves, for their actions portended the destruction of the traditional sex-gender system and the institutions based on it.[24] If we accept this reasoning, we can begin to understand why, in the end, women accepted dismissal from commerce and trade, and why men, sometimes with self-conscious deliberation, arranged it.[25] Most often unconsciously—but with unquestionable success—men may have battled to strengthen the traditional order while women may have struggled, as the economic, social, and political order which shapes the meaning of gender was changing, to establish a new gender identity.

The patriarchal order, as we know, was restored, even renewed, where men gained privileged access to high labor-status. In this exploration of women's exodus from the positions in market production which might have overturned the traditional order, we have witnessed an important part of the process of restoration and renewal. While there is much to learn—almost everything to learn—about the other issues at stake as gender was redefined in the late medieval period, we now know, beyond doubt, how important women's roles in economic production were in requiring such redefinition.

Appendix 1

APPROXIMATE INCOME FROM LEIDEN'S STRIKERYE, 1400–1573

Year	(1) Income	(2) Tax Rate	(3) No. of Cloths	(4) No. of Cloths	(5) No. of Cloths	(6) No. of Cloths
1400	161 lbs.	1/2 g.	9,660			
1413	257				15,420	7,710
1419	529[a]				15,885	10,590
1420	559[b]				16,776	11,184
1426	439				13,193	8,795
1427	551				16,537	11,025
1434	381				11,430	7,620
1449	537				16,118	10,745
1450	562				16,860	11,240
1451	641				19,230	12,820
1452	731				21,930	14,620

SOURCES: All figures from columns (1) are taken from Posthumus, *Geschiedenis*, 1: *Bijlage* VI[A], p. 426

Posthumus used figures reported in the city accounts to obtain income data but he made several adjustments. First, he added to income actually received (the number normally recorded in the accounts) an amount that represented the expenses associated with collecting the tax. This adjustment was necessary because the city often leased the tax out at a net rate exclusive of the leasee's costs. Even when the city collected the tax itself, it entered the collections net of costs. Posthumus based his estimates of such costs on actual figures; the charges were about 600 £ Holl. in 1543. Second, he reported all amounts in £ Holl. of 30 Flemish groten. After 1545, the actual accounts were kept in £ Holl. of 40 groten. I have eliminated shillings and pence.

Posthumus found the tax rates he used in the various pieces of municipal legislation, generally Vroedscap Resoluties, and calculated production using such tax rates and income data; for those periods for which he was unsure of the tax rate he did not provide production figures (1413–69). I have tried to indicate the possible range of production for those years in columns (5) and (6): column (5) assumes 1/2 groot for 1413 and 1 groot through 1469, and column (6) assumes 1 groot for 1413 and 1 1/2 groten through 1469.

According to doc. no. 1103, Posthumus, *Bronnen*, vol. 2, in 1548 the tax rate was raised from 4 1/2 groten to 5 1/2 groten. Posthumus's figures do not reflect the change. Column (4) is a calculation of production that assumes the higher rate.

[a]period of 9 months
[b]period of 3 months

Year	(1) Income	(2) Tax Rate	(3) No. of Cloths	(4) No. of Cloths	(5) No. of Cloths	(6) No. of Cloths
1453	750				22,500	15,000
1454	725				21,750	14,500
1455	752				22,560	15,040
1456	700				21,000	14,000
1457	600				18,000	12,000
1458	652				19,560	13,040
1459	700				21,000	14,000
1460	650				19,500	13,000
1461	676				20,287	13,525
1462	610				18,300	12,200
1463	635				19,050	12,700
1464	602				18,060	12,040
1465	654				19,620	13,080
1466	613				18,390	12,560
1467	613				18,390	12,560
1469	671				20,130	13,420
1470	983	2 g.	14,745			
1471	925		13,875			
1472	1007		15,105			
1473	1140		17,100			
1475	1251		18,765			
1476	1413		21,195			
1477	488[c]		7,235[c]			
1481	549[d]		9,585[d]			
1484	1644		24,675			
1485	1462		21,940			
1486	1295		19,430			
1487	1476		22,140			
1488	1437		21,555			
1491	1451		21,765			
1493	2359	3 g.	23,595			
1494	2380		23,800			
1496	1737	31/2 g.	17,370			
1497	2250		22,500			
1498	3515	41/2 g.	23,430			
1499	3664		24,425			
1500	3509		23,393			
1502	4221		28,141			
1503	4123		27,495			
1504	3345		22,302			

[c]period of 3 months, 10 days
[d]period from 11 November to 17 April

Year	(1) Income	(2) Tax Rate	(3) No. of Cloths	(4) No. of Cloths	(5) No. of Cloths	(6) No. of Cloths
1506	3650		24,333			
1507	3795		25,303			
1508	3715		24,769			
1509	3439		22,926			
1511	3036		20,240			
1512	3691		24,611			
1513	3861		25,740			
1514	3956		27,379			
1515	3939		26,396			
1516	4144		27,626			
1518	3956		26,373			
1519	3568		23,786			
1520	3966		26,440			
1521	4348		28,987			
1522	3242		21,616			
1523	3444		22,967			
1525	3662		24,413			
1526	3147		20,983			
1527	3382		22,550			
1528	3500		23,337			
1529	3687		24,584			
1530	3602		24,017			
1532	2359		15,730			
1533	2465		16,433			
1534	2765		18,441			
1536	1990		12,270			
1537	2897		19,314			
1538	2818		18,790			
1539	2428		16,187			
1540	2350		15,670			
1541	2476		16,507			
1542	2850		19,006			
1543	1920		12,800			
1546	2061		13,742			
1547	1776		11,845			
1548	953		6,355	5,201		
1556	1251		8,335	6,826		
1559	917		6,113	5,002		
1560	1232		8,218	6,723		
1561	964		6,427	5,259		
1562	1160		7,767	6,329		
1563	755		5,035	4,119		

Approximate Income from Leiden's Strikerye, 1400–1573
(Continued)

Year	(1) Income	(2) Tax Rate	(3) No. of Cloths	(4) No. of Cloths	(5) No. of Cloths	(6) No. of Cloths
1564	500		3,335	2,729		
1565	579		3,864	3,164		
1568	536		3,578	2,928		
1570	568		3,792	3,102		
1573	163		1,086	892		

Appendix 2

ARCHIVAL SOURCES SAMPLED IN STUDY OF LEIDEN

Corrextieboeken
These are the city records of the fines and punishments imposed for violations of city ordinances, including industrial, trade, and police ordinances. They begin formally in 1434 when Leiden received jurisdiction over all criminal infractions in the city.* The sample originally chosen included the years 1435–36; 1465–66; 1509–10; and 1540–41. Because they proved useful guides to the cloth business, I later added 1475–76, and 1490–91.

Kenningboeken
These records of appeals in civil cases, like the *Corrextieboeken*, begin in 1434. A *Kenning* was the decision of the *Schepenen* in a civil case brought by one involved party. The plaintiff challenged the defendant to appear before the *Schepenen* by pledging a sum of money; refusal to respond resulted in loss by default. Most cases involved disputes over real property transfers or the validity of legal instruments issued in lower courts. I read the same eight years of these records which I had originally selected from the *Corrextieboeken:* 1435–36; 1465–66; 1509–10; 1540–41.

Wedboeken
These records began in 1477 as preliminary hearings for *Kenningen* and involve similar cases. The years read were 1478, 1479–80; 1510–11; 1527; 1540.

* A partial list of such fines and punishments survives from 1392–95; evidently the city had jurisdiction over some cases prior to 1434 and kept sporadic records, but it is only in 1434 that full records begin.

Rekeningen

The municipal accounts of Leiden were kept by various administrative officers at different periods. Individually they are called the *Burgemeesters Rekeningen, Homans Rekeningen,* and *Tresoriers Rekeningen,* and because each group of officials concerned itself with slightly different aspects of city finances, the respective accounts of each are consequently not identical. In certain years, only one kind of financial officer functioned; in others, two divided the responsibilities of collecting revenue, dispensation, and record-keeping. Each account therefore varies from year to year. All *Rekeningen* that survived up to 1434 have been published.** I examined the accounts for 1399–1400; 1434; 1465–66; 1498–99; 1508–09; 1540–41.

Vroedscap Resoluties

These record the decisions taken in meetings of the *Vroedschap.* I sampled 1451–52; 1465–68; 1508–11; 1540–42.

Aflezingboeken

These record governmental decisions announced to the citizenry. They begin in 1505. I read years 1506–11; 1523–28; 1540–45.

Tax roll of 1498

In 1498 the city imposed a head-of-household tax on all citizens and assessed them at 1 percent of property value. The list of assessments and collections is contained in the *Tresoriers Rekeningen* of 1498.

** M. van Embden, Stadsrekeningen, 2 vols.

Appendix 3

The Population of Leiden in 1498

Posthumus used the tax roll of 1498 to estimate the size and composition of the population of Leiden at that time. As discussed in the body of this study and as indicated by information provided in a later population survey of 1581 (analyzed both by Posthumus, in *Geschiedenis*, vol. 2, and by Daelemans in "Leiden, 1581: Een socio-demografisch onderzoek"), his figures require some modification. These adjustments are discussed below. This table summarizes Posthumus's analysis of Leiden's population based on the roll of 1498 and my revisions of his analysis.

	Posthumus 1498		Revised 1498	
Male heads of household	2,253	19.4%	2,253	16.2%
Married women	1,756	15.1	1,756	12.6
Widowed and single women	880	7.6	880	6.3
Children, male and female, except servants and lodgers	4,327	37.2	4,327	31.0
Servants, all ages and both sexes	1,960	16.8	1,960	14.1
Cloistered and miscellaneous	460	3.9	460	3.3
Lodgers (includes most journeymen and relatives), all ages and both sexes	—		2,300	16.5
Totals	11,636	100%	13,936	100%
Household size	3.6		4.5	

The only change in Posthumus's estimate of the population of Leiden is the addition of 2,300 "lodgers" which represents the dependent population not reflected in the servant category, especially the journeymen living in Leiden. The first category of persons in the group was mostly relatives, and the size of this group has been estimated by reference to Daelemans's analysis of Leiden's population in 1581. At that time, some 500 men, women, and children lived with relatives in a population of perhaps 12,000, when the economy and the population were at a low point. Conservatively, some 300 such persons, 100 of whom were adult men, must have lived in Leiden in 1498. The second category was journeymen, and it is certain that about 2,000 of them lodged in Leiden. The tax roll excluded them, as we have seen, and therefore Posthumus ignored them in his analysis of the labor force, but we have also seen that at any one time *alone* the drapery industry employed at least 1,000 full-time journeymen weavers, fullers and dyers. We know that the industry also employed male journeymen for many other tasks—as pelt sorters, finishers, card makers, warpers, *spoelers*, and so on. We know that many other trades used journeymen as well; in 1581 there were at least 259 such male journeymen—this at a time when the industrial economy was at its lowest point.* It seems, then, quite reasonable to assume that 2,000 journeymen worked in 1498 Leiden.

According to my calculation, the average household size in 1498 was 4.5, a figure larger than that of 1581 (3.9) but not at all out of line with figures obtained in studies of other medieval and early modern cities comparable to Leiden. The adult male work force (nonservant) would then have totaled 4,353 (2,253 male heads of household plus about 2,000 journeymen and perhaps about 100 adult male dependent relatives).

*Posthumus, *Geschiedenis*, 2: pp. 22–30. Daelemans shows that the tax roll itself identifies only 232 adult male journeymen, many of them textile workers (Daelemans, "Een socio-demografisch onderzoek," pp. 181 and 213). Posthumus's additional identifications are all from sources external to the tax roll; in all, he identified occupations for about 86 percent of the adult male population who were heads of households.

Notes

INTRODUCTION

1. The quotation is from p. 19 of the revised edition (1910). This and all other translations in the text, unless otherwise noted, are my own.

2. The quotation in the text is from p. 68. Bücher thought that the feminist movement of the late nineteenth century owed something to a similar demographic imbalance and he obviously hoped this "woman question" would be resolved as that of the fifteenth century had been. As Bücher presented the problem, it could be resolved only if women were to retreat from market production and if the primacy of the household were reasserted. In doing so, women would have to resist the capitalist market economy which rendered all labor a commodity, which pitted women against men in the competition for jobs, and which destroyed centuries of social and ethical development, all leading, as he described it, to a "retreat into barbarity, a disruption of family order which had taken shape since the Reformation, a destruction of the household, in which the woman ruled, and the entry of women into the world of economic production in which they could find places only as the servile members" (p. 75). "Shouldn't we work with all our strength so that all classes of the population are assured the peace and the comfort of the domestic hearth, which strengthens family consciousness and which provides a woman the single sphere where she feels the happiest and in which she creates the value more precious to the nation than whatever increase in production she might achieve with her 'cheap labor' ['billige Hände']?" (p. 72).

3. The three most important were Wilhelm Behagel, "Die gewerbliche Stellung der Frau im mittelalterlichen Köln"; Julius Hartwig, "Die Frauenfrage im mittelalterlichen Lübeck"; and Gustav Schmoller, *Die Strassburger Tucher- und Weberzunft*.

4. Most are from Germany and include Helmut Wachendorf, *Die*

wirtschaftliche Stellung der Frau in den deutschen Städten des späteren Mittelalters; Bruno Kuske, "Die Frau im mittelalterlichen Wirtschaftsleben"; Rudolf Wissel, *Das alten Handwerks Recht und Gewohnheit;* G. K. Schmelzeisen, *Die Rechtsstellung der Frau in der deutschen Stadtwirtschaft;* Gertrud Schmidt, *Die berufstätigkeit der Frau in der Reichsstadt Nürnberg bis zum Ende des 16. Jahrhundert;* Rudolf Endres, "Zur Lage der Nürnberger Handwerkerschaft zur Zeit von Hans Sachs"; Edith Ennen, "Die Frau in der mittelalterlichen Stadtgesellschaft Mitteleuropas" and "Die Frau im Mittelalter"; Margret Wensky, *Die Stellung der Frau in der stadtkölnischen Wirtschaft im Spätmittelalter.*

There is, in addition, less extensive evidence from England, France and the Low Countries. See, for England, Eileen Power, *Medieval Women;* Alice Abram, "Women Traders in Medieval London"; and Mary Anne Kowaleski, "Women's Work in a Market Town: Exeter in the Late Fourteenth Century." Recent studies have also confirmed what historians have long suspected: women were regularly the commercial brewers of late medieval English villages, small towns, and large cities: see Judith M. Bennett, "The Village Ale Wife: Women and Brewing in Fourteenth-century England"; John J. Butt, Jr., "The Transition of Privilege in Medieval Society: A Study of the English Brewers."

Henri Hauser's *Ouvriers du temps passé* of 1897 and Madeleine Guilbert's very recent *Les fonctions des femmes dans l'industrie* both described late medieval women, particularly urban women, as active and valued participants in market production in France. Parisian evidence for this argument is the best. A late thirteenth-century compilation of regulations affecting organized trades in Paris, Etienne Boileau's *Livre des métiers,* for example, indicated that five of one hundred of these *métiers* were exclusively for women. Gustav Fagniez's *Études sur l'industrie et la classe industrielle à Paris au xiiie et au xive siècle* provided additional evidence of the importance of women in the trade and industry of late-thirteenth-century Paris: of some 300 trades named in two tax rolls of 1292 and 1300, fifteen were exclusive to women and about eighty were practiced by both men and women. For the *Livre des Métiers* of Paris, see G. B. Depping, *Réglements sur les arts et métiers de Paris, rédigés au 13e siècle, et connus sous le nom du Livre des Métiers d'Etienne Boileau.* These calculations were made by Madeleine Guilbert, *Les fonctions des femmes dans l'industrie* (the data are from Fagniez); E. Dixon, in "Craftswomen in the *Livre des Métiers*" early drew attention to the importance of women in the trades of Paris. In both late medieval Poitiers and Toulouse, women also appear to have been active in industry and trade: M. de la Fontenelle de Vaudoré, *Les arts et métiers à Poitiers pendant les xiiie, xive et xve siècles;* M. A. Mulholland, *Early Gild Records of Toulouse.*

For the Low Countries, see the economic histories by George Espinas, *La vie urbaine de Douai au moyen âge;* Emile Coornaert, *Un centre industriel d'autrefois: la draperie-sayetterie d'Hondschoote*; G. des Marez, *L'organisation du travail à Bruxelles au xvᵉ siècle*; N. W. Posthumus, *De Geschiedenis van de Leidsche Lakenindustrie*. Also see the more recent work of Jenneke Quast, "Vrouwenarbeid omstreeks 1500 in enkele nederlandse Steden"; idem, "Vrouwen in gilden in Den Bosch, Utrecht en Leiden van de 14e tot en met de 16e eeuw." There are also several unpublished studies on women's work in cities of the southern Low Countries: Christiane Leonard, "De status en de positie van de Gentse vrouw in de xive en de xve eeuw"; A. Baeten, "De vrouw in de mentaliteit van een aantal laat-middeleeuwse auteurs"; Frieda Vandenabeele, "De vrouw in de lakennijverheid in Vlaanderen." A recent study by David Nicholas, *The Domestic Life of a Medieval City*, includes descriptions of women's work in the commerce and crafts in fourteenth-century Ghent. His data by and large accords with the pattern evidenced elsewhere.

5. Two studies stand out, Alice Clark's *The Working Life of Women in the 17th Century* and Eileen Power's *Medieval Women*. Clark investigated the effects of capitalism on women's work in early modern England. She argued that women's opportunities for work were then lessening as compared to their opportunities in the Middle Ages, but she provided only a few examples of women's work in the earlier period. For further discussion of Clark's thesis, see Part 1 above. Eileen Power, like Clark, studied how work organized gender relations but, since she focused on the Middle Ages, she provided much more detail than Clark about medieval women's work. Hers is nevertheless an exploratory survey, not an investigation of theory. For examples of explorations of some of these points, see Lily Braun, *Die Frauenfrage: ihre geschichtliche Entwicklung und wirtschaftliche Seite*; B. Brodmeier, *Die Frau im Handwerk in historischer und moderner Sicht*; J. Barchewitz, *Von der Wirtschaftstätigkeit der Frau in der vorgeschichtlichen Zeit bis zur Entfaltung der Staatswirtschaft*; L. Hess, *Die deutschen Frauenberufe des Mittelalters*; Susan Cahn, *Descent from Paradise*; and Roberta Hamilton, *The Liberation of Women*.

6. Bücher's thesis, or a variation of it, has been unhesitatingly adopted in survey literature: see, for example, Shulamith Shahar, *Die Frau im Mittelalter*, esp. p. 169; Roberta Hamilton, *The Liberation of Women*, esp. p. 32; Frances and Joseph Gies, *Women in the Middle Ages*, esp. pp. 174–75, 183. Also see the scattered comments in Peter Kriedte, Hans Medick, and Jürgen Schlumbohm, *Industrialisierung vor der Industrialisierung*, esp. p. 195.

Many historians primarily concerned with the period after about 1700 seem also agreed that late medieval women had a position in market production better than that available to their later counterparts. See, for example, Richard Vann, "Women in Preindustrial Capitalism," which (esp. p. 203) contrasts women's roles in early modern crafts with the roles they played in earlier days, and Louise Tilly and Joan Scott, *Women, Work and Family*, which, although not specifically concerned with changes in women's work from the Middle Ages to the early modern period, nevertheless describes the work as it existed around 1700 in terms similar to Vann's and draws similar contrasts with the earlier period: see in particular, pp. 49 and 51.

7. For the Ghent case, see Georges Espinas and Henri Pirenne, *Recueil des documents relatifs à l'histoire de l'industrie drapière en Flandre*, vol.2, doc. no. 478; for the Parisian evidence, see Madeleine Guilbert, *Les fonctions des femmes dans l'industrie*.

8. See chaps. 3–6 of this work for details.

9. Natalie Davis, "Women in the *arts méchaniques* in sixteenth-century Lyon"; Louise Tilly and Joan Scott, *Women, Work and Family;* Merry Wiesner Wood, "Paltry Peddlers or Essential Merchants? Women in the Distributive Trades in Early Modern Nuremberg"; E. William Monter, "Women in Calvinist Geneva (1550-1800)."

10. The quotations are from pp. 229 and 233 of Casey's article.

11. Shulamith Shahar offered similar cautionary notes in her *Die Frau im Mittelalter* (see, for example, pp. 174, 175 and 188). Jenneke Quast had another list of qualifications which, again, were not incorporated into her general assessment (see p. 35 of "Vrouwen in gilden"). Madeleine Guilbert's *Les fonctions des femmes dans l'industrie* (pp. 22–24) even more extensively described the constraints under which women labored, but she also treated them parenthetically: women in late medieval French cities had no supervisory or judicial power in their guilds; they did not practice all the traditionally feminine crafts; the rights of widows to their husbands' trades were often severely restricted; guilds were not particularly accessible to women.

12. Kurt Wesoly, "Der weibliche Bevölkerungsanteil," p. 102.

13. Ibid., p. 89.

14. Some historians have concluded from such contradictory evidence that whatever favor women found in late medieval market production was the product of an earlier age; the declines suffered by the urban working woman during the period, the argument continues, were not restricted to them but were part of a general diminution in the powers and prestige of women of all social ranks. For a general statement of this position, see Susan M. Stuard, Introduction, *Women in Medieval Society*. Also see David Herlihy ("Women in Medieval Society," "Land, Family and Women in Continental Europe, 701–1200," and "Life Expectancies for Women in Medieval Society"), who has proposed that women as a group suffered a decline of status in law, in religious thought and practice, and in the teachings of philosophers and that working women also lost access to certain jobs during the period. Among the related causes for the reversals were an unfavorable turn in the sex ratio so that women outnumbered men (the very situation Bücher thought to women's advantage in the workplace) and the economic dislocations of the period caused by depression and the emergence of capitalism. In chaps. 7 and 8, these possibilities are further discussed.

15. Bücher's argument is contained in *Die Frauenfrage*. Margret Wensky, *Die Stellung der Frau*, and N. W. Posthumus, *De Geschiedenis van de Leidsche Lakenindustrie*, vol. 1, suggested that women's physiques might have excluded them from certain tasks and by and large have accounted for the sexual division of labor that then prevailed. Several historians have noted that women's apparent exodus from privileged sectors of market production occurred during the so-called fifteenth-century depression, and some have pointed to instances when beleaguered journeymen whose own jobs were in jeopardy sought women's expulsion; for examples of the reasoning, see Herlihy, "Women in Medieval Society" and "Life Expectancies for Women in Medieval Society," and Susan Cahn, *Descent from Paradise*.

Chapter One

1. Here, as for the peasantry of late medieval and early modern Europe, the family and the household were approximately equivalent. Elsewhere, however, the two were rarely equivalent, if by "family" the nuclear reproductive unit is meant. For an analysis of the differences, see Rayna Rapp et al., "Examining Family History," and Olivia Harris, "Households as Natural Units." In the European past the term "family" was only one of several words or phrases used to designate kin, and often, in fact, did not designate either the nuclear reproductive unit or the co-resident group. J. L. Flandrin, *Families in Former Times*, pp. 4ff., and Michael Mitterauer and Reinhard Sieder, *The European Family*, pp. 5ff., sketch a history of the word "family" and of the other terms used in the European past to designate kin or residential groups.

2. Runtiger's household is described in Edith Ennen, *Frauen im Mittelalter*, pp. 185–86.

3. Laurel Thatcher Ulrich, *Goodwives*, describes a similar pattern in early modern America, emphasizing that women, more than men, regularly combined roles in analytically separate spheres, in the course of a single day moving into and out of the reproductive sphere, the sphere of market production, and the sphere of subsistence production. In this culture, "women's sphere" intersected all these spheres in about equal measure.

4. For a general discussion of the traditional sexual division of labor in Europe, see Edith Ennen, "Die Frau in der mittelalterlichen Stadtgesellschaft Mitteleuropas," and her *Frauen im Mittelalter*, where, p. 87, she comments, "Für den Tätigkeitsbereich der Frauen in ihrem Alltagsleben bestand seit altersher eine geschlechtsspezifische Arbeitsteilung. Sie wies den Frauen allgemein die Binnenwirtschaft zu," and, p. 104, where she describes a similar sexual division of labor in cities. Also see G. K. Schmelzeisen, *Die Rechtsstellung der Frau*, Susan Cahn, *Descent from Paradise*, and Miranda Chaytor, "Household and Kinship," who use a similar analysis. For an evocative description of the "inside" sphere reserved for

women in seventeenth-century New England, see Laurel Thatcher Ulrich, *Goodwives*, chap.1.

Christopher Middleton, "The Sexual Division of Labour in Feudal England"; Gay Gullickson, "The Sexual Division of Labor in Cottage Industry and Agriculture in the Pays de Caux"; Louise Tilly and Joan Scott, *Women, Work and Family*; and Julie A. Mattaei, *An Economic History of Women in America*, describe somewhat different patterns by which labor was divided between men and women in medieval and early modern Western society.

5. For examples, see J. Flandrin, *Families in Former Times*, pp. 116–17. Middleton, "The Sexual Division of Labour in Feudal England," also describes a different sexual division of labor under conditions of manorial production, while Rab Houston and Richard Smith, "A New Approach to Family History?" (p. 128), remark on how commonly the "traditional" division of labor in early modern England was violated.

6. The practice was so widespread that in most cities women acting in their husbands' absences automatically acquired the civil status always accorded adult men but only by exception accorded married women. For references, see n. 24 below.

7. Rose the Regrator was the wife of Avarice described by Langland in *Piers Plowman*; see Eileen Power, *Medieval Women*, and Rodney Hilton, "Lords, Burgesses and Hucksters," for descriptions of this kind of work. For references to sources describing the work of silk makers in Cologne, see chap. 6 below. Lübeck's women merchants are described in J. Hartwig, "Die Frauenfrage im mittelalterlichen Lübeck"; Douai's are described in chap. 7 below.

8. G. K. Schmelzeisen, *Die Rechtsstellung der Frau*, pp. 8ff., and Th. Vogelsang, *Die Frau als Herrscherin im hohen Mittelalter*, provide good evidence detailing the economic, social, and political functions of the medieval elite household. Robert Hajau, "The Position of Noblewomen in the Pays des Coutumes, 1100–1300," somewhat qualifies this view. Descriptions of women's roles in manorial life are more abundant for the late medieval and early modern period; see, for example, surveys such as Eileen Power, *Medieval Women*, and Shulamith Shahar, *Die Frau im Mittelalter*, and sources such as *The Paston Letters*, ed. Norman Davis.

9. See Edith Ennen, *Frauen im Mittelalter*, pp. 87–88, 104, for some descriptive details and for references to representative primary sources.

10. For useful surveys summarizing recent and past research on the history of the Western family, see Michael Anderson, *Approaches to the History of the Western Family, 1500–1914*; Michael Mitterauer and Reinhard Sieder, *The European Family: Patriarchy to Partnership from the Middle Ages to the Present*; and Peter Laslett, "Characteristics of the Western Family Considered Over Time." The recent review essays by Louise A. Tilly and Miriam Cohen, "Does the Family Have a History?" and W. R. Lee, "Past Legacies and Future Prospects: Recent Research on the History of the

Family in Germany," are also helpful. More specific references appear in notes below.

11. E. A. Wrigley, "Family Limitation in Pre-industrial England."

12. Etienne Gautier and Louis Henry, *La Population du Crulai*.

13. Peter Laslett, *Family life and Illicit Love*, pp. 26–28.

14. J. Hajnal, "European Marriage Patterns in Perspective," first identified this pattern as "European" and argued that it was restricted to northwest Europe after about 1400; he offered scattered evidence that the age of marriage in this area had earlier been lower. Scholars have very little evidence to work with from the Middle Ages, other than from a few ruling families, so it has not been possible to establish whether this pattern first emerged at the end of the Middle Ages, as Hajnal believed. Now, however, scholars are coming to believe that it did not and that the link between nuclear families, late marriage-ages, and household economies had been well established long before the sixteenth century when good data are first available: see Peter Laslett, *Family Life and Illicit Love*, pp. 47–48, and the work of Richard Smith to which he refers.

For more extensive evidence on the age at marriage in late medieval and early modern Europe and a discussion of the problems of interpretation, see Peter Laslett and Richard Wall, *Household and Family in Past Time*.

15. J. Hajnal, "European Marriage Patterns." Richard T. Vann, "Wills and the Family in an English Town: Banbury, 1550–1800," provides evidence that the death of parents was not the sole occasion for the marriage of heirs and their setting up new households. Nevertheless, most scholars are agreed that people dependent upon the household economy for subsistence or socioeconomic status married late. For a description of this pattern among Genoa's artisan population, see Diane Owen Hughes, "Urban Growth and Family Structure in Medieval Genoa."

16. The best collections of information on average household size in late medieval and early modern cities are contained in Peter Laslett and Richard Wall, *Household and Family in Past Time*. Also see the data Edith Ennen provides on household size in German and Swiss cities in *Frauen im Mittelalter*, pp. 142ff., and her comments on the meaning of the figures. Flandrin, *Families in Former Times*, argues that the usual household size in early modern France, whether in cities or in the countryside, was between four and six.

17. Daelemans, "Leiden 1581: een socio-demografisch onderzoek," provides detailed information about the relationships between the economic status of a family and the size of the household it constructed. Also see Flandrin, *Families in Former Times*, pp. 53–64. Households of the very rich, even in northern cities, were sometimes very large; one of Cologne's richest fourteenth-century merchant patricians maintained a household with twenty-four to thirty-six members, most of them servants not involved in the household economy as producers but working simply as personal servants: Edith Ennen, *Frauen im Mittelalter*, p. 167. Diane Owen Hughes,

"Urban Growth and Family Structure in Medieval Genoa," shows that artisanal couples (who married much later than their aristocratic neighbors) had fewer children than the rich.

18. When *The World We Have Lost* was first published in 1965, Laslett was criticized for having described this nuclear family as typical of late medieval and early modern Europe. In later work, Laslett has modified his claims for its universality. See, for example, Peter Laslett and Richard Wall, *Household and Family in Past Time*.

Historians of the rural economy have, however, found that most independent peasant households were nuclear. See, for example, Flandrin's comments on pp. 71-74 of *Families in Former Times* and the sources he cites; also see Ennen's summary of recent research on medieval Germany, esp. p. 89, of *Frauen im Mittelalter* (even then, she argues, "Kernfamilien dominieren . . . Grossfamilien sind selten").

19. The best summaries of property arrangements within late medieval urban families are contained in the volume *La Femme* published by the Société Jean Bodin (see in particular the articles by Thieme, Petot and Vandenbossche, and Gilisen). For Germany, see G. K. Schmelzeisen, *Die Rechtsstellung der Frau*, and Edith Ennen, *Frauen im Mittelalter*. For the Low Countries, see J. C. Overvoorde, *De ontwikkeling van den rechtstoestand der vrouw*. Jack Goody, E. P. Thompson, and Joan Thirsk, *Family and Inheritance*, which treats the peasantry, is also very valuable. Ennen's discussion of community property laws, their evolution and variation in Germany, and their significance for women is especially complete. See pp. 94. of her *Frauen im Mittelalter*. In "Die Frau in der mittelalterlichen Stadtgesellschaft Mitteleuropas," p. 11, Ennen pointed out that community property laws provided the basis for urban credit; only assets jointly belonging to a husband and wife rather than, eventually, their families of origin (whose members may not have been residents of the city) could provide adequate security to urban creditors. On this point, also see L. von Winterfeld's comments in "Die stadtrechtlichen Verflechtungen in Westfalen."

20. In "Urban Growth and Family Structure in Medieval Genoa," Diane Owen Hughes describes a similar system among Genoa's artisanal class, where the marriage bond defined the family, and contrasts it with patterns common among the urban aristocracy, where patrilineal ties were supreme.

21. For discussion of the practice, see Suzanne Wemple, *Women in Frankish Society*, Diane Owen Hughes, "From Brideprice to Dowry," G. K. Schmelzeisen, *Die Rechtsstellung der Frau*, and Edith Ennen, *Frauen im Mittelalter*.

22. Flandrin, *Families in Former Times*, and Schmelzeisen, *Die Reschtsstellung der Frau*, provide especially good discussion of the primacy of the household in medieval society. Public authorities in the Middle Ages did not easily recognize individuals as the objects of their regulation and, in order to carry out their functions, were often compelled to create

households where, technically, there were none. In southeastern France, for example, authorities artificially preserved households which no longer had a legal head because they had no other way of regulating tax payments, property transfers, and the like or of conducting elections; they regularly treated widows who maintained the family household as "male" heads of household and accepted oaths, contracts, and tax payments they executed and ballots they cast, although by customary law in the region only men over twenty-five could acquire independent civil status: Flandrin, *Families in Former Times*, pp. 116–17.

23. The standard histories of private law as it affected women all trace these developments: see n. 19 above for references. Ennen cites an example from sixteenth-century Lübeck, where a statute prohibited married women from entering any business transactions without a guardian "except those who have a trade and are accustomed to buying and selling": Edith Ennen, "Die Frau in der mittelalterlichen Stadtwirtschaft Mitteleuropas," p. 15, n.46. Instances like these have led some observers to conclude that, in violation of all tradition, married women in fact regularly acquired independent civil competence. So common did such exceptions seem to Shahar that she made them the rule: "Jede Kauffrau— ob ledig, verwitwet oder verheiratet—konnte vor Gericht selbständig klagen und verklagt werden": Shulamith Shahar, *Die Frau im Mittelalter*, p. 174.

In some areas, however, the convention of feme sole was not accepted. See, for example, chap. 2 below.

24. Traditionally, only single and widowed women could represent themselves in civil proceedings or enter contracts. Married women, who could incur debts to run the household, and defend themselves against criminal charges, otherwise remained legal wards of their husbands, who were described as their "seigneur et maître" (in Gilisen, Société de Jean Bodin, ed., *La Femme*) In almost all urbanized areas of late medieval northern Europe, exceptions to these restrictions rendered them increasingly less onerous. When the husband was absent—at war, on pilgrimage, or on business—wives usually assumed, without being formally deputized, the rights necessary to act for them. The rule that required married women to be represented by guardians in court appearances also seems to have been undermined; for example, while women commonly hired a guardian to represent them in court, they seem to have ignored him in the actual proceedings, when they often conducted their defense or attack themselves.

All observers seem agreed that urban law in cities of the North developed in ways especially favorable to women. In addition to the authorities cited in n. 19 above, see Flandrin, *Families in Former Times*, pp. 71–74. (But also see his discussion, pp. 125–27, concerning other aspects of legal change in France between the thirteenth and the eighteenth centuries and their effects on women.)

Women in Cologne, as we shall see, had extraordinary independence in some aspects of civil life. They could, for example, make wills and contracts, as well as give oaths. At the same time, however, their property was considered as part of the male-controlled household, and they could not easily separate their own assets from those of their husbands. See chap. 2 for a fuller discussion of these points.

25. The notarial records kept in southern Europe from the late Middle Ages on, provide extensive documentation about property relations in marriages, both of aristocrats and ordinary people. Although rich families in the North made marriage contracts and wrote wills, as did some ordinary people, the institutions for registering them systematically were less well-established, until the late sixteenth century, in the North than in the South and only a few document series of this kind have survived outside of England; in general, people in the North relied upon these written records less often than Southerners. Several studies have been made of testamentary practices in the South and their implications for women. See, for example, Susan Stuard, "Women in Charter and Statute Law: Medieval Ragusa/Dubrovnik"; Diane Owen Hughes, "From Brideprice to Dowry"; Stanley Chojnacki, "Dowries and Kinsmen in Early Renaissance Venice."

26. For discussion of the marriage patterns and property arrangements among Italian urban aristocrats and the functions the family came to assume, see Richard Goldthwaithe, "The Florentine Palace as Domestic Architecture"; idem, *Private Wealth in Renaissance Florence*; Diane Owen Hughes, "Urban Growth and Family Structure in Medieval Genoa"; Julius Kirshner and Anthony Molho, "The Dowry Fund and the Marriage Market in Early *Quattrocento* Florence." For statistics on marriage age, see the work of David Herlihy and Christiane Klapisch-Zuber, *Les Tocsans et leurs familles*; in an essay in *Household and Family in Past Time*, p. 272, Klapisch reported that the wives of Italian elites were on average fifteen years younger than their husbands. Also see R. B. Litchfield, "Demographic characteristics of Florentine patrician families," and Julius Kirshner and Anthony Molho, "The Dowry Rund and the Marriage Market in Early *Quattrocento* Florence."

27. The political, social, and economic functions of the Italian urban patriarchal clan have been the subject of many studies. For guides to representative literature, see Jacques Heers, *Family Clans in the Middle Ages*, David Herlihy and Christiane Klapisch-Zuber, *Les Tocsans et leurs familles*, and Diane Owen Hughes, "Urban Growth and Family Structure in Medieval Genoa."

28. Extensive studies of inheritance practices among Europe's peasantry have shown that in many areas daughters inherited land equally with sons. Even where sons were preferred, daughters received portions of the patrimony; sometimes they were dowered at marriage with moveables valued at an equal share of the total patrimony; sometimes they inherited

moveables and a smaller share of the family's land; almost always they enjoyed the rights of sons should there have been no male heirs. In many, perhaps most, peasant families of late medieval and early modern France, wives and husbands shared property and economic responsibilities as they did in the typical northern European city; accordingly, men and women married late, husbands and wives were one another's heirs, women shared production responsibilities beyond the purely domestic; sons and daughters both inherited productive property. Even among rich landed families, particularly on the Continent, daughters often inherited land, although sons were normally preferred. See Emmanuel Le Roy Ladurie, "Family structures and inheritance customs in sixteenth-century France."

29. David Herlihy and Christiane Klapisch-Zuber, *Les Tocsans et leurs familles.*

30. See Christiane Klapisch and Michel Demonet, "A uno pane e uno vino."

31. The northern European patriciate is described in greater detail in the following chapter, where the marriage patterns of Leiden's patriciate are discussed.

32. *Le Ménagier de Paris* has been translated into English and published by Eileen Power in *Medieval People*; for Margaret Paston, see *The Paston Letters*, ed. Norman Davis.

33. For a study of this phenomenon, see David Levine, *Family Formation in an Age of Nascent Capitalism.*

34. Papers by Nancy Adamson and Steve Rappaport delivered in Toronto, Canada, October 1984, at the conference of the Social Science History Association.

35. Roger A. P. Finlay, "Population and Fertility in London, 1580–1650".

36. The importance of men's roles as heads of household in perpetuating patriarchal relations in medieval society, even in families whose members shared economic tasks in an apparently egalitarian manner, is emphasized in Flandrin, *Families in Former Times*, pp. 123. Also see Olivia Harris, "Households as Natural Units," pp. 145ff., for a general discussion of how the "power and authority of the household head is derived not so much from the internal relations of the household, as from the use the state makes of households as legal, economic, administrative and political units" (from p. xv, Introduction, *Marriage and the Market*, the volume in which Harris's article appears).

There is no agreement on a definition of patriarchy or on whether that is the best label for whatever "it" is. In a general sense, the term is often used to describe a system of gender relations where males dominate and where males and male activities are valued both by men and women more than females or female activities. For a definition of male dominance, see Rosaldo, "The Use and Abuse of Anthropology," pp. 393–94. The difficulty with general definitions is that they tend to assign a transcultural meaning to what is a historically rooted phenomenon, obscuring the very problem facing scholars: how, why, and to what extent is male dominance achieved in a particular setting? By restricting the term "patriarchy" to situations in which male dominance is achieved through the father's or the senior male's power in the family, we obtain some needed specificity.

37. The notion that women were "incomplete men" was a legacy from Aristotle; for a general discussion of learned opinion about women during the late medieval period, see Ian Maclean, *The Renaissance Notion of Women*. For a review of the best known misogynistic literature, see Joan Kelly, "Early Feminist Theory and the *Querelle des Femmes*, 1400–1789," Carolyn Lougee, *Le Paradis des Femmes*, chap. 1; Katherine Rogers, *The Troublesome Helpmate*; Eileen Power, *Medieval Women*.

38. The data from Bücher are from pp. 16, 18–19. The anecdotal and uncritical quality of Bücher's work also characterizes even some of the most detailed surveys recently published. For example, Quast, in "Vrouwen in gilden in Den Bosch, Utrecht en Leiden," did not assess the meaning of the data she assembled about women's work; such important facts as whether high economic status was implied by guild membership in each city, how much and what kind of market production was organized into guilds, or whether the statutes investigated accurately reported the activities of guild workers were simply not discussed. Without reference points of this kind, however, her data cannot establish that women held "good" jobs.

39. Other historians have raised similar objections: see, for example, Christopher Middleton, "The Sexual Division of Labour in Feudal England," as well as Rab Houston and Richard Smith, "A New Approach to Family History?"

40. Erich Maschke, "Die Unterschichten der mittelalterlichen Städte Deutschlands," provides an account of the marked differences in the ways identical trades were regarded in medieval cities of Germany.

41. Martin Whyte's recent effort to define the elements of women's status and discover their connections, *The Status of Women in Pre-industrial Societies*, is a useful comment on the complexity of the notion of status. One of his central points is that many elements make up a definition of personal status, including such factors as sexual freedom, control over marriage decisions, power to decide about consumption in the household, authority in child rearing, rights to dowries, and participation in religion. His examination of 93 separate preindustrial cultures shows that women's status, according to any of his 52 measures, is not constant from place to place; moreover, status in one sphere does not predict status in another. But his failure to distinguish labor status in nonmarket societies from labor status in market societies weakens his case because only in the latter would we expect strong correlations between labor status and status in other spheres.

42. Basic readings on the meaning of labor status in market economies

and its relationship to status in other spheres include John Hicks, *A Theory of Economic History*; Karl Polanyi, *The Great Transformation*; idem, "Aristotle Discovers the Economy"; Karl Marx, "The Power of Money in Bourgeois Society," in "The Economic and Philosophic Manuscripts"; idem, "Commodities," "The Buying and Selling of Labor Power," "Co-operation," and "Division of Labor and Manufacture," in *Capital*, vol. 1; Ferdinand Toennies, *Gemeinschaft und Gesellschaft*.

CHAPTER TWO

1. Louise Tilly and Joan Scott, *Women, Work and Family*, p. 12.

2. While producers in this system (which in German is called the *Kaufsystem*) might often have been threatened with a loss of status as merchants sought to take control of their tools and materials, usually by extending credit to them during lean periods (resulting in the *Verlagssystem*), this outcome of the *Kaufsystem* was not inevitable.

For a discussion of these systems, see Peter Kriedte, Hans Medick, and Jürgen Schlumbohm, *Industrialisierung vor der Industrialisierung*, pp. 202–10 and 210–24. Schlumbohm, who wrote these sections, regards the *Kaufsystem* as a precursor of industrial capitalism (proto-industrial capitalism) which took root in the countryside where the peasant families (see in particular his comments on the nature of the family economy there) were particularly vulnerable to merchant capital. As this study will review, artisanal families in cities, while often involved in a similar system, were better protected, mostly by organizations which limited membership, controlled production technology, and amassed the bargaining power of individual artisans or by their location in cities which freed them from dependence on a single merchant. It is for reasons such as these that an urban *Kaufsystem* did not necessarily presage an urban *Verlagssystem*.

3. See in particular their comments in *Women, Work and Family*, p. 21: "The work of individuals was defined by their family positions. An observer of twentieth-century French peasants described their household economy in terms which also portray peasant and artisan families in the seventeenth and eighteenth centuries: 'The family and the enterprise coincide: the head of the family is at the same time the head of the enterprise. Indeed, he is the one because he is the other . . . he lives his professional and his family life as an indivisible entity. The members of his family are also his fellow workers.' But whether or not they actually worked together, family members worked in the economic interest of the family. In peasant and artisan households, and in proletarian families, the household allocated the labor of family members. In all cases, decisions were made in the interest of the group, not the individual. This is reflected in wills and marriage contracts which spelled out the obligations of siblings or elderly parents who were housed and fed on the family property, now owned by the oldest son."

4. See the discussion of the convention of feme sole in chap. 8.

5. Hans Medick made this point in *Industrialisierung vor der Industrialisierung*, pp. 90–119, esp. pp. 112–19. His analysis, elements of which he explicitly drew from Claude Meillassoux, *Femmes, greniers et capitaux*, and from the work of A. V. Chayanov on the peasant family economy (see *Industrialisierung vor der Industrialisierung*, nn. 14, p. 95, and 20, p. 97), focused on rural families whose labor for subsistence was, in early modern Europe, being replaced by labor for wages.

6. Thus, women married to peasants lost their roles as coproducers in the village household when capitalist-owned farms replaced peasant holdings and when industrial commodities brought in by merchants were substituted for village-made craft goods. City women whose husbands fell victims to capitalist competition lost their roles as partners, but the men to whom they were married took on wage work in the ateliers of others. At the same time, Clark argued, the increasing professionalism of the day drove women from certain tasks such as midwifery or teaching which were now reserved for specially educated and trained men, while wives of those merchants, of those artisan-merchants, and of those yeomen who joined the urban or rural bourgeoisie withdrew from economic production because their rich husbands now no longer needed their help.

7. Cahn did acknowledge that some women continued to work in market production under capitalism, but she claimed that the only women who stayed on were those who had to. Middle-class and newly rich women left the labor force, she argued, because they could afford to, because a new ethic made it inappropriate for them to work and because the jobs remaining open to women had been degraded. Just how they had been degraded or why some were chosen for this degradation, she did not explain.

8. Pp. 28–29.

9. M. Coulson, B. Magas, and H. Wainwright, "The Housewife and Her Labour under Capitalism—A Critique," p. 555.

10. The quotation is from Clark, p. 7. Gullickson, in "The Sexual Division of Labor in the Pays de Caux," similarly made no distinction between the family production unit and the family wage economy. Hamilton, *The Liberation of Women*, and Guilbert, *Les fonctions des femmes dans l'industrie*, seem to have equated the family economy with the household workshop. Cahn, *Descent from Paradise*, saw little difference between a family producing for the market and one producing for subsistence, except that in the latter women had important economic functions while in the former they did not, a notion implicit as well in the passages from Zaretsky's and Coulson's studies cited here.

11. While many of these scholars have acknowledged that women continued to work in capitalist market production and that they often performed tasks similar to those of precapitalist society, they have not been able to account for such evidence without giving up the notion that women lost a role in economic production under capitalism. Alice Clark, for

example, alternately ignored this evidence, as in illustrating her general thesis that women lost jobs under capitalism; treated the work as a residual and uninteresting hangover from precapitalist days; or described it as a special creation of capitalism. She drew on the latter strategy to explain why women dominated spinning in early modern England. Its low capital cost, its flexible production schedule, and the ease with which its skills could be mastered made it perfect for the women of the new poor who otherwise had no opportunity for wage work. What had been a fairly respectable and sometimes remunerative trade before capitalism became, after its entrenchment, a refuge for the otherwise unemployable.

12. For important literature on the transition and guides to current scholarship, see Maurice Dobb, *Studies in the Development of Capitalism;* Frederick Krantz and Paul M. Hohenberg, *Failed Transitions to Modern Industrial Society: Renaissance Italy and Seventeenth-Century Holland;* Rodney Hilton, *The Transition from Feudalism to Capitalism;* Robert Brenner, "Agrarian Class Structure and Economic Development in Pre-Industrial Europe," in *Past and Present,* no. 70, and the contributions to the symposium on this article in *Past and Present,* nos. 78, 79, 80 and 97; Peter Kriedte, Hans Medick, and Jürgen Schlumbohm, *Industrialisierung vor der Industrialisierung.*

For older but still valuable analyses, see the work of Henri Pirenne, especially *Histoire de Belgique,* "Villes, marchés et marchands," "Une crise industrielle au xvieme siècle: la draperie urbaine et la nouvelle draperie en Flandre," "Les périodes de l'histoire sociale du capitalisme," *Belgian Democracy;* and George H. Unwin, *Industrial Organization in the Sixteenth and Seventeenth Centuries.*

Marx's best-known comments are in "The German Ideology (Part I)"; *Capital,* 2, chap. 20; *Grundrisse,* p. 512. For a recent discussion of Marx's views on the transition, see R. S. Neale, *Class in English History,* chaps. 3 and 5.

13. Some of these notions were developed by Pirenne; see the references in n. 12 above, especially "Les périodes de l'histoire sociale du capitalisme." On the notion of class consciousness in late medieval and early modern cities, see Robert S. DuPlessis, "Class and Class Consciousness in Western European Cities, 1400-1650." For recent work on class formation in preindustrial Europe, see David Levine, *Family Formation in an Age of Nascent Capitalism;* Peter Kriedte, Hans Medick, and Jürgen Schlumbohm, *Industrialisierung vor der Industrialisierung*; and the articles by Catharina Lis and Hugo Soly ("Policing the Early Modern Proletariat"), Charles Tilly ("Demographic Origins of the European Proletariat"), and David Levine ("Production, Reproduction and the Proletarian Family in England, 1500–1851") in *Proletarianization and Family History,* ed. David Levine.

Marx's most pertinent comments on class formation are in "The German Ideology (Part I)," "The Eighteenth Brumaire of Louis Bonaparte," and *A Contribution to the Critique of Political Economy.* The literature on class theory is vast. General overviews or critiques of class theory include Bendix and Lipset, *Class, Status and Power;* T. Nichols, "Social Class: Official, Sociological and Marxist"; E. P. Thompson, *The Making of the English Working Class,* esp. pp. 9–13; idem, "The Peculiarities of the English"; and idem, *The Poverty of Theory.* Also see Philip Abrams, "History, Sociology, and Historical Sociology" and the references he cites.

14. This reasoning underlies Maurice Dobb's *Studies in the Development of Capitalism,* the work of Henri Pirenne and George Unwin (see n. 12 above) as well as more recent studies such as H. Amman, *Die wirtschaftliche Stellung der Reichsstadt Nürnberg im Spätmittelalter;* H. Aubin, "Formen und Verbreitung des Verlagswesens in der altnürnberger Wirtschaft"; J. Strieder, *Zur Genesis des modernen Kapitalismus;* C. R. Friedrichs, "Capitalism, Mobility and Class Formation in the Early Modern German City"; and F. Irsigler, *Die Wirtschaftliche Stellung der Stadt Köln im 14. und 15. Jahrhundert.*

For literature focusing on the proto-industrial period, see Peter Kriedte, Hans Medick and Jürgen Schlumbohm, *Industrialisierung vor der Industrialisierung,* esp. pp. 202–24.

15. These ideas are discussed in more detail in Robert S. DuPlessis and Martha C. Howell, "Reconsidering the Early Modern Urban Economy: The Cases of Leiden and Lille"; see esp. pp. 49–51 for a description of the main features of small commodity production.

16. Horst Jecht, "Studien zur gesellschaftlichen Struktur der mittelalterlichen Städte."

17. Contemporaries referred to the burghers as an order (*Stand*), but they did not in fact fit Weber's definition of an order: "a collection of individuals identified by assigned, acquired or usurped rights (privileges) and corresponding duties as well as by a similar life-style in accord with the norms of a common 'honor' and by means of a specific esteem" ["eine Gesamtheit von Personen die durch zugeteilte, erworbene oder usurpierte Rechte (Privilegien) und entsprechende Pflichten sowie gleichartige Lebensführung nach den Normen einer gemeinsamen 'Ehre' und durch eine spezifische Wertschätzung gekennzeichnet ist"], in Erich Maschke, "Die Schichtung der mittelalterlichen Stadtbevölkerung Deutschlands als Problem der Forschung," p. 369. Maschke's work on the social structure of late medieval cities appears in several other places as well; see "Die Unterschichten der mittelalterlichen Städte Deutschlands" and "Mittelschichten in deutschen Städten des Mittelalters." Also see the volume edited by Erich Maschke and Jürgen Sydow, *Städtische Mittelschichten;* Gerd Wunder, "Unterschichten der Reichsstadt Hall"; and Werner Schnyder, "Soziale Schichtung und Grundlagen der Vermögensbildung in den spätmittalterlichen Städten."

For Mousnier's analysis of the social structure of early modern Europe, see Roland Mousnier, "Le concept de la classe sociale et l'histoire"; idem,

Problèmes de stratification sociale: actes du colloque international; idem, *Les Hiérarchies sociale de 1450 à nos jours;* Roland Mousnier, J. P. Labatut, and Y. Durant, *Problèmes de stratification sociales: deux cahiers de la noblesse pour les États Généraux de 1649–1651*.

18. The term "patriciate" has been given no precise definition. The traditional description emphasized the constitutional aspects of the elite's rule; a patriciate was "eines engen, abgeschlossen Kreises alter Familien, die vor allem in den grossen traditionsreichen Städten wohnen und dort, wenn auch nicht politische Ämter, so doch viele Ehrenämter bekleiden." But more recently historians emphasized the social and economic status and roles of the elite, differentiating between a "true" or "strict" patriciate (*eigentlich* or *eng*) and a broad (*weit*) patriciate sometimes described simply as a merchant patriciate without inherited or legally conferred claims to rule. The first is a "sozial zunehmend zusammengeschlossene, manchmal auch rechtlich zusammengefasste, fest gefügte und durchaus einheitlich gewordene, je länger, je mehl ständisch hervorragende und damit zu immer grösserer Abschliessung gelangte erste Sozialgruppe der städtischen Bevölkerung." The second describes "eine sozial mobilere, in ihrer Zusammensetzung wesentlich labilere, nicht so hermetische abgeschlossene Sozialgruppe . . . , die nicht ausschliesslich am Stadtregiment beteiligt war und nicht den Anspruch hatte, ständig in einem der führenden Gremien der städtischen Verwaltung vertreten zu sein." Because there is no generally accepted definition of a patriciate and because historians have often referred to a patriciate without defining it, some historians have begun to avoid the term and to adopt, as Wolfgang Herborn did in his study of fourteenth- and fifteenth-century Cologne, the deliberately imprecise term "Führungsschicht" (very close to the English "ruling elite") on the grounds that only for a period of its history did this political elite approximate a "politically and economically homogeneous stratum [*Schicht*]"—the group for which Herborn reserves the term "patriciate." It is in this more precise sense that the term patriciate has been used in my study. Herborn, *Die politische Führungsschicht*, pp. 48ff., gives a fuller summary of the origins and various meanings of the term. All quotations in this note are from that work, pp. 52, 53, 56, and 202.

Deutsches Patriziat, ed. Hellmuth Rössler, contains a collection of essays on the urban patriciates of Germany and the Low Countries which explores the meaning of the term and the significance of this elite in urban history of the period.

19. ". . . eine Gesamtheit von Personen . . . deren Lebenschancen ökonomisch durch die Verfügung über wirtschaftliche Güter (Vermögen, Einkommen) oder der Fehlen derselben unter Bedingungen des Marktes, sowie durch die gleiche Interessenlage bestimmt sind und die ein Bewusstsein ihrer Lage haben." Maschke, "Die Schichtung der mittelalterlichen Stadtbevölkerung," p. 370.

20. ". . . eine sich horizontal durch ein soziales System hindurchzieh-

ende Anzahl von Personen, die auf grund [sic] der Wertung bestimmter Merkmale als ungefähr gleichwertig und im Vergleich zu anderen Gruppen als höher oder tiefer, darüber oder darunter stehend gelten." Ibid., p. 373.

21. See Appendix 3 for a discussion of the household size in Leiden.

22. Sterling Lamet, "Men in Government," Appendix C/II, supplies the data from which this conclusion can be drawn. In six mid-sixteenth century marriages for which the birth date of both bride and groom are known (if not the date of the marriage itself), men were on average two years older than the women. In two of the cases, the wives were older than their husbands. A group of seven men living during the same period were, on average, thirty-six when the first child of each was born, a figure which suggests a marriage age of about thirty-five; for six men whose marriage age is known, the average was thirty-two. One woman was thirty-six when her second child was born. (She is the only woman about whom we have such information.)

23. See Thieme in *La Femme* and J. C. Overvoorde, *De ontwikkeling van den rechtstoestand der vrouw.*

24. See preface and chap. 6.

CHAPTER THREE

1. Posthumus, *De Geschiedenis van de Leidsche Lakenindustrie,* 1: 286 and 360–61.

2. Jenneke Quast, "Vrouwen in gilden in den Bosch, Utrecht en Leiden," and "Vrouwenarbeid omstreeks 1500 in enkele nederlandse steden."

3. Leiden apparently began using English wool with the first settlement of the English wool Staple at Calais in 1346, but the city's drapers seem not to have established regular access to it until the 1380s; the earliest surviving treaty between Leiden and Staple merchants dates only from 1421.

4. The most useful measure of the spectacular rise of Leiden's industry in the fifteenth century is the strikerye, the excise tax collected by the city on wool cloth sealed for export (Appendix 1). In the third quarter of the fifteenth century, England was exporting the equivalent of about 8,000–10,000 sacks of wool annually; Leiden was buying between 70 and 100 percent of the pelts included in that total or between 10 and 20 percent of the total. English raw wool exports were at this time only about one-third of the mid-fourteenth-century volume, a decline which reflected the growing importance of wool cloth production in England. By mid-sixteenth century, they had again fallen by two-thirds.

Leiden's import figures for the period can be found in Posthumus, *De Geschiedenis van de Leidsche Lakenindustrie,* vol. 1, App. 5. England's export figures are from Carus-Wilson and Coleman, *England's Export Trade, 1275–1547.*

5. The history of Leiden's drapery and the textile industry which succeeded it is provided by N. W. Posthumus, *Geschiedenis*, 3 vols., and *Bronnen tot de Geschiedenis van de Leidsche Textielnijverheid*, 6 vols.

6. Examples of Hansa demands for consistency and quality include the following: Posthumus *Bronnen*, 1, doc. nos. 50, 80, 268, 270, 322 (7, 13–15), 326–30, 334(7), 357, 358, 365, 369, 370, and 418.

7. While many documents suggest that Leideners sometimes used Continental wools for sealed cloths, the production of such cloths seems to have been in violation of agreements with Staplers which from 1469 restricted Leiden's drapers to use of English wool bought at Calais. The treaty containing these restrictions was consistently renewed until the 1520s, when the unavailability of sufficient good-quality English wool forced Leiden to consider Spanish wool, but was again renewed in 1536 and remained in effect until 1548. (The collection of documents covering this exchange are reproduced by Posthumus in *Bronnen*, vols. 1 and 2: doc. nos. 400, 402, 435, 453, 454, 501, 596, 643, 867, 868, 869, 901, 999, and 1068; see also doc. nos. 903, 921 and 985 regarding Leiden's temporary decision during the 1520s to use Spanish wool.) In addition, since the Hansa would take only cloth made of English wools, it seems unlikely that Leiden could have had much of a market for cloth of Continental wools.

The records of taxed imported pelts show that *verkens* (Continental pelts) were regularly imported through 1484: Posthumus, *Geschiedenis*, 1, App. 5, pp. 421ff. Moreover, the *Keurboeken* of 1446–51, 1472–1541, and 1543–72 all contain elaborate provisions for inspecting and testing *verkens*. For further evidence of the continued use of *verkens*, see Posthumus, *Bronnen*, vols. 1 and 2: doc. nos. 58 (8, 9), 203, and 292. For evidence of local sales of good-quality cloth made of *verkens*, see ibid., vol. 2: doc. no. 747.

8. In the 1530s, English exports averaged over 100,000 cloths per year, as compared to 30,000 a century earlier: Carus-Wilson and Coleman, *England's Export Trade, 1275–1547*.

9. A 1531 appeal to the city government by a group of drapers testifies to their difficulties, not just with the wool tax, but with all city imposts on the production process. The document claimed that a draper making his 240-cloth quota would pay 93 gold guldens in excess taxes; that is, 93 guldens more than a draper in other (unspecified) cities would pay: Posthumus, *Bronnen*, 2: doc. no. 964.

10. The population that had once directly depended on the drapery—in 1500, at least one-half of the city—left or took up other economic activities. According to a 1581 population survey of Leiden, there were only twenty-one male wool-cloth weavers—masters, journeymen, and apprentices—among 2,053 adult men identified by trade in Leiden (about 86 percent of the adult male population). Figures are based on those reported in Posthumus, *Geschiedenis*, 2: pp. 20–30.

11. Population figures are from van Maanen, "De Vermogensopbouw van de Leidse bevolking"; also see Posthumus, *Geschiedenis*, 2.

12. For example, see Posthumus, *Bronnen*, 2, doc. no. 667: 1491 account of three men who bought wool for the city; ibid, 2, doc. no. 954: 1529 decision to set up a dyeworks; ibid, 1, doc. no. 166 (III-27): 1446–51 ordinance regarding government ownership of drying frames (*ramen*). The Rekeningen of 1451–55 also record the city's decision to build fifty-seven new drying frames and lease them to drapers who did not own their own. Posthumus, *Bronnen*, 1, doc. no. 254.

13. The best description of Leiden's governmental structure during this period remains Blok's *Geschiedenis eener Hollandsche stad*, 2 vols.

14. In 1449, Philip of Burgundy delegated the Vroedschap and the Gerecht to choose a Council of Forty to nominate aldermen, and this body quickly became identified with the Vroedschap, which until that time had generally counted about eighty members. Like its predecessor, this smaller Vroedschap drew its membership from former members of the Gerecht and retained, even strengthened, its legislative powers.

15. Lamet's "Men in Government" is the best source of information about the character of Leiden's late-sixteenth-century patriciate and a good guide to secondary material about the elite in seventeenth-century Leiden. For a general discussion of the social structure of cities in the Low Countries during the late Middle Ages, see Jan A. van Houtte, "Gesell-schaftliche Schichten in den Städten der Niederlande."

16. These measures, the only ones we have of the links between the drapery and the government, were derived from two lists of names, one of Gerecht members who served during those years and another of drapers active during the same period. The lists of drapers' names were compiled using various city accounts, administrative and judicial records. The list of Gerecht members was compiled using a file made over the last two centuries and stored in the library of Leiden's municipal archive: G.A.L. Bibliotheek, Leiden en omg., 1503f, "Namen van Vroedschappen, 1358–1794"; this compilation was supplemented by G. Ryckhuysen, *Wapenkaart, behelzende alle de Wapens en Naamen van de edele groot achtbaare Heeren Veertigen der Stad Leyden,* and Lamet, "Men in Government."

Earlier historians of medieval Leiden discussed the connections among wealth, cloth production, and political power in the city, but they did not have the data for measuring these connections. See Blok, *Geschiedenis eener Hollandsche Stad*, vols. 1 and 2; Posthumus, *Geschiedenis*, vol.1.

17. Men's family relations could be identified in most cases only if they had adopted a family name; in the fifteenth century this practice was still rare, even among the elite.

18. For the sources of these data, see n. 16 above.

19. Laws prohibiting simultaneous office-holding and draping were regularly issued and upheld; they are reproduced in Posthumus, *Bronnen*, 1: doc. nos. 244 and 440. The repeal is in ibid., 3: doc. no. 6 (65).

20. Data assembled from Lamet, "Men in Government."

21. Often, for example, some family members concentrated on government while others produced cloth; in the mid-sixteenth century this pattern was evident, for example, in the families Paedze, Van der Laen, Symonsz, von Boschuysen, and Stoop Kerstantsz Mast; see n. 16 above for the sources of these data.

22. This information, too, is owed to Lamet's "Men in Government." Their investments in the countryside did not, however, ally them with Holland's feudal class. They seem to have been investors in rural properties, nothing more. Des Marez reported a similar pattern of investment by the patriciate of late medieval Brussel; see G. des Marez, *L'organisation du travail à Bruxelles au xve siècle*, pp. 188–89; D. Nicholas's *Town and Countryside* reported a similar pattern for Ghent.

23. Blok, *Geschiedenis eener hollandsche stad*, vols. 1 and 2, still the best history of medieval and early modern Leiden, provides a detailed history of politics in Leiden.

24. For a description of Leiden's brotherhoods, see Overvoorde, "De ordonnanties van de Leidsche ambachtsbroederschappen."

25. Leiden's "craft" system was briefly described by Posthumus, *Geschiedenis*, 1, and contrasted with what he regarded as the quite different system of the seventeenth century in *Geschiedenis*, vol. 2. Van Dillen, "Gildewezen en publiekrechtelijke bedrijfsorganisatie," provides an analytical summary of the structure and functions of guilds in the northern Low Countries during the period; there he lists the attributes typical of guilds, and it is instructive to note how few of them belonged to Leiden's ambachten. In *Der Kaiser und die Zunftverfassung in den Reichsstädten bis zum Tode Karl IV*, Lentze provided a four-part categorization scheme for ranking artisanal organizations according to their corporative power. The ambachten of Leiden would have been included in the category of those with least corporative power.

26. At informal quarterly hearings; at *poortdingen* (hearings between citizens) arbitrated by aldermen; or at *gewone rechtsdagen buiten het poortding* (regular court days in addition to citizens' hearings) with the aldermen sitting as judges (in *Vierschaar*).

27. There were no independent courts treating economic matters, since the craftsmen and merchants of Leiden had no corporative power and there were no lower municipal courts in which such cases might first be heard. The government-appointed wardens of the cloth industry brought their charges directly to the aldermen, who recorded their punishments in these Corrextieboeken.

28. The principal publications of these documents, or studies which have them, are Posthumus, *Geschiedenis*, 2 vols; Posthumus, *Bronnen*, 6 vols.; de Blecourt and Wijs, *Kenningboek der stad Leiden, 1553/1570*; Blok, *Leidsche rechtsbronnen uit de middeleeuwen;* Meerkamp van Embden, *Stadsrekeningen van Leiden (1390–1434);* Hamaker, *De Middeneeuwsche*

keurboeken van de stad Leiden; and Osinga and Gelinck, *Kenningboek der stad Leiden, 1570–80.*

29. For the quotation, see G.A.L., Archief der Secretarie I, 384, Vroedscapboek E, fol. 13r–v.

30. For Hondschoote, see Coornaert, *Un centre d'autrefois;* for Ghent, see Prevenier, "Bevolkingscijfers en professionele strukturen der bevolking van Gent en Brugge"; for Ypres, see Pirenne, "Les dénombrements de la population d'Ypres," and van Werveke, "De Omvang van de Ieperse Lakenproductie in de veertiende eeuw." Also see W. Prevenier, "La démographie des villes du comté de Flandre aux xive et xve siècles".

31. Posthumus could provide occupational identifications for only about 37 percent of the householders taxed, and a close study of the tax roll shows that almost half of the identifications came from outside sources. The tax roll is included in the treasurer's account of 1497–98: G.A.L., Archief der Secretarie I, Rekeningen van de tresoriers, 1497–98, #578, fols. 27v–99. See Howell, "Women's Work in Urban Economies of Late Medieval Northwestern Europe," chap. 3, for a detailed analysis of the tax roll and a critique of Posthumus's analysis of it. According to Posthumus, *Geschiedenis,* 1, p. 373 (citing v. Mieris, *Handvesten,* p. 435), *dienstboden* (servants), *joncvrouwen* (female servants) and *knechts* (servants or journeymen) were excluded from the tax. (The prologue to the tax roll itself specifically makes no such exclusion: fol. 27.) But, in n. 1, p. 373, *Geschiedenis,* vol. 1, Posthumus speculated that by *knechts,* journeymen were not meant since the usual words for such workers were *cnapen* or *gesellen,* and thus he implied that trade journeymen were included on the roll. It is apparent, however, that journeymen were excluded, for only one person on the tax roll itself was named as a journeyman. It is also apparent that journeymen were referred to as *knechten.* For example, the *Keurboek* of 1472–1541, in a 1530 addition, spoke of dyers' *meesterknechts* and *ketelknechts:* Posthumus, *Bronnen,* 1: doc. no. 440 (VII-38). In all probability, journeymen were excluded from the tax because they were not heads of households but lodgers in the homes of others; see Posthumus, *Geschiedenis,* 1, chap. 5.

32. The *Draperiekeurboeken* are reproduced in Posthumus, *Bronnen,* 1 and 2: doc. nos. 132, 166, 263, 440, 1034, 1214. In his study of Ypres' production, "De Omvang van de Ieperse Lakenproductie in de veertiende eeuw," van Werveke similarly worked from production figures derived from cloth seal purchases to construct a possible labor force profile. Others have modified and extrapolated from his work: see Demey, "Proeve tot raming van de bevolking en de weefgetouwen te Ieper"; Nicholas, "The Population of 14th Century Ghent"; Prevenier, "Bevolkingscijfers en professionele strukturen der bevolking van Gent en Brugge." Postan, "Some Economic Evidence of the Declining Population in the Later Middle Ages," tried similar computations for England.

33. Finishers could not be included because there is no reliable way to

estimate their number. There were, however, very few finishers in Leiden until the sixteenth century, when Leiden began to finish foreign cloth, especially English cloth. The traditional drapery of Leiden was not highly finished and most of the necessary work could be done by fullers.

By the sixteenth century, some of the functions of the drapers had already been taken on by *uutreeders* who prepared the cloth for sale, underwrote the production of small-draper weavers, and managed sales for them. Many *uutreeders* had emerged from the group of large drapers, and of course their emergence signifies the end of the old way of doing business.

34. Posthumus's analysis was based on the tax roll of 1498 (in which he found names of 127 drapers: Posthumus, *Geschiedenis,* 1, p. 298), and on ordinances which limited the output of individual drapers. The relevant legislation is in Posthumus, *Bronnen,* 1 and 2: doc. nos. 263 (II-32, 40), 440 (III-39, 45, 46), 549, 623, 707. The limits imposed varied between 160 and 240 cloths a year but were sometimes dropped for short periods; the limitation upon the number of looms a draper could employ was more consistently in force and was always set at two.

35. Of some 200 large drapers named in government records dated between 1491 and 1500, for example, only a quarter were normally at Calais on their own account in a given year. The remainder, it seems, either had temporarily left off production, were producing cloth with wool brought in previous years, or were buying only small quantities through syndicates.

36. Legislation beginning in 1406 set the minimum investment required of a venturer to Calais; the minimum set in 1469 implied a production level of between sixty-six and one hundred cloths. The legislation is contained in Posthumus, *Bronnen,* 1 and 2: doc. nos. 58 (VII-4), 166 (II-3, 20), 263 (I-26), 410; in 1469 the minimum was 200 nobels which would have purchased between 10,000 and 15,000 pelts. For prices, see Posthumus, *Bronnen,* 1: no. 667: (accounts of merchants at Calais).

I have assumed that fifteen pelts were used per cloth. Posthumus estimated that twenty-one pelts were used per cloth: *Geschiedenis,* 1: p. 276; he derived his estimate from a complaint of 1531 by a group of drapers to the magistrate about the high taxes Leiden's drapers had to pay. The first article claims that a draper making his allotted output would pay 36 gold Karolusgulden in pelt taxes in a year: Posthumus, *Bronnen,* 2: no. 964. Posthumus referred (in a note to the text of this complaint) to the 190-cloth/year ceiling imposed in 1498. Although Posthumus did not account for his arithmetic, I assume that, using the tax of 20 st./100 pelts then in effect, he figured that a 36-Karolusgulden tax implied 3,600 pelts (1 Karolusgulden = 20 stuivers: van der Wee, *The Growth of the Antwerp Market,* 1, pp. 110–11; Posthumus, *Bronnen,* 2: nos. 984 and 987 [city accounts of 1533 and 1534 where actual conversion rates are indicated]). A draper producing 190 cloths from 3,600 pelts would have used nineteen pelts per cloth. Posthumus somehow figured twenty-one. It seems, however, that the limitation in effect in 1531 was not 190 cloths but 240: Posthumus, *Bronnen*, 2: no. 707. At 240 cloths per draper, the correct number is fifteen pelts/cloth.

It should be acknowledged that records upon which Posthumus heavily relied in his study—city accounts which listed the amount of wool imported, both by drapers working for their own account and by those buying for syndicates, and which are perhaps the most single important piece of evidence we have about the drapery in Leiden—suggest that drapers typically made more than 200 cloths a year. For example, in fiscal year 1497–98 sixteen of the twenty-six journeyers not part of a syndicate bought wool which could have been made into well over 200 cloths. A close examination of these records indicates, however, that most of these large purchases were for inventory, not for immediate production. See Howell, "Women's Work in Urban Economies of Late Medieval Northwestern Europe," chap. 3.

37. A good many of the drapers at Calais were not buying for themselves but for syndicates; in 1497–98, thirty of the sixty-eight ventures were organized as syndicates. If, as other evidence indicates, the average syndicate had at least twelve members, then the average member of each made *no more* than thirty-seven cloths. The figures on syndicate size are derived from Posthumus, *Bronnen*, 1: doc. no. 97; *Bronnen*, 2: no. 663; *Geschiedenis*, i, p. 225, n. 2. The regulations of 1446–51, which apportioned drying and stretching frames among drapers according to their production volume, set minimum levels and required, even, that any draper assigned part of a frame make at least thirty cloths, implying that some made fewer: Posthumus, *Bronnen*, 1: doc. no. 166 (III-27). Another ordinance of 1446 prohibited a draper from hiring a frame on an annual basis unless he made at least 40 cloths annually; Posthumus, *Bronnen*, i, no. 166 (III-2). Other records attest to the presence of a large number of small producers, some of them responsible only for ten to twenty cloths per year, who made up the remainder—close to half—of annual production. Judicial records contain even better evidence of the importance of small drapers. The Corrextieboeken for 1490 and 1491 (the only two years of the decade from 1490 to 1500 for which they survive) named sixty-five drapers, only twenty-seven of whom appear elsewhere as large drapers, and the Scoutsrekeningen surviving for eleven of the seventeen years from 1487 to 1501 name one hundred drapers, only forty-seven of them large producers; Corrextieboeken of 1490 and 1491; Posthumus, *Bronnen*, 2: doc. nos. 603, 638, 664, 713, 733, 739, 745, 750, 766, 776, 781. Both series contain records of fines for offenses of the same sort, such has having work done illegally outside the city, producing cloth *te groff* (too coarse), falsifying cloth quality, or disobeying import regulations. But, oddly, they contain few overlapping records. See Howell, "Women's Work," for a discussion of this oddity.

38. Some regulations speak of small drapers who did their own weaving; others describe drapers who simultaneously plied another trade like dyeing or carpentry; still others suggest that many worked only intermittently in supervising cloth production and interspersed draping with full-time weaving. On drapers as weavers, see Posthumus, *Bronnen*, 1: doc. no. 166 (V-19), *Keurboek* of 1446–51, where a 1448 ordinance forbade weavers who produced cloth to weave for wages; the ordinance was repeated in the *Keurboek* of 1453 but was explicitly annulled in 1458; ibid., doc. no. 888, *Aflezing* of 1520: forbade both drapers and weavers to produce white *lappen* (cloths of nonregulation size); ibid., doc. no. 1034 (IV-24), *Keurboek* of 1541, 1547 addition: forbade drapers with looms in their houses to weave or have woven any cloth of Continental wools; this provision was effectively repeated in the 1568 *Keurboek* (no. 1214 [III-17]) where the reference to drapers doing their own weaving was even more explicit.

The *Scoutsrekeningen* lend support to this claim, for many of the individuals fined as drapers in these records were also described as weavers. Between 1487 and 1503, 42 draper-weavers were named, that is, individuals who at one time paid a fine for improper weaving and at another time for improper draping or who were named as weavers but whom other sources also identify as drapers; on the same rolls, 80 individuals were named as drapers, and for them no evidence was found to indicate that they also wove, and 67 weavers were named for whom we have no evidence that they produced cloth.

Posthumus, in *Geschiedenis*, 1, p. 301, named eleven individuals whom he found to have acted as drapers at one time and as weavers at another time.

39. This estimate finds support in several calculations. One is based on the regulations which limited producers to an output of about 200 cloths per year and to the exclusive employment of two looms (or four weavers, since each loom required the work of two weavers). The implication of these figures is that a full-time weaver or journeyman on average produced fifty cloths per year; at this rate, 480 weavers could have made 24,000 cloths. If, however, 100 to 150 of the weavers worked part-time, devoting the remainder of their time to cloth production, the total number would have to rise, perhaps to 550 or 600. This is a minimum figure, for surely many ostensibly full-time weavers did not attain a 50-cloth per year production rate.

Wage legislation from 1545, when piece rates were first set for weavers, provides a way of testing this assumption. The given piece rate of 19 to 25 stuivers suggests that, assuming a minimum wage of 4 stuivers per day for each skilled weaver (equal to the minimum earned by fullers, somewhat above that of *vellendeelers* [semiskilled pelt sorters] and somewhat below that of bricklayers) and a 240-day working year, there would have to have been a full-time weaving force of 550. (The wage levels are from Blok, *Geschiedenis eener Hollandsche Stad,* 2: p. 286; Posthumus, *Geschiedenis,* 1: p.

330, n. 1; and Posthumus, *Bronnen*, 2: doc. no. 1034 (II-8.) The 240-day estimate is from van Werveke, "De Omvang van de Ieperse Lakenproductie in de veertiende eeuw"; it is a widely accepted estimate of the maximum medieval work year.)

A survey of Holland and Friesland taken by the Hapsburg government in 1514 provides another test. A weaver interviewed there claimed that in 1496 there were 350 looms operating full-time in Leiden, a figure that had steadily fallen to 200 in 1514: Fruin, ed., *Informatie up den staet faculteyt ende gelegenheyt van de steden ende dorpen van Hollant ende Vrieslant*, pp. 245–46. Although his figures may well be suspect, it is interesting that he considered 200 looms (which implies at least 400 weavers) a low figure.

At a minimum, then, alongside the 150–200 large drapers in late fifteenth-century Leiden, and the 200–300 small drapers and draper-weavers, there were some 450 weavers who themselves produced no cloth but who wove in the employ of others.

40. In 1447, when only about 10,000 cloths were produced, sixty-two masters and 280 journeymen took a loyalty oath after a strike. In the following five and a half years, 35 new fullers were registered in the *Poorterieboeken* and 448 new fullers' names were added to the list of signers of the loyalty oath. In the unlikely event that no fullers left Leiden during the period, the city had around 791 fullers by 1453, of whom at least 97 were masters: Posthumus, *Bronnen*, 1: doc. no. 190. A 1479 loyalty oath signed by master fullers after yet another walkout (when production may have doubled to 20,000) had 125 signers; in the next twenty-two months another twenty-one names were added, bringing the total to 146: ibid., doc. no. 529. At a 1:4 master:journeyman ratio, there were thus 730 fullers in Leiden in 1480.

We have additional sources for estimating the number of fullers as well. The 1541 complaint used for estimating weavers' production rates implies a work rate of five man-days/cloth and a total work force of 500: Posthumus, *Geschiedenis*, 1: p. 330, n. 1; a fourteenth-century regulation which demanded that a master fuller make no more than one cloth (of double length) in two days implies, assuming a three-man team, a fulling work force of 600: *Bronnen* 1: doc. no. 11-B (5). A 1497 addition to the 1472-1541 *Keurboek* complained that "once" 108 master fullers operated in Leiden but that in 1497, the time of the ordinance, only 70 were in business: ibid., 1: doc. no. 440 (VI-41). Assuming the average 1:4 ratio of masters to journeymen, there were "once" 540 fullers in Leiden but by 1497 (when production was near its peak) only 350. The survey of 1514 claimed that the master-fuller population of Leiden in 1500 was 150 (implying a 750 population; production in that year topped 23,000); Fruin *Informatie up den staet faculteyt ende gelegenheyt van de steden ende dorpen van Hollant ende Vrieslant*, p. 246. Both estimates are probably exaggerations, but it is interesting that both implied that a master-fuller population of 150 was high, a conclusion in accord with the estimate worked out here.

41. Using price regulations established for dyeing cloth in the sixteenth century, and estimating that each member of the "official" three-man work team earned a daily wage rate of 9.5 groten, we can calculate that there were at least 225 dyers in Leiden, 75 of them master dyers and 150 of them journeymen. This estimate excludes apprentices, wives, and casual help. Further, it assumes that only half of Leiden's sealed cloth was dyed and that Leiden's dyers did no work on foreign cloth. While the first assumption has a basis in fact, the second is surely unrealistic since there is convincing evidence that, while they did not dye foreign cloth in the fifteenth century, Leideners often dyed English cloth in the sixteenth century as well as voerlaken. Posthumus, *Bronnen*, 1: no. 12 (186): 1396 *Keur* which prohibits dyeing any cloth not made of English wool; Posthumus, *Bronnen*, 1: no. 74 (68): 1435 *Keur* which forbids dyeing cloth in Leiden (except cheap cloth) which does not bear the city's seal; Posthumus, *Bronnen*, 1: nos. 166 (VII-1), 263 (VI-1), 440 (VII-1): later Keurboeken which repeat the 1435 prohibition; Corrextieboek 1466, fol. 114v and 113: fines of drapers who dyed foreign cloths.

See, for the sixteenth-century changes, documents such as Posthumus, *Bronnen*, 2: doc. nos. 1034 (VI-23), 1177, 1184, 1186, 1187: Keurboeken of 1541, its 1544 addition, Vroedscap Resolutie of 1562 and 1563, two *Aflezingen* of 1563 which clearly indicate that Leiden's drapers were actively seeking foreign, particularly English, dyeing business and were dyeing voerlakens. Also, a 1562 addition to the Keurboeken of 1472 exemplifies the increasingly rigid dyeing standards associated with dyeing: Posthumus, *Bronnen*, 1: doc. no. 440 (VII-37).

42. See Appendix 3 for the population estimate.

43. For Pirenne's ideas, see his *Medieval Cities*; idem, *Histoire de Belgique*; "Villes, marchés et marchands au moyen âge"; "Une crise industrielle au xvie siècle: la draperie urbaine en Flandre"; "Les périodes de l'histoire sociale du capitalisme"; *Belgian Democracy*.

44. Posthumus acknowledged that the city government preserved some economic independence for the small entrepreneur who survived not only as an artisan but also as a draper. For example, on p. 275, *Geschiedenis*, vol. 1, he remarked that, given the production limits on drapers of 160–240 cloths per year, it is "difficult to speak of large entrepreneurial undertakings." Rather, "small production was the reality." He noted that many drapers produced far less than the maximum number of cloths. Elsewhere (p. 121), he noted the measures taken to restrict capital accumulation such as production maximums, limitations on the number of looms, etc.

In examining the drapers as a group, however, he emphasized the large entrepreneurs, for him the group that determined the character of Leiden's industry and the social mode of production in the city. Accordingly, the form of production typical of medieval industry where "craft production [was] the single existing mode of production . . . and the craftsman the almost only existing type of producer" had been superseded by the second half of the fourteenth century by "domestic industry, which had given craft production an entirely different character": ibid., p. 269. In this system, production was controlled by a merchant-entrepreneur, the draper, who made all other workers—combers, spinners, weavers, fullers, dyers—dependent on him and whose primary objective was sales growth: "The character of the cloth industry bore totally the imprint of the domestic industrial system, in which the motivating force of the production system was not providing for the needs of a smaller or greater circle of individuals but the accumulation of profit through sales volume": ibid, p. 271. This argument was repeated in the introduction to the later *Bronnen*, pp. xxx, xvi-xvii: He remarked there that Leiden's industry, as early as the late fourteenth century, demonstrated a pattern entirely different from the usual medieval one where "economically independent masters, if necessary supported by a few journeymen, worked with raw materials they had bought themselves and sold [their products] at a fixed price to their buyers." Instead, "here the industry had received a capitalist character, according to which the main object was the making of profit for the entrepreneur-draper; an entirely new production system, the domestic industrial system, appears to have arisen."

45. Posthumus discussed the issue in general in *Bronnen*, 1: pp. xvii–xviii, and gave a general history of the fullers' status in Leiden in *Geschiedenis*, 1: chap. 5. Fullers' strikes in 1372, 1391, and 1393 are mentioned in the sources, and there is good evidence, most of it reproduced in the *Bronnen*, of fifteenth- and sixteenth-century actions; see, too, Posthumus, *Geschiedenis*, 1: p. 272.

46. Posthumus, *Geschiedenis*, 1: pp. 278, 333, 305 and 352.

47. For evidence of the kind of wage exploitation to which fullers were subject—and which the government restricted—see Posthumus, *Bronnen*, 1: doc. nos. 11, 28, 74, 132, 263, and 440. For limits on the size of fulling shops, also see ibid, doc. no. 74 (VII-118), 132 (V-11[1]), 166 (VI-10), 263 (V-13), and ibid, 2: doc. no. 1214 (V-8).

48. For examples of restrictions on spinning in the countryside or outside the Rijnland, see ibid., 1: doc. nos. 132 (IV-27), 411, 419 (7 and 21), 420, 424, and 425.

49. See, for example, Corrextieboek 1475–76: fols. 254v(1), 254v(2); 254v(3); 256(2); 257v(2); 267(2); 279v(1); 274(3); 274(4) (all fines for too many looms).

There are many cases of falsifying drapers' marks (*nopteyken*) in an attempt to avoid production limits: for example, Corrextieboek 1475: fols. 261v(2), and 262 where a weaver was fined for counterfeiting one draper's mark at another's request. Another example is found in the Corrextieboek 1491, fol. 39v(1), of wardens using the wool purchases recorded in the Rekeningen to check whether or not drapers were violating production limits. Similar fines for overproduction occur in Corrextieboek 1491, fol. 33v(2), Corrextieboek 1510, fol. 36v(2), Corrextieboek 1541, fol. 188.

Posthumus, *Bronnen*, 2: doc. no. 552, lists a similar 1482 fine, and no. 745 lists a 1497 fine by the Schout for the same offense.

Posthumus, *Bronnen*, 2: doc. nos. 574 and 582, lists fines of merchants at Calais who bought too much wool (above the amount registered). Corrextieboek 1491, fol. 43(1 and 2), contains similar cases.

50. Posthumus, *Bronnen*, 1 and 2:, doc. nos. 74 (VII-24), 120, 132 (II-1, 12, 14 15), 151, 166 (II-26), 263 (I-9, 25, 26, and 30), 397, 401, 402, 440 (II-9 and 30), 1034 (II-6), and 1214 (III-4 and 6). (Except for short periods or under special circumstances, as indicated by some of these documents, drapers were not permitted to deal in wool); ibid., doc. nos. 499, and 954; Vroedscapboek, na F, fols. 14v , 21.

51. Kenningboek 1465, fols. 104, 106v, 107v, 124v, 129.

52. Irsigler, "Soziale Wandlungen in der Kölner Kaufmannschaft."

53. Espinas, *Origines du capitalisme*, 2: pp. 130–31, n. 1.

54. Zorn, *Augsburg*, p. 155; also see Blendinger, "Versuch einer Bestimmung der Mittelschicht in der Reichsstadt Augsburg."

55. de Meyer, in Blockmans' *Studien betreffende de sociale strukturen te Brugge, Kortrijk en Gent*, 1: p. 174.

56. Soly, *Urbanisme en kapitalisme te Antwerpen*.

57. The Augsburg data is from Zorn, *Augsburg*, pp. 184–85. Even during the sixteenth century, when huge fortunes were accumulated in other cities, Leideners remained modestly wealthy. See the discussion in Posthumus, *Geschiedenis*, 1: pp. 390–97, on the apparent declines in the fortunes of the rich and in the economy in the early sixteenth century. Also see his comments about the scarcity of large fortunes even at the very end of the century when industry was quickly reviving and immigration was high: Posthumus, *Geschiedenis*, 2: p. 178.

Two surviving marriage contracts from the period emphasize the modest size of the fortunes owned by Leiden's sixteenth-century elite. One contract which involved the children of two prominent families settled assets yielding just 36 Karolusgulden annually and the other, which involved equally important citizens, listed total properties of just 2,500 Karolusgulden. In 1550, when Jacob Willemsz van der Burch (later a member of the Vroedschap and in 1584 listed in a forced loan as one of Leiden's richest residents) married, he brought to the marriage property valued at about 2,200 Karolusguldens which produced an income of about 60 Karolusguldens; his bride, a member of the important van der Laen family, brought property yielding 36 Karolusguldens. The couple undoubtedly had other sources of income but it is likely that their marriage settlement would have treated only the significant portion of their property: Lamet, "Men in Government," pp. 209–10, and Posthumus, *Geschiedenis*, 2, p. 175. In another important marriage of 1556, between Allert Willemsz van Sassenhem (he would later serve on the Vroedschap) and Janetgen Ghysbrechtsdr., the groom brought property worth 1000

Karolusgulden, and his bride 1,500 Karolusgulden: Lamet, "Men in Government," pp. 210–11.

58. For Jecht's analysis, see Part 1 above.

59. Bothe, *Beiträge zur Wirtschafts- und Sozialgeschichte der Reichsstadt Frankfurt,* and "Die Entwicklung der direkten Besteurung."

60. Scribner, "Civic Unity and the Reformation in Erfurt."

61. Eitel, *Die oberschwäbische Reichsstädte.*

62. Jecht, "Studien zur gesellschaftlichen Struktur"; see chap. 2 above for a fuller discussion of Jecht's argument.

63. In 1623 only three of fifty-four taxpayers with taxable property over 20,000 guldens were in textiles (out of 607 identified by occupation on the tax roll of 1,829 individuals); in 1644 none of the twenty-eight with property over 20,000 guldens fit the description (out of 504 identified by occupation or on a tax roll of 1,684 individuals); in 1675 just eight of sixty-four with property over 20,000 guldens were in textiles (out of 783 identified in a tax roll of 2,071 individuals): Posthumus, *Geschiedenis,* 2, pp. 968–71. Posthumus would have tended to have identified taxpayers in this industry in particular since he collected a lot of information about such people from other sources.

64. Ibid., p. 102.

65. Ibid., pp. 138–39.

66. Ibid., pp. 532–33.

67. Ibid., 3: pp. 532–33.

68. Ibid., p. 537.

69. The Gerecht refused to stop them despite a petition by irate small drapers: ibid., p. 114.

70. Ibid., pp. 138–39.

71. Ibid., pp. 575. From 1638 to 1650, Leiden imported about 5,000 youngsters to work as apprentices (p. 601).

72. These points are more fully developed in DuPlessis and Howell, "Reconsidering the Early Modern Urban Economy."

Chapter Four

1. The 1446 Keurboek (Posthumus, *Bronnen,* 2: doc. no. 166) is introduced by the phrase, "These are the rules of the [female] comber and spinner." This section is a virtual repeat of previous Keurboeken and is almost identical to similar sections in subsequent books. An early reference to women working in other low-skilled textile trades appears in the 1363 Keurboek: "First, if any draper hired any maid for day wages to *ofsteken* [separate wool from pelts], to sort wool or to trim cloths who did not show up as promised but took another job, the maid is fined 2 shillings." Later ordinances similarly referred to women doing this kind of work.

2. See Howell, "Women's Work in Urban Economies of Northwestern Europe," chap. 4.

3. The Correxties listed by Posthumus in the *Bronnen,* vols. 1 and 2,

named a total of 106 individuals, one of whom was a woman; the Scoutsrekeningen named 187 individuals, one of whom was female.

4. Posthumus, *Bronnen*, 1: doc. no. 190.

5. Ibid., doc. no. 529: 21 more masters registered in 1479 and 1480, but all were men.

6. See Howell, "Women's Work in Urban Economies of Northwestern Europe," chap. 4.

7. Posthumus, *Bronnen*, 1: doc. no. 508 (C-22). The December 1478 agreement settling the dispute kept this provision: ibid., doc. no. 525(15).

8. A regulation of 1396 referred to women who illegally produced cloth: "Likewise, so must no one working for day wages, whether *offsteecsters* [(female) separators of wool from pelts], dyers' journeymen or [female] combers produce cloth. . . ." But women cloth producers were normally described as though entirely legitimate. For the regulation, see Posthumus, *Bronnen*, 1: doc. no. 12 (128-5). The essence of the prohibition is repeated in Keurboeken of 1406 and 1415: ibid., 1: doc. nos. 58 (vii-59) and 74 (vii-51).

9. Ibid., doc. no. 67: a bot was equal to about 1.2 English nobels, enough for about 80 percent of a cloth, assuming the wool was of good Calais quality.

10. A half-cloth was the standard Leiden product; it measured about 20 ells. For the reference, see ibid., 1: doc. no. 79.

11. Ibid., 1: doc. no. 97.

12. Ibid., 1: doc. no. 135.

13. Ibid., 1: doc. no. 463.

14. Ibid., 1: doc. no. 476.

15. Ibid., 2: doc. no. 663.

16. Ibid., 2: doc. no. 874.

17. Ibid., 2: doc. no. 1118.

18. Although the three computations use similar data, they are not directly comparable. The first is a complete analysis of Correxties issued during the sampled years. The second was constructed from Correxties Posthumus published, and we cannot assume that his selection was representative of the actual array of cases. A test (made by comparing the selections Posthumus made with all Correxties during the years I sampled) suggests, however, that his selection did not overemphasize one kind of fine with respect to another or favor one sex over another. As discussed in Howell, "Women's Work," chap. 3, the Schout's fines were imposed according to a somewhat different system and were incomplete for many of the years listed.

The sources for these computations were the Corrextieboeken and Posthumus, *Bronnen*, vols. 1 and 2. The cases were separated into three categories according to the general character of the offense. The first was for a simple violation of quality-control regulations such as use of inferior dyes, poor finishing work, or crude weaving. The fiscal 1475 *Corrextieboek* provides a typical example: fol. 261v (1): "Thus Phillips Adrianensz had a second wool [cloth] on the frame that was judged to have been woven with too coarse yarns . . . which is contrary to the regulations and as a result of which the aforesaid Phillips shall have 1,000 stones added to the city walls at 24 *placken* per thousand. . . ." The second was for deliberate falsification of shoddy workmanship, attempts to counterfeit inspection seals, etc. The fiscal 1510 Corrextieboek provides examples typical of these offenses: fol. 29 (2): "Thus Clais Gherytsz van Bockam had a cloth on the frame with an imperfection covered with chalk; this is a case of deception in the drapery which the magistrate will tolerate neither from him nor anyone else. . . ."; fol. 35v (1): "Thus Jan Veen had a green [cloth] on the frame which the wardens marked with a cross; the cross was stricken out and the wardens did not recognize it . . . ." The third category (omitted here) treated violations in purchasing or importing wool, an activity in which women were not involved.

19. For example, thirty-five black cloths so identified (Leiden's best dyed cloth) were mentioned in 1475–76; six, or 17 percent, were owned by women.

20. Of twenty-five fines assessed in 1475 and 1476 for violations of manufacturing ordinances, four were assessed of women, and the fines women paid were exactly like those paid for similar violations by men. Of ten assessed in these years for deliberate falsification of poor workmanship, six were of women; in two of these cases, the women's fines were higher than the men's (one was for using another draper's sign, an apparent attempt to exceed production requirements, the other for using stolen wool, both of which were very serious offenses).

21. Posthumus, *Bronnen*, 1: doc. nos. 14, 16, 18, 20–22, 24–26, 35–39, 41, 42, 44, 46, 48, 49, 52, 55–57, 59, 60, 62, 63, 66, 68, 70, 75, 77, 83–85, 89, 90, 94–96. Averages were compiled using only those purchases for which complete information was available: the sex and name of the merchant (except in one case where the seller was identified as *een wyve uut Leyden*), the amount purchased (where a whole cloth was assumed to be 40 ells long and a half cloth 20 ells long), and the price (converted into Flemish groten at exchange rates implied by the accounts themselves or derived from other contemporary accounts).

22. There is no way to compile a complete list of drapers who operated at this time. A record from 1424 contained the names of forty-two individuals who had invested in a failed Calais venture (Posthumus, *Bronnen*, 1: no. 97), but none of the names was the same as any of the fifty-two retailers' names.

For the ordinances regulating late fourteenth- and early fifteenth-century cloth sales, see ibid., 1: doc. nos. 11 (A), 12 (128 [15, 19, 20]), and 58 (VII-64 and 70).

23. Ibid., 2: doc. no. 508 (C-22 and 25); also see doc. nos. 509 (22–23 and 25) and 525 (15 and 16).

24. Ibid., 2: doc. no. 713; for similar cases see ibid., doc. nos. 745 and 776.

Years linked by slashes, as in 1493/94, indicate fiscal years beginning in the first calendar year listed and ending in the second.

25. Ibid., doc. no. 810.

26. Ibid., 2: doc. no. 1034 (VI-7 and 25).

27. See, for example, ibid., 1: doc. no. 440 (VII-37).

28. Ibid., 2: doc. nos. 561, 818, and 1013: In the sampled Corrextieboeken, there were ten cases that dealt with dyers; no women were mentioned. In all the Schout's fines listed for the years available from 1487 through 1503, only four dyers' names appeared, all male.

29. Ibid., 2: doc. no. 919.

30. One very short set of mid-fourteenth century regulations of this industry also exists (ibid., 2: no. 1182, n. 2). It seems that the city government had once regulated the linen industry but later ignored it as the wool cloth industry expanded. Only at the demise of the wool cloth industry, when Leiden's drapers, workers, and government turned to the linen cloth industry as a way to create jobs and revenues, did linens again become a governmental concern.

31. Ibid., 2: doc. no. 1182.

32. Ibid.

33. The founding legislation, unlike that giving official status to the already existing brotherhood of the linen weavers, required that the producer-workers set up a brotherhood so they could participate in official city pageants. The legislation is printed in ibid., 2: doc. nos. 1179 and 1215; for earlier ruminations about the advisability of legalizing the trade, see ibid., doc. nos. 1143 and 1173.

34. Ibid., 2: doc. nos. 1222 and 1184.

35. 500 roeden = ca. 1 mile; the business descriptions in the records indicate that these were not "cottage industries" controlled by in-town merchant capitalists but were small, independent, and probably somewhat marginal household-based industries very much like many cloth-producing businesses within the city: Posthumus, "Een zestiendeeuwsche Enqueste naar de Buitenneringen rondom de Stad Leiden."

36. Excluding textiles, the numbers are 76 percent, 26 percent, and 34 percent for women and 38 percent, 32 percent, and 12 percent for men.

37. The economic status of twenty-four of the forty-seven women in the table with identified trades was unknown.

38. According to the population figures worked out in Appendix 3, this would mean that about two-thirds of widowed and single females who headed households worked in market production.

39. Since tables 1 and 3 only by chance included servants among the individuals named, it must be taken as strong evidence of the importance of this group in Leiden that even a few women servants were named. The 1498 tax roll normally excluded servants from its list. The Corrextieboe-

ken normally mentioned servants only in the course of the case description, usually because the servant delivered or collected a cloth for his/her draper-employer or, in some cases, because the servant failed to inform his/her employer of orders delivered by the government to the employer; when the employer failed to carry out the order, the employer was fined. Few of the cases, as might be expected, involved fines of the servants themselves. *All* the servants mentioned in the Corrextieboeken were female.

40. See Appendix 3, where an estimate of 1,960 servants in 1498 Leiden was derived, 80 percent of them women. In Zurich in 1357, 338 of 1,055 households had servants or apprentices living in, 74 percent of them female: Nabholz and Hegi, *Die Steurbücher von Stadt und Landschaft Zürich.* Also see Laslett, *Households and Family in Past Time,* for an extensive discussion of servants in the "northern European family."

41. These activities are amply documented by Posthumus, *Geschiedenis,* vol. 1.

42. Others have previously suggested that there was such an inverse correlation; in particular, see G. K. Schmelzeisen, *Die Rechtsstellung der Frau in der deutschen Stadtwirtschaft.* More recent commentators include Quast, "Vrouwen in gilden," p. 27, Guilbert, *Les fonctions des femmes dans l'industrie,* pp. 21–31, and Power, *Medieval Women,* pp. 62–65. But none of these writers has traced the links in specific cases and none has shown how the family and its female members lost labor status as work entered politics.

The idea that women are denied a place in economic production when it is linked to politics has been developed, in a more general formulation, by theoreticians who distinguish between private and public realms and argue that women are by definition excluded from the public, where politics resides. This argument is briefly summarized in Jaquette, "Women and Modernization Theory."

Others have quite rightly pointed out that the content in neither sphere is constant and that no single human activity—including political activity—belongs exclusively to a private or a public realm. Joan Kelly in "The Doubled Vision of Feminist Theory: A Postscript to the Woman and Power Conference," for example, argues in part that *"woman's place is not a separate sphere or domain of existence but a position within social existence generally.* It is a subordinate position, and it supports our social institutions at the same time that it serves and services men. Women's place is to do women's work—at home and in the labor force. And it is to experience sex hierarchy—in work relations and in personal ones, in our public and our private lives. Hence our analyses, regardless of the tradition they originate in, increasingly treat the family in relation to society; treat sexual and reproductive experience in terms of political economy; and treat productive relations of class in connection with sex hierarchy" (p. 221; emphasis in original). Zillah Eisenstein, in *The Radical Future of Liberal Feminism,* makes a similar argument: "Nevertheless there is no constant meaning to the terms *public and private* other than their sexual identification, and even this identity takes on particular meaning within the specific culture and society one is examining" (p. 26).

To place women in a private sphere composed of specific activities and to place men in a public sphere composed of different activities thus seems unjustifiable. But it seems entirely reasonable to treat formal participation in government as a public activity, perhaps the quintessential public activity, and foolish to disregard the abundant evidence we have which argues that women were usually absent from this sort of public activity in western Europe.

43. Posthumus, *Bronnen*, 2: doc. no. 1118.

44. Ibid., 2: doc. nos. 810, 1119, and 1189.

45. Ibid., 2: doc. no. 1212.

46. Article 10, ibid., 2: doc. no. 1179, required that "no [female] carders, [female] combers, weavers, [female] spinners of wool yarn or other workers, men or women, or children, for whom the parents are held responsible, who work in the aforesaid textile production, may work in the drapery." None of the other twenty-three articles, or any of the ten additions dated 1563, mentioned women.

47. For examples both of the rules and their enforcement dating from 1363/84 to 1568/85 see Posthumus, *Bronnen*, 1 and 2: doc. nos. 12, 103, 263, 440, 525, 603, 763, 773, 1036–39, and 1214.

48. Ibid., 1: doc. no. 263 (V-29).

49. Ibid., doc. no. 508 (C-25). Also see, however, the drapers' reply, doc. no. 509 (A-26), in which it is argued that "it has always been the custom here in Leiden that the fullers and their wives, their domestic servants and helpers take cloth from the frames."

50. Some children were certainly at home and probably performed domestic chores; but it is unlikely that many over the age of fifteen or sixteen had remained, because they would certainly have been helping in the family business and, thus, would have been mentioned in the survey.

CHAPTER FIVE

1. Behagel, "Die gewerbliche Stellung der Frau im mittelalterlichen Köln," published in 1910.

2. Kuske published extensively on trade in late medieval Cologne; the publications of most direct use in this study are "Die Frau im mittelalterlichen Wirtschaftsleben" and the four-volume document collection, *Quellen zur Geschichte des Kölner Handels und Verkehrs im Mittelalter;* for a more detailed listing, see the bibliography in Irsigler, *Die wirtschaftliche Stellung der Stadt Köln;* Wachendorf, *Die wirtschaftliche Stellung der Frau in den deutschen Städten des späteren Mittelalters.*

3. Both quotations are from Wensky, "Die Stellung der Frau in Familie,

Haushalt und Wirtschaftsbetrieb im spätmittelalterlichen-frühneuzeitlichen Köln," pp. 9 and 22.

4. Wensky, *Die Stellung der Frau*, pp. 318–19: "Im spätmittelalterlichen Köln gab es kaum Wirtschaftszweige, in denen Frauen nicht zu finden waren. Nur einige wenige Zünfte (Schneider, Harnischmacher, Tuchscherer) legten Frauen Arbeitsbeschränkungen auf, und auch das nur zeit-bzw teilweise. . . . Die grosse Selbständigkeit, die Kölner Frauen in Handel und Gewerbe genossen, ist in keiner anderen deutschen Stadt des Spätmittelalters erreicht worden. . . . Die Verwaltung und Struktur der Frauenzünfte ergibt Unterschiede zu den ubrigen Zünften nur insofern, dass diese Gewerbe fast ausschliesslich Frauen zu ihren Mitgliedern zählten."

5. The data in support of this reasoning are entirely contained in *Die Stellung der Frau*, but it was only in a talk delivered in Cologne in 1979, "Die Stellung der Frau in Familie, Haushalt und Wirtschaftsbetrieb im spätmittelalterlichen-frühneuzeitlichen Köln" and in an English translation of a short description of the women's guilds, "Women's Guilds in Cologne in the Later Middle Ages," that she developed the point. See, however, comments in *Die Stellung der Frau* such as that on p. 180.

6. Bibliographies of literature and sources on Cologne have been published regularly since 1951; bibliographies published before then covered the years 1911–34 and 1934–38, the latter of which were published in vols. 1–5 of the *Jahrbuch der Arbeitsgemeinschaft des Rheinischen Geschichtsvereins* (1935–40); all others are in the *Jahrbuch des Kölnischen Geschichtsverein.*

7. Hansen, "Das Archiv und die Bibliotheek der Stadt Köln," is the last published attempt at an inventory. Issued in 1894, it is now out-of-date. Since 1882, the *Mitteilungen aus der Stadtarchiv von Köln* has regularly published registers of important dossiers.

Although the municipal archive has in some respects been well used, it has by no means been fully exploited. To be sure, certain topics of special concern in this study have been well treated by some carefully edited published source collections. Foremost among the collections are Walter Stein's on the urban constitution and administration, Knipping's on its finance, Heinrich von Loesch's on the guilds, Keussen's on the topography and the university, and Bruno Kuske's on economic activity, especially long-distance trade: Stein, ed., *Akten zur Geschichte der Verfassung und Verwaltung der Stadt Köln im 14. und 15. Jahrhundert*; von Loesch, *Die Kölner Zunfturkunden*; Keussen, *Topographie der Stadt Köln in Mittelalter*; Kuske, *Quellen zur Geschichte des Kölner Handels und Verkehrs im Mittelalter.* Also see Irsigler, *Die wirtschaftliche Stellung der Stadt Köln*, pp. 7–9 for a discussion of these source collections and their use for economic and social history.

Some extensive document series from the late medieval and early modern periods remain largely unexamined in systematic scholarship; approximately 335 volumes of the *Ratsprotokolle*, the most important source of constitutional history; the *Briefbücher* (governmental correspondence) which comprises 210 volumes; and the *Rechnungen* (accounts) which require 1,384 volumes. The *Schreinsurkunden* and *Amtleutebücher*, a massive collection from the Middle Ages originating at the parish level, have also been virtually unused. The first, made up of *Schreinskarten* and *Schreinsbücher*, contain records of land and real property transfers in Cologne and related documentation; in addition to being a potential source of information about the economy and social structure, they tell us about the political development of the city, for they are witness that communal life in Cologne began at the parish level. The first four volumes of the continuous series of the *Ratsprotokolle*, which begins in 1396, are known as *Ratsmemoriale* or *Libri registrationum Senatus;* they continue until 1522. The *Ratsmemoriale* also contain *Morgensprachen* issued before 1440. There is also a broken series of *Ratsmemoriale*, then called *Eidbücher*, from 1335 to 1387. The figure of 335 volumes for the *Ratsprotokolle* is Stehkämper's, "Das historische Archiv der Stadt Koln"; Stein counted 248 in *Akten zu Geschichte der Verfassung und Verwaltung der Stadt Köln im 14. und 15. Jahrhundert.*

From 1135 when the *Schreinskarten* began (and from 1220 when the *Schreinsbücher* superseded them), until the late thirteenth and early fourteenth centuries, when the *Schöffen* and then later the council began to assume such functions and displace these *Sondergemeinen*, the *Schreinsurkunden* were the only official records of land transfers. Although it never was made obligatory to record transactions here, it was so common to do so that already by the twelfth century an entry served not just as a record of a record but as the record itself and as an enforceable claim or contract. That these parishes, half-secular, half-religious organizations could, by registering a property transfer, give it legitimacy, is evidence of the communal authority they bore. The parishes also were the city's original units of defense, a job they retained for centuries; there is evidence too that taxes were assessed and collected by parishes and that they performed the judicial functions of interpreting and enforcing property and inheritance law and of granting citizenship.

8. Von Loesch, *Die Kölner Zunfturkunden.* A list of the dossiers in the *Zunftabteilung* in Cologne's archives not published by von Loesch is contained in *Mitteilungen aus der Stadtarchiv von Köln*, no. 33.

9. Kuske, *Quellen*, 4 vols.

10. For a discussion of these sources, see chap. 6, nn. 38, 57 and 59.

11. Irsigler, "Kölner Wirtschaft im Spätmittelalter," offers a good overview of the economy of Cologne in the Middle Ages.

12. The Italian trade is described in some detail in Irsigler, *Die wirtschaftliche Stellung der Stadt Köln.*

13. For a good description of the eastern trade in wool cloth, see Militzer, "Tuchhandel," esp. p. 270.

14. Some historians have pointed out that during this time there were

certain social groups, certain industries, and certain geographic areas which prospered both in relative and absolute terms. For example, artisans in favored industries like luxury cloth and metal goods are thought to have benefited from low prices for housing and food, strong demand for their specialized wares and the success of their guilds in protecting their interests. A few scholars have even been persuaded that this was not a century of depression but, instead, a time of reorganization brought about by the population shifts and the associated shifts in assets and income flows.

There is an extensive literature on the depression of the Renaissance. For an introduction, see Cipolla, Lopez, and Miskimin, "The Economic Depression of the Renaissance"; Postan, *Medieval Agriculture and General Problems;* Abel, *De Wüstungen des ausgehenden Mittelalters;* Bridbury, *Economic Growth: England in the Later Middle Ages.* The latter study has particular relevance to a debate about the fortunes of English towns in the late Middle Ages. Carus-Wilson, *The Expansion of Exeter at the Close of the Middle Ages* and Bridbury, ibid., represent the position that there was no widespread depression, while recent studies by Platt, *The English Medieval Town,* and Reynolds, *An Introduction to the History of English Medieval Towns,* have taken the opposite view. For a discussion of the literature and an empirical study of the conditions of prosperity in one place, see Gottfried, *Bury St. Edmunds and the Urban Crisis.*

15. Wilhelm Schönfelder, in *Die wirtschaftliche Entwicklung Kölns von 1370–1513,* has argued that Cologne suffered severe economic setbacks during this period. Population in the city, he claimed, fell 30 to 40 percent; wool cloth sales, linen and coarse cloth production, wine sales, and the spice trade all declined. Guild entrance requirements were also tightened, and many trades saw severe unemployment. Thus, for Schönfelder, the fifteenth century was a time of retreat for the rich and of suffering for the poor. Franz Irsigler and Hermann Kellenbenz have attacked both Schönfelder's evidence and his reasoning. The measures of decline Schönfelder used, they argued, are misleading, and they claimed that he ignored the abundant evidence of prosperity in Cologne. See Irsigler's comments on Schönfelder's work in "Kölner Wirtschaft im Spätmittelalter," *Die wirtschaftliche Stellung der Stadt Köln,* and "Soziale Wandlungen"; for Kellenbenz, see "Wirtschaftsgeschichte Kölns im 16. und beginnenden 17. Jahrhundert" in his *Zweijahrtausende Kölner Wirtschaft,* and "Die wohlhabensten Bürger."

16. For wool cloth production, see Irsigler, *Die wirtschaftliche Stellung der Stadt Köln,* pp. 10–15, 40ff; for barchent, *Tirtei,* and silk, ibid., pp. 15–40. For sales of imported wool cloths, see table 5, chap. 6 below. For silk prices, see Wensky, *Die Stellung der Frau,* pp. 193–95.

17. For the history of the industry, see Koch, *Geschichte des Seidengewerbes in Köln.*

18. The bases of this analysis are Irsigler's *Die wirtschaftliche Stellung der Stadt Köln* and Arentz, *Die Zersetzung des Zunftgedankens.*

19. Irsigler provided evidence that members of the *Wollamt,* the guild of wool weavers which became a dominant *Gaffel* after 1396, were in all three kinds of markets as early as the second half of the fourteenth century. Because weavers in eastern Europe in the fourteenth century led cloth-trading ventures he concluded that they ran putting-out operations. See Irsigler, *Die wirtschaftliche Stellung der Stadt Köln,* pp. 53–58, esp. p. 57: "Die aus dem Rahmen einer zweifellos wohlhabenden Zunft durch ihre kaufmannische Initiative fast herausgewachsenen Weber-Verleger standen den Kölner Berufskaufleuten in keiner Weise nach." In *Ursachen und Folgen,* Militzer has questioned Irsigler's assumptions, arguing in part that participation in long-distance trade is not necessarily evidence of a putting-out system: see pp. 126–32. See the section on capitalism in Cologne of this chapter for their debate.

20. For earlier rulings on the Gewandschnitt which allowed weavers limited rights to sell cloth in Cologne, see von Loesch, *Die Kölner Zunfturkunden,* 2: nos. 734 and 738. After their defeat in 1371, the weavers lost these rights. The Gewandschnitt began, in the thirteenth century, as a patrician organization to which foreign cloth merchants from places like Tournai or Maline, belonged; by the mid-fourteenth century, Cologners alone controlled sales, and patrician merchants then still managed sales themselves. During the fourteenth century, however, tailors and a special branch of their trade, pants makers, began to circumvent the Gewandschneider and deal directly with importers. In 1378, the Gewantschnitt was opened to those who could pay the 10 Gulden fee (certain groups, including wool weavers, were disqualified); thereafter, the trade was dominated by pants makers, tailors, and cloth cutters. In 1396 cloth wholesaling in Cologne was open to all, but long-distance merchants never dominated it again. See Irsigler, *Die wirtschaftliche Stellung der Stadt Köln,* pp. 62–65.

Irsigler provided some good statistical evidence indicating the extent of weavers' participation in wholesale trade in Cologne: of the 133 Gewandschneider who appeared in records from 1414 to 1442, 95 can be identified according to the Gaffel to which they belonged: 39 belonged to the Wollamt or the Schneideramt; 31 belonged to a Gaffel associated with commerce alone; the rest were spread among other "craft" Gaffeln: ibid., pp. 71–72.

21. Irsigler, *Die wirtschftliche Stellung der Stadt Köln,* p. 58.

22. The total import figures for wine are from Irsigler, *Die wirtschaftliche Stellung der Stadt Köln,* pp. 24–25. Despite its decline in the fifteenth century, wine remained an important part of local and long-distance trade. Even in the late fifteenth century, when wine imports through Cologne had fallen dramatically, they were still larger than spice imports.

The late fourteenth-century figures are directly from Herborn and Militzer, *Der Kölner Weinhandel,* pp. 13–14.

23. In 1372 the *Weinbrüderschaft,* at origin already a patrician organization, was closed to any without family connections, and in 1386 even inheritance rights were abolished: Lau, *Die Entwicklung der kommunale Verfassung.* Also see Irsigler, *Die wirtschaftliche Stellung der Stadt Köln,* pp. 240–45.

24. The 1390–92 figures are from Herborn and Militzer, *Der Kölner Weinhandel,* pp. 13ff.; the 1420/21 figures are from Irsigler, *Die wirtschaftliche Stellung der Stadt Köln,* table 74, p. 254. Irsigler argued, p. 255, that from 1390/92 to 1420/21 wine sales became more concentrated in the hands of large merchants, reporting that in the former years 8.2 percent of merchants did 46.7 percent of the business as compared to 25 percent who did 74.4 percent of the trade in 1420/21. Irsigler's own 1390/92 figures (table 69, p., 247) included only the numbers of merchants in one of seven categories of importers, while Herborn and Militzer's 1390/92 figures (table 1, p. 13) gave both the amounts imported and the number of merchants in each of six categories; neither table for 1390/92 is therefore directly comparable to Irsigler's 1420/21 table, which used seven categories and provided both numbers of merchants and imported volumes. (Irsigler cited Herborn and Militzer for his table 69 but did not explain why his presentation of the 1390/92 data differed from theirs.) The best we can do, it seems, is substitute, for Irsigler's 8.2 percent (categories VI and VII) from the 1390/92 figures, which accounted for 46.7 percent, Herborn and Militzer's 5.6 percent, which accounted for 37.3 percent (Category I), or their 13.2 percent, which accounted for 59.8 percent (Categories I and II). (We might also compare the smaller of these [5.6 percent and 37.3 percent, respectively] with the 1420/21 figure of 3 percent and 19.8 percent, respectively.)

Thus, my own reading of the same data Irsigler used is that wine sales were *not* more concentrated in 1420/21 than in 1390/92. In the later years, the top 3 percent of merchants imported 19.8 percent and the top 24.7 percent took in 74.4 percent; in the earlier years, the top 5.6 percent took in 37.3 percent, the top 13.2 percent took in 59.8, and the top 27.2 percent took in 81 percent.

Years linked by slashes, as in 1414/15, refer to fiscal years beginning in the first calendar year listed and ending in the second.

25. Irsigler, *Die wirtschaftliche Stellung der Stadt Köln,* pp. 265-65.

26. Lau, *Die Entwicklung der kommunale Verfassung.* Lau is the basic source for the constitutional history of this period, but see also Herborn, *Die politische Führungsschicht.*

27. von Loesch, *Die Kölner Zunfturkunden,* p. 25, emphasized this point and its consequences for artisanal economic independence: "Trotz seines weiten Absatzkreises ist Köln's Gewerbe im Mittelalter im wesentlichen auf der Stufe des Handwerks stehengeblieben."

28. Rental prices from Wensky, *Die Stellung der Frau,* p. 41 and nn. 73 and 75; for wages, see Irsigler, "Kölner Wirtschaft im Spätmittelalter," p. 304, where he reported that in 1374 a skilled carpenter earned some 160 Mark in a 260–day year.

29. Only *Altschuhmacher* and *Lederzurichter* had not won *Zunftzwang* by the end of the fourteenth century.

30. Mickwitz used the term *Beitrittszwang* to characterize this limited sort of membership control and to distinguish it from true *Zunftzwang*, which involved full rights to choose members as well as to prohibit practice of the craft by nonmembers: Mickwitz, *Die Kartellfunktionen der Zünfte.* For more on the corporative status of Cologne's guilds, both before and after 1396, see Militzer, *Ursachen und Folgen,* section 5.

31. In 1326, the wool weavers won limited rights to retail their own cloth in Cologne and in 1352 won full rights to sell their own (but not imported) cloth; the right was taken away in 1372 after the overthrow of the weavers' government: see von Loesch, 2: nos. 734 and 738 (pp. 481–82) and Arentz, *Die Zersetzung des Zunftgedankens,* p. 15. After 1396, anyone could join the Gewandschnitt, but few weavers did so.

32. The twenty-two Gaffeln, and an indication of the number of representatives each sent to the council, are listed below (asterisks signify merchant Gaffeln; Aren is often treated as a merchant Gaffel).

Wollamt (4)	Schmiede (2)
*Eisenmarkt (2)	Schilderer (1)
*Schwarzhaus (2)	Steinmetzen (1)
Goldschmiede (2)	Backer (1)
Brauer (2)	Fleischamt (1)
Gurtler (2)	Schneider (1)
Fischer (2)	Schuhmaker (1)
*Windeck (2)	Sarworter (1)
Buntworter (2)	Kannengiesser (1)
*Himmelreich (2)	Fassbinder (1)
Aren (Riemenschneider) (2)	Ziechenweber (Leinenweber) (1)

33. "Unsere Untersuchung uber die Zusammenhänge zwischen Handel, Kapital und Patriziat in Köln endigt deshalb mit dem Ergebnis, dass die Kölner Patrizier ihre auf Reichtum berühende Herrenstellung nicht angestammten Grundbesitz, sonder Handelsgewinn verdankten": von Winterfeld, "Handel, Kapital und Patriziat in Köln bis 1400" (p. 80). This question was more famously addressed by Strieder in *Zur Genesis des modernen Kapitalismus:* were urban patricians originally merchants or rentiers, that is, did their wealth come from trade alone or had these families obtained their capital from landholdings? Strieder's findings paralleled von Winterfeld's. The question had social as well as economic significance, of course, for a finding that the elite's origins were in land

would have, Strieder thought, implied aristocratic, not plebian, origins of early modern capitalism.

34. Steinbach, "Zur Sozialgeschichte von Köln im Mittelalter," p. 682; for Boinbroke, see Espinas, *Origines du capitalisme*, 1: pp. 212–20, esp. n. 4, pp. 213–44, and "Jehan Boin Broke. Bourgeois et drapier Douaisien."

35. Strait, *Cologne in the Twelfth Century*, esp. chap. 5.

36. Ibid., chap. 5; Steinbach, "Zur Sozialgeschichte von Köln im Mittelalter," p. 677; von Winterfeld, "Handel, Kapital und Patriziat in Köln bis 1400"; see, too, Herborn's studies of the lives and ancestries of individual patrician families in the thirteenth century in his *Die politische Führungsschicht*.

37. Steinbach, "Zur Sozialgeschichte von Köln im Mittelalter," p. 677.

38. Herborn, *Die politische Führungsschicht*; Steinbach, "Zur Sozialgeschichte von Köln im Mittelalter," p. 679, claimed that intermarriage between merchants and nobles was progressively less frequent by the late fourteenth century.

39. "Nirgends begegneten [wir] jedoch industrieelle Betriebe under der Leitung Kölner Patrizier": von Winterfeld, "Handel, Kapital und Patriziat in Köln bis 1400," p. 80.

40. Herborn, *Die politische Führungsschicht*, p. 285.

41. Ibid., p. 286. The acreage conversions are roughly figured, based on Wielandt, "Münzen, Gewichte und Masse bis 1800"; the liter conversion (1 Malter = 150 l is from Irsigler, "Getreidepreise, Getreidehandel und städtische Versorgungspolitik," p. 572. In "Kölner Wirtschaft im Spätmittelalter," p. 304, he reckoned the Malter of Cologne at 164 l and used the same conversion in "Getreide- und Brotpreise, Brotgewicht und Getreideverbrauch." For a discussion of the Malter as a unit of grain measure in late medieval Germany, see Wielandt, *"Münzen, Gewichte und Masse bis 1800."*

42. Militzer, *Ursachen und Folgen*, p. 68. Militzer pointed out that not all patricians were so rich and cited a few examples of individuals with quite modest holdings in Cologne; he also conceded, however, that these members of the patriciate very likely had nonurban property as well.

43. Herborn, *Die politische Führungsschicht*, p. 289.

44. Irsigler, *Die wirtschaftliche Stellung der Stadt Köln*, p. 178.

45. Ibid., p. 146.

46. Ibid., pp. 87–88.

47. In many of these trades, the division of labor was particularly far advanced and the split between producer-merchants and workers quite marked. Ibid., pp. 167 and 165: "In fast allen Bereichen der Kölner Waffenfabrikation ist—verstärkt seit der zweiten Halfte des 15. Jahrhunderts—ein stärker Trend zum Übergang von der Urproduktion zur Verlegerlungstechnik zu beobachten. Hand in Hand damit geht die verlegerische Zusammenfassung des ländlichen zum Teil auch kleinstädt-

ischen Handwerks durch Kölner Kaufleute und die führenden Kräfte des Handwerks."

48. Ibid., pp. 203 and 209.

49. Irsigler's argument rested on the proposition that the 200 looms which operated in Cologne during the 1370s could not have produced the 10,500 cloths sold annually in those years, since, as he computed it, maximum annual capacity per loom was thirty-five to forty cloths. The weavers, he reasoned, who sold this cloth must have commissioned some of it from weavers outside Cologne. Militzer argued that a weaver with one loom could easily have produced some fifty cloths per year and that commissioned production was therefore not necessary. Because neither Irsigler nor Militzer apparently realized how much production rates per artisan could vary in the medieval wool textile industry, neither provided sufficient information about the weaving process in Cologne to evaluate his own argument. Hence, we cannot know whether, as Militzer charged, *Wollamt* members of the fourteenth century rarely worked through a rural putting-out system. The answer, however, does not seem crucial, since, even if Militzer was correct, it would not weaken Irsigler's thesis substantially. After all, Irsigler had good evidence about the extent of the putting-out system in fifteenth-century Cologne, evidence which Militzer and other historians have not challenged.

Irsigler's data are in *Die wirtschaftliche Stellung der Stadt Köln*, esp. p. 43; Militzer's is in "Zur Kölner Tuchproduktion." Also see p. 144 of *Ursachen und Folgen*. Militzer also argues that the *Verlag* system rests upon a system of credit in which the lender advances production capital to commissioned workers who then lose "Eigentumsrechte an den Tüchen": Militzer, *Ursachen und Folgen*, p. 128, n. 657. Because he found little evidence of these financial arrangements in the *Schreinsbücher* between 1360 and 1410, he argued that members of the Wollamt were simply buying production in the city and the region and selling it in Cologne and beyond: see esp. p. 128, n. 657. Agreeing with the earlier scholars von Loesch and Arentz, Militzer would place the real beginnings of the *Verlag* system in the Wollamt in the fifteenth century: for von Loesch, see *Die Kölner Zunfturkunden*, Introduction, p. 25, for Arentz, see *Die Zersetzung des Zunftgedankens*, p. 93; both are cited in Militzer, *Ursachen und Folgen*, p. 127.

One of Militzer's assumptions in his calculation seems particularly odd. He considered one weaver as capable of operating two looms at full capacity. This simply could not have been the case. Two looms would have employed at least two weavers, and very likely four, unless the technology of weaving cloth in Cologne (where, at 1.16 meters, cloth was close to standard width) differed markedly from technology in the Low Countries, England, and elsewhere in Germany, where looms used two workers.

50. Militzer, *Ursachen und Folgen*, p. 69. The figures for Augsburg are from Blendinger, "Versuch einer Bestimmung der Mittelschicht in der

Reichsstadt Augsburg." Militzer's data were based only on the value of real property owned in Cologne, but he argued (pp. 67–68) that real property ownership, while not indicative of total wealth, is indicative of *relative* wealth. He also argued that the property tax registers available for so many other cities are not necessarily more reliable guides to total property owned or any more comparable, one to another, than these data. While these points seem well taken, it is not clear that the absolute levels of property ownership reckoned by Militzer are comparable to those derived from Augsburg's tax rolls, or even that Militzer's sample of the *Schreinsbücher* provided enough information about the property distribution among nonpatrician residents of Cologne to warrant the kind of comparisons he made with other cities for which tax information is available. Most damaging to Militzer's case is the omission of patrician property holdings; including this group would certainly have yielded a much more highly skewed distribution table, one even more skewed, probably, than Augsburg's.

51. See n. 7 above for a description of the *Schreine*. Much of the information about the *Sondergemeinden* is based on Beyerle, "Die Anfange," but see also Planitz and Buyken, *Die Kölner Schreinsbücher des 13.–14. Jahrhunderts;* Keussen, *Topographie der Stadt Köln;* Buyken and Conrad, *Die Amtleutebücher der Kölnischen Sondergemeinden;* Hoeniger, *Kölner Schreinsurkunden des 12. Jahrhunderts.* Militzer excluded important groups of property owners. One group consisted of clerics, nobles, and foreign residents who did not make use of the *Schreinsbücher.* As mentioned above, he omitted patricians, whose property transfers were too numerous and too complex to be conveniently analyzed and who held a good deal of their property outside Cologne, so that in any case the *Schreinsbücher* were a poor guide to their holdings.

52. For purposes of his study, Militzer defined the patriciate as Herborn did in *Die politische Führungsschicht* and as they both did in their joint study of the wine trade, *Der Kölner Weinhandel:* those whose families were represented in the pre-1396 Schöffen College, the Richerzeche, and the Small Council.

53. In Militzer, *Ursachen und Folgen*, p. 137, from the *Limburger Chronik.* See Militzer, p. 137, for a fuller description of these houses and the importance of the Wollamt in the mid-fourteenth century. After 1396 the Wollamt managed sales from the "New Hall" which had been built to replace the two guild houses destroyed in the defeat of the weavers in 1371.

54. For the older interpretation, see Lau, *Die Entwicklung der kommunale Verfassung;* Arentz, *Die Zersetzung des Zunftgedankens;* Mollat and Wolff, *Ongles bleus.*

55. Irsigler, *Die wirtschaftliche Stellung der Stadt Köln*, p. 317. These are only the goods for which he was taxed on the *Eisen- und Kraut Wage.* Other kinds of goods—wool, for example—came through a different trade hall

and some goods—raisins and dates, for example—were not taxed: see Kuske, *Quellen*, 3, p. 100, and "Kaufhäuser und Märkte." The goods listed in the surviving records are only those on which the excise taxes had not yet been paid, and it is quite possible that he imported other goods on which he promptly paid taxes and for which, therefore, we have no records. See chap. 6, n. 59, for a discussion of the use of these excise tax records in measurement of import volumes.

56. Irsigler, *Die wirtschaftliche Stellung der Stadt Köln*, p. 316.

57. Ibid., p. 144.

58. Ibid., p. 124.

59. Wensky, *Die Stellung der Frau*, p. 308–9.

60. Ibid., pp. 313–15.

61. See chap. 6 for discussion of the problem of including linen weavers in this category.

62. We have no direct measure of Cologne's population of servants and apprentices, but comparisons with other cities suggest that the 20 percent figure assumed here is not high. In Leiden in 1581, when the economy was weak and the industrial labor force small, 6 percent of the population were servants and another 8 percent were "lodgers," many of these students at the new university and many others among them journeymen: see chap. 3. In 1449 in Nuremberg, then a prosperous trade and industrial city like Cologne but probably less devoted to industry, almost 18 percent of the population fell into this category: figures cited in Maschke, "Die Unterschichten der mittelalterlichen Städte Deutschlands." In 1497 in Basel the figure was 17 percent: ibid.; in 1357 Zürich, 27 percent of the households had servants or apprentices living in; there were 388 servants or apprentices distributed among 1,055 households: Nabholz, *Die Steuerbücher von Stadt und Landschaft Zürich*. For a full discussion of the importance of servants in the late medieval and early modern household, see Laslett, *Household and Family in Past Time*.

63. Von Loesch, *Die Kölner Zunfturkunden*, 1 and 2: doc. nos. 516, 551 (2, 4, and 38).

64. Irsigler, *Die wirtschaftliche Stellung der Stadt Köln*, p. 219.

65. See Wesoly's documentation of the frequency with which this occurred in certain German towns: "Der weibliche Bevölkerungsanteil."

66. For a general discussion of the problem, see Maschke, "Die Unterschichten der mittelalterlichen Städte Deutschlands." In 1429 in Basel, Maschke reports, 66 percent of the individuals in the lowest category of taxpayers on a property tax roll were women. In 1498 in Leiden, about 33 percent of the people in the lowest category (those considered too poor to pay a tax) were women, but, overall, women made up only about 22 percent of the taxpayers; most of the poor women were single or widowed. In Frankfurt am Main in 1495, 62 percent of the women taxpayers paid less than 6 shillings while only 35 percent of the

men did. The Frankfurt data are derived from Bothe, "Die Entwicklung der direkten Besteurung" and *Beiträge zur Wirtschaft- und Sozialgeschichte.*

67. Militzer, *Ursachen und Folgen,* pp. 75ff.

68. Ibid., p. 80.

69. Ibid., p. 89; see too Militzer and Herborn, *Der Kölner Weinhandel,* in which the notion of "Abkömmlichkeit," borrowed from Weber, is discussed further.

70. Militzer, *Ursachen und Folgen.*

71. But, see Herborn's study, "Verfassungsideal," discussed later in this chapter, which showed how individuals not representing the interests of artisans came to dominate government in Cologne in the course of the fifteenth century.

72. Herborn, *Die politische Führungsschicht,* p. 298.

73. ·Ibid., p. 321.

74. For the details, see ibid., chap. 7.

75. ". . . die neue Führungsschicht nach 1396 noch weitaus stärker activ im Handel tätig war als der alter Patrizierstand. . . . der Reichtum öffnete wiederum den Zutritt zur politischen führenden Schicht und zu führenden städtischen Ämtern und zu einer Spitzenstellung im Rat, . . . Die neue Führungschicht was eine Geldaristokratie. Die ständische Herkunft blieb sekundar. Kriegerische Auseinandersetzungen untereinander gab es nicht. Die wirtschaftlichen Voraussetzungen hatten den Vorrang und entschieden über politischen Karrieren. In der ersten Hälfte des 15. Jahrhunderts spielte sich innerhalb der Familien dieser neuen Führungsschicht eine erhebliche Fluktuation ab": Ibid., p. 409.

76. Herborn, "Verfassungsideal."

77. For details on the split among the nonpatrician merchants during the takeover, see ibid., esp. p. 33.

78. Ibid., pp. 38–39. Still later, the less powerful Gaffeln won more places in the Gebrech, partly because they revolted in the early 1480s (with the support of a few of the old patriciate who were looking for a way back into government); although one outcome was some accommodation with these dissident industrial Gaffeln, another was ostracism of the merchant Gaffeln with whom the patriciate had been associated and an increase in the power of those remaining. Another factor that helped to concentrate the office of Bürgermeister in a few hands, despite the apparent widening of the composition of the Gebrech, was Cologne's late-fifteenth-century financial crises; Herborn argued that only rich merchants could have managed Cologne during such times: ibid., esp. p. 44. The financial crisis was largely a result of the costs of the defense of Neuss.

79. Herborn, "Bürgerliches Selbstverstandnis."

80. Irsigler, "Kölner Kaufleute im 15. Jahrhundert."

81. "Rationalität und Grosszügigkeit, Masshalten und masslosses Gewinnstreben, Sicherheitsbedürfnis und Riskofreudigkeit zugleich":

Ibid., p. 87. Maschke's article is "Das Berufsbewusstsein des mittelalter-lichen Fernkaufmanns."

Chapter Six

1. This information is from Wensky, *Die Stellung der Frau*, table 4, pp. 116–34.
2. Ibid., p. 138.
3. Ibid., pp. 138–39. For more on the Rinck family, see Irsigler, "Hansekaufleute", esp. p. 317; cited in Wensky, p. 138.
4. Wensky, *Die Stellung der Frau*, p. 141.
5. Ibid., p. 161; Kuske, *Quellen*, 2: no. 84.
6. Wensky, *Die Stellung der Frau*, p. 143.
7. Ibid., p. 143–45.
8. Ibid,, p. 143.
9. Ibid., p. 149; Kuske, *Quellen*, 2:, no. 1227.
10. Wensky, *Die Stellung der Frau*, p. 149. His second wife began her apprenticeship in 1465 but did not register as a mistress until 1487, the year of her marriage. There are several other recorded instances of men remarrying into the trade, as there are instances of silk mistresses whose first and second husbands were silk merchants.
11. Kuske, *Quellen*, 4: p. 257; Wensky, *Die Stellung der Frau*, p. 160.
12. Wensky, *Die Stellung der Frau*, pp. 146–48.
13. This information is derived from ibid., table 4, pp. 116–34.
14. Ibid., table 8, p. 177. The number of women in the next decade rose: six of the top forty-eight importers were women and they accounted for about 8 percent of imports. (This excludes Grietgen van der Bruch who was listed with her husband; together they brought in about 28 percent.) In the 1470s four women (excluding the female member of another pair) accounted for about 6 percent. Between 1491 and 1495, two women with just over 1 percent of the market were counted among the top 24 importers.

The husbands of silk makers accounted for between 15 percent of volume at the low and 40 percent of volume at the high, or just 18 percent if Johann Liblar is excluded, who took almost 25 percent of the 1470–80 imports and 22 percent of those between 1491 and 1495.

15. See ibid., pp. 171–72, 183–86, for examples of women's direct involvement in the export of silk fabrics; some women even traveled to fairs at Frankfurt am Main and Antwerp and dealt directly with merchants abroad. Much of Wensky's data is from Kuske, *Quellen*, vol. 2.
16. Wensky, "Women's Guilds in Cologne in the Later Middle Ages," p. 637.
17. Ibid., p. 638. In 1438 the council permitted members of one of the two guilds to transfer freely to the other.
18. von Loesch, *Die Kölner Zunfturkunden*, 2: no. 378; Wensky, "Die

Stellung der Frau in Familie, Haushalt und Wirtschaftsbetrieb im spätmittelalterlichen-frühneuzeitlichen Köln," p. 19.

19. The statistical data is derived from Wensky, *Die Stellung der Frau*, table 4, pp. 116–34.

20. Ibid. All thirty-two men were, of course, council members, for it was by virtue of their membership in the council that we have records of their Gaffel affiliation. Other men related to silk mistresses were elected to the council as Gebrech members (and were therefore not identifiable by Gaffel); many may have been members of the traditional merchant Gaffeln since, as Herborn has shown, the merchant Gaffeln tended to be disproportionately represented in the Gebrech during part of this period: see Herborn, "Verfassungsideal."

21. As explained elsewhere, they were probably exchanging cloths from England for silk. We have another measure of the artisanal roots of the merchant families involved in the silk business: twenty-five of the men who were husbands or fathers of silk mistresses can be identified as Gewandschneider; of the thirteen whose Gaffel memberships could be identified, only one was a member of a merchant Gaffel, and only five more belonged to the Goldschmiede, Wollamt, or Aren (Riemenschneider), Gaffeln which by then were dominated by trading interests. (Aren is often counted as a merchant Gaffel.) The rest were in Gaffeln which had not yet entirely shed their craft beginnings.

In "Kölner Wirtschaft im Spätmittelalter," table 15, p. 307, Irsigler provided another demonstration of this point. Of 227 men from Cologne associated with the Hansa and regularly doing business in London, Bruges, and Antwerp in 1476/77, 131 were members of craft Gaffeln (Goldschmiede, Fassbinder, Fischamt, Aren, Gürtelmacher, Harnischmacher, Wollamt, Schmiede, Buntwörter, Schneider).

22. This was a report written by Gerard von Wesel, a council member, found in von Loesch, *Die Kölner Zunfturkunden*, 2: doc. no. 661, and discussed in Wensky, *Die Stellung der Frau*, pp. 168ff.

23. Wensky, *Die Stellung der Frau*, p. 100.

24. Wensky argued that the *Transfixbrief* unmistakably demonstrates that around 1500 the silk industry was strongly oriented toward the putting-out system: ibid., pp. 196–97.

25. Wensky's "Women's Guilds in Cologne in the Later Middle Ages," pp. 648–50, provides a good description of this guild.

26. These data are from Wensky, *Die Stellung der Frau*, pp. 164–66.

27. For thirty-three of the women on Wensky's list of ninety-six active mistresses, we have the apprenticeship records. All but ten of the thirty-three are *known* to have had fathers or husbands in trade or on the council.

28. Wensky, "Women's Guilds in Cologne in the Later Middle Ages," pp. 632–38.

29. Ibid., p. 633.

30. See Wensky, *Die Stellung der Frau*, p. 15; Stein, *Akten zur Verfassung*, 1: doc. no. 52; Lau, *Die Entwicklung der kommunale Verfassung*, p. 200.

31. Originally, many luxury goods had apparently not been made for the market as such but on order for the archbishop (and sometimes the city of Cologne) by women in rich convents and in the homes of merchants and well-to-do artisans.

32. See Wensky, *Die Stellung der Frau*, pp. 85–89, and the sources she cites.

33. Ibid., p. 89, citing Ennen's report of contemporary sources. Wensky points out that the skilled crafts that belonged to women were related, in that women from all three crafts worked on Borten. The silk spinners and weavers made the fabric (these were apparently not exclusively female trades until about 1400); the yarn makers provided the linen thread used in embroidery; the gold spinners provided the gold fiber. Nothing, it seems, that went into the "Kölner Borten" was made by men then, except perhaps the cartoon for the design, which was often provided by a member of the Malerzunft.

34. The craft was then called the Wappensticker, referring to the coat of arms, which had become one of the main products. It is possible that men specialized in this kind of work, while women continued the embroidery of Borten and the articles for liturgical wear that had earned them their place in the trade. Although males dominated the Wappensticker, the guild maintained its close association with the silk makers, and at times during the fifteenth century was even supervised by the same council officer: see ibid., pp. 92–95.

35. In "Wirtschaftsgeschichte Kölns im 16. und beginnenden 17. Jahrundert," in his *Zwei Jahrtausende Kölner Wirtschaft*, Kellenbenz briefly describes these industries.

36. See von Loesch, *Die Kölner Zunfturkunden*, Introduction, for a history of the guilds, in which this argument is elaborated; for the Riemenschneider statutes, see ibid., 1: doc. nos. 53A and 53B.

37. See ibid., Introduction, pp. 133ff., for Cologne's brotherhoods.

38. These figures are based on my reading of the documents published by von Loesch, *Die Kölner Zunfturkunden*, and of Wensky's (*Die Stellung der Frau*) summary of her reading of documents from this collection and from a few unpublished dossiers.

The count excludes the Goldspinnerinnen/Goldschlager, the Garnmacherinnen, the Seidemacherinnen, and the Seidespinnerinnen.

The nine were the Altschuhmacher, Bronzegiesser, Dachdecker, Schreiner/Kistenmacher, Kumtmacher, Seilmacher, Steinmetzen, Tirteiweber, and Weissgerber: see Wensky, *Die Stellung der Frau*, pp. 33 and 47.

39. Wensky had the same comment: Wensky, *Die Stellung der Frau*, p. 33.

40. For the hatmakers, see von Loesch, *Die Kölner Zunfturkunden*, 1: doc.

no. 38; for the cloth cutters, ibid., 1: doc. no. 74; for the sword makers, ibid., 1: doc. no. 648. Two of the three otherwise permitted women limited participation. The cloth cutters allowed one year's widows' rights in 1293: ibid., 1: doc. no. 73 (21). A council order of 1462 implied that wives and servants helped in the business: ibid., 2: doc. no. 705. The hatmakers permitted limited widows' rights in the 1378 statute: ibid., 1: doc. no. 38 (6 and 19).

41. Harnischmaker: von Loesch, *Die Kölner Zunfturkunden*, 2: doc. no. 516 (1494); Wensky, *Die Stellung der Frau*, p. 35; the language suggests that women had been used as piece- or wage-workers, not that they had been full mistresses.

Lederzurichter: von Loesch, *Die Kölner Zunfturkunden*, 2: doc. nos. 551–52 (1500–15); Wensky, *Die Stellung der Frau*, p. 46; the reference is to "Magden" who did low-skilled work. Later brotherhood ordinances permitted limited widows' rights.

Lohgerber: the statutes do not mention women but a 1465 list of members counted one widow among twenty-nine men: von Loesch, *Die Kölner Zunfturkunden*, 2: doc. no. 566 (1465); Wensky, *Die Stellung der Frau*, p. 46.

Maler: von Loesch, *Die Kölner Zunfturkunden*, 1: doc. no. 52 (1449); Wensky, *Die Stellung der Frau*, p. 49; statute language implies widows' rights but there is no explicit provision.

Riemenschneider: von Loesch, *Die Kölner Zunfturkunden*, 1: doc. nos. 53A, 53B; Wensky, *Die Stellung der Frau*, pp. 46–47; a widow could continue the family business until she married outside the trade and could keep (male) apprentices as long as she kept a journeyman.

Sattelmacher: von Loesch, *Die Kölner Zunfturkunden*, 1: doc. no. 55 (1397); Wensky, *Die Stellung der Frau*, p. 47; a widow could continue the family business until she married outside the trade.

42. Wensky, *Die Stellung der Frau*, p. 34, and von Loesch, *Die Kölner Zunfturkunden*, 1: doc. nos. 103–8.

43. Kannengiesser: Wensky, *Die Stellung der Frau*, pp. 35–36; von Loesch, *Die Kölner Zunfturkunden*, 1: doc. no. 41.

Kupferschläger: Wensky, *Die Stellung der Frau*, p. 36; von Loesch, *Die Kölner Zunfturkunden*, 1: doc. no. 43.

Scharzenweber/Decklackenweber: Wensky, *Die Stellung der Frau*, p. 39; von Loesch, *Die Kölner Zunfturkunden*, 1:i, doc. nos. 11 and 12.

Schuhmaker: Wensky, *Die Stellung der Frau*, p. 47; von Loesch, *Die Kölner Zünfturkunden*, 1: doc. no. 60, and ii, doc. no. 636.

Böttcher: Wensky, Die Stellung der Frau, p. 48; von Loesch, *Die Kölner Zunfturkunden*, 1: doc. nos. 5 and 84 and ii, doc. nos. 234 and 237.

Drechsler: Wensky, *Die Stellung der Frau*, pp. 48–49; von Loesch, *Die Kölner Zunfturkunden*, 1: doc. nos. 13–16.

44. Barbiere: Wensky, *Die Stellung der Frau*, p. 52; von Loesch, *Die Kölner Zunfturkunden*, 1: doc. nos. 3, 81–83, ii, doc. no. 216.

Schmiede: Wensky, *Die Stellung der Frau*, pp. 36–37; von Loesch, *Die Kölner Zunfturkunden*, 1: doc. nos. 56 and 80.

Färber: Wensky, *Die Stellung der Frau*, pp. 44–45; von Loesch, *Die Kölner Zunfturkunden*, 1: doc. nos. 18–20, ii, doc. no. 309; Kuske, *Quellen*, 2: p. 104, 123, 129, and 149.

45. The guild statutes of 1397 expressly provided full widows' rights and extended guild membership to daughters' husbands: von Loesch, *Die Kölner Zunfturkunden*, 1: doc. no. 57. In 1426, the council first restricted women who sewed old underwear to work with cheap fabrics and in 1445 allowed them to manufacture new underwear only out of cheap fabrics: ibid., 2: doc. nos. 616 and 619; also see Wensky, *Die Stellung der Frau*, pp. 50–52.

46. Fish merchants were not organized as a guild until 1505: von Loesch, *Die Kölner Zunfturkunden*, 2: doc. no. 20A; according to Bruno Kuske, "Der Kölner Fischhandel von 14. bis 16. Jahrhundert," the *Fischmengergaffel* formed in 1396 was a political organization without economic identification. Nevertheless, the trade had long been regulated and from early on women were forbidden to sell fish unless they were whole. See Stein, *Akten zur Verfassung*, 2: doc. nos. 504, 114, and Kuske, *Quellen*, 2: doc. no. 878. Also see Wensky, *Die Stellung der Frau*, pp. 286–88.

47. Beutelmacher: Wensky, *Die Stellung der Frau*, pp. 45–46; von Loesch, *Die Kölner Zunftunkunden*, 1: doc. no. 4.

Taschenmacher: Wensky, *Die Stellung der Frau*, p. 47; von Loesch, *Die Kölner Zunfturkunden*, 1: doc. no. 70.

Buntwörter: Wensky, *Die Stellung der Frau*, pp. 49–50; von Loesch, *Die Kölner Zunfturkunden*, 1: doc. nos. 44 and 45. This trade also granted widows' rights: von Loesch, *Die Kölner Zunfturkunden*, 2: doc. no. 545.

Fleischhauer: Wensky, *Die Stellung der Frau*, pp. 56–57; von Loesch, *Die Kölner Zunfturkunden*, 1: doc. no. 21, ii, doc. no. 341. These statutes and the occasional list of names of butchers suggest that women were accepted as members of the craft but that few indeed practiced it. They did, however, dominate one of its lesser specialties, the sale of cheap cuts of meat.

48. Wensky, *Die Stellung der Frau*, pp. 53–54; von Loesch, *Die Kölner Zunfturkunden*, 1: doc. nos. 2 and 80, 2: doc. nos. 168, 168A, 174, and 181B. Also see Knipping, *Stadtrechnungen*, 1: pp. 14, 77, and 91.

49. For this analysis of the brewing industry and the guild, see Irsigler, *Die wirtschaftliche Stellung der Stadt Köln*, pp. 273. Also see Wensky, *Die Stelllung der Frau*, pp. 54–56.

50. In 1471, Keutebier production, which the council had long been trying to suppress, presumably to protect hopped beer production and the old Grutbier makers (the city collected a royalty on its production), was authorized: Irsigler, *Die wirtschaftliche Stellung der Stadt Köln*.

51. According to Irsigler, ibid., 17 of the total 80 to 121 beer producers in Cologne had some 67 percent of the market. The biggest importers of hops, however, were foreigners.

52. See Wensky, "Der Stellung der Frau in Familie, Haushalt und Wirtschaftsbetrieb im spätmittelalterlichen-frühneuzeitlichen Köln": Maria, aunt of Hermann Weinsberg, was a linen and wine merchant.

53. Erich Maschke, "Die Unterschichten der mittelalterlichen Städte Deutschlands."

54. See the discussion on the origins of silk making above.

55. For details on the needle makers and the belt makers, see Irsigler, *Die wirtschaftliche Stellung der Stadt Köln*, esp. pp. 116–18. See Wensky, *Die Stellung der Frau*, tables 35 and 36, pp. 228 and 229, for women's participation in bronze imports.

56. Von Loesch, *Die Kölner Zunfturkunden*, 1: doc. no. 109, and Wensky, *Die Stellung der Frau* (with corrections to von Loesch), p. 35, n. 30.

57. Part of the records have been published in Bruno Kuske, *Quellen zur Geschichte des Kölner Handels und Verkehrs im Mittelalter*, vol. 3; the remaining records are summarized in Irsigler, *Die wirtschaftliche Stellung der Stadt Köln*, and in Wensky, *Die Stellung der Frau.*

58. Wool had its own marketplace (the *Wollküche*). Some important dry goods, such as *Krapp* (a chemical used in textile dyeing), came through the *Kaufhaus auf dem Alten Markt* instead of the *Malzbüchel*; others may have been traded on this market as well: Kuske, *Quellen*, 3: p. 100; also see idem, "Kaufhauser und Markte."

59. Irsigler and, following him, Wensky noted this limitation, and Irsigler was usually careful to point out that his data referred only to minimum imports. Irsigler also, on p. 26, *Die wirtschaftliche Stellung der Stadt Köln*, cited Kuske's calculations (in *Quellen*, 2: p. 41) that actual imports in 1493–94 were two and one-half to three times higher than those indicated by the Akzisestundung records. But neither he nor Wensky systematically investigated the meaning of the omissions from the lists, and both generally used them as rough guides to the structure of import trade in Cologne.

The reader should keep in mind the following points when reading both Irsigler's and Wensky's tables: (1) Individuals not making use of the Akzisestundung were in all likelihood large merchants who had less need of the credit offered by the city. Kuske suggested that this was the case around the 1470s, for firms such as the van der Burgs and Vurbergs which were active in Italian trade appeared only occasionally on the lists: *Quellen*, 2: p. 41. Another group of large merchants not on the lists were foreigners, most of them from firms specializing in carrying trade, and most from upper Germany.

(2) Other Cologners, however, seem usually to have taken advantage of the right to credit. The Gewandschmitt tax records for 1426 to 1431, for example (a period when cloth wholesaling was no longer the preserve of old families, who usually dealt in large volume, but was shared by the many smaller merchants and merchant-producers emerging in the fifteenth century), can be compared with the city's *total* income booked from this

tax: the sums owed were less than 5 percent smaller than the sums booked. See, in particular, Irsigler, *Die wirtschaftliche Stellung der Stadt Köln*, p. 68, n. 300. For a similar point regarding wine imports in the second half of the fifteenth century, see ibid., table 78, p. 262.

(3) We do not have a complete list of the goods *not* traded on the *Malzbüchel* and we do not know whether all goods supposedly traded there were actually registered. We do know that fluctuations in tax policies could distort the records. See, for example, the description of how taxes on lead imports were changed during the late fifteenth century: Kuske, *Quellen*, 2: pp. 543ff., 656, 683, and 690; Irsigler, *Die wirtschaftliche Stellung der Stadt Köln*, pp. 132, n. 102, and pp. 133–35.

60. The records of cloth sales are reproduced in Irsigler, *Die wirtschaftliche Stellung der Stadt Köln*, and Wensky, *Die Stellung der Frau*.

61. The records of wine sales are in Wensky, *Die Stellung der Frau*, and Irsigler, *Die wirtschaftliche Stellung der Stadt Köln*, but for the late fourteenth century, see the more detailed records in Herborn and Militzer, *Der Kölner Weinhandel*.

62. Wensky, *Die Stellung der Frau*, tables 32, 34, 36, 38, pp. 224, 227, 229, and 231.

63. Ibid., p. 223.

64. Ibid., p. 224.

65. Ibid., p. 225.

66. Ibid., p. 226.

67. Ibid., pp. 234–36.

68. Ibid., p. 237.

69. See ibid., pp. 238–39 for the data on which this conclusion is based.

70. Ibid., pp. 254–55.

71. By way of comparison, one of Cologne's largest merchants, Heinrich Struyss, imported some 62,000 Gulden of silk between August 1493 and November 1495.

72. Wensky, *Die Stellung der Frau*, pp. 222–23, offers similar comments.

73. Kuske, *Quellen*, 2: pp. 100–142.

74. The figures on women's share of imports are taken from Wensky, table 13, pp. 195–96; her figure for total spice imports agrees with Irsigler, *Die wirtschaftliche Stellung der Stadt Köln*, table 876, p. 290, but at least the volumes for pepper and the amount of that spice handled by Wensky reported on differ from Irsigler's figures in table 90, p. 299. Part of the difference may be that Irsigler included pepper weighed in units other than pounds. These figures assume conversions of Sack to pounds as 200:1 (see n. 76 below), without conversion of other units. Accordingly, women handled 10,281 lbs. of pepper out of 111,542 (9.2 percent); 6,969 lbs. of ginger out of 64,154 (10.9 percent); and 191 lbs. of saffron out of 3,469 (5.5 percent).

In the next decade, women handled only 6,745 lbs. of pepper out of

123,499 (5.5 percent); 8,854 lbs. of ginger out of 98,209 (9.0 percent); and 60 lbs. of saffron out of 3,269 (1.8 percent): ibid., table 19, pp. 205–6.

In the 1470s, they handled 3.0 percent of the pepper and 7.2 percent of the ginger but none of the saffron: ibid., table 25, p. 210.

75. Ibid., table 13, pp. 195–96, and table 15, pp. 199–200.

76. This conversion is implied by Irsigler's table 90, p. 299, *Die wirtschaftliche Stellung der Stadt Köln*, where he treated Helmslegern's 29 Sack of pepper as 5,800 pounds.

77. For Helmslegern's imports, see Wensky, *Die Stellung der Frau*, table 15, pp. 199–200; for totals, see Irsigler, *Die wirtschaftliche Stellung der Stadt Köln*, table 90, p. 299.

78. These figures are derived from Wensky, *Die Stellung der Frau*, table 13, pp. 195–96.

79. Ibid., tables 28–30, pp. 218–20. A 1491–95 list of *purchasers* of these goods shows that women were more important as local distributors of dyes and chemicals: ibid., table 31, p. 221.

80. Ibid., pp. 194–217.

81. Ibid., pp. 217–23; 223–34.

82. Ibid., pp. 199–200.

83. Ibid., p. 203.

84. Ibid., pp. 210–11.

85. Ibid., pp. 228–32.

86. Ibid., pp. 233–35. The taxable value of her steel imports from 1497 through 1509 was almost 7,000 Gulden.

87. Ibid., pp. 234–36.

88. Ibid., pp. 210–11.

89. Ibid., pp. 203–4.

90. Ibid., p. 225.

91. Ibid., p. 208.

92. Ibid., p. 211.

93. Ibid., p. 223.

94. Ibid., pp. 224–25.

95. The fee effectively restricted membership to the well-to-do, but after 1396 the membership was increasingly made up of artisans and merchant-producers rather than specialists in long-distance trade: Irsigler, *Die wirtschaftliche Stellung der Stadt Köln*, pp. 64–65. Wool weavers were not well represented in the group of Gewandschneider, although after 1396 the commerce denied them in 1371 was again permitted them. For a sketch of the history of this occupation and its changing social and economic composition, see ibid., pp. 62ff.

96. Von Loesch, *Die Kölner Zunfturkunden*, 1: doc. no. 98.

97. The raw data are from city accounts printed in Knipping, *Stadtrechnungen*, 1: p. 45, and from records of the cloth halls in StaK Zunft 29, 485, 486.

98. Wensky, *Die Stellung der Frau*, pp. 243ff.

99. See Irsigler, *Die wirtschaftliche Stellung der Stadt Köln*, p. 71, and Wensky, *Die Stellung der Frau*, pp. 244–45.

100. Wensky, *Die Stellung der Frau*, pointed out that this decline corresponds with a decrease in the number of women admitted to citizenship in the early sixteenth century. Since citizenship was required for membership in the Gewandschnitt (but for few other trades), we can assume that the two declines were related.

101. Of the ninety-six members of the Seideamt analyzed by Wensky, twenty-three had direct connections to the Gewandschnitt: see ibid., pp. 116–34.

102. Table 5 reminds us that Cologne's Gewandschneider handled few sales of domestically produced cloth. The best source of information about these sales, an isolated record of excise taxes paid by *purchasers* of wool cloth produced in Cologne during eight months of 1428 and 1429, shows that two of the sixteen largest members of the Wollamt selling cloth were women; the sixteen accounted for some 38 percent of sales and the two women for 3 percent. These women may have been widows of masters but may also have belonged to the Wollamt by virtue of another trade. A 1417 list of Gaffeln members who contributed to a forced loan named eighteen female Wollamt members; at least one of these eighteen women (there were 135 men) was a yarn maker; von Loesch, *Die Kölner Zunfturkunden*, 1: no. 80, p. 209. See also Wensky's corrections, *Die Stellung der Frau*, p. 43, no. 86.

Although after 1396 Cologne's wool weavers were permitted membership in the Gewandschnitt, few took advantage of the opportunity, and normally they continued to sell their cloth themselves, usually at regional trade fairs. Irsigler has suggested that the difficulty of the combination of cloth production with management of a wholesale outlet that had to keep regular hours, the high cost of membership in the Gewandschnitt, and perhaps a certain aversion to dealing in cloth made elsewhere explain the wool weavers' infrequent participation in the trade. The Gewandschneider did not themselves sell much Cologne-produced wool cloth, doubtless because the weavers managed their own sales energetically at least from the fourteenth century on; for a fuller discussion of the outlets for Cologne-produced wool cloth, see Irsigler, *Die wirtschaftliche Stellung der Stadt Köln*, pp. 51ff.

103. Wensky, *Die Stellung der Frau*, tables 55–56, pp. 262 and 263–64.

104. Herborn and Militzer, *Der Kölner Weinhandel*, p. 37, commented that "selbständiges Handel ohne Rückhalt des Gatten blieb eher Aushahme als Regel. . . ."

105. Wensky, *Die Stellung der Frau*, tables 58–61, pp. 265–67.

106. Figures are from ibid., table 63, p. 271, and Irsigler, *Die wirtschaftliche Stellung der Stadt Köln*, table 80, p. 265.

107. Wensky, *Die Stellung der Frau*, pp. 271–72.

108. Ibid., table 65, pp. 274–75.

109. Ibid., tables 66–68, pp. 277–79.

110. See in particular Wensky's biographical sketch of Bielgen Pyll, ibid., p. 280.

111. Ibid., table 69, pp. 281–82.

112. These figures are derived from Irsigler, *Die wirtschaftliche Stellung der Stadt Köln*, table 69, p. 247; table 74, p. 254; table 80, p. 265.

113. Wensky, *Die Stellung der Frau*, pp. 256–57, and table 52, p. 256.

114. Ibid., p. 283.

115. For example, see Kuske, *Quellen*, 1: doc. nos. 130, 683, 895, 1005, 1093, and Wensky, *Die Stellung der Frau*, pp. 284–85.

116. See Wensky, *Die Stellung der Frau*, pp. 19–20; Stein, *Akten zur Verfassung*, 1: doc. no. 86; Kuske, *Quellen*, 2, doc. no. 188.

117. Fygen von Weinsberg (married 1516), partner to her husband in the wine trade and in a linen-dyeing enterprise, bore eleven live children; another woman of the same generation who was independently active in the linen trade and in the Weinzapf had thirteen; a silk dealer traveled to the fairs at Frankfurt am Main, leaving at least three children under the age of six at home: Wensky, "Die Stellung der Frau in Familie, Haushalt und Wirtschaftsbetrieb im spätmittelalterlichen-frühneuzeitlichen Köln," p. 12.

118. In ibid., Wensky provided a few details that illustrate this point.

119. We do not have precise counts for either city. In Leiden, it will be recalled, it was estimated that only about 200 women could have been employed in high-status work in the drapery, which was not only the largest employer in the city by far but the source of most high-status jobs. In Cologne, a city almost three times as large, at any one time 200 silk makers, yarn makers, and gold spinners were enrolled, another group of almost the same size was involved in the Staple trade, and the forty-odd traditional guilds had at least 100 mistresses. If we add the hundreds of women grocers, brokers, toll collectors, pawnbrokers, innkeepers, midwives, and minor city employees (Wensky, *Die Stellung der Frau*, has some examples of women who held these jobs), we easily can arrive at a total of some 1,000 women working in high-status positions.

120. The lists of wool importers paying the excise tax in Leiden include an occasional woman's name, almost always that of a widow of a large draper; other records sometimes name a large draper's widow as a producer. See chap. 4 for details.

121. Kellenbenz, "Wirtschaftsgeschichte Kölns im 16. und beginnenden 17. Jahrhundert," in his *Zweijahrtausende Kölner Wirtschaft*, pp. 335 and 357.

CHAPTER SEVEN

1. See also Herman van der Wee and Erik van Mingroot, "The Charter of the Clothiers' Guild of Lier, 1275," and the references they cite.

2. Among the names on a 1419–34 list of 117 wool importers, for

example, 12 were large merchants who accounted for 58 percent of all import transactions (33 transactions per importer). The remaining 105 importers accounted for the rest (less than 3 transactions per importer). Another record from 1419–32 provided the names of 227 weavers who were judged to have imported inferior wools for cloth manufacture; records from the same period indicate that the wool purchases of these people were also small, averaging about 3 transactions per weaver.

3. See in particular his *La vie urbaine de Douai au moyen âge*, 2: p. 699.

4. Espinas's principal study of the Boinbroke operation is "Jehan Boine Broke. Bourgeois et drapier Douaisien." See also Espinas's comments in *La vie urbaine de Douai au moyen âge*, 2: p. 697, and his *Les origines du capitalisme*.

5. Espinas, *La vie urbaine de Douai au moyen âge*, 2: pp. 1012–13. See also Espinas and Pirenne, *Recueil des documents relatifs à l'industrie drapière en Flandre*, 1(2): doc. no. 218 (1).

6. The ordinances regularly prohibited merchants from extending credit to workers, accepting their work as collateral on a loan, renting them houses, or, in general, operating a truck system. See, for example, Espinas and Pirenne, *Recueil des documents relatifs à l'industrie drapière en Flandre*, 1(2): doc. nos. 282, 239 (50), and 224 (10–11).

The nonlegislative documents published in this collection (primarily wills, contracts, and records of civil suits) give evidence of the existence of a substantial artisanal class. Admittedly, many of the documents record the debts owed by these artisans and small merchants, but we need not take this to mean that these people were marginally viable entrepreneurs. The medieval economy was not a cash economy, but it made very heavy use of debt instruments; the ability to participate in the economy might just as readily be read as evidence of financial soundness as of financial precariousness. (Espinas, *La vie urbaine*, 2: p. 1029, argued that many of the debts owed by the artisans mentioned in these documents were the property of wool/cloth merchants, but he supplied no independent confirmation of his suspicion. The debts were in the area of 3 to 5 Flemish pounds, about equal to the wholesale price of a good—but not luxury—cloth of Douai, and probably worth more than half the annual wage of a skilled construction worker.)

7. See Espinas, *La vie urbaine*, 2: p. 969, and his comments on p. 971. Ordinances mentioning women weavers include doc. nos. 235 (11, 13, 19), 256 (8, 11, 18), 328 (24); for fullers and finishers (*foulons, pareurs, tondeurs* or *tendeurs*), see doc. nos. 239 (34), 240 (2), 328 (6); for one of many references to dyeing, see doc. no. 231 (1); for warping, see, for example, doc. no. 234 (8); both *ourdres* and *ourderesses* are regularly mentioned in the ordinances.

8. For one of the many examples, see ibid., doc. no. 223 (1 and 2).

9. Ibid., doc. nos. 224 (6, 9, 12, 19), 227 (1), 228 (3), 229 (56 and 57), 231 (1, 2 and 12), 234 (8), 235 (5, 6, 9, 13, 14, 15, 16, 24), 238 (4–10), 239 (7, 35, 51), 240 (3, 10, 20), 243 (5, 6, 8, 10), 275 (4, 10, 11), 276 (9, 25), 278

(1, 2), 315 (9), 348 (1, 2, 5), 349 (1, 6, 8). 380 (A-1, 7, 17, 18, 21, 23, 25), 384 (E-8, 11), 386 (G-2), 388 (I-8).

10. Ibid., doc. no. 234 (8): "Et que nus ourderes ne ourderesse, ne hom ne feme, ne soit si hardis ke il ourde drap ne couverture a home ne a feme, s'il n'est borgois ur borgoise de le vile, sor ce meisme forfait, se ce n'est par le conseil et par le congiet des eschevins en le hale."

11. Ibid., doc. no. 239 (7): "Et que drapiers ne drapiere n'envoit sen drap au maistre, s'il n'envoie le bure avoec, sor 20s."

12. For example, ibid., doc. nos. 229 (1, 6, 7, 9, 11, 20, 22), 276 (10, 11), 337 (3–6); 380 (1), 389 (2, 3), all of which refer to women buying and selling wool, dyes, and other raw materials. See also the following references to women cloth merchants: doc. nos. 231 (4, 5), 321 (6, 8), 323 (1–3), 324, 337 (1, 2, 9), 349 (10, 11), 380 (A-7), 381 (B-1).

Further, the regulations treating brokerage always mentioned women (brokers arranged sales between city producers and visiting merchants). Their functions seem to have been analogous to those of Leiden's sixteenth-century *uutreeders* and Courtrai's fifteenth-century *makelaars:* see doc. no. 321 (4, 5, 6, 8).

A list of fees from 1324 for renting stalls to sell at retail in Douai's *basse halle* named sixteen women among the sixty-three retailers; in a list almost its duplicate, thirteen of fifty-two retailers were women; ibid., doc. no. 338. In the *basse halle*, cloth was sold by the piece; according to Espinas, few of the names on this list were patrician and many may have been finishers (*tondeurs*).

But two similar lists named those who rented *quariel* in the *haute halle* where cloth was sold at wholesale; one of nine persons on the first list was a woman, and one of eight on the second was a woman. These merchants were certainly from some sort of economic elite.

A document of 1331–33 that listed fees due for past sales both in the wholesale cloth hall and at retail confirm the impression that it was not just women from small household shops who dealt in cloth. The list of the wholesaling fees due from 1326 named women as three among the total of six; the list of retail sales fees from 1327 and 1328 indicate that twelve of fifty-eight retailers were women: see ibid., doc. no. 341.

13. The family production unit may occasionally have survived for centuries in this region. In *Ladies of the Leisure Class,* Bonnie Smith reported that as late as the early nineteenth century women of the *Nord* actively managed family-owned capitalist industrial firms. She describes (chap. 3) these women as "capitalists of the first order" and contrasts them with their late-nineteenth-century descendants who were truly "ladies of the leisure class." The *Nord* was, of course, historically Flemish, having come to the French only as a consequence of Louis XIV's wars with Spain. Is it possible that the women running capitalist enterprises there in the early nineteenth century perpetuated a tradition that had direct roots in the late Middle Ages?

14. Ibid., doc. no. 229 (32), p. 47: "Et se li lainne n'estoit bien tinte de tele couleur con li drapiers u li drapiere aroit diviset au tinterier u a se feme u a sen maistre vallet."

15. Ibid., doc. no. 385 (11).

16. Ibid., doc. no. 250.

17. The principal studies and collections of sources used for this analysis were the following: F. Bothe, *Beiträge zur Wirtschafts- und Sozialgeschichte der Reichsstadt Frankfurt*; idem, "Die Entwicklung der direkten Besteurung in der Reichsstadt Frankfurt bis zur Revolution 1612–1614"; idem, "Frankfurter Patriziervermögen im 16. Jahrhundert"; idem, "Frankfurts Wirtschaftsleben im Mittelalter"; idem, *Geschichte der Stadt Frankfurt am Main*; K. Bücher, *Die Bevölkerung von Frankfurt a.M. im 14. und 15. Jahrhundert*; idem, *Frankfurts wirtschaftlichsoziale Entwicklung vor dem dreissigjahrigen Kriege und der Fettmilchaufstand (1612–1616)*; A. Dietz, *Frankfurter Bürgerbuch*; W. Kallmorgen, *Siebenhundert Jahre Heilkunde in Frankfurt am Main*; G. L. Kriegk, *Deutsches Bürgerthum im Mittelalter*, 2 vols.; idem, *Frankfurter Bürgerzwiste und Zustande im Mittelalter*; H. Mauersberg, *Wirtschafts- und Sozialgeschichte zentraleuropäischer Städte in neuer Zeit; dargestellt an den Beispielen von Basel, Frankfurt a.M., Hamburg, Hannover und München*; K. Bücher and B. Schmidt, eds., *Frankfurter Amts- und Zunfturkunden bis zum Jahre 1612* ("Zunfturkunden bis zum Jahre 1612"); G. Witzel, "Gewerbegeschichtliche Studien zur niederlandischen Einwanderung in Deutschland im 16. Jahrhundert."

18. For this argument, see Bothe, "Frankfurts Wirtschaftsleben im Mittelalter."

19. In 1600, approximately 2,500 people from Flanders, Brabant, and Hainault lived in Frankfurt. In the late sixteenth century Frankfurt also was established as a center of Jewish settlement. In 1542, there may have been about 300 to 500 Jews in the city but by 1605 there were about 2,100. In 1600 these two groups made up over a fifth of the city's population, which by some estimates reached almost 20,000 (estimated in Dietz, *Frankfurter Bürgerbuch*, pp. 187ff.). The numerical importance of Netherlanders in the population of Frankfurt is borne out by scattered pieces of information: from 1606 through 1613, 13 percent of all registered baptisms in Frankfurt were of Netherlandish children; for the period 1591–5, 15 percent of all registered deaths were of Netherlanders.

20. G. Witzel, "Gewerbegeschichtliche Studien," p. 145, reports that of 195 Netherlandish immigrants in 1556, 103 were textile workers, and of 417 in 1557, 226 had occupations of this sort.

21. For discussions of these industries, see Dietz, *Frankfurter Bürgerbuch*, p. 144; Bothe, *Geschichte der Stadt Frankfurt am Main*, pp. 104–12; idem, *Die Entwicklung der direkten Besteurung in der Reichsstadt Frankfurt*, pp. 225–33.

22. F. Bothe, *Geschichte der Stadt Frankfurt am Main*, pp. 110–11; idem, *Die Entwicklung der direkten Besteurung in der Reichsstadt Frankfurt*, p. 162.

23. A group of lists of citizen and tax rolls surviving from the four-

teenth to the seventeenth centuries illustrates these economic and social changes more precisely. In 1387, the date of the first list, over 80 percent of the adult male population worked as artisans while only 7 percent worked in commerce or the professions. The largest production sectors were clothing and cleaning (17 percent), food (16 percent), and wool cloth production (17 percent). Only 1 percent of the adult men named in this survey of heads of household (which identified the occupations of about 60 percent of the men named on the role [2,900 in a total population estimated at 10,000]) were wage workers. In 1586, only 21 percent of adult males were in the three areas of clothing, food, and wool textiles combined while 5 percent of the adult males were wage workers in unspecified trades, 13 percent were silk workers (most of them wage workers), and 15 percent produced agricultural products for market (95 percent of the men named on the roll were identified by occupation [1,919 men named in a total population of about 14,400]). By 1607, only 55 percent of the male heads of household identified by trade were in the skilled crafts but 26 percent were in commerce or the professions (87 percent of the men on the roll were identified by occupation [1,565 men named in a total population estimated at 17,900]). Data for these statistical summaries are from: Bücher, *Die Bevölkerung von Frankfurt a.M.*, pp., 66, 141–47, 96, 214–25, and 520; Bothe, *Beiträge zur Wirtschafts- und Sozialgeschichte der Reichsstadt Frankfurt*, pp. 153–58; idem, *Frankfurts wirtschaftliche-soziale Entwicklung*, pp. 50–157, 121*–136*.

24. Bücher, *Die Bevölkerung von Frankfurt am Main*, p. 146, provides evidence that as early as the late fourteenth century, the organized work force included almost all skilled artisans. Of 1,353 independent adult men identified by occupation (excluding merchants, professionals, city officials, and other nonartisans), only 13 practiced trades not listed as subject to guild regulations; 77 belonged to the guild associated with their occupation, 8 belonged to no guild, and 2 belonged to a guild associated with a foreign occupation. The increasing volume of guild-associated legislation during the fifteenth century suggests that the number of unorganized artisans would have shrunk during the fifteenth century.

25. This development is illustrated by the ordinances of the *Schneider*, one of Frankfurt's largest and most important guilds (which for long periods of time included the *Seidensticker* and the *Tuchscherer* or *Gewandschneider*). Three major codifications were produced during the period. The first, in 1377, part of the second *Handwerkerbuch* issued in that year, contained the rewritten ordinances of the guilds that survived the abortive revolution of 1366 and those of new or recombined guilds. (The first *Handwerkerbuch*, begun in 1355, contained the ordinances of the contemporary guilds, including two sets of regulations for the *Schneider*, one from 1352 and one from 1355.) The second codification, contained in the third *Handwerkerbuch*, reissued and reformulated regulations first issued in 1479, was made soon after 1479. The third was issued in 1588.

Each codification was amended and supplemented over the intervening years.

The developments I have described, while best appreciated through a close reading of the articles themselves, can be suggested by contrasting several of their features:

(1) The ordinances became longer and more detailed. The issue of 1377 contained 19 articles (that of 1352 contained 25, that of 1355, 7); the 1479 issue contained 41; the 1588 issue, 83.

(2) The guild increasingly came under the control of the council and the mayors of Frankfurt, and even came to be described almost as an agent of the government. The ordinances of 1352 were apparently issued by the authority of the masters alone; the first article began, "Die sint die gesetzede, die wir, die meystere, die snydere und die duchschere zu Frankinford, die die zunft hant, umb gemeinen nutz unsirs handwerckis undir uns gesast und gemacht, alse von stucke hernach stet geschrebin" (1: no. 1, p. 500).

Those of 1377 were prefaced by an acknowledgment of the council's authority; the Prologue said, "Nota daz hernach geshriben stet, sint die gesetze der snydere, der sydenstydkere und der gewantscherer, alse in die der rad irleubet und irneuewet hat" (1: no. 1, page 504). The first and fourth articles required regular oaths to the emperor and the council (doubtlessly in response to the 1366 uprising), and that fines collected by the guild be split with the city and that masters maintain gear for defense of the city. The revisions of 1479 added the point that the guild's legislative and judicial authority was derived from the council and forbade meetings without the council's knowledge and approval (nos. 2 and 6).

(3) Entrance requirements for masters became more elaborate. In 1377, new masters had to swear an oath, be a citizen, provide gear to outfit themselves for defense of the city, and pay 3 lbs. *heller* and 1/4 wine (nos. 1, 2, 4 and 8). The rules remained unchanged in 1479, but in 1588 new entrants had to prove their own and their wives' legitimacy; produce a masterpiece and provide 1/4 wine in order to offer it, a gift they gave again along with an 8 shilling fine if they failed; stand before the council as a candidate for citizenship; and swear separate oaths to the city and to the guild. If accepted, they paid 3 lbs. *heller,* 1/4 wine for themselves, another 1 Gulden for their wives, and 16 shillings for a bucket (for the fire brigade).

(4) The requirements for trainees escalated even more rapidly. In 1377, the sole reference to apprentices had them paying 5 shilling to the guild (no. 11). In 1479, they paid 10 shillings and swore an oath (nos. 20 and 34); in 1588 apprentices had to prove their legitimacy, masters were limited to one apprentice and two journeymen, and journeymen had to have been employed for two years before gaining a mastership (64, 65, 74, and 79).

Each of these changes may have had a different origin, but together they undoubtedly contributed to the organizational changes of the sort I call the business and political organization of work.

26. The ordinances of the coopers, fishers, gardeners, cloth and wool workers, linen and fustian workers, shippers, smiths, tailors, and slaters and tilers all refer to or explicitly include women as full-fledged trade members. The ordinances of the bakers, merchant retailers (*Gewandschneider*), furriers, tanners, butchers, cobblers, saddlers, painters, shoemakers, masons, cartwrights, and carpenters do not mention women.

27. The regulations of the fishers' and tailors' guilds continued to include women throughout the period but the linen workers mentioned women only up to 1550.

28. The bathing house workers made up the only guild that continued to refer to women practitioners; the wooden-shoe makers, the hatmakers, the cabinet makers, and the glovers included women during the fifteenth century but not afterwards; the two guilds of barbers and brewers and of goldsmiths never mentioned women.

29. The bookbinders, book printers, potters, ferrymen, belt makers, silk and lace makers, rope makers, and shearers seem to have excluded them.

30. The usual phrases are "das handwerck halten" (or "treiben"), "in das hantwerg gewand sein," "das hantwerg haben." For examples, see Karl Bücher and Benno Schmidt, eds., *Frankfurter Amts- und Zunfturkunden bis zum Jahre 1612*, 1: nos. 13, 19 and 32, p. 191; no. 35, p. 506; no. 9, p. 291; no. 23, p. 462; nos. 9 and 10, pp. 511–12; no. 9, p. 435; 2: no. 35, p. 157; no. 132, p. 173; no. 114, p. 205; no. 8, p. 2; no. 313, p. 211.

There were rare exceptions. A late sixteenth-century ordinance of the *Hosenstricker, Teppich- und Barrettmacher,* for example, referred to a *maisterin*; 1: no. 12, p. 258.

31. Ibid., 2: no. 3, pp. 75–76 (*Steindecker*); no. 114, p. 205 (*Wollenweber*).

32. Ibid., 2: no. 131, p. 211.

33. Ibid., 1: no. 14, pp. 512–13 and no. 11, p. 512.

34. Ibid., 1: no. 9, p. 291.

Also see 1: no. 2, p. 91 (dated 1355) which extends similar rights to daughters of coopers, and 1: no. 10, p. 5 (dated ca. 1479) extending entrance rights to daughters of tailors.

35. Ibid., 1: no. 10, p. 4: "Des glichen sollen die witfrauwen, so in handtwerckern und sunst mit narung, wie obstet, versehen sein sollen, iren harnesch in obgemelter maissen halten, domit sie ander manspersonen zu der stat Franckfort noitturft rustig machen moge." See also, for example, 1: no. 11, p. 512, which extended widows' rights to wives of tailors (dated ca. 1479): "Item die witwen, den ire menner zu zyden abegangen sin, sollen, obe sie wollen, dwile sie off iren witwestule sitzen und den erberlich halten, alles das recht han, als ire mennere hatten, off das sie sich und ihre kinde desterbass generen mogen, doch as sie den harnesch halde und einen redelichen knecht bestelle, der mit solichem

harnesch dem rade zu sinen und der stede gescheffte bereit und gewertig sij."

36. For examples, see ibid., 1: no. 9, p. 92; no. 59, p. 107; no. 61, p. 107; no. 62, p. 109; no. 9, p. 183; nos. 2 and 3, p. 203; no. 5, p. 205; no. 93, p. 314; nos. 9 and 14, pp. 351–52; no. 7, p. 424; no. 10, p. 425; no. 18, p. 426; no. 10, p. 435; no. 5, p. 443; no. 4, p. 450; no. 9, p. 453; no. 10, p. 479; no. 1, p. 527, no. 9, p. 530; ibid., 2: no. 22a, pp. 32–33; no. 4, p. 47; no. 3, pp. 75–76; no. 10, p. 78; nos. 4 and 5, pp. 90–91; no. 31, p. 108; no. 6, pp. 116–17; no. 10, p. 140; no. 10, p. 227; no. 10, p. 243; no. 9, p. 74; no. 3, p. 84; no. 9, p. 253; no. 11, p. 253; no. 49, pp. 271–72; no. 3, p. 4; no. 51, p. 14; no. 11, p. 19; no. 11, p. 153; no. 8, pp. 167–68; no. 5, p. 66; ibid., 1: no. 8, pp. 126–27; no. 6, p. 134; no. 18, p. 177, no. 3, p. 255; no. 7, pp. 257–58, no. 5, p. 257; no. 37, p. 416; no. 43, p. 418.

The practice does not appear to have declined at the end of the period.

37. Ibid., 1: no. 19, p. 506.

38. Ibid., 1: no. 15, p. 513.

39. Ibid., 2: no. 35, p. 157.

40. Ibid., 1: no. 4, p. 182.

41. The situation in fourteenth-century Ghent, where guilds staked a claim for political power, seems to have resembled that in fifteenth-century Cologne. From Ghent, we have a suit that shows that women were already being excluded from the dyers' guild. The suit was brought before Ghent's *Schepenen* in 1367: Espinas and Pirenne, *Recueil de documents relatifs à l'industrie drapière en Flandre*, 2: doc. no. 478.

42. See p. 169 and n. 25 above where I argue that the increasing specificity and restriction evident in later guild ordinances reflects a change in the powers and structure of guilds.

43. Bücher and Schmidt, *Frankfurter Amts- und Zunfturkunden bis zum Jahre 1612*, 1: no. 34, p. 412.

44. Ibid., 2: no. 132, p. 173.

45. Ibid., 1: no. 41, p. 417.

46. Ibid., 2: no. 42, p. 417.

47. Ibid., 1: nos. 51 and 54, pp. 419–20.

48. Few of the primary and secondary sources published about cities of the period yield enough specific information about the political and economic context of women's work to conduct even the cursory tests possible in the cases of Lier, Douai, and Frankfurt am Main. The occasional study does, however, offer glimpses of women with high-status positions in market production where conditions were apparently unlike those in any of the five cities investigated in my study. Whether the pattern of women's work suggested in these cases can be explained by the hypothesis applied in my study probably cannot be known without additional archival research.

Fifteenth-century Brussels appears to be one such instance. According to G. des Marez (whose *L'organisation du travail à Bruxelles* of 1904 remains the standard for late medieval Brussels as Posthumus's work is for Leiden or Espinas's for Douai), women there regularly participated in market production. They produced cloth, both the heavy *draperie* that had dominated fourteenth-century industry in Brussels and the new drapery that expanded in the fifteenth century. They did so with the permission of the *gilde*, which regulated the textile industry and, therefore, des Marez concludes, did so as its members. Women practiced skilled crafts and were described as mistresses in several of the corporate craft guilds (the *métiers*) which achieved recognition after 1421. In at least one *métier* (the *gantiers*), they formally apprenticed.

An interpretation of these data must await further research. It is not clear that registration with the *gilde* implied membership in it; the extent of women's participation in the developing *métiers* needs to be made more precise, as does any change in women's participation from the fourteenth to the fifteenth centuries; the relationship between the artisan or merchant family and the public organizations which oversaw commerce and industry needs illumination; modifications in the social organization of work during the late-fourteenth-century decline of long-distance trade and of the traditional drapery need study. Des Marez's investigation, focused as it was on somewhat different issues, leads us to, but cannot answer, these questions.

F. Favresse's later *L'avènement du régime démocratique à Bruxelles* takes up some of these questions, but not with an eye towards examining women's place in the sociopolitical structure of Brussels.

Another city which deserves further investigation is fourteenth-century Ghent. Although most records concerning the drapery (which dominated Ghent's economy) have not survived, records of other sorts reveal that women were active in commerce, in retailing, and in the crafts, even after the so-called guild revolutions of the period. For a description of women's work in the city, see D. Nicholas, *Domestic Life in a Medieval City*.

CHAPTER EIGHT

1. See in particular his comments on pp. 69–70 in *Die Frauenfrage im Mittelalter*.

2. To be sure, not all share this view. Some have questioned the extent of the *Frauenfrage* or even its existence. For a discussion of the literature on both sides, see Edith Ennen, "Die Frau in der mittelalterlichen Stadtgesellschaft Mitteleuropas," p. 13; for further references and a critique, see Kurt Wesoly, "Der weibliche Bevölkerungsanteil."

Others have even considered the oversupply of women responsible for their *departure* from market production in cities. David Herlihy has taken this view, claiming that, as part of a general loss of status caused by the excess numbers, women steadily lost labor status throughout the late Middle Ages; see in particular "Women in Medieval Society" and "Life Expectancies for Women in Medieval Society."

3. See chap. 5, esp. n. 14, for a discussion of the literature on late medieval depression or the "depression of the Renaissance." See also Hans van Werveke, "Ambachten en erfelijkheid," for evidence of the increased exclusivity of guilds in the Low Countries at the end of the Middle Ages.

4. For evidence that the relative oversupply of women persisted in Europe well beyond 1500, see Edith Ennen, "Die Frau in der mittelalterlichen Stadtgesellschaft Mitteleuropas," n. 40; Roger Mols, *Introduction à la démographie historique des villes d'Europe du xivme au xviiime siècle;* and J. Verbeemen, "De Werking van economische factoren op de stedelijke demografie der xviie en der xviiie eeuw in de zuidelijke Nederlanden," which offer extensive evidence that the oversupply of women in cities in the southern Low Countries was just as marked during the seventeenth and eighteenth centuries.

5. Women accounted for between ca. 19 percent and 28 percent of head-of-household taxpayers in fifteenth-century Frankfurt am Main and accounted for about 23 percent in Leiden in 1498. (The Frankfurt data are taken from Bücher, *Frauenfrage*, p. 76; readers interested in more detail should compare Bücher's figures with those reported in Friedrich Bothe, "Die Entwicklung der direkten Besteuerung," pp. 106*–108*).

Women made up between 16 percent and 24 percent of fourteenth century head-of-household taxpayers in Frankfurt and accounted for 20 percent of taxpayers in 1607. (The fourteenth-century figures are from Bücher, *Die Frauenfrage;* the seventeenth-century figure is from Bothe, "Die Entwicklung der direkten Besteuerung," pp. 120*–35*.)

6. N. Z. Davis, "Women in the *arts méchaniques* in sixteenth-century Lyon," p. 145.

7. N. W. Posthumus, *Geschiedenis van de Leidsche Lakenindustrie*, 1: pp. 360-61.

8. Wensky, *Die Stellung der Frau.*

9. See chap. 1 above for a discussion of these changes.

10. Petot and Vandenbossche, "Le statut de la femme dans les pays coutumiers français du xiiie au xviie siècle," in *La Femme*, ed. Société de Jean Bodin.

11. Gilissen, "Le statut de la femme," in ibid.

12. Casey, "The Cheshire Cat," p. 247, n. 15.

13. See Barbara Diefendorf, "Widowhood and Remarriage."

14. Bonnie Smith, *Ladies of the Leisure Class*, found, however, that in the *Nord* urban women from rich merchant families actively joined in the management of family businesses until early in the nineteenth century.

15. This notion pervades several disciplines. See, for example, the literature on the "domestic-labour debate": W. Secombe, "The Housewife and Her Labour," J. Gardiner, "Women's Domestic Labour," M. Coulson et al., "The Housewife and her Labour," and W. Secombe, "Reply." See Paul Smith, "Domestic Labour and Marx's Theory of Value" and T. Fee, "Domestic Labour: An Analysis of Housework and Its Relationship to the

Productive Process," for reviews of and contributions to the debate; sociological literature as represented by Talcott Parsons, "A Revised Analytical Approach to the Theory of Social Stratification" and *Essays in Sociological Theory* (see also Veronica Beechey, "Women and Production: a Critical Analysis of some Sociological Theories of Women's Work," for a critique of Parsons); and economists such as W. Elliott Brownlee, "Household Values, Women's Work and Economic Growth, 1800–1930"; Martha N. Frauendorf, "The Labor Force Participation of Turn-of-Century Married Women"; Richard C. Edwards, Michael Reich, and David Gordon, eds., *Labor Market Segmentation.*

For a Marxist-feminist attack on the notion that women derive their class position from the family and thus presumably play no active role in forming classes, see Jackie West, "Women, Sex, and Class." She argued that women's place in the labor process (under capitalism) both determines the nature of the class structure *and* makes class members of women. She does not deny that women play special roles in economic production because they are subject to a particular division of labor by sex which restricts their access to the paid labor market (or makes it different from men's). West's analysis implies that the family is not a unit in the social hierarchy and that husband and wife, son and daughter, need not belong to the same class. It follows that a woman's status in the social hierarchy was not independent of, but bound to, her place in economic production. Even conceding West's point, we may still find, however, a discrepancy between a woman's class as measured by standard of living, life-style, and ideology, and as measured by the objective conditions of her work.

16. These tendencies were also present in the late Middle Ages. At the moment when family firms established permanent operations, women were often excluded. In *Die Familie in der deutschen Stadt des späten Mittelalters*, Maschke showed that the family unit once served most effectively in long-distance trade carried on in German commercial cities (see pp. 54ff.), but that in the case of the Fugger and other family firms which established permanent operations outside their home cities, it became common to write women family members out of the firm: "weibliche und geistliche Mitglieder der Familie ausgezahlt wurden und als Gesellschafter ausschieden. Die Gesellschaftskapital blieb bei Mannestamme" (p. 64).

17. Lawrence Stone, *The Family, Sex and Marriage*, has offered a well-known version of this argument. The family of early modern England became a rigidly hierarchical and patriarchal institution which subordinated women, thanks to the emergence of the national state, the teachings and institutional structure of Protestantism, the explosion and institutionalization of learning, and changes in property law. Stone argues, however, that this family structure was short-lived, and he proposes that it was superseded by companionate marriages. In this respect, he presents a thesis fundamentally at odds with the idea, widely accepted among feminist scholars, that the early modern period was the beginning of a

subordination peculiar to bourgeois women which lasted well into the twentieth century.

18. The decision from a court case of 1367 in Ghent forbade a dyer's daughter from joining the guild in spite of her family claim to a place. Two centuries later almost the same arguments were heard in Dordrecht about a *wantsnijder's* daughter—and the same decision was reached. For Ghent, see G. Espinas and H. Pirenne, *Recueil des documents relatifs à l'industrie drapière en Flandre*, 2: doc. no. 478; for Dordrecht, see Overvoorde, *Rekeningen van de gilden van Dordrecht*, p. 198 (cited in Jenneke Quast, "Vrouwenarbeid omstreeks 1500 in enkele nederlandse steden"); see also the Paris case of 1399 (G. Fagniez, *Documents relatifs à l'histoire de l'industrie et du commerce en France*, 1: pp. 172–73).

19. Many versions of the Noah cycle of plays in fifteenth-century England, for example, portray Mistress Noah as a shrewish, unattractive, bossy tradeswoman (who, by the way, had better sense and management skills than her husband). Katherine Rogers, *The Troublesome Helpmate*, offers a guide to some of the misogynistic literature emanating from bourgeois culture in the late Middle Ages. As Joan Kelly pointed out in "Early Feminist Theory and the *Querelle des Femmes*, 1400–1789," the misogynistic themes of this literature proved inspiring for writers of the literature read in aristocratic circles, for example, Jan de Meung's section of the *Roman de la rose* (1277).

20. Prologue, *Canterbury Tales*.

21. *Een scoon spel van Mariken van Niemeghen*, ed. P. Leendertz, Jr., p. 287.

22. Sarah Melhado White, "Sexual Language and Human Conflict in Old French Fabliaux," p. 185.

23. A case from early fifteenth-century Paris seems to combine exactly these tensions. A woman who had been variously a successful hatmaker, weaver, and cloth merchant (or retailer), who employed her own apprentices and owned her own house, was reprimanded for dressing above her station (a violation of sumptuary laws) and ordered to move from her residence on the grounds that she was a prostitute and madam. The testimony summarized suggests that she was charged as much for her cheeky aggressiveness as for actual deeds: G. Fagniez, *Documents relatifs à l'histoire de l'industrie et du commerce en France*, 1: pp. 204–5.

24. Hans Medick, in Kriedte, Medick, and Schlumbohm, *Industrialisierung vor der Industrialisierung*, pp. 133–37, and in "The Proto-industrial Family Economy," proposed a similar interpretation, and evidence he offered from early modern rural society (where women in peasant families worked as wage-earning weavers) suggests that the sex-gender system was in flux because of women's enhanced earning power.

25. This study has quoted several of the many instances recorded in documents of this period when legislation was deliberately changed to exclude women or when courts deliberately ruled that women were

"henceforth" not to practice a particular trade. Occasionally we find excuses being made for the exclusion: in Ghent, when a woman was forbidden to carry on her father's dyeing trade, it was argued that it had not been traditional for sons and daughters to inherit from their parents (see n. 18 above); in England in 1461, it was claimed that weaving ought to be reserved for men because only they defended the king and his realm and because only they were sufficiently learned in the trade (*The Little Red Book of Bristol*, ed. F. B. Bickley, 2: pp. 127–28).

Works Cited

PRIMARY SOURCES

Manuscript

Leiden, Gemeente Archief

Oude Rechterlijke Archief
4. *Corrextieboeken* A,B,C,D,F,H
41. *Kenningboeken* A,C,H,L
42. *Wedboeken* 1477–1496, 1506–1515, 1526–1527, July 1539–October 1540

Archief der Secretarie I
C. Archief van Poortmeesters en Burgemeesters 536
D. Archief van den Tresorier-ordinaries 578, 579, 588, 589, 623.
Nos. 381–84: *Vroedscap Resoluties* 1449–58, 1465–1504, 1508–22, 1522–53.
Nos. 387 and 388: *Aflezing boaken* 1505–28, 1528–70

Printed Sources

Bickley, F. B., ed. *The Little Red Book of Bristol.* Bristol: 1900.
de Blécourt, A. S., and Wijs, J. J. A., eds. *Kenningboek der stad Leiden, 1553/1570.* Werken der Vereeninging tot uitgaaf der Bronnen van het Oud-Vaderlandsche Recht, series 3, no.6. Utrecht: 1936.
Blok, Petrus Johannes, ed. *Leidsche rechtsbronnen uit de middeleeuwen.* Vereeninging tot uitgave der Bronnen van het Oud-Vaderlandsche Recht, series 1, no. 6. The Hague: 1884.
Bothe, Friedrich. *Beiträge zur Wirtschafts- und Sozialgeschichte der Reichsstadt Frankfurt.* Leipzig: 1906.
——. "Die Entwicklung der direkten Besteuerung in der Reichsstadt

Frankfurt bis zur Revolution 1612–1614." *Staats- und sozialwissenschaftliche Forschungen* 26, no.2 (1906).

———. *Frankfurts wirtschaftlich-soziale Entwicklung vor dem Dreissigjahrigen Kriege und der Fettmilchaufstand, 1612–1616*. Veröffentlichungen der historischen Kommission der Stadt Frankfurt a. M., vol. 7. Frankfurt am Main: 1920.

Bücher, Karl, and Schmidt, Benno, eds., *Frankfurt Amts- und Zunfturkunden bis zum Jahre 1612*. Veröffentlichungen der historischen Kommission der Stadt Frankfurt a.M., vol. 6. Frankfurt am Main: 1914.

Buyken, Thea, and Conrad, Hermann, eds. *Die Amtleutebücher der Kölnischen Sondergemeinden*. Publikationen der Gesellschaft für Rheinische Geschichtskunde 45 (1936).

Carus-Wilson, E. M. and Coleman, O, eds. *England's Export Trade 1275–1547*. Oxford: 1963.

Chaucer, Geoffrey. *The Canterbury Tales*. Trans. Nevill Coghill. Harmondsworth: 1951.

Davis, Norman, ed. *The Paston Letters*. Oxford and New York: 1983.

Depping, G. B., ed. *Règlements sur les arts et métiers de Paris, rédigés au 13e siècle et connus sous le nom de Livre des Métiers d'Étienne Boileau*. Paris: 1837.

Dietz, Alexander, ed. *Frankfurter Bürgerbuch*. Frankfurt am Main: 1897.

van Embden, A. Meerkamp, ed. *Stadsrekeningen van Leiden (1390–1434)*. Werken uitgegeven door het historisch Genootschap, vols. 32 and 34, series 3. Amsterdam: 1913 and 1914.

Espinas, Georges and Pirenne, Henri, eds. *Recueil des documents relatifs à l'histoire de l'industrie drapière en Flandre: des origines à l'époque bourguignonne*. 4 vols. Brussels: 1906.

Fruin, Robert, ed. *Informatie up den staet faculteyt ende gelegenheyt van de steden ende dorpen van Hollant ende Vrieslant om daernae te reguleren de nyeuwe schiltaele gedaen in de jaere 1514*. Leiden: 1866.

Hamaker, H. G., ed. *De Middeneeuwsche keurboeken van de stad Leiden*. Leiden: 1873.

Hoeniger, Robert, ed. *Kölner Schreinsurkunden des 12. Jahrhunderts*. Gesellschaft für rheinische Geschichtskunde, Publikationen I. Bonn: 1884.

Irsigler, Franz, ed. "Getreide- und Brotpreise, Brotgewicht und Getreideverbrauch." In "Köln vom Spätmittelalter bis zum Ende des Ancien Regime." In *Zwei Jahrtausende Kölner Wirtschaft*, vol. 1, ed. H. Kellenbenz. Cologne: 1975.

Knipping, Richard. *Die Kölner Stadtrechnungen des Mittelalters mit einer Darstellung der Finanzverwaltung*, 2 vols. Publikationen der Gesellschaft für Rheinische Geschichtskunde, vol. 15. (Bonn: 1897–98).

Kuske, Bruno, ed. *Quellen zur Geschichte des Kölner Handels und Verkehrs im Mittelalter*. 4 vols. Publikationen der Gesellschaft für Rheinische Geschichtskunde, vol. 33 (Bonn: 1917–24).

Leendertz, P., ed. *Een scoon spel van Mariken van Niemeghen*. Leiden: 1907.

von Loesch, Heinrich, ed. *Die Kölner Zunfturkunden nebst anderer Kölner*

Gewerbeurkunden bis zum Jahre 1500. Publikationen der Gesellschaft für Rheinische Geschichtskunde, vol. 22 (Bonn: 1907).

Nabholz, Hans, and Hegi, Friedrich, eds. *Die Steuerbücher von Stadt und Landschaft Zürich des xiv. und xv. Jahrhunderts.* Zürich: 1918.

Osinga, M. D., and Gelinck, W. S., eds. *Kenningboek der stad Leiden 1570–80.* Oud Vaderlandsche Rechtsbronnen. Werken der Vereeninging tot uitgaaf der bronnen van het Oud-Vaderlandsche Recht, second series, vols. 23 and 24. Utrecht: 1928-30.

Overvoorde, J. C. *Rekeningen van de gilden van Dordrecht (1438–1600).* The Hague: 1894.

Planitz, Hans, and Buyken, Thea, eds. *Die Kölner Schreinsbücher des 13. und 14. Jahrhunderts.* Publikationen der Gesellschaft für Rheinische Geschichtskunde, vol. 46 (Weimar: 1937).

Posthumus, N. W., ed. *Bronnen tot de Geschiedenis van de Leidsche Textielnijverheid.* 6 vols. Rijksgeschiedkundige Publicatiën, nos. 8, 14, 18, 22, 39, 49. The Hague: 1910–22.

―――. "Een zestiendeeuwsche Enqueste naar de Buitenneringen rondom de Stad Leiden." *Bijdragen en Mededeelingen van het Historisch Genootschap,* vol. 33. Amsterdam: 1912.

Stein, Walter, ed. *Akten zur Geschichte der Verfassung und Verwaltung der Stadt Köln im 14. und 15. Jahrhundert.* 2 vols. Publikationen der Gesellschaft für Rheinische Geschichte, vol. 10. (Bonn: 1893–95).

SECONDARY SOURCES

Abel, Wilhelm. *Die Wüstungen des ausgehenden Mittelalters.* 2d ed. Stuttgart: 1955.

Abram, Alice. "Women Traders in Medieval London." *Economic Journal* 28 (1916).

Abrams, Philip. "History, Sociology, and Historical Sociology." *Past and Present* 87 (1980).

Adamson, Nancy. "Female Life Cycles in Early Modern London." Paper read at the Social Science History Association Annual Meeting, Toronto, Canada, 1984. Typescript.

Ammann, H. *Die wirtschaftliche Stellung der Reichsstadt Nürnberg im Spätmittelalter.* Nuremberg: 1970.

Anderson, M. *Approaches to the History of the Western Family, 1510–1914.* London: 1980.

Arentz, Ludwig. *Die Zersetzung des Zunftgedankens.* Veröffentlichungen der Kölnischen Geschichtsverein, vol. 12. Cologne: 1935.

Aubin, H. "Formen und Verbreitung des Verlagswesens in der Altnürnberger Wirtschaft." In *Beiträge zur Wirtschaftsgeschichte Nürnbergs,* vol. 2. Nuremberg: 1967.

Baeten, A. "De vrouw in de mentaliteit van een aantal laat-middeleeuwse auteurs: Een konfrontatie tussen het theoretisch-abstrakt beeld en de reele rol van de vrouw in de samenleving." Licenciaatsverhandeling, Rijksuniversiteit te Gent, 1972.

Barchewitz, J. *Von der Wirtschaftstätigkeit der Frau in der vorgeschichtlichen Zeit bis zur Entfaltung der Stadtwirtschaft.* Breslau: 1937.

Beechey, Veronica. "Women and Production: A Critical Analysis of Some Sociological Theories of Women's Work." In *Feminism and Materialism: Women and Modes of Production*, ed. by Annette Kuhn and Ann Marie Wolpe. London: 1978.

Behagel, Wilhelm. "Die gewerbliche Stellung der Frau im mittelalterlichen Köln." *Abhandlungen zur mittleren und neuren Geschichte* 23 (1910).

Bendix, Reinhard, and Lipset, Seymour Martin, eds. *Class, Status and Power: Social Stratification in Comparative Perspective.* 2d ed. New York: 1966.

Bennett, Judith M. "The Village Ale Wife: Women and Brewing in Fourteenth-century England." Paper read at the American Historical Association Annual Meeting, Washington, D. C., December 1982. Typescript.

Beyerle, Konrad. "Die Anfange des Kölner Schreinswesens." *Zeitschrift der Savigny-Stiftung für Rechtsgeschichte*, Germanische Abteilung 51 (1931).

Blendinger, Friedrich. "Versuch einer Bestimmung der Mittelschicht in der Reichsstadt Augsburg vom Ende des 14. bis zum Anfang des 18. Jahrhunderts." In *Städtische Mittelschichten*, ed. E. Maschke and J. Sydow. Veröffentlichungen der Kommission für geschichtliche Landeskunde in Baden-Wurtemberg, series B., vol. 69, Stuttgart: 1972.

Blockmans, W., et al. *Studien betreffende de sociale strukturen te Brugge, Kortrijk en Gent in de 14e en 15e eeuw. Standen en Landen* 54 (1971), 57 (1972), and 63 (1973).

Blok, Petrus Johannes. *Geschiedenis eener Hollandsche Stad.* 2 vols. The Hague: 1910–18.

Bois, G. "Against the Neo-Malthusian Orthodoxy." *Past and Present* 79 (1978).

Bothe, Friedrich. "Frankfurter Patriziervermögen im 16. Jahrhundert." In *2. Ergänzungsheft des Archivs für Kulturgeschichte.* Berlin: 1908.

———. "Frankfurts Wirtschaftsleben im Mittelalter." *Zeitschrift für de gesamte Staatswissenschaft* 93 (1932).

———. *Frankfurts wirtschaftlich-soziale Entwicklung vor dem Dreissigjahrigen Kriege und der Fettmilchaufstand (1612–1616).* Veröffentlichungen der historische Kommission der Stadt Frankfurt a.M., vol. 7. Frankfurt am Main: 1920.

———. *Geschichte der Stadt Frankfurt am Main.* Frankfurt am Main: 1923.

Braun, Lily. *Die Frauenfrage, ihre geschichtliche Entwicklung und wirtschaftliche Seite.* Leipzig: 1901.

Brenner, Robert. "Agrarian Class Structure and Economic Development in Pre-industrial Europe." *Past and Present* 70 (1976).

————. "The Agrarian Roots of European Capitalism." *Past and Present* 97 (1982).

Bridbury, A. R. *Economic Growth: England in the Later Middle Ages.* London: 1962.

Brodmeier, B. *Die Frau im Handwerk in historischer und moderner Sicht.* Forschungsberichte aus dem Handwerk 9. Münster i. W.: 1963.

Brownlee, W. Elliott. "Household Values, Women's Work and Economic Growth, 1800–1930." *Journal of Economic History* 39 (1979).

Brunner, E. C. G. *De Order op de Buitennering van 1531.* Utrecht: 1918.

Bücher, Karl. *Die Bevölkerung von Frankfurt am Main im 14. und 15. Jahrhundert.* Tubingen: 1886.

————. *Die Frauenfrage im Mittelalter.* 2d rev. ed. Tübingen: 1910.

Butt, John J., Jr. "The Transition of Privilege in Medieval Society: A Study of the English Brewers." Ph.D. dissertation, Rutgers University, 1982.

Cahn, Susan. *Descent from Paradise: The Fall of Women in Sixteenth and Seventeenth-Century England.* Forthcoming.

Carus-Wilson, E. M. *The Expansion of Exeter at the Close of the Middle Ages.* Exeter: 1963.

Casey, Kathleen. "The Cheshire Cat: Reconstructing the Experience of Medieval Women." In *Liberating Women's History,* ed. Berenice A. Carroll. Urbana, Chicago, and London: 1976.

Chaytor, Miranda. "Household and Kinship: Ryton in the late 16th and 17 centuries." *History Workshop* 10 (1980).

Chojnacki, Stanley. "Dowries and Kinsmen in Early Renaissance Venice." In *Women in Medieval Society,* ed. Susan M. Stuard. Philadelphia: 1976.

Cipolla, Carlo; Lopez, R. S.; and Miskimin, Harry. "The Economic Depression of the Renaissance." *Economic History Review* 16 (1964).

Clark, Alice. *The Working Life of Women in the Seventeenth Century.* London: 1919.

Cooper. J. P. "In Search of Agrarian Capitalism." *Past and Present* 80 (1978).

Coornaert, Emile. *Un centre industriel d'autrefois: la draperie-sayetterie d'Hondschoote (xive–xviiie siècle).* Paris: 1930.

Coulson, M., Magas, B., and Wainwright, H. " 'The Housewife and Her Labour under Capitalism'—A Critique." *New Left Review* 89 (1975).

Croot, P., and Parkert, D. "Agrarian Class Structure and Economic Development." *Past and Present* 78 (1978).

Daelemans, F. "Leiden 1581: een socio-demografisch onderzoek." *A. A. G. Bijdragen* 19 (1975).

Davis, Natalie. "Women in the *arts méchaniques* in sixteenth-century Lyon." In *Lyon et l'Europe. Hommes et sociétés.* Mélanges d'histoires offerts à Richard Gascon. Lyon: 1980.

Demey, J. "Proeve tot raming van de bevolking en de weefgetouwen te Ieper van de 13e tot de 17e eeuw." *Revue belge pour philologie et histoire* 28 (1950).

Diefendorf, Barbara B. "Widowhood and Remarriage in Sixteenth-century Paris." Paper read at The Fifth Annual Conference on the History of Women, June 1981. Typescript.

van Dillen, J. G. "Gildewezen en publiek rechtlijke bedrijfsorganisatie." *Historische Studies* 19 (1964).

Dixon, E. "Craftswomen in the *Livre des métiers.*" *Economic Journal* 5 (1895).

Dobb, Maurice. *Studies in the Development of Capitalism.* 2d rev. ed. London: 1946.

DuPlessis, Robert S. "Class and Class Consciousness in Western European Cities 1400–1650," *Radical History Review* 3, no. 1–2 (1975).

DuPlessis, Robert S., and Howell, Martha C. "Reconsidering the Early Modern Urban Economy: The Cases of Leiden and Lille." *Past and Present* 94 (1982).

Ebeling, Dietrich, and Irsigler, Franz. "Getreideumsatz, Getreide- und Brotpreise in Köln, 1368–1797." *Mitteilungen aus dem Stadtarchiv von Köln* 65 (1976).

Edwards, Richard C.; Reich, Michael; and Gordon, David, eds. *Labor Market Segmentation.* Massachusetts: 1975.

Eisenstein, Zillah R. *The Radical Future of Liberal Feminism.* New York and London: 1981.

Eitel, Peter. *Die oberschwäbische Reichstädte im Zeitalter der Zunftherrschaft.* Stuttgart: 1970.

Endres, R. "Zur Lage der Nürnberger Handwerkerschaft zur Zeit von Hans Sachs." *Jahrbuch für frankische Landesforschung* 37 (1977).

Ennen, Edith. *Frauen im Mittelalter.* Munich: 1984.

———. "Die Frau im Mittelalter." *Kurtrierisches Jahrbuch* 21 (1981).

———. "Die Frau in der mittelalterlichen Stadtgesellschaft Mitteleuropas." *Hansische Geschichtsblätter* 98 (1980).

Espinas, Georges. *Les origines du capitalisme,* 2 vols. Paris: 1933–49.

———. "Jehan Boine Broke. Bourgeois et drapier Douaisien." *Vierteljahrschrift für Sozial- und Wirtschaftsgeschichte* 2 (1904).

———. *La vie urbaine de Douai au moyen âge.* 2 vols. Paris: 1913.

Fagniez, Gustave. *Documents relatifs à l'histoire de l'industrie et du commerce en France.* 2 vols. Paris: 1898–1919.

———. *Études sur l'industrie et la classe industrielle à Paris au xiii* et au xiv* siècle.* Bibliotheque de l'École des hautes études. Sciences philologiques et historiques 33. Paris: 1877.

Favresse, F. *L'avènement du régime démocratique à Bruxelles pendant le moyen âge (1306–1403).* Académie royal de Belgique. Classe des lettres. Mémoires. Coll. in 8o. 2d series, vol. 3. Brussels: 1932.

Fee, T. "Domestic Labour: An Analysis of Housework and its Relationship to the Productive Process." *Review of Radical Political Economics* (Summer 1980).

Finlay, Roger A. P. "Population and Fertility in London, 1580–1650." *Journal of Family History* 4 (1979).

Flandrin, J. L. *Families in Former Times: Kinship, Household, and Sexuality.* Cambridge and New York: 1979.

de la Fontenelle de Vaudoré, M. *Les arts et métiers à Poitiers pendant les xiiie, xive et xve siècles.* Poitiers: 1837.

Frauendorf, Martha Norby. "The Labor Force Participation of Turn-of-Century Married Women." *Journal of Economic History* 39 (1979).

Friedrichs, C. R. "Capitalism, Mobility and Class Formation in the Early Modern German City." *Past and Present* 69 (1975).

Gardiner, J. "Women's Domestic Labour." *New Left Review* 89 (1975).

Gautier, Etienne, and Henry, Louis. *La population de 'Crulai'.* Paris: 1958.

Gies, Frances and Joseph. *Women in the Middle Ages.* New York: 1978.

Goldthwaite, Richard. "The Florentine Palace as Domestic Architecture." *American Historical Review* 77 (1972).

————. *Private Wealth in Renaissance Florence.* Princeton: 1968.

Goody, Jack; Thompson, E. P.; and Thirsk, Joan. *Family and Inheritance; Rural Society in Western Europe, 1200–1800.* Cambridge: 1976.

Gottfried, Robert. *Bury St. Edmunds and the Urban Crisis.* Princeton: 1982.

Guilbert, Madeleine. *Les fonctions des femmes dans l'industrie.* Paris and The Hague: 1966.

Gullickson, Gay. "The Sexual Division of Labor in Cottage Industry and Agriculture in the Pays de Caux." *French Historical Studies* 12, no. 2 (1981).

Hajau, Robert. "The Position of Noblewomen in the Pays des Coutumes, 1100–1300." *Journal of Family History* 5, no. 2 (1980).

Hajnal, J. "European Marriage Patterns in Perspective." In *Population in History*, ed. D. V. Glass and D. E. C. Everley. London: 1965.

Hamilton, Roberta. *The Liberation of Women: a Study of Patriarchy and Capitalism.* London: 1978.

Hansen, Joseph. "Das Archiv und die Bibliotheek der Stadt Köln." In *Festschrift zur 23. Jahresversammlung des Hansischen Geschichtsverein in Köln.* Cologne: 1894.

Harris, Olivia. "Households as Natural Units." In *Of Marriage and the Market*, ed. Kate Young, Carol Wolkowitz, and Roslyn McCullagh. 2d ed. London: 1984.

Hartwig, Julius. "Die Frauenfrage im mittelalterlichen Lübeck." *Hansische Geschichtsblätter* 14 (1908).

Hauser, Henri. *Ouvriers du temps passé.* Paris: 1899; reprint, 1927.

Heers, Jacques. *Family Clans in the Middle Ages.* Amsterdam, New York and Oxford: 1977.

Herborn, Wolfgang. "Bürgerliches Selbstverstandnis im spätmittelalterlichen Köln. Bermerkungen zu zwei Hausbüchern aus der ersten Hälfte des 15. Jahrhunderts." In *Die Stadt in der europäischen Geschichte.* Festschrift Edith Ennen, ed. W. Besch et al. Bonn: 1972.

————. "Verfassungsideal und Verfassungswirklichkeit in Köln während der ersten zwei Jahrhunderte nach inkrafttreten des Verbundbriefes von 1396, dargestelt am Beispiel des Bürgermeisteramtes." In *Städtische Führungsgruppen und Gemeinde in der werdenden Neuzeit,* ed. Wilfried Ehbrecht. Vienna: 1980.

———. *Die politische Führungsschicht der Stadt Köln im Spätmittelalter.* Bonn: 1977.

Herborn, Wolfgang, and Militzer, Klaus. *Der Kölner Weinhandel. Seine sozialen und politischen Auswirkungen im ausgehenden 14. Jahrhundert.* Sigmarigen: 1980.

Herlihy, David. "Land, Family and Women in Continental Europe, 701–1200." *Traditio* 18 (1962).

———. "Women in Medieval Society." In *The Social History of Italy and Western Europe, 700–1500.* London: 1978.

———. "Life Expectancies for Women in Medieval Society." In *The Social History of Italy and Western Europe, 700–1500.* London: 1978.

Herlihy, David, and Klapisch-Zuber, Christiane. *Les Tocsans et leurs familles: une étude du "castasto" florentin de 1427.* Paris: 1978.

Hess, L. *Die deutschen Frauenberufe des Mittelalters.* Munich: 1908.

Hicks, John. *A Theory of Economic History.* Oxford: 1969.

Hilton, Rodney H. "Lords, Burgesses and Hucksters." *Past and Present* 97 (1982).

———. *The Transition from Feudalism to Capitalism.* London: 1978.

———. "A Crisis of Feudalism." *Past and Present* 80 (1978).

Houston, Rab, and Smith, Richard. "A New Approach to Family History?" *History Workshop* 14 (1982).

van Houtte, Jan. "Gesellschaftliche Schichten in den Städten der Niederlande." In *Untersuchungen zur gesellschaftlichen Struckturen der mittelalterlichen Städte in Europa,* ed. Th. Mayer. Reichenau Vortrage 1963–64. Constance and Stuttgart: 1966.

Howell, Martha C. "Women's Work in Urban Economies of Late Medieval Northwestern Europe: Female Labor Status in Male Economic Institutions." Ph.D. dissertation, Columbia University, 1979.

Hughes, Diane Owen. "Urban Growth and Family Structure in Medieval Genoa." *Past and Present* 66 (1975).

———. "From Brideprice to Dowry in Medieval Europe." *Journal of Family History* 3, no.3 (1978).

Irsigler, Franz. "Getreidepreise, Getreidehandel und stadtische Versorgungspolitik in Köln, vornehmlich im 15. und 16. Jahrhundert." In *Die Stadt in der europaischen Geschichte.* Cologne: 1972.

———. "Hansekaufleute. Die Lübecker Veckinschusen und de Kölner Rinck." In *Hansa in Europa, Brücke zwischen den Märkten. 12. bis 17. Jahrhunderts.* Cologne: 1973.

———. "Kölner Kaufleute im 15. Jahrhundert. Die Akten des Prozess Rosenkrantz/Viejof als Quelle für die Kölnischen Handelsgeschichte." *Rheinische Vierteljahrsblätter* 36 (1972).

———. "Kölner Wirtschaft im Spätmittelalter." In *Zwei Jahrtausende Kölner Wirtschaft,* ed. Hermann Kellenbenz. 2 vols. Cologne: 1975.

———. "Kölner Wirtschaftsbeziehungen zum Oberrhein vom 14. bis 16. Jahrhundert." *Zeitschrift für die Geschichte des Oberrheins* 121, new series 82 (1974).

———. "Soziale Wandlungen in der Kölner Kaufmannschaft im 14. und 15. Jahrhundert." *Hansische Geschichtsblätter* 92 (1974).

———. *Die wirtschaftliche Stellung der Stadt Köln im 14. und 15. Jahrhundert. Struckturanalyse eines spätmittelalterlichen Exportgewerbe und Fernhandelstadt.* Vierteljahrschrift fur Sozial- und Wirtschaftsgeschichte, Beiheft 65. Wiesbaden: 1979.

Jahrbuch der Arbeitsgemeinschaft der rheinische Geschichtsverein 1–5 (1935–40).

Jaquette, Jane S. "Women and Modernization Theory. A Decade of Feminist Criticism." *World Politics* 1 (1982).

Jecht, H. "Studien zur gesellschaftlichen Struktur der mittelalterlichen Städte." *Vierteljahrschrift für Sozial- und Wirtschaftgeschichte* 19 (1926).

Kallmorgen, Wilhelm. *Siebenhundert Jahre Heilkunde in Frankfurt am Main.* Frankfurt am Main: 1936.

Kellenbenz, Hermann, ed. *Zwei Jahrtausende Kölner Wirtschaft.* 2 vols. Cologne: 1975.

———. "Die wohlhabendsten Kölner Burger um 1515." In *Geschichte in der Gesellschaft.* Festschrift fur Karl Bosl. Stuttgart: 1974.

Kelly, Joan. "The Doubled Vision of Feminist Theory: A Postscript to the Women and Power Conference." *Feminist Studies* 5 (1979).

———. "Early Feminist Theory and the *Querelle des Femmes,* 1400–1789." *Signs* 8, no.1 (1982).

Keussen, Hermann. *Topographie der Stadt Köln im Mittelalter.* 2 vols. Bonn: 1910.

Kirshner, Julius, and Molho, Anthony. "The Dowry Fund and the Marriage Market in Early *Quattrocento* Florence." *Journal of Modern History* 50, no. 3 (1978).

Klapisch, Christiane, and Demonet, Michel. "A une pano e uno vino. structure et développement de la famille rural Toscane (debut du 15e siècle)." *Annales. E.S.C.* 27.

Koch, Hans. *Geschichte des Seidengewerbes in Köln vom 13. bis 18. Jahrhundert.* Staats- und Sozialwissenschaftliche Forschungen, ed. G. Schmoller and M. Sering, vol. 128. Leipzig: 1907.

Kowaleski, Mary Anne. "Women's Work in a Market Town: Exeter in the Late Fourteenth Century." Paper read at the Annual Meeting of the American Historical Association, Washington, D.C. December 1982. Typescript.

Krantz, Frederick, and Hohenberg, Paul M. *Failed Transitions to Modern Industrial Society: Renaissance Italy and Seventeeth-Century Holland.* Montreal: 1975.

Kriedte, Peter; Medick, Hans; and Schlumbohm, Jürgen. *Industrialisierung vor der Industrialisierung.* Göttingen: 1978.

Kriegk, Georg Ludwig. *Frankfurter Bürgerzwiste und Zustände im Mittelalter.* Frankfurt am Main: 1862.

———. *Deutsches Bürgerthum im Mittelalter.* 2 vols. 1868–71; reprint, Frankfurt am Main: 1969.

Kuske, Bruno. "Kaufhäuser und Märkte im mittelalterlichen Köln." In *Mitteilungen der Industrie und Handelskammer zu Köln* 17 (1962).

———. "Der Kölner Fischhandel vom 14. bis 17. Jahrhundert." *Westdeutsche Zeitschrift* 24 (1905).

———. "Die ¦Frau im mittelalterlichen deutschen Wirtschaftsleben." *Zeitschrift für handelwissenschaftliche Forschung* 11, no. 3 (1959).

Lamet, Sterling. "Men in Government: The Patriciate of Leiden, 1550–1600." Ph.D. dissertation, University of Massachusetts, 1979.

Laslett, Peter. "Characteristics of the Western Family Considered Over Time." In *Family Life and Illicit Love in Earlier Generations,* ed. Peter Laslett. Cambridge: 1977.

———. *The World We Have Lost.* New York: 1965.

———, ed. *Family Life and Illicit Love in Earlier Generations.* Cambridge: 1977.

———, and Wall, Richard, eds. *Household and Family in Past Time.* Cambridge: 1972.

Lau, Friedrich. *Entwicklung der kommunalen Verfassung und Verwaltung der Stadt Köln bis zum Jahre 1396.* Bonn: 1898.

Lee, W. R. "Past Legacies and Future Prospects: Recent Research on the History of the Family in Germany." *Journal of Family History* 6, no.2 (1981).

Leonard, Christiane. "De status en de positie van de Gentse vrouw in de xive end de xve eeuw. Een juridische en sociale benaering." Licenciaatsverhandeling, Rijksuniversiteit te Gent, 1967.

Le Roy Ladurie, Emmanuel. "Family Structures and Inheritance Customs in Sixteenth-Century France." In *Family and Inheritance: Rural Society in Western Europe, 1200–1800,* ed. Jack Goody; E. P. Thompson; and Joan Thirsk. Cambridge: 1976.

———. "A Reply to Professor Brenner." *Past and Present* 79 (1978).

Lentze, Hans. "Der Kaiser und die Zunftverfassung in den Reichsstädten bis zum Tode Karls IV." *Untersuchungen zur Deutschen Staats- und Rechtsgeschichte* 145 (1933).

Levine, David. *Family Formations in an Age of Nascent Capitalism.* New York: 1977.

———. ed. *Proletarianization and Family History.* New York: 1984.

Litchfield, R. B. "Demographic Characteristics of Florentine Patrician Families, 16th to the 19th Centuries." *Journal of Economic History* 29, no.2 (1969).

Lopez, R. S., and Miskimin, Harry A. "The Economic Depression of the Renaissance." *Economic History Review*, 2d series, 14 (1962).

Lougee, Carolyn. *Le Paradis des Femmes: Women, Salons, and Social Stratification in Seventeeth-Century France*. Princeton: 1976.

van Maanen, R. C. J. "De Vermogensopbouw van de Leidse bevolking in het laatse kwaart van de zestiende eeuw." *Bijdragen en Mededeelingen betreffende de Geschiedenis der Nederlanden* 93, no.1 (1978).

Maclean, Ian. *The Renaissance Notion of Woman*. Cambridge: 1980.

des Marez, G. *L'organisation du travail à Bruxelles au xve siècle*. Mémoire de l'académie royale de Belgique 65. Brussels: 1904.

Marx, Karl. *Capital*. 3 vols. Reprint, New York: 1967.

———. *A Contribution to the Critique of Political Economy*, ed. Maurice Dobb. New York: 1970.

———. "The Economic and Philosophic Manuscripts." In *Karl Marx. Selected Writings*, ed. David McLellan. Oxford: 1977.

———. "The Eighteenth Brumaire of Louis Bonaparte." In Karl Marx and Frederick Engels. *Selected Works*. 2 vols. Moscow: 1962.

———. "The German Ideology (Part I)." In *Pre-capitalist Economic Formations*, ed. E. J. Hobsbawm. New York: 1965.

———. *Grundrisse*. Reprint, Harmondsworth: 1973.

Maschke, Erich. "Das Berufsbewusstsein des mittelalterlichen Fernkaufmanns." In *Miscellanea Medievalia*. Veröffentlichungen des Thomas-Instituts an der Universität Köln 3. Cologne: 1964.

———. "Mittelschichten in deutschen Stadten des Mittelalters." In *Städtische Mittelschichten*, ed. Erich Maschke and Jürgen Sydow. Veröffentlichungender Kommission für geschichtliche Landeskunde in Baden-Wurtemberg, series B, vol. 69, Stuttgart: 1972.

———. "Die Schichtung der mittelalterlichen Stadtbevölkerung Deutschlands als Problem der Forschung." In *Städte und Menschen*, Vierteljahrschrift für Sozial- und Wirtschaftsgeschichte, Beiheft 68. Wiesbaden: 1980.

———. "Die Unterschichten der mittelalterlichen Städte Deutschlands." In *Die Stadt des Mittelalters*, ed. Carl Haase, vol. 3. Darmstadt: 1973.

———. *Die Familie in der deutschen Stadt des späten Mittelalters*. Sitzungsberichte der Heidelberger Akademie der Wissenschaften. Heidelberg: 1980.

Mattaei, Julie A. *An Economic History of Women in America*. New York: 1982.

Mauersberg, Hans. *Wirtschafts- und Sozialgeschichte zentraleuropäischer Städte in neuer Zeit; dargestellt an den Beispielen von Basel, Frankfurt a. M., Hamburg, Hannover und München*. Göttingen: 1960.

Medick, Hans. "The Proto-industrial Family Economy: The Structural Function of Household and Family during the Transition from Peasant Society to Industrial Capitalism." *Social History* 3 (1976).

Meillassoux, Claude. *Femmes, greniers et capitaux*. Paris: 1975.

Mickwitz, Gunnar. *Die Kartellfunktionen der Zünfte und ihre Bedeutung bei der*

Entstehung des Zunftwesens. Commentationes Humanarum Litterarium 8, no. 3. Helsingfors: 1936.

Middleton, Christopher. "The Sexual Division of Labour in Feudal England." *New Left Review* 113–14 (1979).

Militzer, Klaus. "Berechunungen zur Kölner Tuchproduktion des 14.–17. Jahrhunderts." *Jahrbuch des Kölnischen Geschichtsverein* 51 (1980).

———. "Tuchhandel und Tüchhandler Kölns in Osterreich und Ungarn um 1400." *Blätter für deutsche Landesgeschichte* 114 (1978).

———. *Ursachen und Folgen der innerstadtischen Auseinandersetzung in Köln in der zweiten Hälfte des 14. Jahrhunderts.* Cologne: 1980.

Mitterauer, Michael, and Sieder, Reinhard. *The European Family: Patriarchy to Partnership from the Middle Ages to the Present.* Rev. ed. Chicago and Oxford: 1982.

Mollat, Michel, and Wolff, Phillippe. *Ongles bleus, Jacques et Ciompi. Les révolutions populaire en Europe aux xive et xve siècles.* Paris: 1970.

Mols, Roger. *Introduction à la démographie historique des villes d'Europe du xivme au xviime siècle.* 3 vols. Louvain: 1954–56.

Monter, William. "Women in Calvinist Geneva (1550–1800)." *Signs* 6, no. 2 (1980).

Mousnier, Roland. "Le concept de la classe sociale et l'histoire." *Revue d'histoire économique et sociale* 48 (1970).

———, ed. *Problèmes de stratification sociale: actes du colloque international.* Paris: 1968.

Mousnier, Roland; Labatut, J-P.; and Durand, Y. *Problèmes de stratification sociale: deux cahiers de la noblesse pour les États Généraux de 1649–1651.* Paris: 1965.

Mulholland, Sister Mary Ambrose. *Early Gild Records of Toulouse.* New York: 1941.

Neale, R. S. *Class in English History.* Oxford: 1981.

Nicholas, D. M. *The Domestic Life of a Medieval City: Women, Children, and the Family in Fourteenth-Century Ghent.* Lincoln, Neb.: 1985.

———. "The Population of 14th Century Ghent." *Handelingen van der Maatschappij voor Geschiedenis en Oudheidkunde te Gent* 24 (1970).

———. *Town and Countryside: Social, Economic, and Political Tensions in Fourteenth-Century Flanders.* Bruges: 1971.

Nichols, T. "Social Class: Official, Sociological and Marxist." In Evans, J.; Irvine, J.; and Miles, I. *Demystifying Social Statistics.* London: 1978.

Overvoorde, J. C. "De Leidsche ambachtsbroederschappen." In *Rechtshistorische opstellen aangeboden aan Prof. Mr. S. J. Fockema Anreae.* Haarlem: 1914.

———. *De ontwikkeling van den rechttoestand der vrouw volgens het oud-germaansche en het oud-nederlandsche recht.* Rotterdam: 1891.

———. "De ordonnanties van de Leidsche ambachtsbroederschappen." *Verslagen en Mededeelingen van de Vereeniging tot uitgave der bronnen van het Oud-Vaderlandsche Recht* 6, no.5 (1914).

Parsons, Talcott. "A Revised Analytical Approach to the Theory of Social Stratification." In *Class, Status and Power: Social Stratification in Comparative Perspective*, ed. Reinhard Bendix and Seymour Martin Lipset. Glencoe, Ill.: 1953.

———. *Essays in Sociological Theory.* New York: 1954.

Pirenne, Henri. *Belgian Democracy.* Manchester: 1915.

———. *Histoire de Belgique.* 7 vols. Brussels: 1900–1932.

———. "Les périodes de l'histoire sociale du capitalisme." *Bulletin de l'académie royale de Belgique.* Classe des Lettres (1914).

———. *Medieval Cities: Their Origins and the Revivial of Trade.* Princeton: 1925.

———. "Une crise industrielle au xvie siècle: la draperie urbaine et la nouvelle draperie en Flandre." *Bulletin de l'académie royale de Belgique.* Classe des Lettres (1905).

———. "Villes, marchés et marchands au moyen âge." *Revue historique* 67 (1898).

———. "Les dénombrements de la population d'Ypres au xve siècle." *Vierteljahrschrift für Sozial- und Wirtschaftsgeschichte* 1 (1903).

Platt, Colin. *The English Medieval Town.* London: 1976.

dePoerck, G. *La draperie médiévale en Flandre et en Artois.* 3 vols. Werken uitgegeven door de faculteit van de wijsbegeerte en letteren, Rijksuniversiteit te Gent, nos. 110–12. Bruges: 1951.

Polanyi, Karl. "Aristotle Discovers the Economy." In *Trade and Market in the Early Empire*, ed. Karl Polanyi, Conrad M. Arensberg, and Harry W. Pearson. Chicago: 1957.

———. *The Great Transformation: The Political and Economic Origins of our Time.* 1944; rev. ed., Boston: 1957.

Postan, Michael M. *Essays on Medieval Agriculture and General Problems.* Cambridge: 1973.

———. "Some Economic Evidence of the Declining Population in the Later Middle Ages." *Economic History Review*, 2d series, 2 (1950).

Postan, Michael M., and Hatcher, J. "Population and Class Relations in Feudal Society." *Past and Present* 78 (1978).

Posthumus, N. W. *De Geschiedenis van de Leidsche Lakenindustrie.* 3 vols. The Hague: 1908 and 1939.

Power, Eileen. *Medieval Women*, ed. Michael M. Postan. Cambridge: 1975.

———. *Medieval People.* London and New York: 1963.

Prevenier, Walter. "Bevolkingscijfers en professionele strukturen der bevolking van Gent en Brugge in de 14de eeuw." *Studia Historica Gandensia* 196 (1975).

———. "La démographie des villes du comte de Flandre aux xive et xve siècles." *Revue de Nord* 65, no. 257 (1983).

Quast, Jenneke. "Vrouwen in gilden in Den Bosch, Utrecht en Leiden van de 14e tot en met de 16e eeuw." In *Fragmenten vrouwengeschiedenis*, ed. Wantje Fritschy. Vol. 1. The Hague: 1980.

————. "Vrouwenarbeid omstreeks 1500 in enkele nederlandse steden." *Jaarboek voor Vrouwengeschiedenis*. Nijmegen: 1980.

Rapp, Rayna; Ross, Ellen; and Bridenthal, Renate. "Examining Family History." In *Sex and Class in Women's History*, ed. Judith L. Newton; Mary P. Ryan; and Judith R. Walkowitz. London: 1983.

Rappaport, Steve. "Male Life Cycles in Early Modern London." Paper read at the Social Science History Association Annual Meeting, Toronto, Canada, 1984. Typescript.

Reynolds, Susan. *An Introduction to the History of Medieval English Towns*. Oxford: 1977.

Rogers, Katherine M. *The Troublesome Helpmate: The History of Misogyny in Literature*. Seattle: 1968.

Rosaldo, M. Z. "The Use and Abuse of Anthropology: Reflections on Feminism and Cross-cultural Understanding." *Signs* 5, no.3 (1980).

Rössler, Hellmuth, ed. *Deutsches Patriziät 1430–1740*. Schriften zur Prolematik der deutschen Führungsschichten in der Neuzeit, vol. 3. Limburg/Lahn: 1968.

Ryckhuysen, G. *Wapenkaart, behelzende alle de Wapens en Naamen van de edele groot achtbaare Heeren Veertigen der Stad Leyden*. Leiden: 1758.

Schmelzeisen, Gustav K. *Die Rechtsstellung der Frau in der deutschen Stadtwirtschaft*. Stuttgart: 1935.

Schmidt, Gertrud. *Die Berufstätigkeit der Frau in der Reichsstadt Nürnberg bis zum Ende des 16. Jahrhundert*. Beitrag zur Wirtschaftsgeschichte Nürnbergs. Erlangen: 1950.

Schmoller, Gustav. *Die Strassburger Tucher- und Weberzunft. Urkunden und Darstellung*. Strassburg: 1879.

Schnyder, Werner. "Soziale Schichtung und Grundlagen der Vermögensbildung in den spätmittelalterlichen Städten der Eidgenossenschaft." In *Aldeutsches Bürgertum II*, ed. Heinz Stoob. Wege der Forschung 417. Darmstadt: 1978.

Schönfelder, Wilhelm. *Die wirtschaftliche Entwicklung Kölns von 1370–1513*. Cologne: 1970.

Scribner, R. W. "Civic Unity and the Reformation in Erfurt." *Past and Present* 66 (1975).

Secombe, W. "The Housewife and Her Labour under Capitalism." *New Left Review* 83 (1974).

Shahar, Shulamith. *Die Frau im Mittelalter*. Königstein/Ts.: 1981.

Smith, Bonnie G. *Ladies of the Leisure Class: The Bourgeoises of Northern France in the Nineteenth Century*. Princeton 1981.

Société de Jean Bodin. *La Femme*. Récueils de la Société de Jean Bodin pour l'histoire comparative des institutions, vols. 11–13. Brussels: 1959-62.

Soly, Hugo. *Urbanisme en kapitalisme te Antwerpen in de 16e eeuw*. Pro Civitate, series in octavo, no. 47. Brussels: 1977.

Stehkämper, Hugo. "Das historische Archiv der Stadt Köln und sein neues Haus." *Mitteilungen aus dem Stadtarchive Köln* 60 (1971).

Steinbach, F. "Zur Sozialgeschichte von Köln im Mittelalter." In *Spiegel der Geschichte*, Festgabe fur Max Braubach zum 10. April 1964. Münster: 1964.

Stone, Lawrence. *The Family, Sex and Marriage in England, 1500–1800.* London: 1977.

Strait, Paul. *Cologne in the Twelfth Century.* Gainesville, Fla.: 1974.

Strieder, Jacob. *Zur Genesis des modernen Kapitalismus. Forschungen zur Entstehung der grossen bürgerlichen Kapitalvermögen am Ausgang des Mittelalters und zu Beginn der Neuzeit, zunächst in Augsburg.* 2d ed. Munich and Leipzig: 1935.

Stuard, Susan. "Women in Charter and Statute Law: Medieval Ragusa/Dubrovnik." In *Women in Medieval Society*, ed. Susan Stuard. Philadelphia: 1976.

———, ed. *Women in Medieval Society.* Philadelphia: 1976.

Thompson, E. P. *The Making of the English Working Class.* London: 1963.

———. "The Peculiarities of the English." In *The Socialist Register*, ed. R. Miliband and J. Saville. London: 1965.

———. *The Poverty of Theory.* London: 1978.

Tilly, Louise, and Cohen, Miriam. "Does the Family Have a History?" *Social Science History* 6 (1982).

Tilly, Louise, and Scott, Joan W. *Women, Work and Family.* New York: 1978.

Tönnies, Ferdinand. *Gemeinschaft und Gesellschaft; Grundbegriffe der reinen Soziologie.* 8th rev. ed. Darmstadt: 1963.

Ulrich, Laura Thatcher. *Goodwives: Image and Reality in the Lives of Women in Northern New England, 1650–1750.* Oxford: 1983.

Unwin, G. H. *Industrial Organization in the Sixteenth and Seventeenth Centuries.* Oxford: 1904.

Vandenabeele, Frieda. "Die vrouw in de lakennijverheid in Vlaanderen (xiie-xive siecle)." Licenciaatsverhandeling, Rijsuniversiteit te Gent, 1955.

Vann, Richard T. "Wills and the Family in an English Town: Banbury 1550–1800." *Journal of Family History* 4, no.4 (1979).

———. "Women in Preindustrial Capitalism." In *Becoming Visible: Women in European History*, ed. Renate Bridenthal and Claudia Koonz. Boston: 1977.

Verbeemen, J. "De Werking van economische factoren op de stedelijke demografie der xviie en der xviiie eeuw in de zuidelijke Nederlanden." *Revue Belge de philologie et d'histoire* 34 (1956).

Vogelsang, Thilo. *Die Frau als Herrscherin im hohen Mittelalter.* Göttingen, Frankfurt, Berlin: 1954.

Wachendorf, H. *Die wirtschaftliche Stellung der Frau in den deutschen Städten des späteren Mittelalters.* Quakenbrück: 1934.

van der Wee, Herman. *The Growth of the Antwerp Market*. 3 vols., Paris, Louvain and The Hague: 1963.

———. "Die Wirtschaft der Stadt Lier zu Beginn des 15. Jahrhunderts." In *Beiträge zu wirtschafts-und Stadtsgeschichte: Festschrift für Hektor Ammann*, ed. Hermann Aubin. Wiesbaden: 1965.

van der Wee, Herman, and van Mingroot, Erik. "The Charter of the Clothiers' Guild of Lier, 1275." In *Cloth and Clothing in Medieval Europe: Essays in Honor of Professor G. M. Carus-Wilson*, ed. N. R. Hapte and K. G. Pontina. London: 1983.

Wemple. Suzanne. *Women in Frankish Society: Marriage and the Cloister, 500-900*. Philadelphia: 1981.

Wensky, Margret. *Die Stellung der Frau in der stadtkölnischen Wirtschaft im Spätmittelalter*. Cologne and Vienna: 1980.

———. "Die Stellung der Frau in Familie, Haushalt und Wirtschaftsbetrieb im spätmittelalterlichen-frühneuzeitlichen Köln." Paper read in Cologne, 1979.

———. "Women's Guilds in Cologne in the Later Middle Ages." *The Journal of European Economic History* 11, no.3 (1982).

van Werweke, Hans. "Ambachten en erfelijkheid." *Mededeelingen van de Koninklijke Vlaamse Academie voor Wetenschappen, Letteren en schone Kunsten van Belgie*. Klasse der Letteren en der Moreele en Staatkundige Wetenschappen, vol. 4, no.1 (1942).

———. "De Omvang van de Ieperse Lakenproductie in de veertiende eeuw." *Mededeelingen van de Koninklijke Vlaamse Academie voor Wetenschappen, Letteren en schone Kunsten van Belgie*. Klasse der Letteren, vol. 2 (1947).

Wesoly, Kurt. "Der weibliche Bevölkerungsanteil im spätmittelalterlichen und frühneuzeitlichen Städten und die Betätigung von Frauen in zünftigen Handwerk (insbesondere am Mittel- und Oberrhein)." *Zeitschrift für die Geschichte des Oberrheins* 128, new series 89 (1980).

West, Jackie. "Women, Sex and Class." In *Feminism and Materialism. Women and Modes of Production*, ed. Annette Kuhn and AnnMarie Wolpe. London, Boston, and Henley: 1978.

White, Sarah Melhado. "Sexual Language and Human Conflict in Old French Fabliaux." *Comparative Studies in Society and History* 24, no.2 (1982).

Whyte, Martin King. *The Status of Women in Preindustrial Societies*. Princeton: 1978.

Wielandt, Friedrich. "Münzen, Gewichte und Masse bis 1800." In *Handbuch der deutschen Wirtschafts- und Sozialgeschichte*, ed. Hermann Aubin and Wolfgang Zorn, vol. 1. Stuttgart: 1971.

Wiesner [Wood], Merry. "Paltry Peddlers or Essential Merchants? Women in the Distributive Trades in Early Modern Nuremberg." *The Sixteenth Century Journal* 12, no.2 (1981).

von Winterfeld, L. "Die stadtrechtlichen Verflectung in Westfalen." In *Der Raum Westfalen*, vol.2, p. 1, ed. H. Aubin and F. Petri. Munster: 1955.

———. "Handel, Kapital und Patriziät in Köln bis 1400." *Pfingstblätter der Hansische Geschichtsverein* 16 (1925).

Wissell, Rudolf. *Des alten Handwerks Recht und Gewohnheit*. 2 vols. Berlin: 1929.

Witzel, Georg. "Gewerbegeschichtliche Studien zur niederlandischen Einwanderung in Deutschland im 16. Jahrhundert." *Westdeutsche Zeitschrift für Geschichte und Kunst* 39 (1910).

Wrigley, E. A. "Family Limitation in Preindustrial England." *Economic History Review* 19, 2d series (1966).

Wunder, Gerd. "Die Sozialstruktur der Reichsstadt Schwäbisch Hall im späten Mittelalter." In *Untersuchungen zur gesellschaftlichen Struktur der mittelalterlichen Städte in Europa*, ed. Theodor Mayer. Constance: 1966.

Wunder, Heide. "Peasant Organization and Class Conflict in East and West Germany." *Past and Present* 78 (1978).

Zaretsky, Eli. *Capitalism, the Family and Personal Life*. New York: 1976.

Zorn, Wolfgang. *Augsburg. Geschichte einer deutschen Stadt*. Augsburg: 1972.

Index

Akzisestundung, 138–44
Ambachten, 73, 74, 162, 165, 167; role of, 56–57; exclusion of women from, 87–91, 130
Amsterdam, 45, 88, 91
Antwerp, 45, 163, 182; Cologne trade with, 100, 125, 140, 157; wealth distribution in, 65–66
Artisans: of Cologne, 98–101, 103; in family production unit, 28; of Leiden, 56, 60–64, 68–69; loss of labor status by, 35, 42; in medieval craft production, 34–35; and small commodity production, 38–39. *See also* Ambachten; Gaffeln; Guilds
Atfange, Druitgin zo dem, 139, 146
Attendarne, Druytgen van, 125
Augsburg, 39; wealth distribution in, 65, 66, 67, 112

Bakers, in Cologne, 135
Barchent production: in Cologne, 100, 101, 110, 111; in Leiden, 66
Barde, Greta zom, 145
Basel, wealth distribution in, 67
Becker, Grietgen, 125
Beer trade, in Cologne, 101–3, 135–36
Behagel, Wilhelm, 95
Belt makers, in Cologne, 22, 136, 137
Berchem, Grietgen van, 125
Berchem, Jacob van, 125

Bergen op Zoom, 91, 157
Boele, Druytgin van, 125
Boinbroke, Jean, 108, 164–67
Boschhuysen, Jacop van, 54
Brabant, 100
Brauerzunft, 135
Brielle, 68
Broelmann, Cathringin, 145
Brotherhoods, in Cologne, 99, 133
Bruges, 45, 91; Cologne trade with, 100, 157; uprisings in, 69; wealth distribution in, 65
Bücher, Karl, 1–5, 13, 22, 26, 95, 174
Burg, Alf van der, 146
Burg, Grietgen van der, 114, 146
Bürgermeister, of Cologne, 117–19
Bürgerschaft, 40
Byse, Bartholomeus, 114

Cahn, Susan, 31
Calais, and Leiden trade, 51, 52, 60, 61, 69, 88, 91, 92, 156–57
Cambridge Group for the History of Population and Social Structure, 12
Capitalism: in Cologne, 110–23, 127–29, 155–58, 179, 180; development of, in medieval cities, 33–43; in Douai, 164–67; and family economy, relationship between, 27–33, 179–80; in Frankfurt am Main, 172–73; in Leiden, 62–68, 94, 179

Capitalism, the Family and Personal Life (Zaretsky), 31
Casey, Kathleen, 3
Chaucer, Geoffrey, 182
"Cheshire Cat: Reconstructing the Experience of Medieval Women, The" (Casey), 3
Cities, late medieval: capitalism in, 35–37; community property laws in, 14, 177, 178; gender and population in, 174–75; medieval craft production in, 34–35; small commodity production in, 37–39; social and political stratification in, 40–43; women's work in, 1–6
Clans, Italian, 16–17
Clark, Alice, 30–31, 32, 179
Classes: absence of in medieval cities, 40–41; in capitalism, 36, 37. See also *Schichten*
Cleve, Niesgin van, 125
Coarse cloth industry, in Leiden, 75, 85
Cologne, 95–123, 181; capitalism in, 110–23, 127–29, 155–58, 179, 180; changes in economy of, 101–4; constitutional history of, 104–8; documents on, 98–99; growth of trade in, 99–100; patriciate in, 108–10; wealth distribution in, 65, 66–67, 112. See also Guilds; Patriciate; Weavers; Women's work; Wool cloth trade, in Cologne
Colyton, England, marriage age in, 13
Community property law, 14, 153, 177, 178
Conninxz, Jan, 54
Corrextieboeken, 57, 64, 70, 72, 74, 76–85
Coulson, M., 31–32
Council, of Cologne, 105. See also Large Council, of Cologne; Small Council, of Cologne
Crulai, France, marriage age in, 13

Davis, Natalie, 175–76
Demographics: of household economy, 12–14; and labor status of women, 174–75
Depression of the Renaissance, 101
Descent from Paradise (Cahn), 31

Dordrecht, 100, 157
Douai, 10, 11, 26, 108, 182; study of women's work in, 45–46, 163–67, 173, 176, 179, 180
Dowries, 14–16, 18
Draperiekeurboeken, 60
Drapery: in Douai, 164–67; in Lier, 163–64
—, in Leiden, 180; documents on, 57–59; history of, 50–52; "new," 50, 67–68; organization of artisans in, 56–57; and patriciate, 52–56; size and importance of, 49, 59–62; small commodity production in, 87–94; structure of, 62–69. See also Coarse cloth industry, in Leiden; Women's work; Wool cloth trade, in Cologne
Dutch Revolt, 50, 52
Dyers: in Douai, 165; in Leiden, 70, 73–74, 85

Échevins, 165
Economic status: and labor status, 25; of Leiden women, 77, 85–87
Economic system, 5, 27
Eisenmarkt (Gaffel), 118, 127–28
England, 168; Cologne trade with, 100–104, 120–21, 126, 147; destruction of family economy in, 30–31; legal status of women in, 177; Leiden trade with, 50–52; marriage age in, 18–19
Erfurt, wealth distribution in, 66
Espinas, Georges, 108, 164–67
Export-import trade. See Trade, long-distance

Family economy: characteristics of, 9–11; varieties of, 27–30; as used by Alice Clark, 30–32
Family production unit: and capitalism, 30–37, 179–80; characteristics of, 27–30; in Cologne, 44, 124–58; in Douai, 166–67; in Frankfurt am Main, 172–73; in Leiden, 43–44, 75–76, 87–94; and sexual division of labor, 176–77; and small commodity production, 37–43; and women's labor status, relationship between, 43, 178–83. See also Household economy

Feme sole, 15, 20, 29
Finance: and Cologne patriciate, 108–10; and urban elites, 39
Finishers: in Douai, 165; in Leiden, 56, 62, 73, 88–90
Fish sellers, 134–35, 171
Flanders, 51, 100, 163–65
France, legal status of women in, 177, 178
Frankfurt am Main, 4, 10, 22, 26, 120, 125, 157; wealth distribution in, 66, 67; study of women's work in, 45–46, 163, 167–73, 175, 176
Frauenfrage im Mittelalter, Die (Bücher), 1–5, 95
Fullers, in Douai, 165, 166
—, in Leiden: in ambachten, 56, 88, 91; condition of, 63; numbers of, 60, 61–62; protests by, 58, 62, 63; women as, 70–71, 73, 75, 85, 87, 88
Furstenberg, Druytgen, 125

Gaffeln, 136, 145; organization of, 106, 107; political power of, 118–22; and women's guilds, 127–31
Garnmacherinnen. See Yarn makers, in Cologne
Gebrech, 107, 118
Gelre, Johann van, 145–46
Gelre, Lempgin van, 145–46
Geneva, 3
Gerecht, 53–56, 63, 165
Gerestorp, Gutgyn van, 139, 146
Geschiedenis van de Leidsche Lakenindustrie (Posthumus), 59–63
Geschlechtsvormundschaft, 15
Gesellen, 128
Gewandschneider. See Wool cloth trade, in Cologne
Ghent, 2, 45, 69, 181; size of textile industry in, 59
Goeswijns, Griete, 72
Gold production, in Cologne, 106, 126, 129–31, 134, 137; women's work in, 97, 124–32, 155–56
Goldspinnerinnen. See Gold production, in Cologne
Goldschläger. See Gold production in, Cologne

Gorlitz, 67
Guilds, 33, 56, 162, 180; in Frankfurt am Main, 168–73; and labor status, 25; in Lier, 163; and medieval craft production, 34; and small commodity production, 38
—, in Cologne: and capitalist development, 115–16; political power of, 105–7, 117; traditional, women in, 95, 133–37, 153–54; women's, 95, 97, 124–33, 153–54. See also Ambachten; Gaffeln

Hajnal, John, 13–14, 44
Hamburg, 100
Hamilton, Roberta, 31
Hansa, 33, 51–52, 69, 99, 100, 156–57
Helmslegern, Karyssen under, 141, 143, 145, 146
Herborn, Wolfgang, 117–20
Himmelreich (Gaffel), 127–28
Homan, 56
Hondschoote, 51–52, 59
Household economy: characteristics of, 9–16; deviations from pattern of, 16–19; and family production unit, 27; and patriarchal system, 19–21, 161; women's work in, 10–11. See also Family production unit; Family economy

Irsigler, Franz, 101–2, 110–13, 119, 121, 128, 147, 150
Italy, household economy in, 16–18

Jecht, Horst, 39, 66

Kampen, 100
Kaufbeuren, wealth distribution in, 66–67
Kemper, Johan, 111
Kenningboeken, 57, 64, 71–72, 74, 84
Keurboeken, 70, 71
Kuske, Bruno, 95, 99
Kuylen, Styngen zo der, 151

Labor status, of women: and capitalism, 30–37; in Cologne, 152–58; and family production unit, 28, 30, 33, 43; hypothesis on conditions affecting, 43; and legal system, 177–78; in Leiden, 70, 75–76, 85–94; in medieval craft production, 34–35; and small commodity production, 37–43; in urban market economies, 21–26
Langland, 10
Large Council, of Cologne, 105–7, 117, 118, 150
Laslett, Peter, 14
Legal status, of women, 177–78
Leiden, 5, 49–69, 181; capitalism in, 62–68, 94, 179; documents on, 57–59, 189–90; government structure in, 52–57; importance of drapery in, 49, 59–62; income from strikerye of, 185–88; introduction to study of, 43–46; population of, 62, 191–92; wealth distribution in, 64–67. *See also* Drapery; Patriciate; Weavers; Women's work
Liberation of Women, The (Hamilton), 31
Liège, 68
Lier, women's work in, 45–46, 163–64, 167, 179
Linen, 66, 140, 170–71; weaving of, 74, 88, 89, 135–37
Loesch, Heinrich von, 98–99
Lohgerber Gesellen, 115
Loubach, Tryngen, 125
Lübeck, 10
Lutzenkirchen, Fygen, 125
Lynge, Tryngin van, 145
Lyons, 3, 26, 175–76

Maastricht, 68
Marijke van Nijmegen (play), 182
Marital status, of women: and civil status, 15; and labor status, 41–43; in Leiden, 76–77, 85–87; in women's guilds of Cologne, 124–27
Market production: and family production unit, 27–29; in household economies, 9–10, 13; and labor status, 21–26; in late medieval period, 30–43; women's entry into, 19–21. *See also*

Capitalism; Family production unit; Small commodity production
Marriage age: in Cologne, 44; in England, 18–19; in family economies, 29–30; in Italy, 16, 17; in Leiden, 43–44; in northern household economies, 13–14
Marriage goods, 14
Marx, Karl, 41
Marxists, 35; on destruction of family economy, 31–32
Maschke, Erich, 40–43, 92–93, 112, 113, 121, 136
Medieval craft production, 34–35, 37, 42–43, 69, 180
Memmingen, wealth distribution in, 66–67
Ménagier de Paris, Le, 18
Merll, Grietgen van, 150, 151
Metals, raw, Cologne trade in, 139
Militzer, Klaus, 112–13, 116–17
Mittelschicht, 41–42; in Cologne, 113, 116, 155; in Leiden, 92–94
Moubach, Guetgen van, 152
Mousnier, Roland, 40
Mulhausen i. Th., 67
Muntgeld payments, 15

Needlemakers, of Cologne, 136–37
Nuremberg, 3, 22, 111; wealth distribution in, 66–67
Nyle, Styngen van, 151

Oberschicht, 112–13, 116
Overstolz, Werner, 119–20
Overstolz family, 108, 119–20

Paris, 2, 45, 181–82
Passamentier loom, 68
Patriarchal system, 20–21, 161, 178–83
Patriciate: in Douai, 164–66; in Frankfurt am Main, 168; in late medieval cities, 17–18, 40–43
—, of Cologne, 127, 146, 156; and merchant capitalist class, relationship between, 112, 114, 116–20; origin and membership of, 108–10

—, of Leiden: as large producers, 61; political and economic power of, 53–56; and small commodity production, 64–69

Philip the Good, 50, 53, 55

Pirenne, Henri, 62, 108

Posamentier, 173

Posthumus, N. W., 49–50, 59–63, 66, 70, 72, 74, 84, 176

Prague, 100

Pressburg, 100

Privilege, of Leiden, 53, 56, 57

Property, in household economies, 14–18

Putting-out system, 32, 35, 42, 103, 104

Quast, Jenneke, 49–50

Rat. *See* Council, of Cologne

Ravensburg, 111; wealth distribution in, 66–67

Real estate holdings: of Cologne patriciate, 108–9; of Leiden patriciate, 65

Rederijkers, 182

Regensberg, 10

Regents, 53

Renaissance, depression of the, 101

Richerzeche, 105–7, 119–20

Rose the Regrator, 10

Runtiger, Margarete, 10

St. Ursula brotherhood, 73, 88–89

Schecters, Hilgin, 139, 146

Schepenen, 53–55, 164

Schichten, 41–42; in Cologne, 112–16. See also *Mittelschicht; Oberschicht; Unterschicht*

Schöffen College, 105, 107–8, 119–20

Schout, 53, 54, 71

Schrijnmechers, Neegin, 114

Schutz, Conrad, 111

Schwarzhaus (Gaffel), 127–28

Scott, Joan, 27, 29

Scoutsrekeningen, 72, 73

Sectam, Johan van, 114

Seideamt, 125, 126, 128, 129, 147

Seideweberinnen. *See* Silk makers, in Cologne

Servants: Cologne women as, 114–16; Leiden women as, 84, 85

Sex-gender system, 5, 27

Sexual division of labor, traditional, 175–77, 181

Silk embroiderers, in Cologne, 131–32, 135, 136

Silk makers, in Cologne, 101–2, 122, 162; women as, 11, 97, 124–32, 154–56, 158

Sloegins, Johan (Jan), 120

Small commodity production: definition and characteristics of, 34, 37–40; and family production, 180; in Leiden, 64–69, 87–94; and patrician rule theory, 42–43

Small Council, of Cologne, 105–7, 112

Spice trade, in Cologne, 100, 112, 140–46, 155–56

Stellung der Frau in der stadtkölnischen Wirtschaft im Spätmittelalter, Die (Wensky), 98–99

Strasbourg, 22

Struyss, Heinrich, 114

Subsistence production: family production unit versus, 27–29; in household economies, 9–10, 13; and labor status, 25

Survey of 1540, of Leiden suburbs, 75–83

Tailors, 134, 171, 172

Tax rolls: Cologne, 137–38; Leiden, 63, 65, 70, 76–86

Tilly, Louis, 27, 29

Tirtei production, 101

Trade, long-distance: of Leiden, 50–52; and market production development, 33, 35, 39–40

—, of Cologne: change in, during fifteenth century, 101–4; growth of, 99–100; and new merchant elite, 110–12, 118–21; patriciate in, 108–10, 113; women in, 97, 137–52, 156–58, 162

Trade fairs, 100–101, 168–69

Unterschicht, 113–16

Venice, 100, 120–21
Verbundbrief, 106, 119
Vienna, 100
Voerlaken production, 75, 89–90
Vroedschap, 53–59
Vurberg, Heinrich, 125

Wachendorf, Helmut, 4, 95
Wachendorp, Yrmgin, 146
Walloons, 52, 67–68, 168
Wantsnijders, women as, 71–73
Wappensticker. *See* Silk embroiderers, in Cologne
Waveren, Stina, 147
Weavers: in Douai, 165; in Frankfurt am Main, 170–171; in Lier, 163–64; status of, 22–23, 25
—, in Cologne: and change in wool cloth industry, 103–4; political power of, 104–7, 113; women as, 134–37
—, in Leiden: in ambachten, 56, 88, 91; condition of, 63; numbers of, 59–62; women as, 70, 73, 87–89. *See also* Drapery; Wool cloth trade, in Cologne
Weber, Max, 40
Wee, Herman van der, 163–64
Weinbrüderschaft, 104, 152
Weinsberg, Hermann van, 44
Weinsburg, Christian von, 158
Wensky, Margret, 95–96, 98–99, 124–29, 134–35, 150–51, 155–56, 176
Wesoly, Kurt, 4
Widows. *See* Marital status, of women
Wine trade, in Cologne, 100, 102, 104, 108; women's work in, 138, 147–52, 154–56
"Wirtschaft der Stadt Lier zu Beginn des 15. Jahrhunderts, Die" (van der Wee), 163–64
Wirtschaftliche Stellung der Frau in den deutschen Städten des Spätmittelalters, Die (Wachendorf), 4
Wirtschaftliche Stellung der Stadt Köln, Die (Irsigler), 101–2, 110
Wollamt, 103–7, 113, 145
Women's work: in Douai, 163–67, 173, 176, 179, 180; and economic/demographic conditions, 174–75; in family production unit, 28–30; in Frankfurt am Main, 163, 167–73, 175, 176; in household economy, 10–16; labor status of, 21–26; in late medieval cities, issue of, 1–6; and legal system, 177–78; in Lier, 163–64, 167, 179; outside northern European model, 16–19; and patriarchal system, 19–21, 161, 178–83; and sexual division of labor, 175–77
—, in Cologne, 2, 5, 10, 11, 22, 26, 124–58, 179–81; in export-import trade, 97, 137–52, 156–58, 162; introduction to study of, 43–46; and other cities compared, 96–97, 130, 137, 154–57, 163–73; pattern of, and family production unit, 152–58, 161–63; and sexual division of labor, 176; and traditional guilds, 133–37, 153–54; and underclass status, 114–15; and wealth, 114; and women's guilds, 124–33, 153–54
—, in Leiden, 5, 49–50, 70–94, 179, 181; and categorization by economic and marital status, 76–87; and economic conditions, 175; introduction to study of, 43–46; and numbers of women in drapery, 62; and other cities compared, 96–97, 130, 137, 154–57, 163–73; pattern of, and family production unit, 87–94, 161–63; reliability of records concerning, 58–60, 71; and sexual division of labor, 176; types of, 70–75, 83–85; and wealth, 65, 66
Wool cloth trade, in Cologne, 111, 113, 118, 176; growth of, 100, 101; patriciate in, 108; and silk mistresses, relationship between, 125, 126, 128; transformation of, 103–4; women in, 146–47, 154–56. *See also* Drapery; Voerlaken production; Weavers
Working Life of Women in the 17th Century, The (Clark), 30–32
World We Have Lost, The (Laslett), 14

Yarn makers, in Cologne, 97, 124, 127, 129–30, 132, 155–56

Index

York, 3
Ypres, 45, 69; size of textile industry in, 59
Yss, Niesgin, 139

Zaretsky, Eli, 31
Zoenboeken, 57
Zunftzwang, 106
Zutphen, Durgin van, 145